*HEH HEH HEH...*

叶 恭弘

Time goes by so fast…It's been a year since the series started, and this is the last volume of *Pretty Face*. Like it did for Rando, this year has passed like a dream. Many thanks to everyone—my editors and staff, and you who are reading this book right now—for giving me this incredible experience!

—Yasuhiro Kano, 2003

Yasuhiro Kano made his manga debut in 1992 with *Black City*, which won *Weekly Shonen Jump*'s Hop★Step Award for new artists. From 1993 to 2001, he illustrated Mugen's serialized novels *Midnight Magic* in *Jump Novel* magazine, and also produced a manga adaptation. *Pretty Face* appeared in *Weekly Shonen Jump* from 2002 to 2003. Kano's newest series, *M x O*, began running in *Weekly Shonen Jump* in 2006.

# PRETTY FACE
## VOL. 6

**The SHONEN JUMP ADVANCED Manga Edition**

STORY AND ART BY
YASUHIRO KANO

Translation & English Adaptation/Anita Sengupta
Touch-up Art & Lettering/Eric Erbes
Design/Hidemi Dunn
Editor/Jason Thompson

Editor in Chief, Books/Alvin Lu
Editor in Chief, Magazines/Marc Weidenbaum
VP of Publishing Licensing/Rika Inouye
VP of Sales/Gonzalo Ferreyra
Sr. VP of Marketing/Liza Coppola
Publisher/Hyoe Narita

PRETTY FACE © 2002 by Yasuhiro Kano. All rights reserved. First published in Japan in 2002 by SHUEISHA Inc., Tokyo. English translation rights arranged by SHUEISHA Inc. The stories, characters and incidents mentioned in this publication are entirely fictional.

Printed in the U.S.A.

Published by VIZ Media, LLC
P.O. Box 77010
San Francisco, CA 94107

SHONEN JUMP ADVANCED Manga Edition
10 9 8 7 6 5 4 3 2 1
First printing, June 2008

www.viz.com

www.shonenjump.com

# Pretty Face

## Vol. 6

STORY & ART BY
YASUHIRO KANO

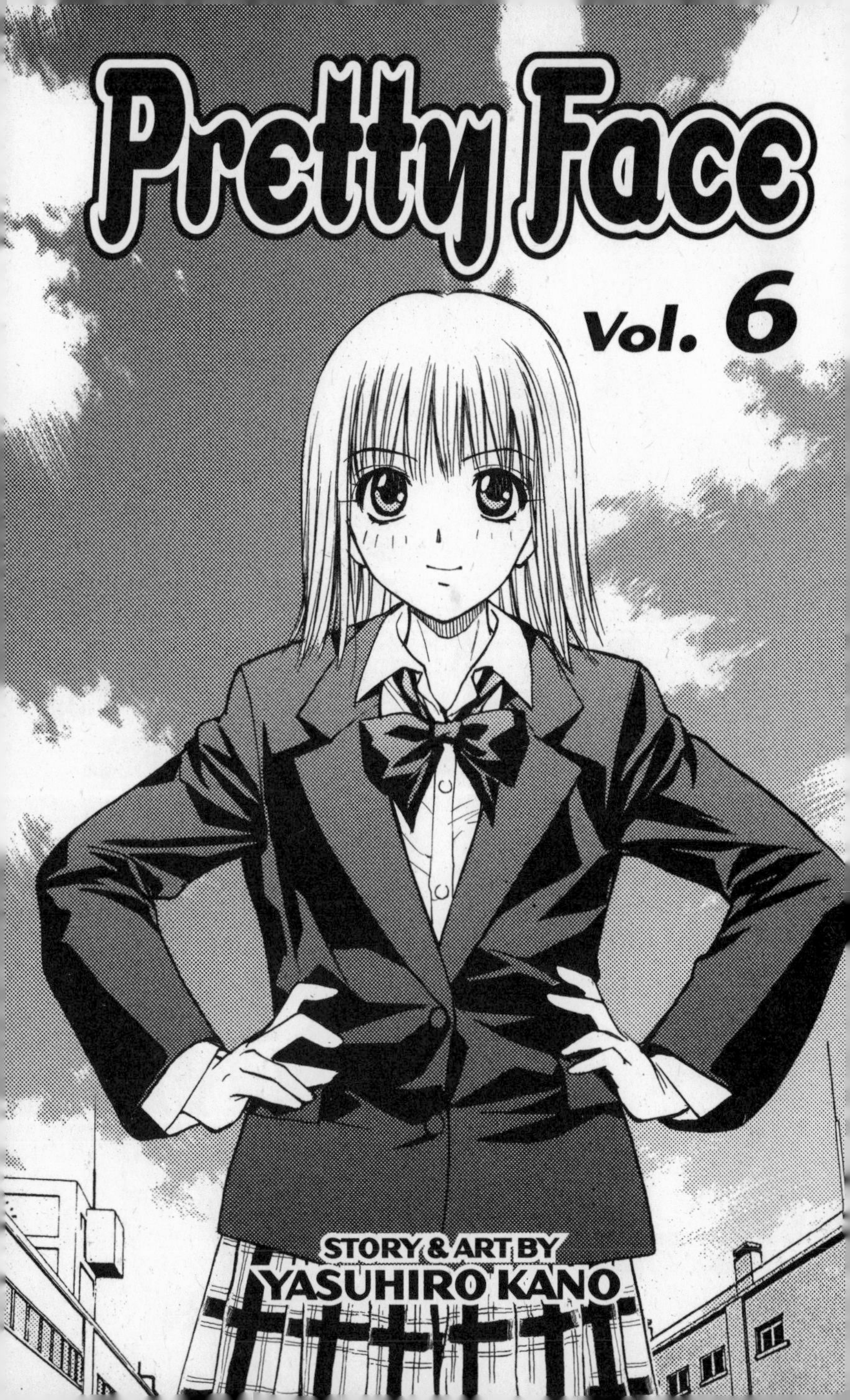

# CHARACTERS

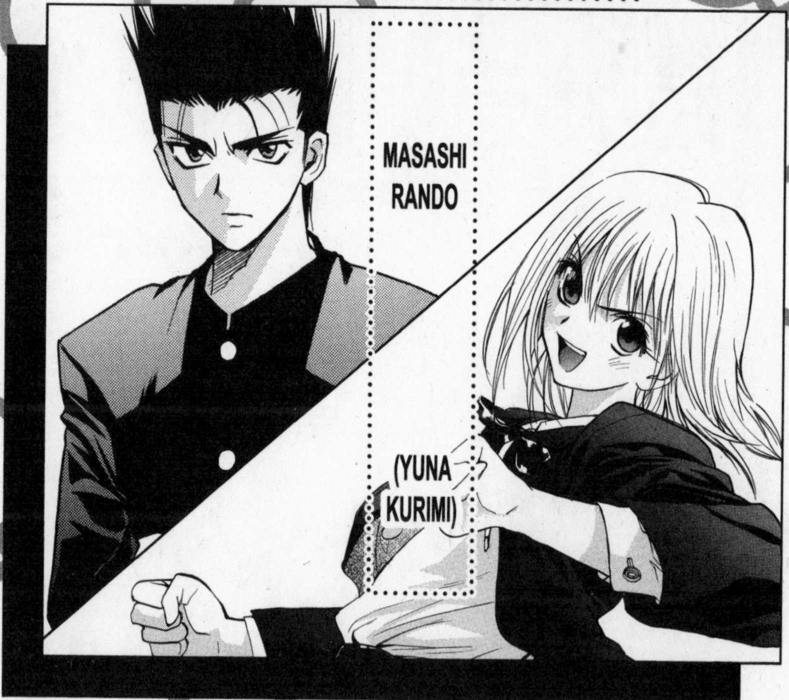
MASASHI RANDO
(YUNA KURIMI)

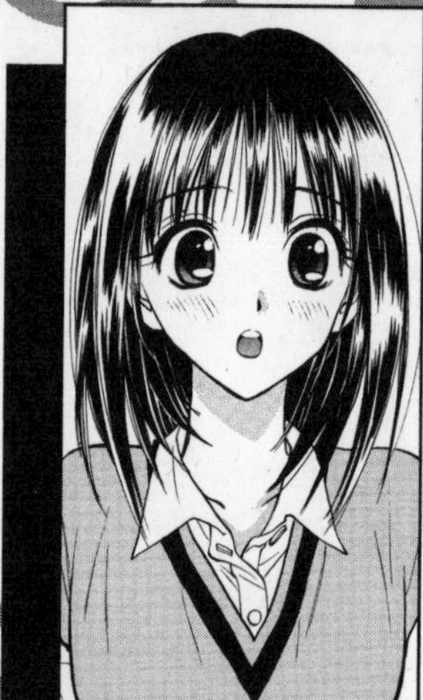

RINA KURIMI

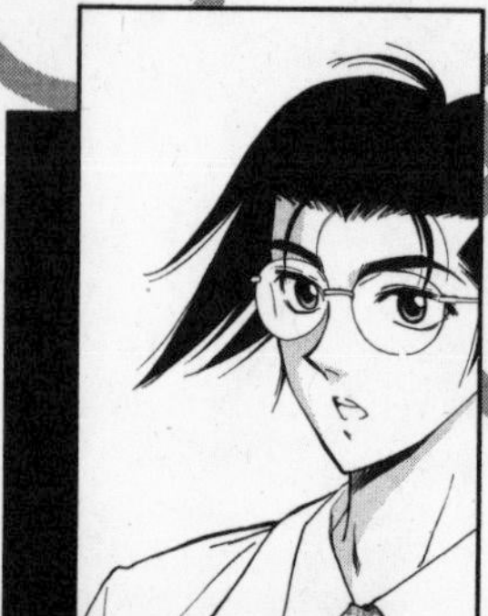

DR. MANABE

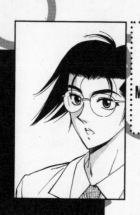

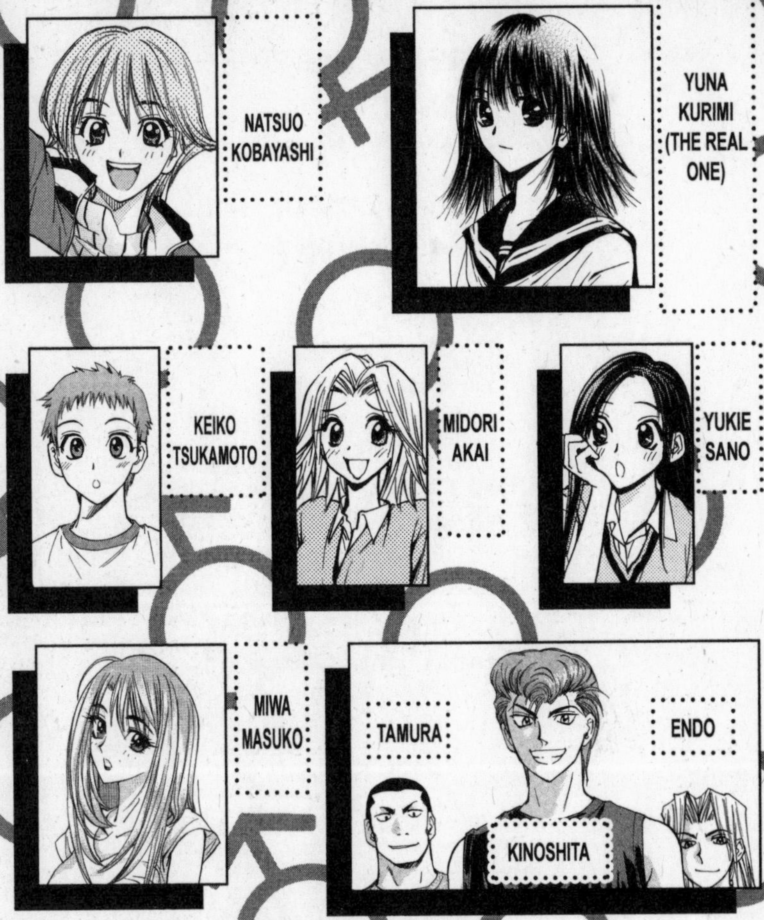
YUNA KURIMI (THE REAL ONE)
NATSUO KOBAYASHI
YUKIE SANO
MIDORI AKAI
KEIKO TSUKAMOTO
ENDO
KINOSHITA
TAMURA
MIWA MASUKO

# STORY

On the way home from a karate tournament, teenage badass Masashi Rando is caught in a horrible bus accident. When he wakes up from his coma a year later, his disfigured face has been reconstructed into the image of *Rina Kurimi, the girl he has a crush on!* Not knowing what Rando originally looked like, the mad plastic surgeon Dr. Manabe used a photo in Rando's wallet as the model for his resconstruction. Abandoned by his friends and parents, Rando is mistaken for Rina's long-lost twin sister and adopted into her family. Struggling with his impure feelings for Rina, Rando tries to be a good "big sister" until he can find the real Yuna Kurimi. But will he ever find her? And will he ever get his *real* face back?

# PRETTY FACE
## Vol. 6
### CONTENTS

# Chapter 46: I'll Nurse You (Natsuo Style)

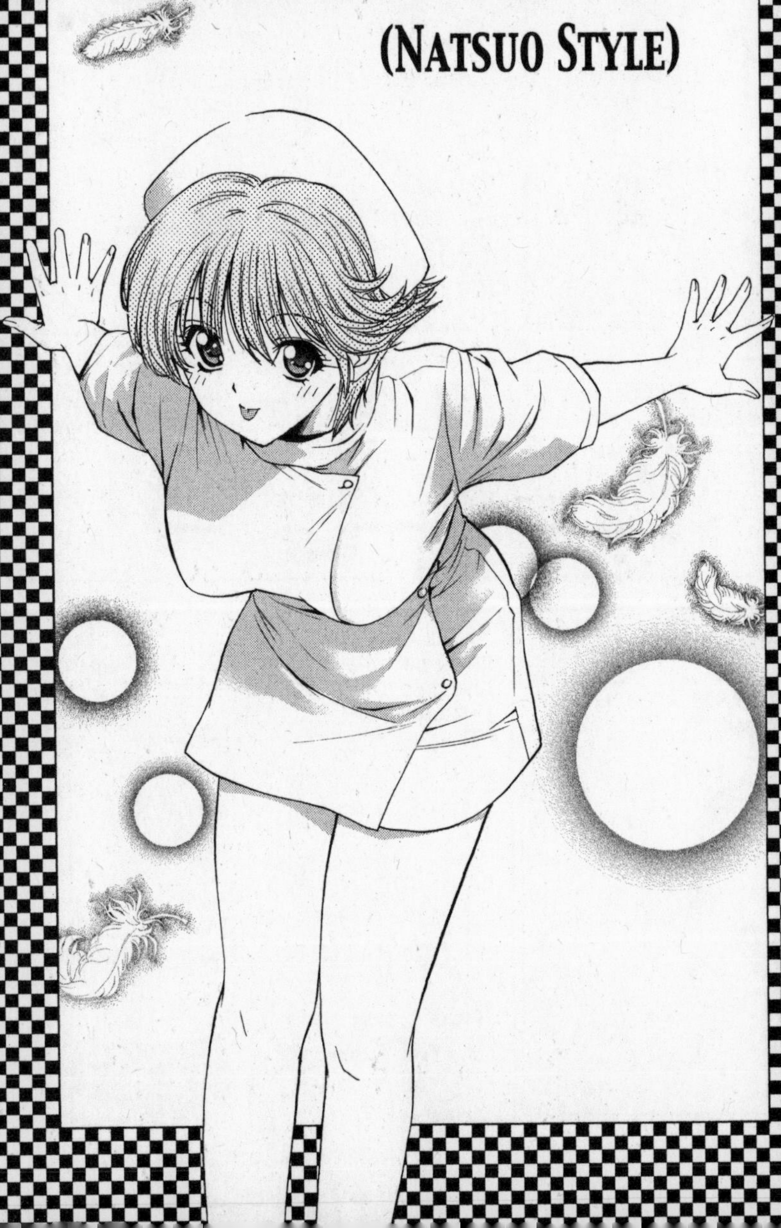

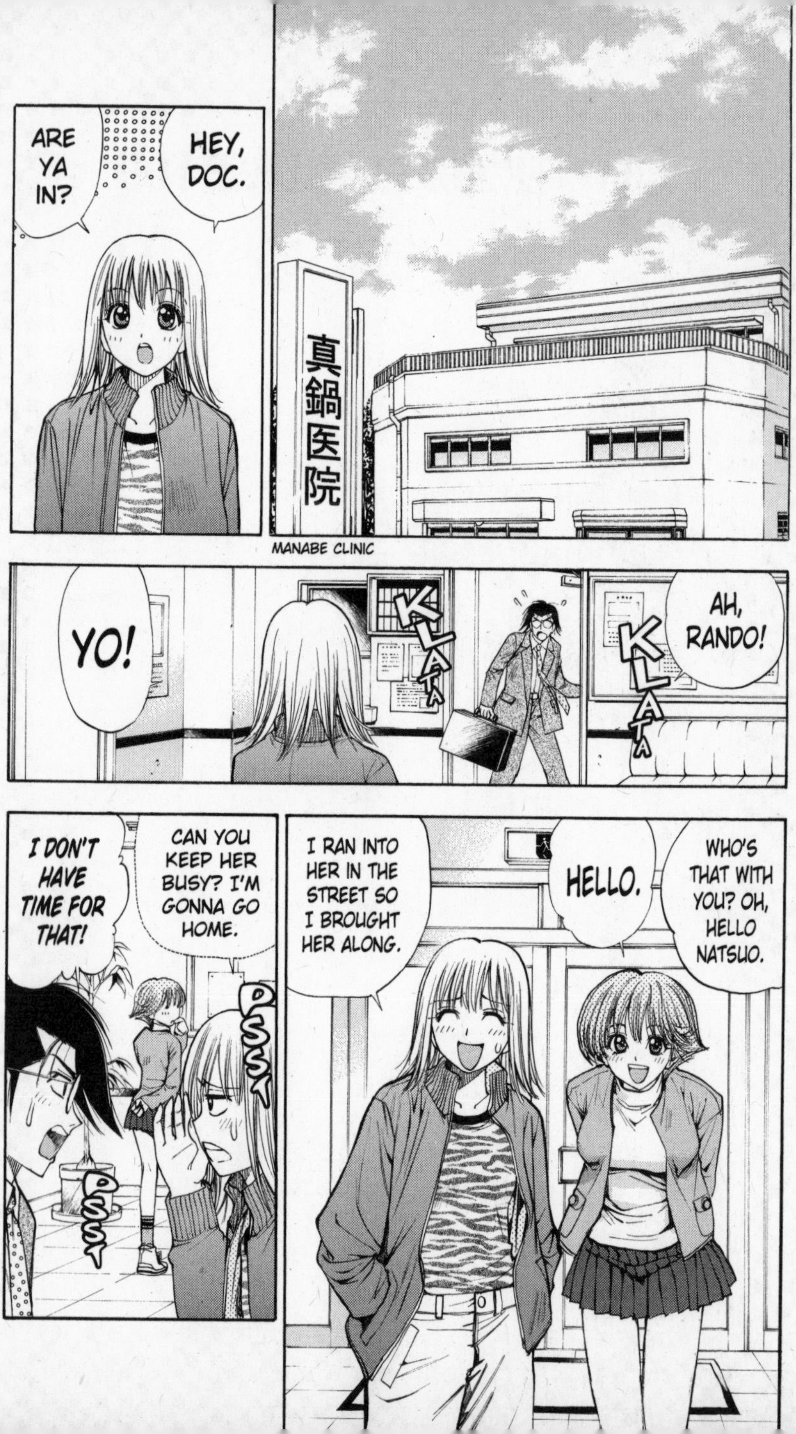
真鍋医院
MANABE CLINIC
HEY, DOC.
ARE YA IN?
AH, RANDO!
KLATA
KLATA
YO!
WHO'S THAT WITH YOU? OH, HELLO NATSUO.
HELLO.
I RAN INTO HER IN THE STREET SO I BROUGHT HER ALONG.
CAN YOU KEEP HER BUSY? I'M GONNA GO HOME.
PSST
I DON'T HAVE TIME FOR THAT!
PSST

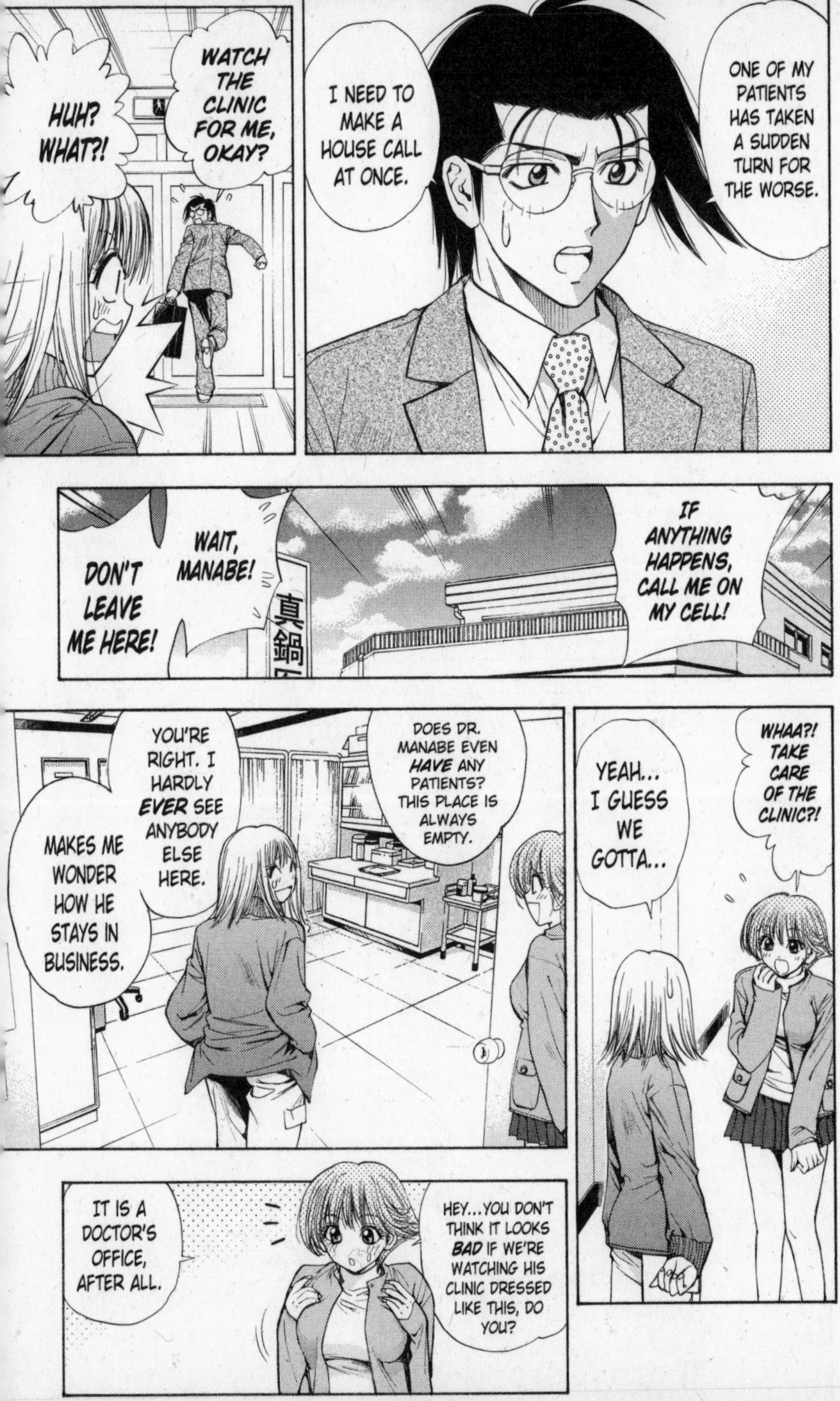
ONE OF MY PATIENTS HAS TAKEN A SUDDEN TURN FOR THE WORSE.
I NEED TO MAKE A HOUSE CALL AT ONCE.
WATCH THE CLINIC FOR ME, OKAY?
HUH? WHAT?!
IF ANYTHING HAPPENS, CALL ME ON MY CELL!
WAIT, MANABE!
DON'T LEAVE ME HERE!
WHAA?! TAKE CARE OF THE CLINIC?!
YEAH... I GUESS WE GOTTA...
DOES DR. MANABE EVEN *HAVE* ANY PATIENTS? THIS PLACE IS ALWAYS EMPTY.
YOU'RE RIGHT. I HARDLY *EVER* SEE ANYBODY ELSE HERE.
MAKES ME WONDER HOW HE STAYS IN BUSINESS.
HEY...YOU DON'T THINK IT LOOKS *BAD* IF WE'RE WATCHING HIS CLINIC DRESSED LIKE THIS, DO YOU?
IT IS A DOCTOR'S OFFICE, AFTER ALL.

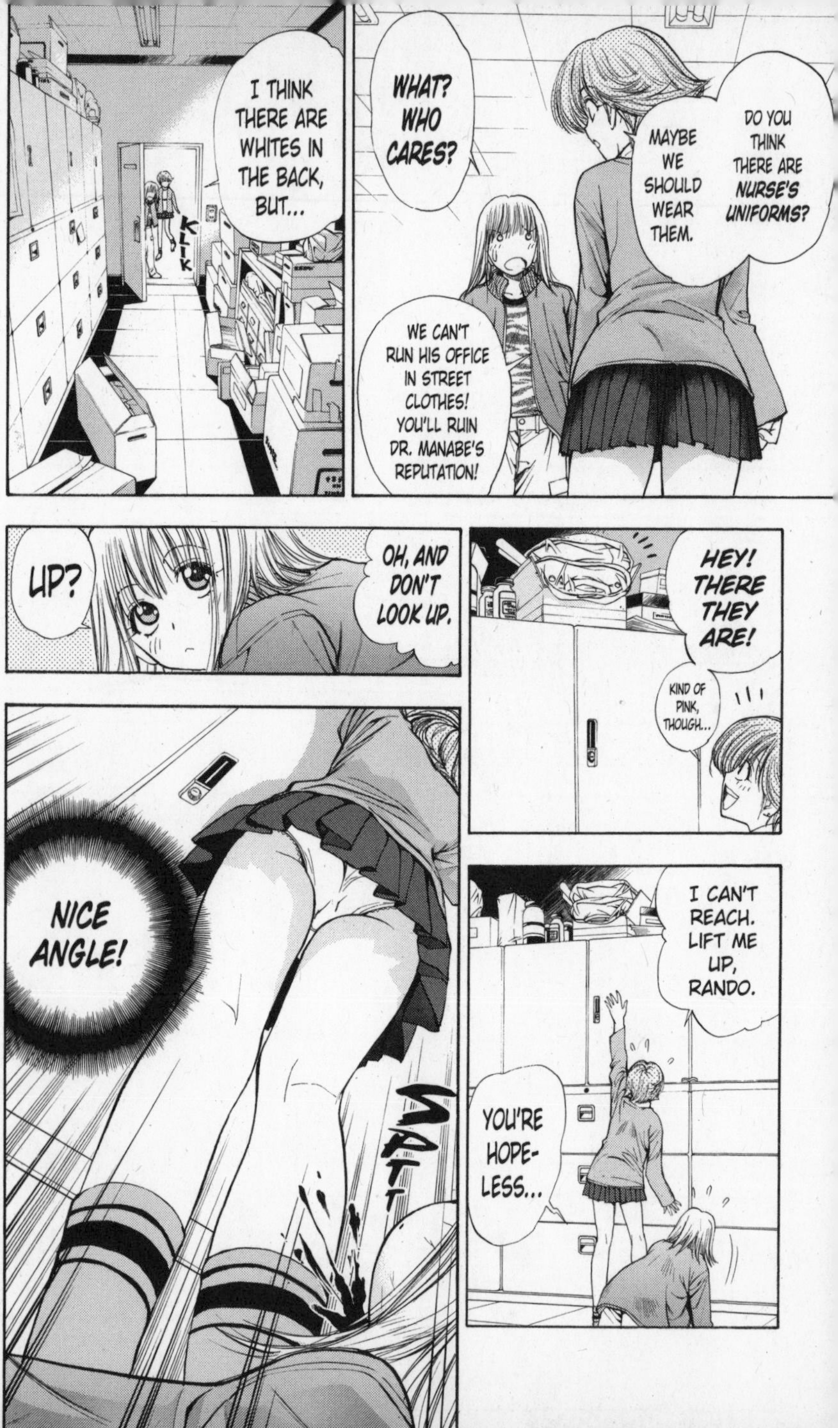
DO YOU THINK THERE ARE NURSE'S UNIFORMS?
MAYBE WE SHOULD WEAR THEM.
WHAT? WHO CARES?
WE CAN'T RUN HIS OFFICE IN STREET CLOTHES! YOU'LL RUIN DR. MANABE'S REPUTATION!
I THINK THERE ARE WHITES IN THE BACK, BUT...
KLIK
HEY! THERE THEY ARE!
KIND OF PINK, THOUGH...
I CAN'T REACH. LIFT ME UP, RANDO.
YOU'RE HOPE-LESS...
OH, AND DON'T LOOK UP.
UP?
NICE ANGLE!
SPLTT

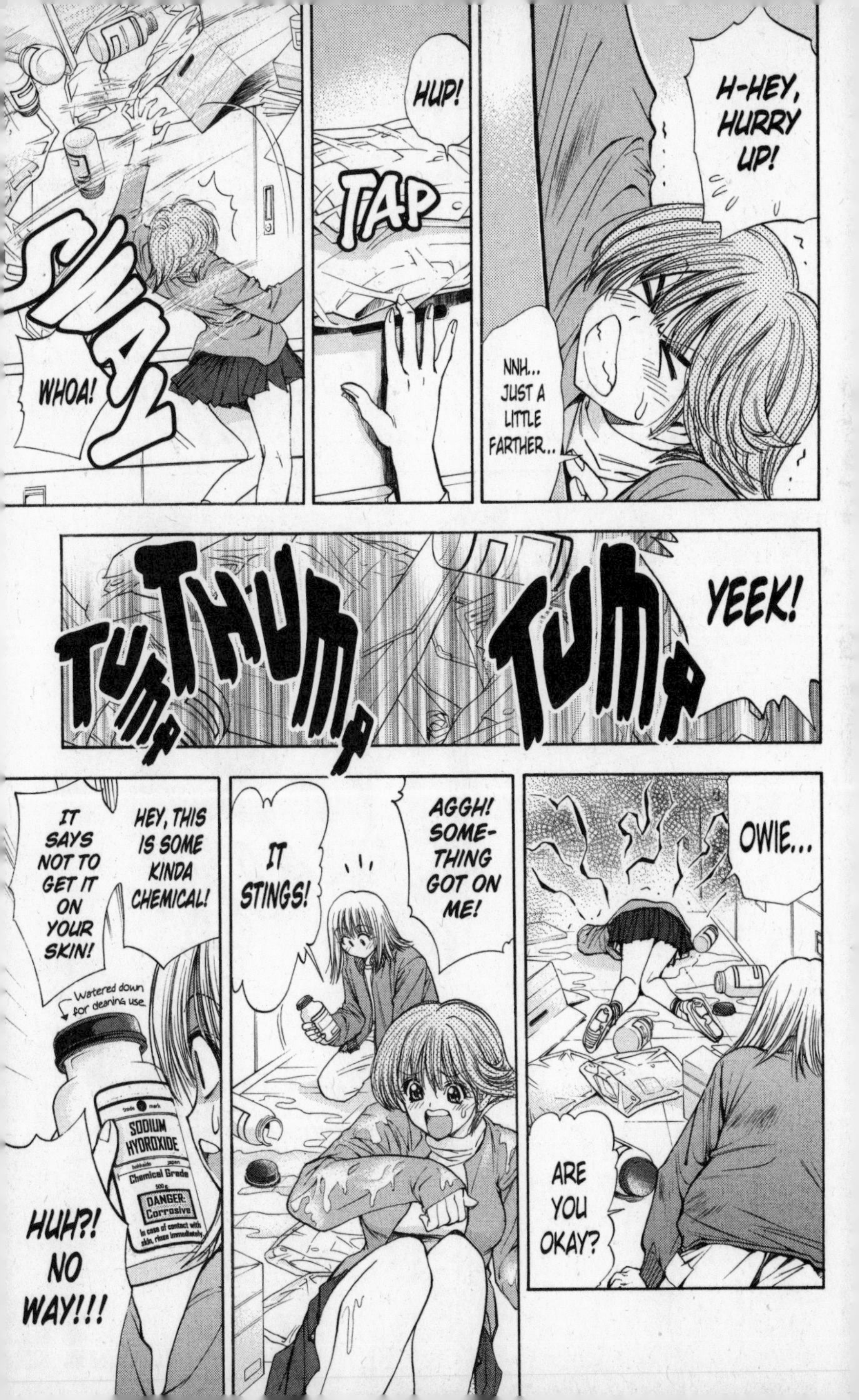
H-HEY, HURRY UP!
NNH... JUST A LITTLE FARTHER...
HUP!
TAP
SWAY
WHOA!
YEEK!
TUMP
THUMP
TUMP
OWIE...
ARE YOU OKAY?
AGGH! SOME-THING GOT ON ME!
IT STINGS!
HEY, THIS IS SOME KINDA CHEMICAL!
IT SAYS NOT TO GET IT ON YOUR SKIN!
Watered down for cleaning use
SODIUM HYDROXIDE
Chemical Grade
DANGER: Corrosive
In case of contact with skin, rinse immediately.
HUH?! NO WAY!!!

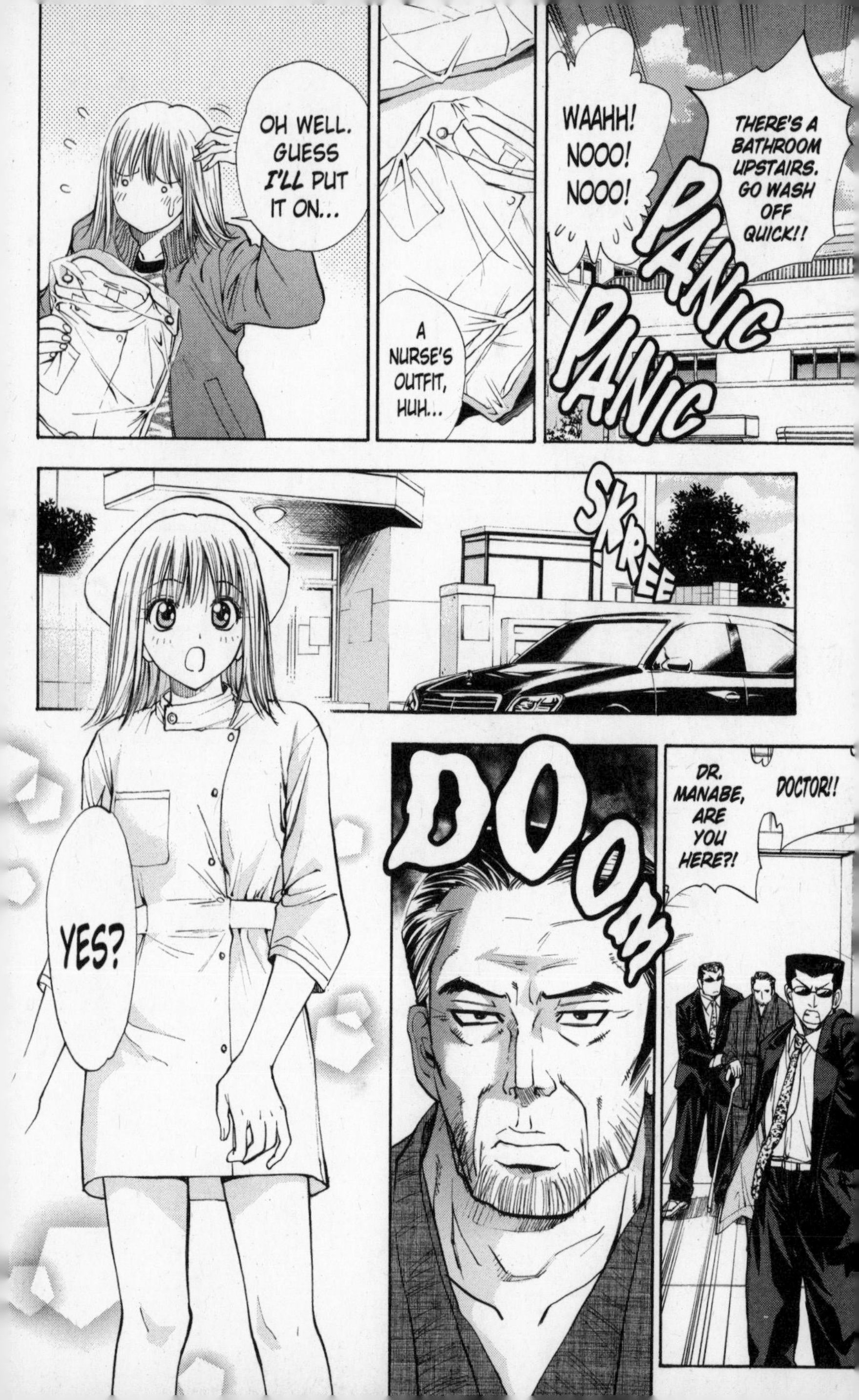
THERE'S A BATHROOM UPSTAIRS. GO WASH OFF QUICK!!
WAAHH! NOOO! NOOO!
PANIC
PANIC
A NURSE'S OUTFIT, HUH...
OH WELL. GUESS *I'LL* PUT IT ON...
SKREE
DOCTOR!!
DR. MANABE, ARE YOU HERE?!
DOOOM
YES?

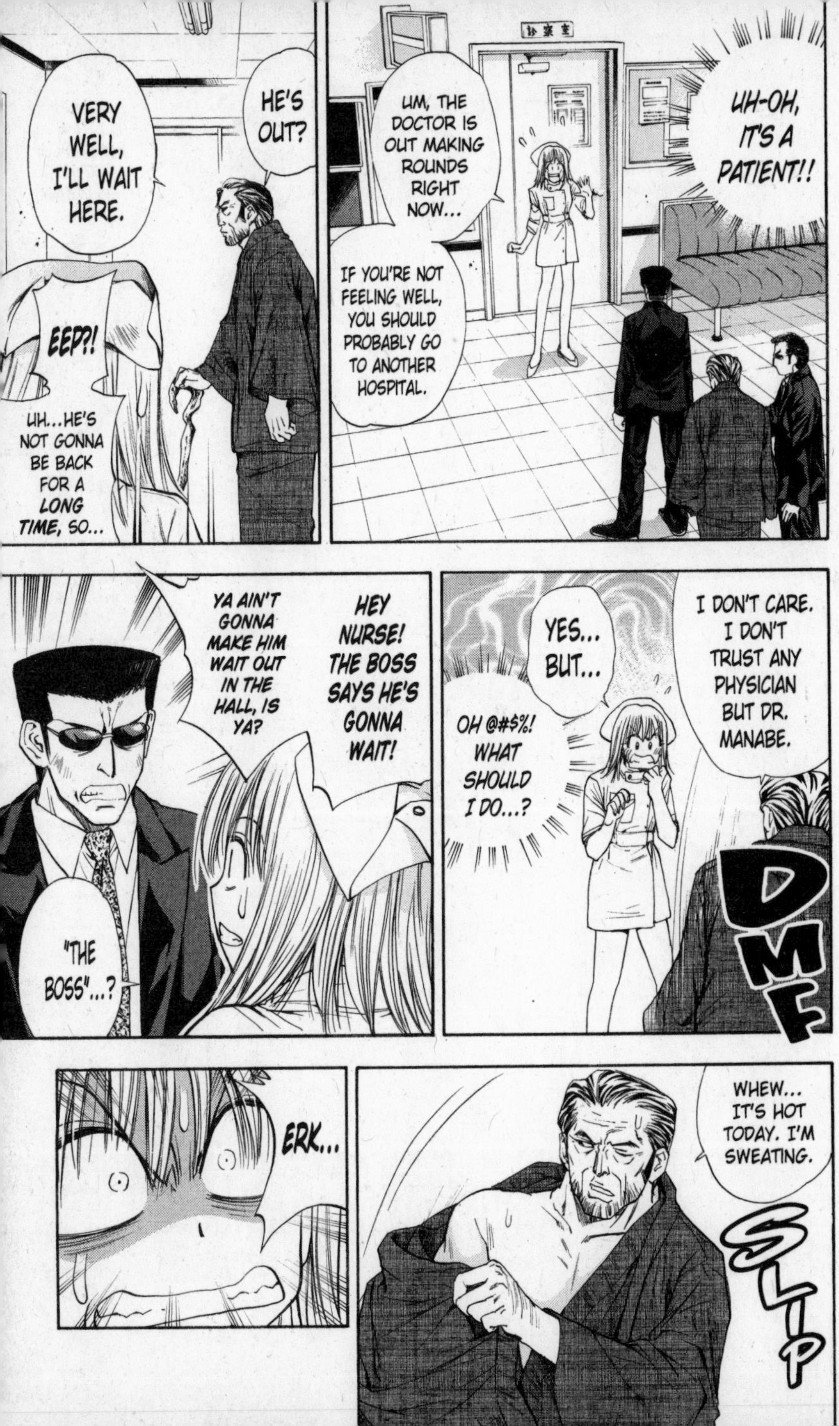

UH-OH, IT'S A PATIENT!!
診察室
UM, THE DOCTOR IS OUT MAKING ROUNDS RIGHT NOW...
IF YOU'RE NOT FEELING WELL, YOU SHOULD PROBABLY GO TO ANOTHER HOSPITAL.
HE'S OUT?
VERY WELL, I'LL WAIT HERE.
EEP?!
UH...HE'S NOT GONNA BE BACK FOR A LONG TIME, SO...
I DON'T CARE. I DON'T TRUST ANY PHYSICIAN BUT DR. MANABE.
YES... BUT...
OH @#$%! WHAT SHOULD I DO...?
DMF
HEY NURSE! THE BOSS SAYS HE'S GONNA WAIT!
YA AIN'T GONNA MAKE HIM WAIT OUT IN THE HALL, IS YA?
"THE BOSS"...?
WHEW... IT'S HOT TODAY. I'M SWEATING.
SLIP
ERK...

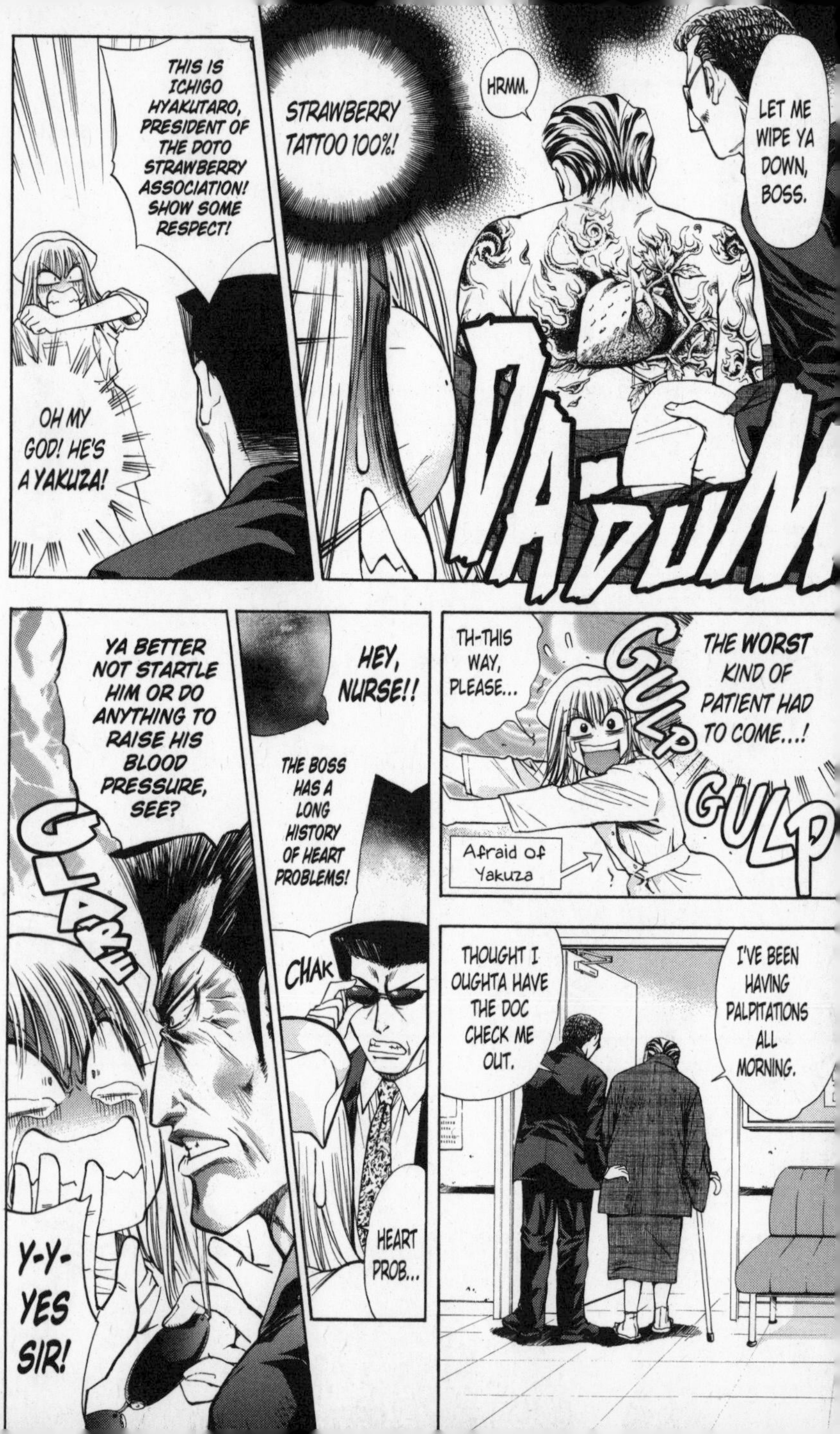
LET ME WIPE YA DOWN, BOSS.
HRMM.
STRAWBERRY TATTOO 100%!
DA-DUM
THIS IS ICHIGO HYAKUTARO, PRESIDENT OF THE DOTO STRAWBERRY ASSOCIATION! SHOW SOME RESPECT!
OH MY GOD! HE'S A YAKUZA!
THE WORST KIND OF PATIENT HAD TO COME...!
GULP
GULP
TH-THIS WAY, PLEASE...
Afraid of Yakuza
I'VE BEEN HAVING PALPITATIONS ALL MORNING.
THOUGHT I OUGHTA HAVE THE DOC CHECK ME OUT.
HEY, NURSE!!
THE BOSS HAS A LONG HISTORY OF HEART PROBLEMS!
CHAK
HEART PROB...
YA BETTER NOT STARTLE HIM OR DO ANYTHING TO RAISE HIS BLOOD PRESSURE, SEE?
GLARE
Y-Y-YES SIR!

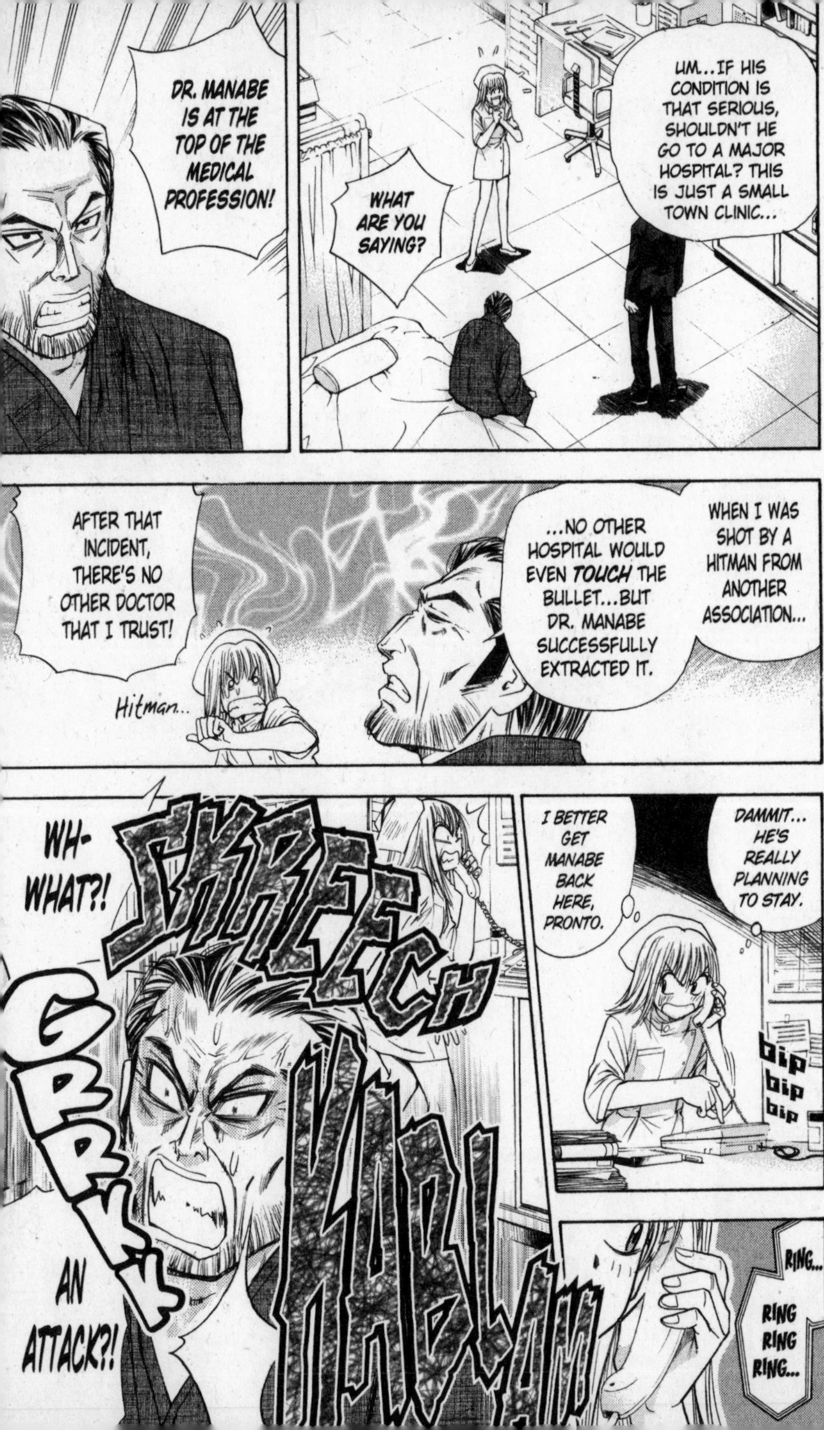

UM...IF HIS CONDITION IS THAT SERIOUS, SHOULDN'T HE GO TO A MAJOR HOSPITAL? THIS IS JUST A SMALL TOWN CLINIC...
WHAT ARE YOU SAYING?
DR. MANABE IS AT THE TOP OF THE MEDICAL PROFESSION!
WHEN I WAS SHOT BY A HITMAN FROM ANOTHER ASSOCIATION...
...NO OTHER HOSPITAL WOULD EVEN TOUCH THE BULLET...BUT DR. MANABE SUCCESSFULLY EXTRACTED IT.
AFTER THAT INCIDENT, THERE'S NO OTHER DOCTOR THAT I TRUST!
Hitman...
DAMMIT... HE'S REALLY PLANNING TO STAY.
I BETTER GET MANABE BACK HERE, PRONTO.
bip bip bip
RING... RING RING RING...
SKREECH
WH-WHAT?!
AN ATTACK?!

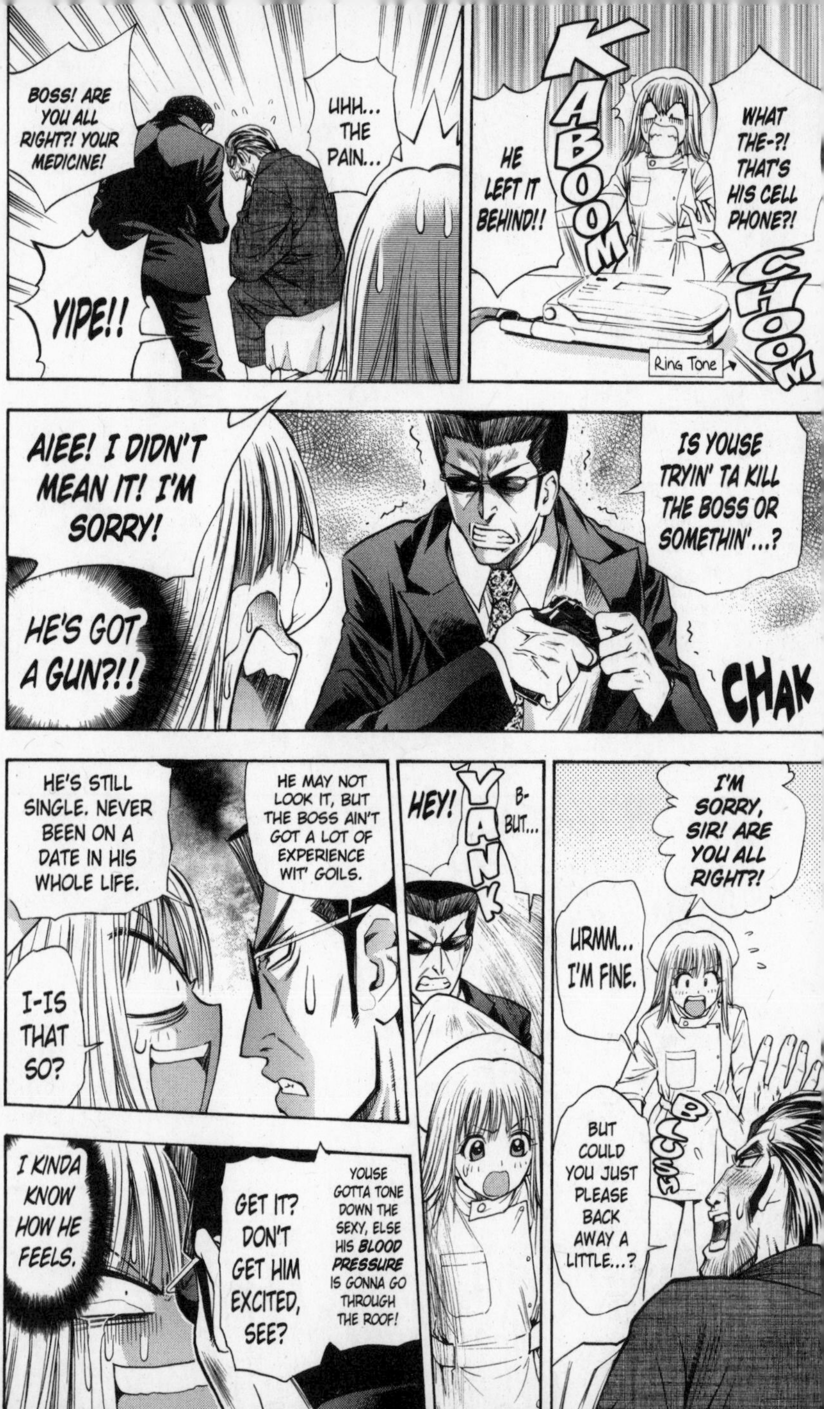
KABOOM
WHAT THE-?! THAT'S HIS CELL PHONE?!
HE LEFT IT BEHIND!!
CHOOM
Ring Tone
UHH... THE PAIN...
BOSS! ARE YOU ALL RIGHT?! YOUR MEDICINE!
YIPE!!
IS YOUSE TRYIN' TA KILL THE BOSS OR SOMETHIN'...?
AIEE! I DIDN'T MEAN IT! I'M SORRY!
HE'S GOT A GUN?!!
CHAK
I'M SORRY, SIR! ARE YOU ALL RIGHT?!
URMM... I'M FINE.
BUT COULD YOU JUST PLEASE BACK AWAY A LITTLE...?
B-BUT...
YANK
HEY!
HE MAY NOT LOOK IT, BUT THE BOSS AIN'T GOT A LOT OF EXPERIENCE WIT' GOILS.
HE'S STILL SINGLE. NEVER BEEN ON A DATE IN HIS WHOLE LIFE.
I-IS THAT SO?
YOUSE GOTTA TONE DOWN THE SEXY, ELSE HIS BLOOD PRESSURE IS GONNA GO THROUGH THE ROOF!
GET IT? DON'T GET HIM EXCITED, SEE?
I KINDA KNOW HOW HE FEELS.

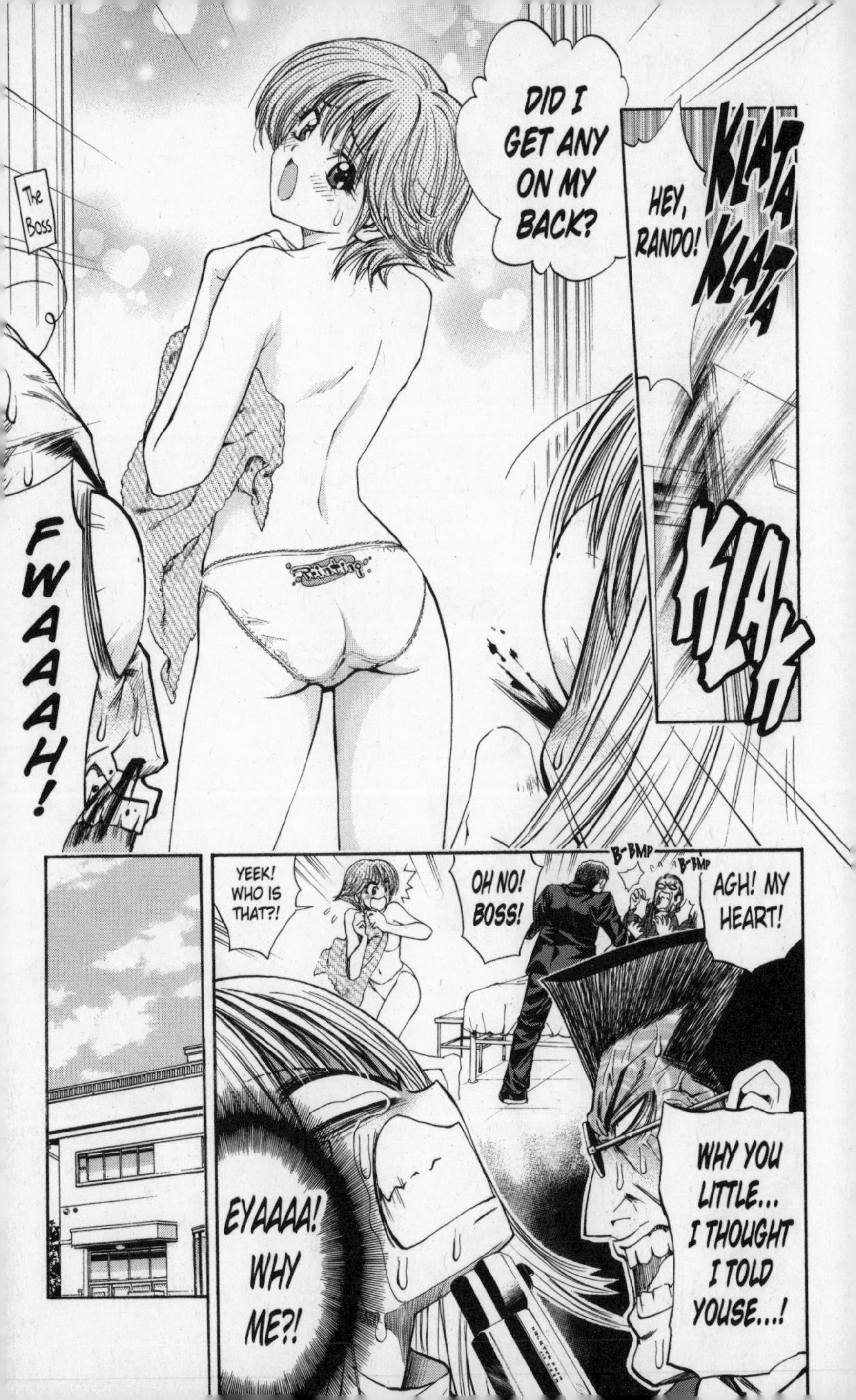
HEY, RANDO!
KLATA KLATA KLATA
KLAK
DID I GET ANY ON MY BACK?
The Boss
FWAAAAH!
B-BMP B-BMP
AGH! MY HEART!
OH NO! BOSS!
YEEK! WHO IS THAT?!
WHY YOU LITTLE... I THOUGHT I TOLD YOUSE...!
EYAAAA! WHY ME?!

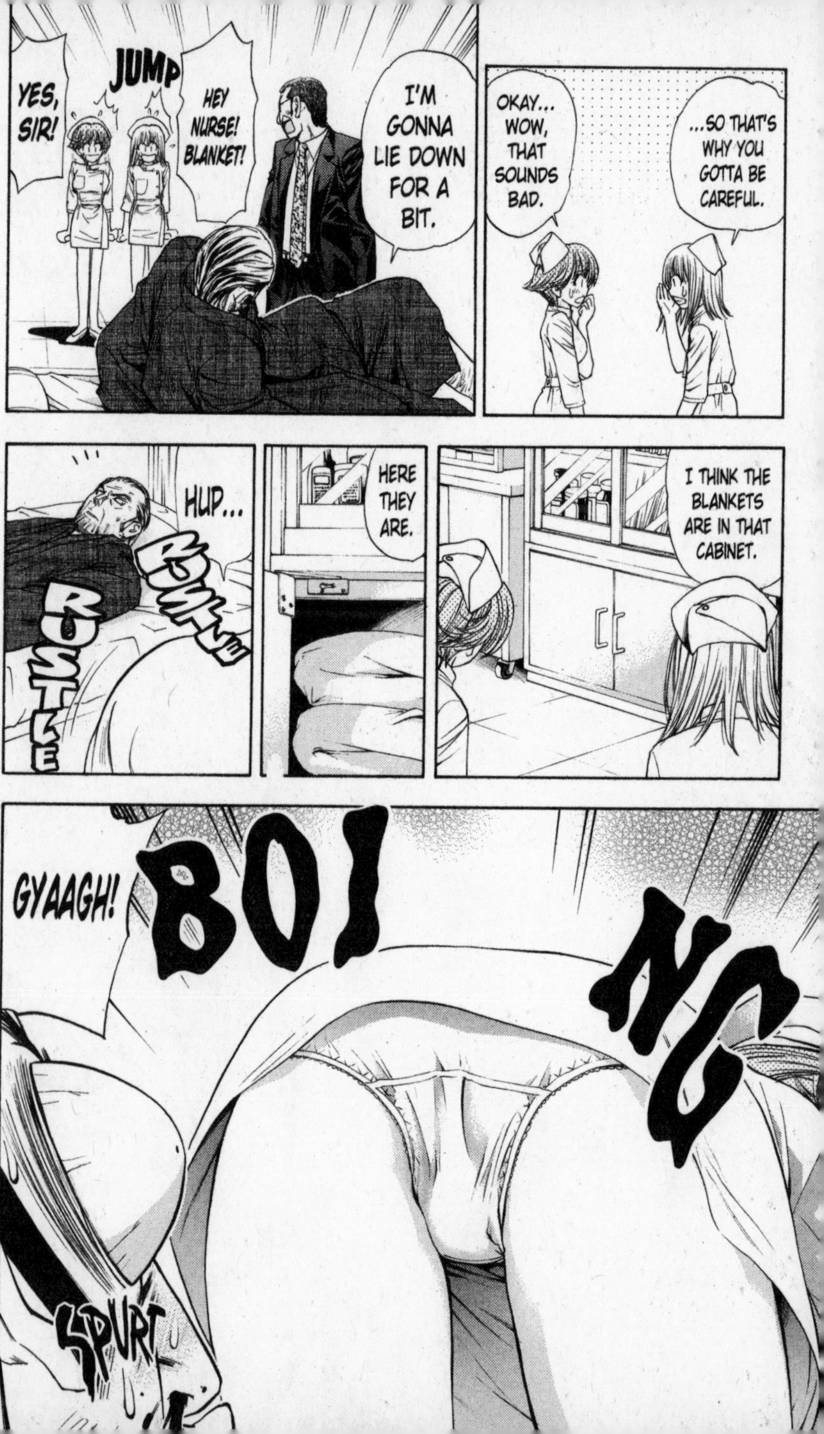
...SO THAT'S WHY YOU GOTTA BE CAREFUL.
OKAY... WOW, THAT SOUNDS BAD.
I'M GONNA LIE DOWN FOR A BIT.
HEY NURSE! BLANKET!
JUMP
YES, SIR!
I THINK THE BLANKETS ARE IN THAT CABINET.
HERE THEY ARE.
HUP...
RUSTLE
BOING
GYAAGH!
SPURT

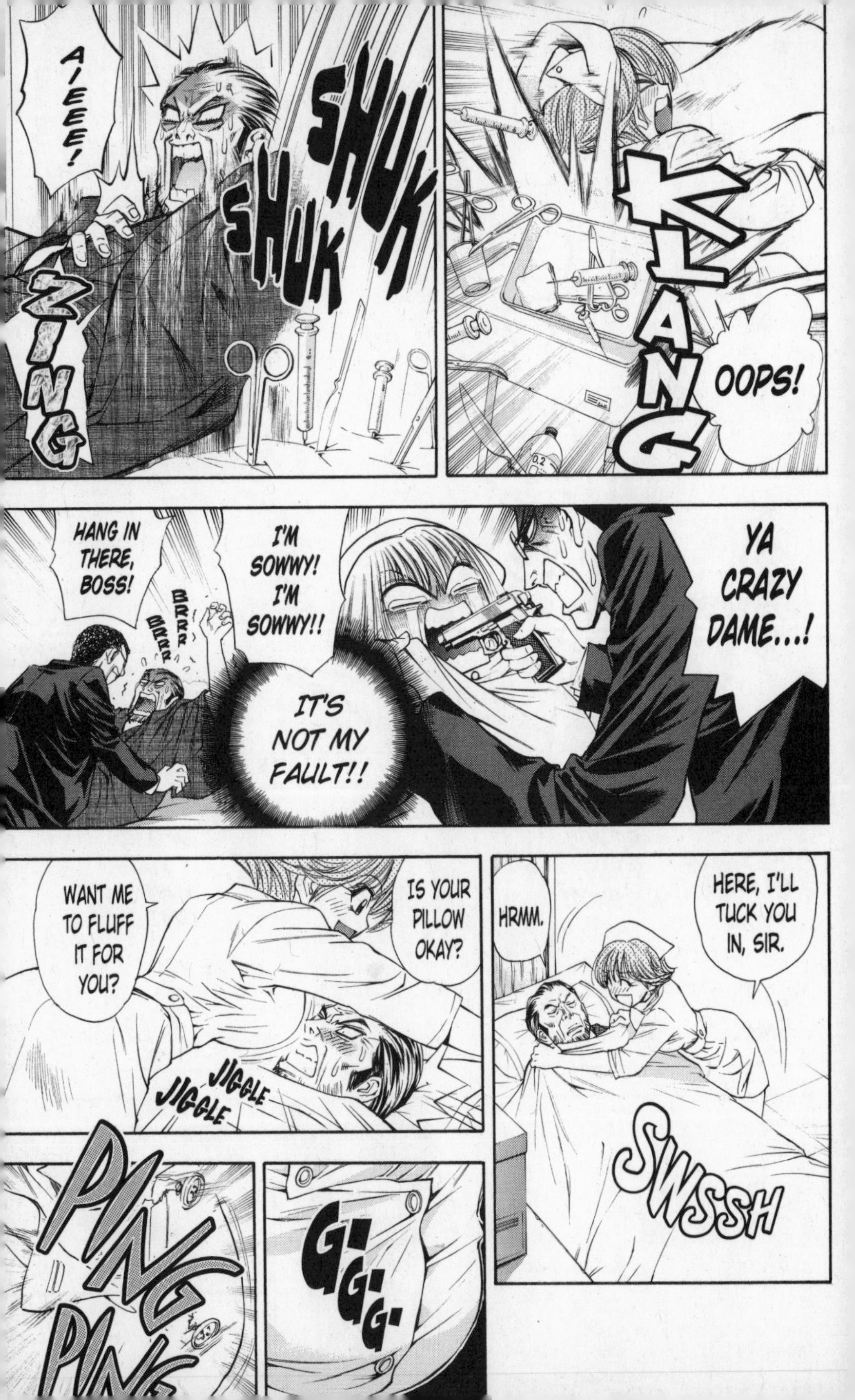
KLANG
OOPS!
SHUK SHUK
AIEEE!
ZING
YA CRAZY DAME...!
I'M SOWWY! I'M SOWWY!!
HANG IN THERE, BOSS!
BRRR BRRR
IT'S NOT MY FAULT!!
HERE, I'LL TUCK YOU IN, SIR.
HRMM.
SWSSH
IS YOUR PILLOW OKAY?
WANT ME TO FLUFF IT FOR YOU?
JIGGLE JIGGLE
GGGG
PING PING

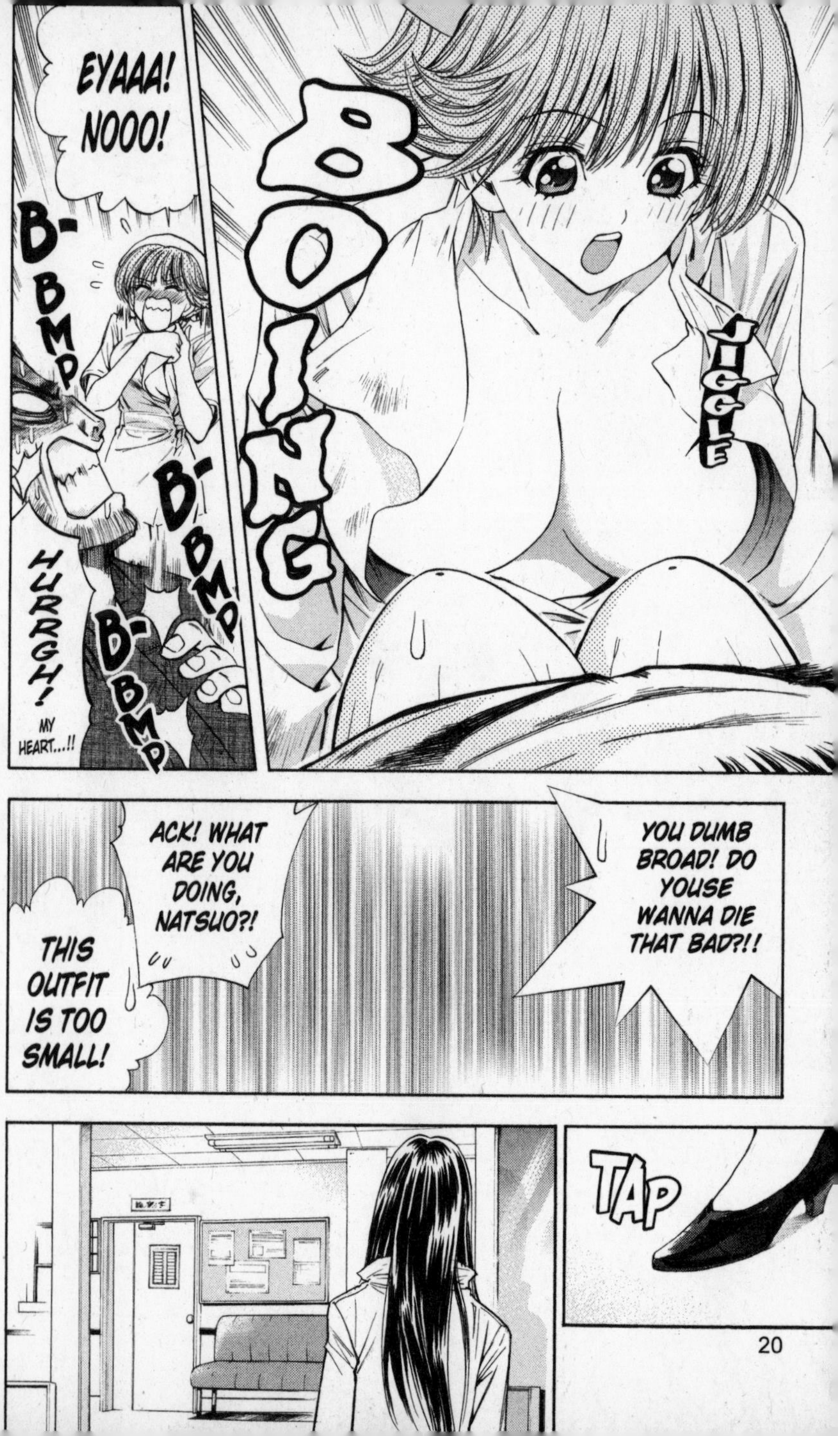
BOING
JIGGLE
EYAAA! NOOO!
B-BMP
B-BMP
HURRGH!
B-BMP
MY HEART...!!
YOU DUMB BROAD! DO YOUSE WANNA DIE THAT BAD?!!
ACK! WHAT ARE YOU DOING, NATSUO?!
THIS OUTFIT IS TOO SMALL!
TAP

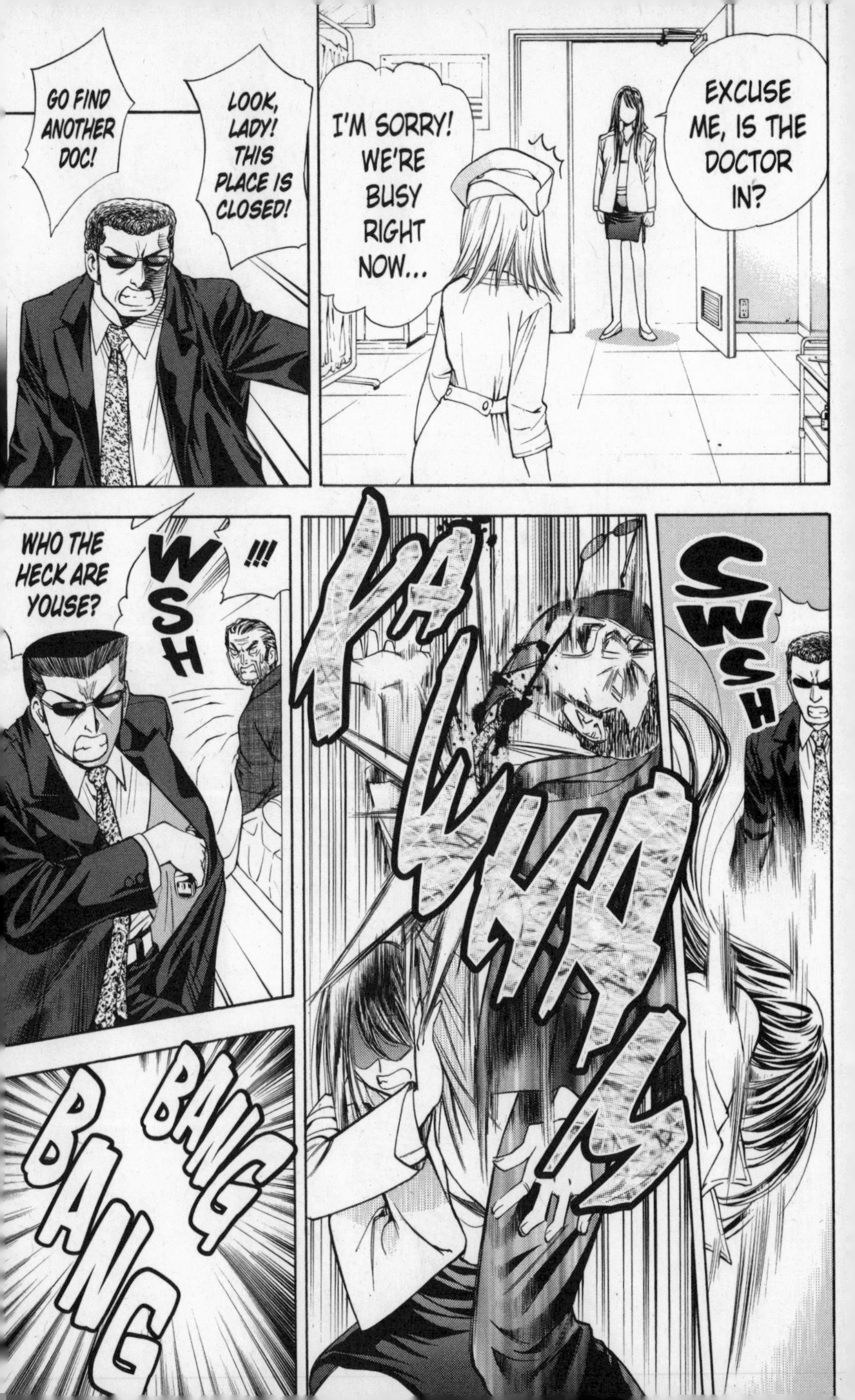
EXCUSE ME, IS THE DOCTOR IN?
I'M SORRY! WE'RE BUSY RIGHT NOW...
LOOK, LADY! THIS PLACE IS CLOSED!
GO FIND ANOTHER DOC!
SWSH
WSH !!!
WHO THE HECK ARE YOUSE?
BANG
BANG
BANG

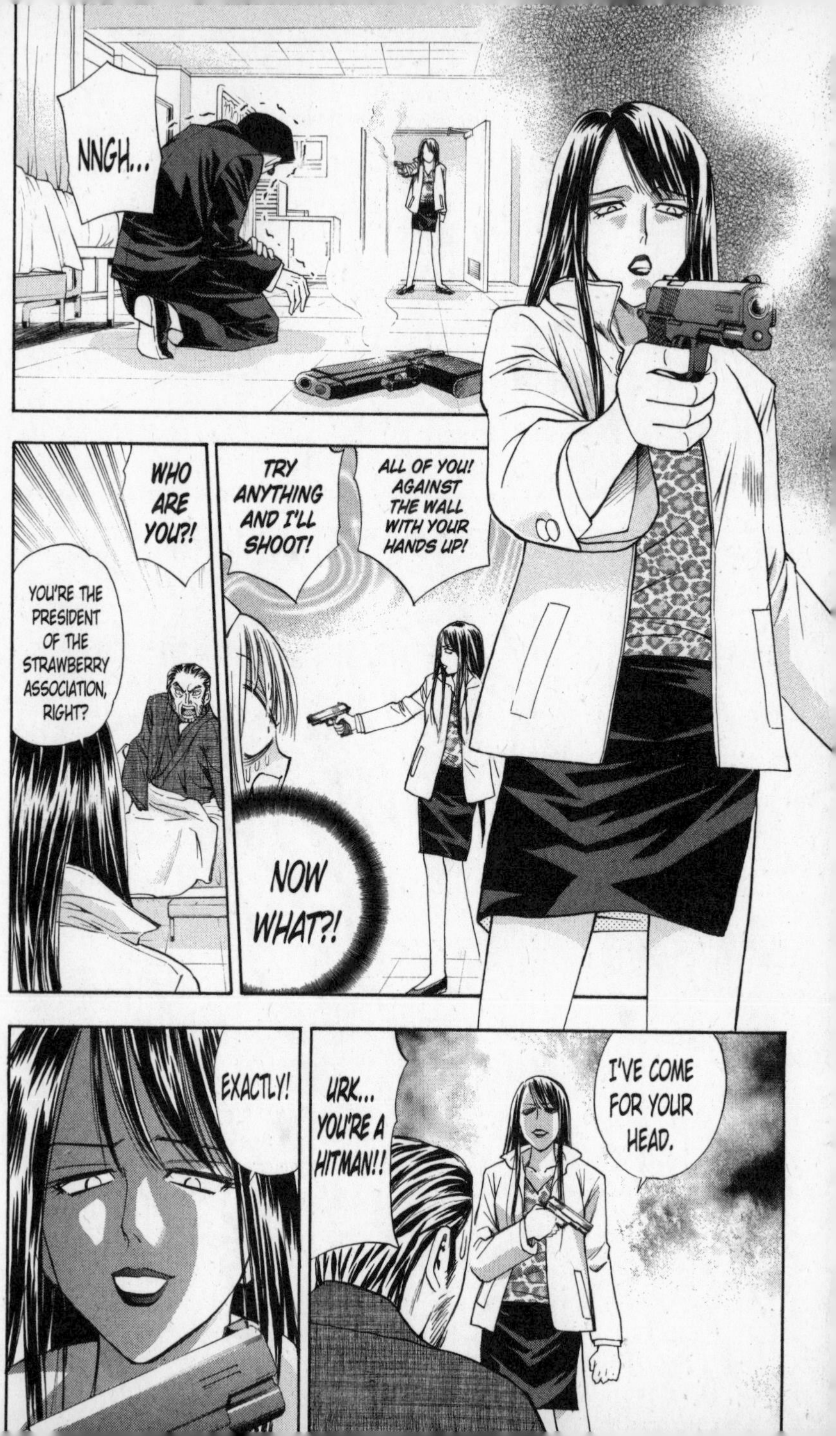
NNGH...
ALL OF YOU! AGAINST THE WALL WITH YOUR HANDS UP!
TRY ANYTHING AND I'LL SHOOT!
NOW WHAT?!
WHO ARE YOU?!
YOU'RE THE PRESIDENT OF THE STRAWBERRY ASSOCIATION, RIGHT?
I'VE COME FOR YOUR HEAD.
URK... YOU'RE A HITMAN!!
EXACTLY!

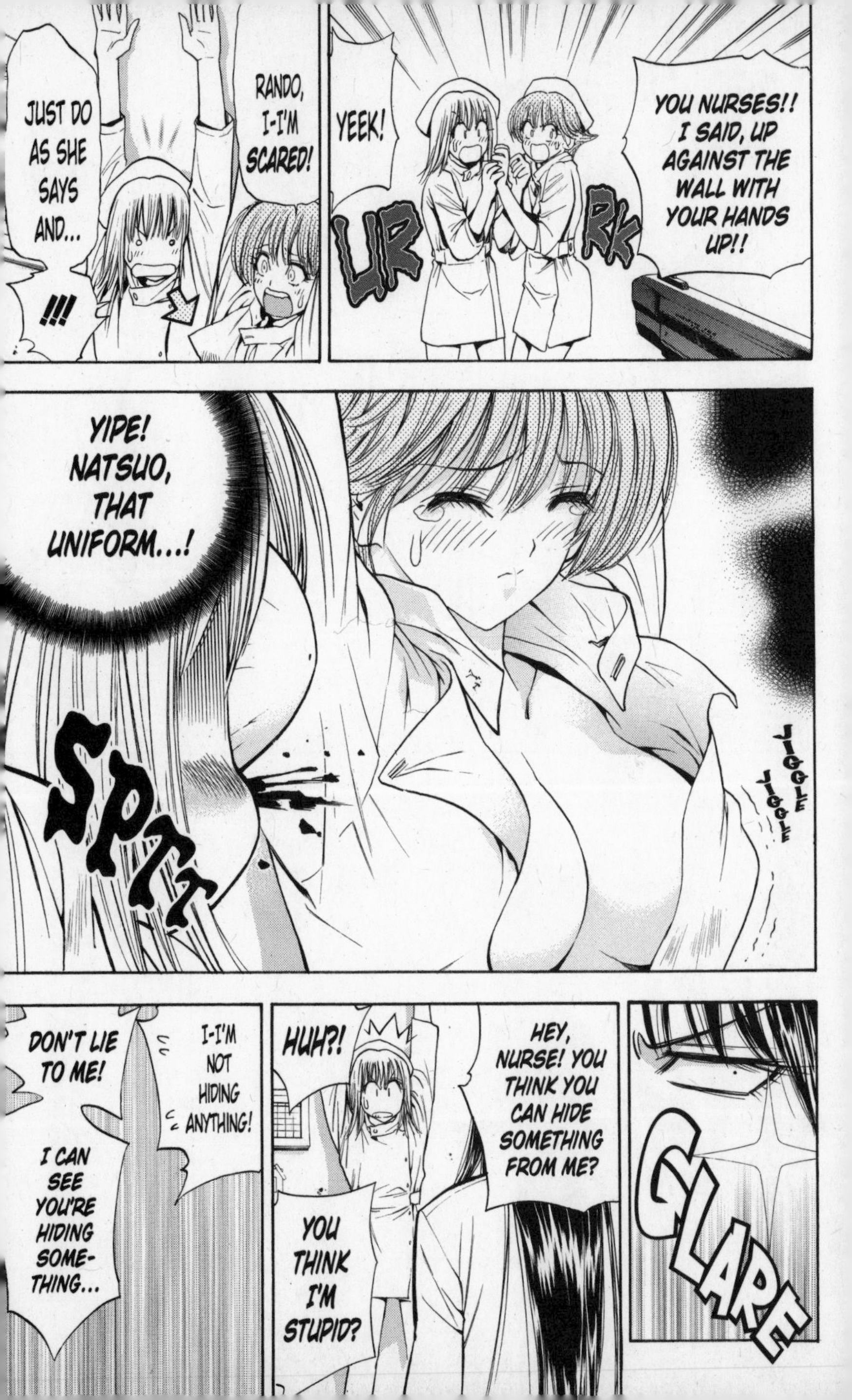
YOU NURSES!! I SAID, UP AGAINST THE WALL WITH YOUR HANDS UP!!
UR
RK
YEEK!
RANDO, I-I'M SCARED!
JUST DO AS SHE SAYS AND...
!!!
YIPE! NATSUO, THAT UNIFORM...!
JIGGLE
JIGGLE
SPTTT
GLARE
HEY, NURSE! YOU THINK YOU CAN HIDE SOMETHING FROM ME?
HUH?!
YOU THINK I'M STUPID?
I-I'M NOT HIDING ANYTHING!
DON'T LIE TO ME!
I CAN SEE YOU'RE HIDING SOME-THING...

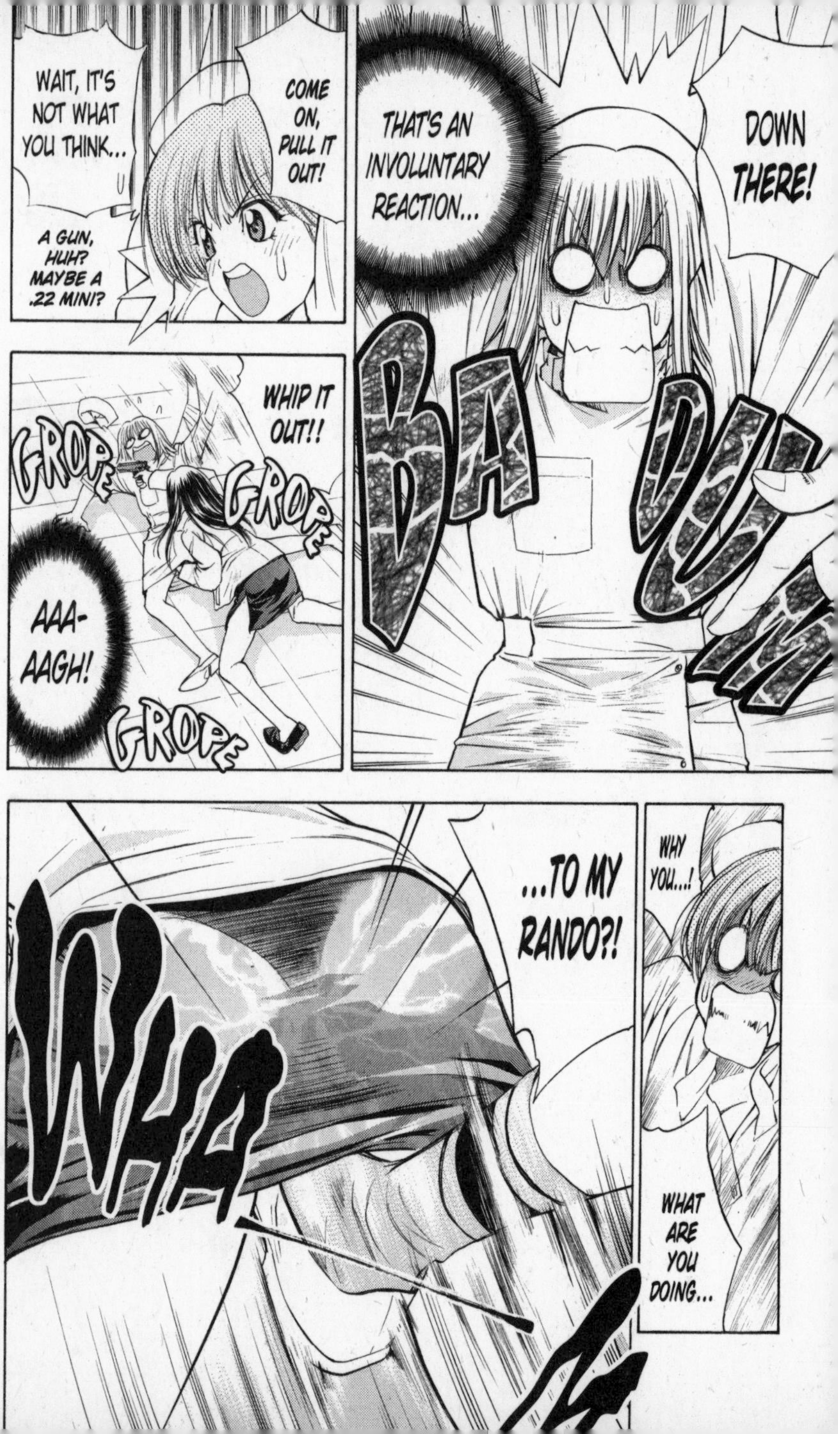
DOWN THERE!
THAT'S AN INVOLUNTARY REACTION...
BA DUM
COME ON, PULL IT OUT!
WAIT, IT'S NOT WHAT YOU THINK...
A GUN, HUH? MAYBE A .22 MINI?
WHIP IT OUT!!
GROPE
GROPE
AAA-AAGH!
GROPE
WHY YOU...!
WHAT ARE YOU DOING...
...TO MY RANDO?!
WHAP

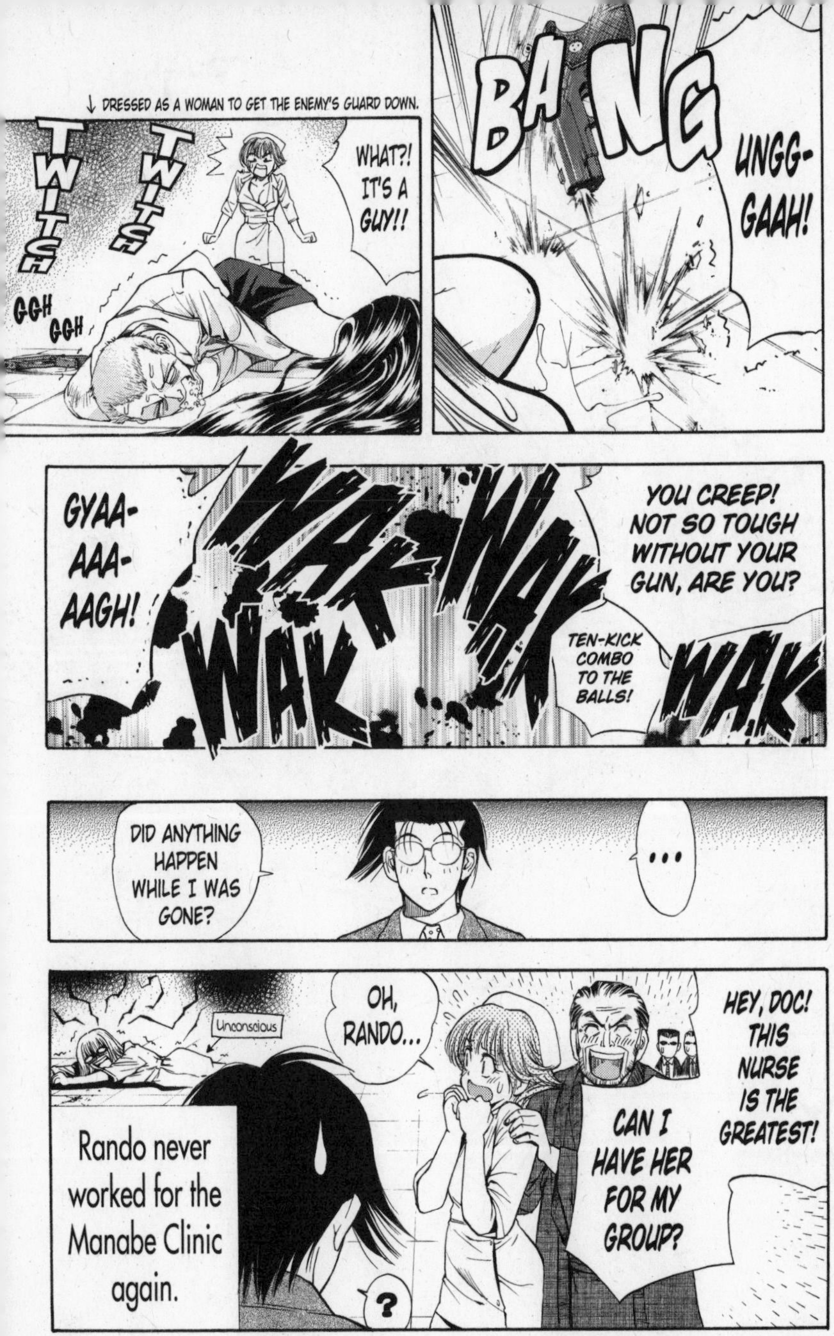
BANG
UNGG-GAAH!
↓ DRESSED AS A WOMAN TO GET THE ENEMY'S GUARD DOWN.
TWITCH
TWITCH
WHAT?! IT'S A GUY!!
GGH GGH
WAK
YOU CREEP! NOT SO TOUGH WITHOUT YOUR GUN, ARE YOU?
TEN-KICK COMBO TO THE BALLS!
WAK WAK WAK
GYAA-AAA-AAGH!
...
DID ANYTHING HAPPEN WHILE I WAS GONE?
HEY, DOC! THIS NURSE IS THE GREATEST!
CAN I HAVE HER FOR MY GROUP?
OH, RANDO...
Unconscious
?
Rando never worked for the Manabe Clinic again.

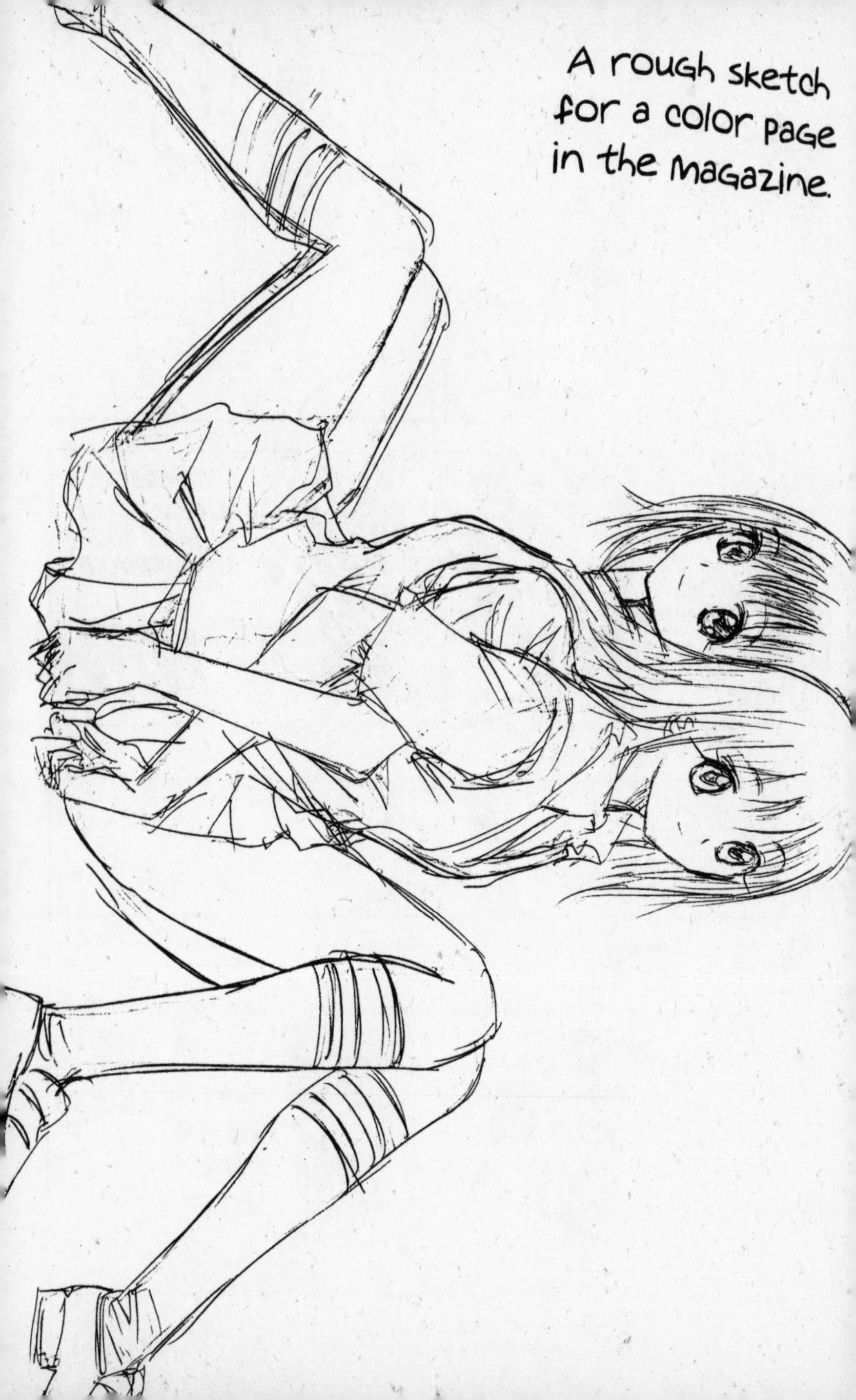

A rough sketch for a color page in the magazine.

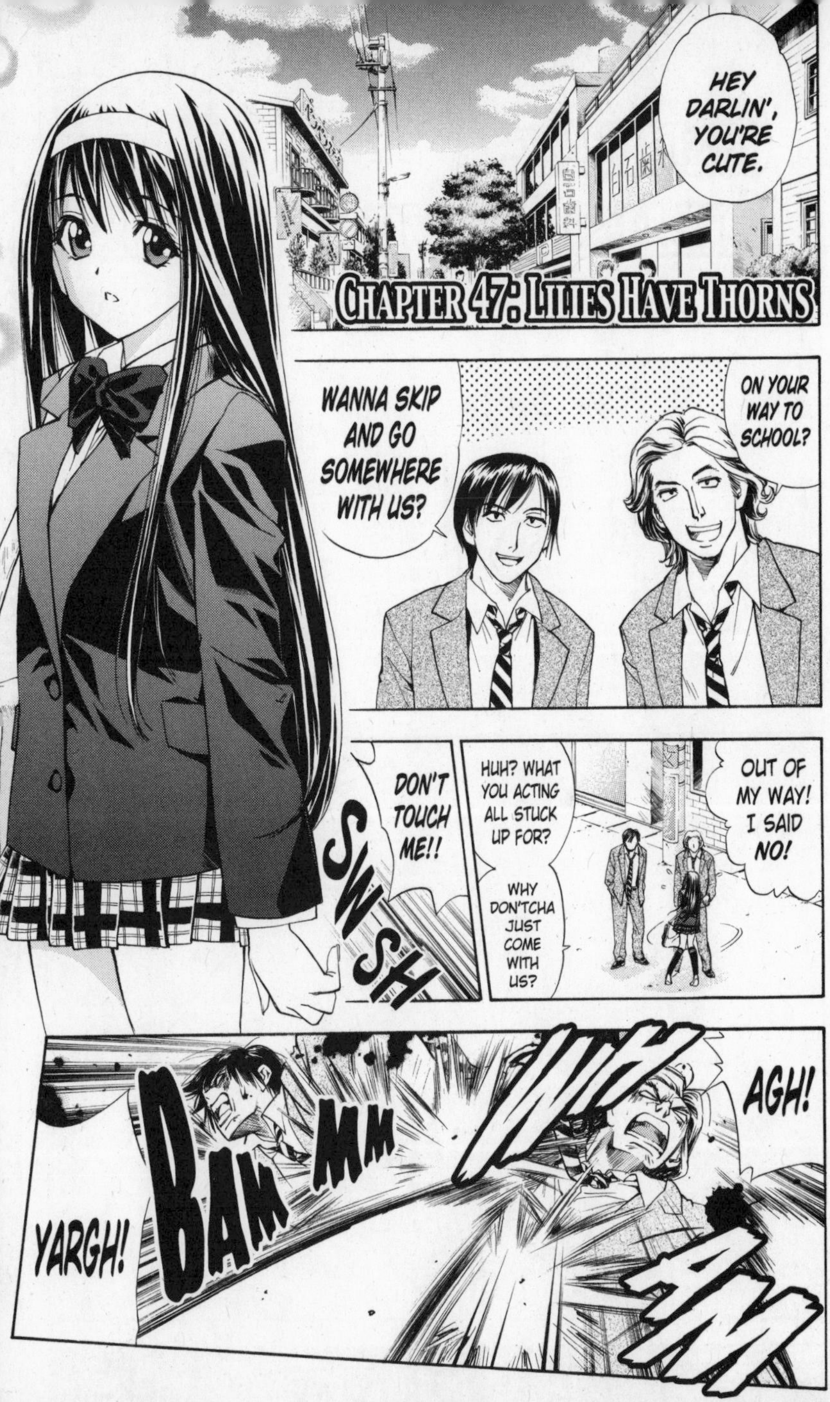
HEY DARLIN', YOU'RE CUTE.
CHAPTER 47: LILIES HAVE THORNS
ON YOUR WAY TO SCHOOL?
WANNA SKIP AND GO SOMEWHERE WITH US?
OUT OF MY WAY! I SAID NO!
HUH? WHAT YOU ACTING ALL STUCK UP FOR?
WHY DON'TCHA JUST COME WITH US?
DON'T TOUCH ME!!
SWISH
AGH!
WHAM
BAMMM
YARGH!

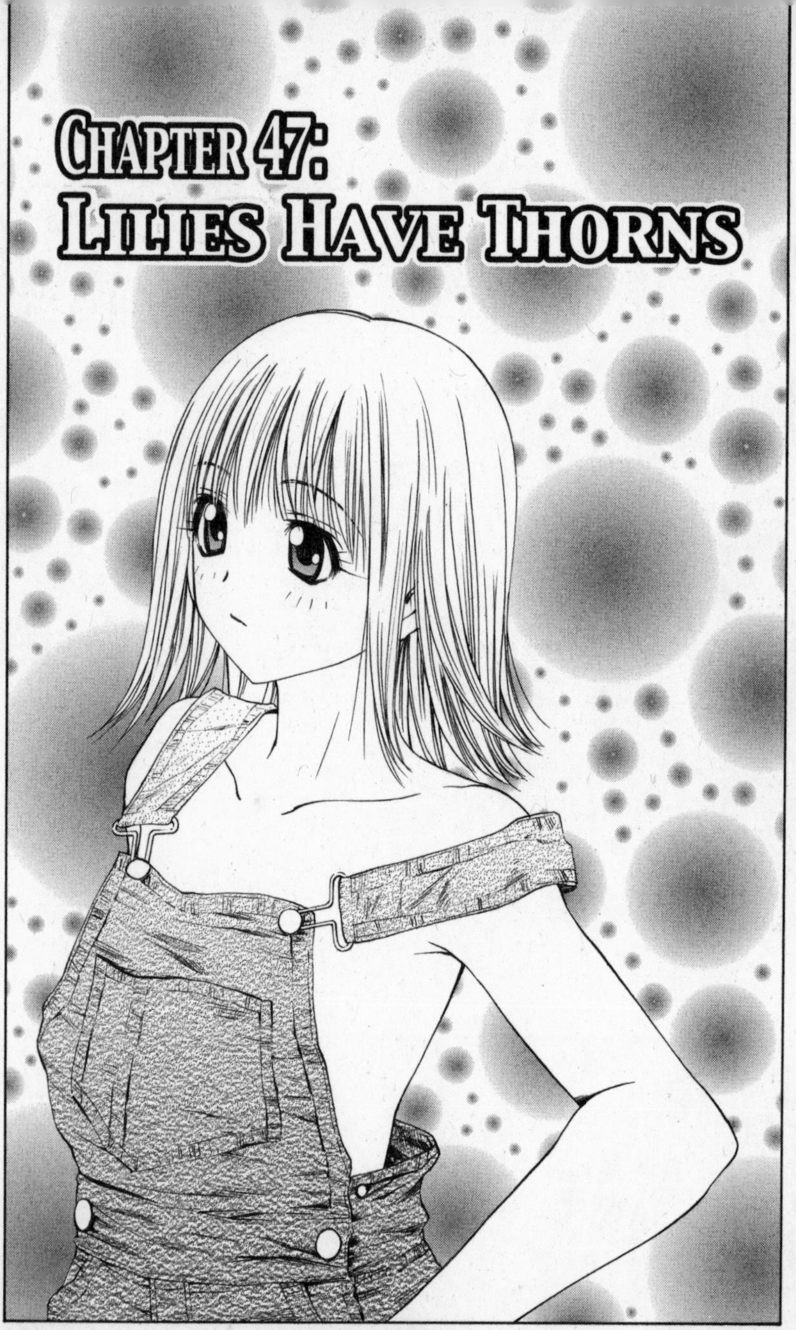
CHAPTER 47:
LILIES HAVE THORNS

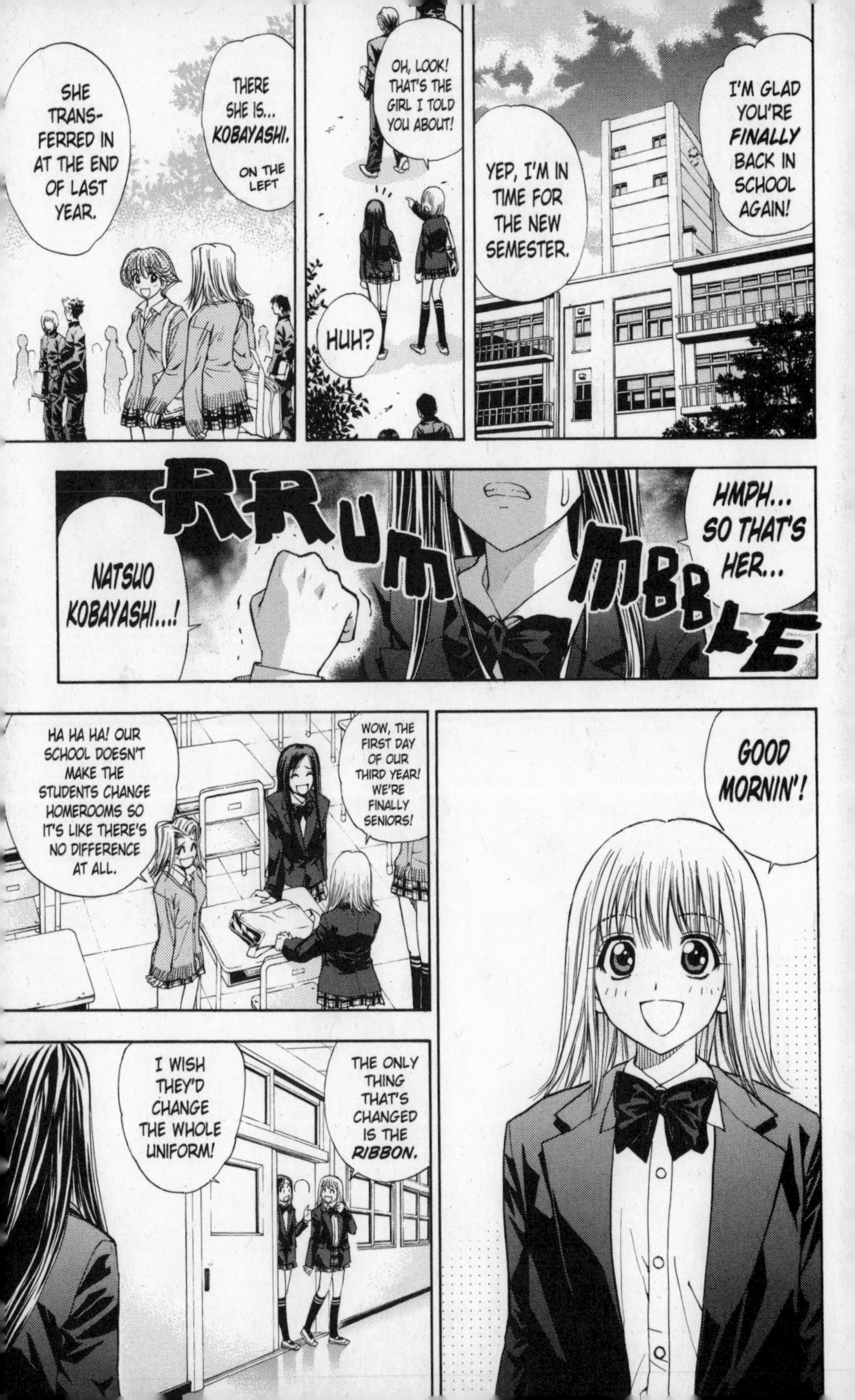
I'M GLAD YOU'RE FINALLY BACK IN SCHOOL AGAIN!
YEP, I'M IN TIME FOR THE NEW SEMESTER.
OH, LOOK! THAT'S THE GIRL I TOLD YOU ABOUT!
HUH?
THERE SHE IS... KOBAYASHI.
ON THE LEFT
SHE TRANSFERRED IN AT THE END OF LAST YEAR.
HMPH... SO THAT'S HER...
RRUMMBBLE
NATSUO KOBAYASHI...!
GOOD MORNIN'!
WOW, THE FIRST DAY OF OUR THIRD YEAR! WE'RE FINALLY SENIORS!
HA HA HA! OUR SCHOOL DOESN'T MAKE THE STUDENTS CHANGE HOMEROOMS SO IT'S LIKE THERE'S NO DIFFERENCE AT ALL.
THE ONLY THING THAT'S CHANGED IS THE RIBBON.
I WISH THEY'D CHANGE THE WHOLE UNIFORM!

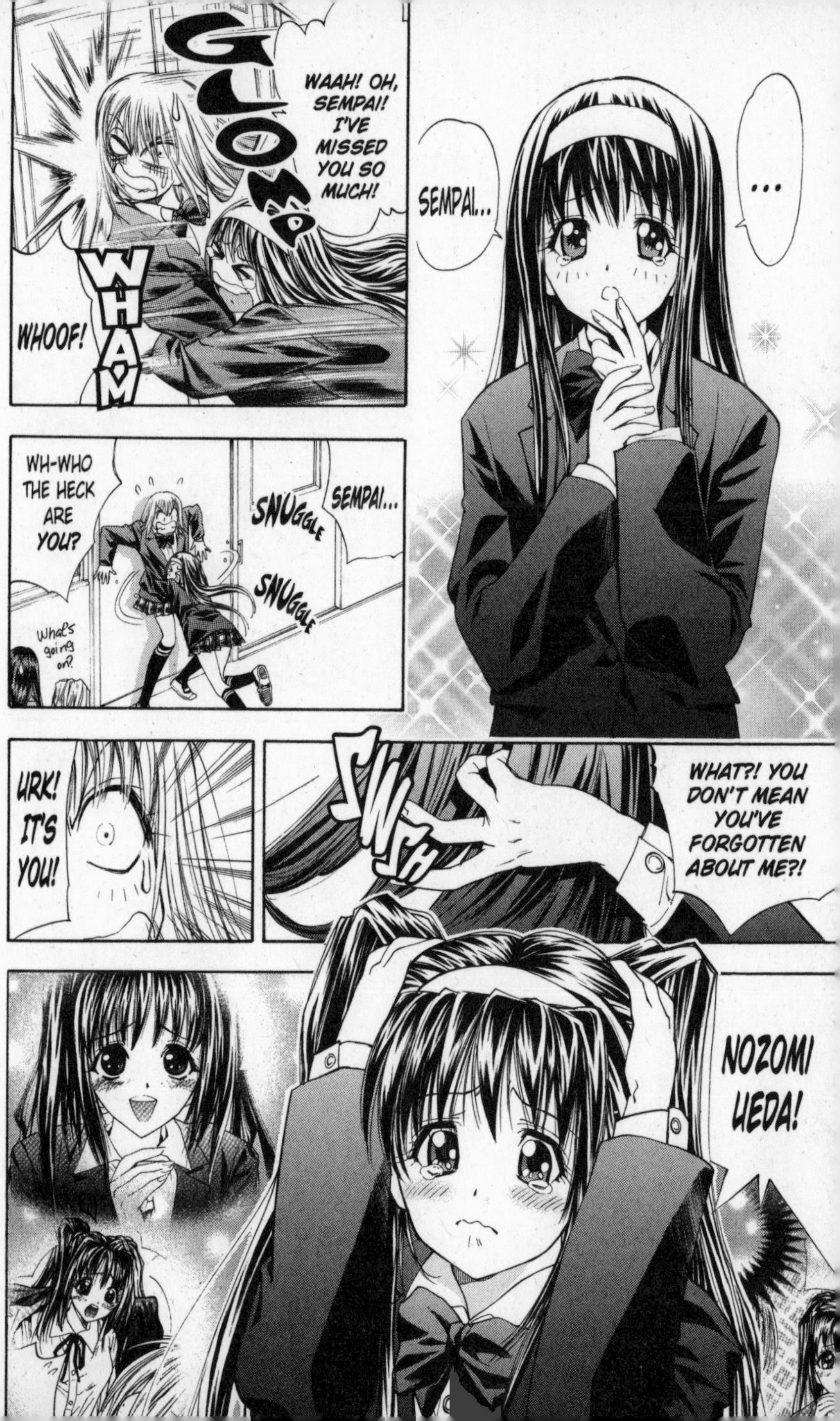
...
SEMPAI...
GLOMP
WAAH! OH, SEMPAI! I'VE MISSED YOU SO MUCH!
WHAM
WHOOF!
SEMPAI...
SNUGGLE
SNUGGLE
WH-WHO THE HECK ARE YOU?
What's going on?
SWISH
WHAT?! YOU DON'T MEAN YOU'VE FORGOTTEN ABOUT ME?!
URK! IT'S YOU!
NOZOMI UEDA!

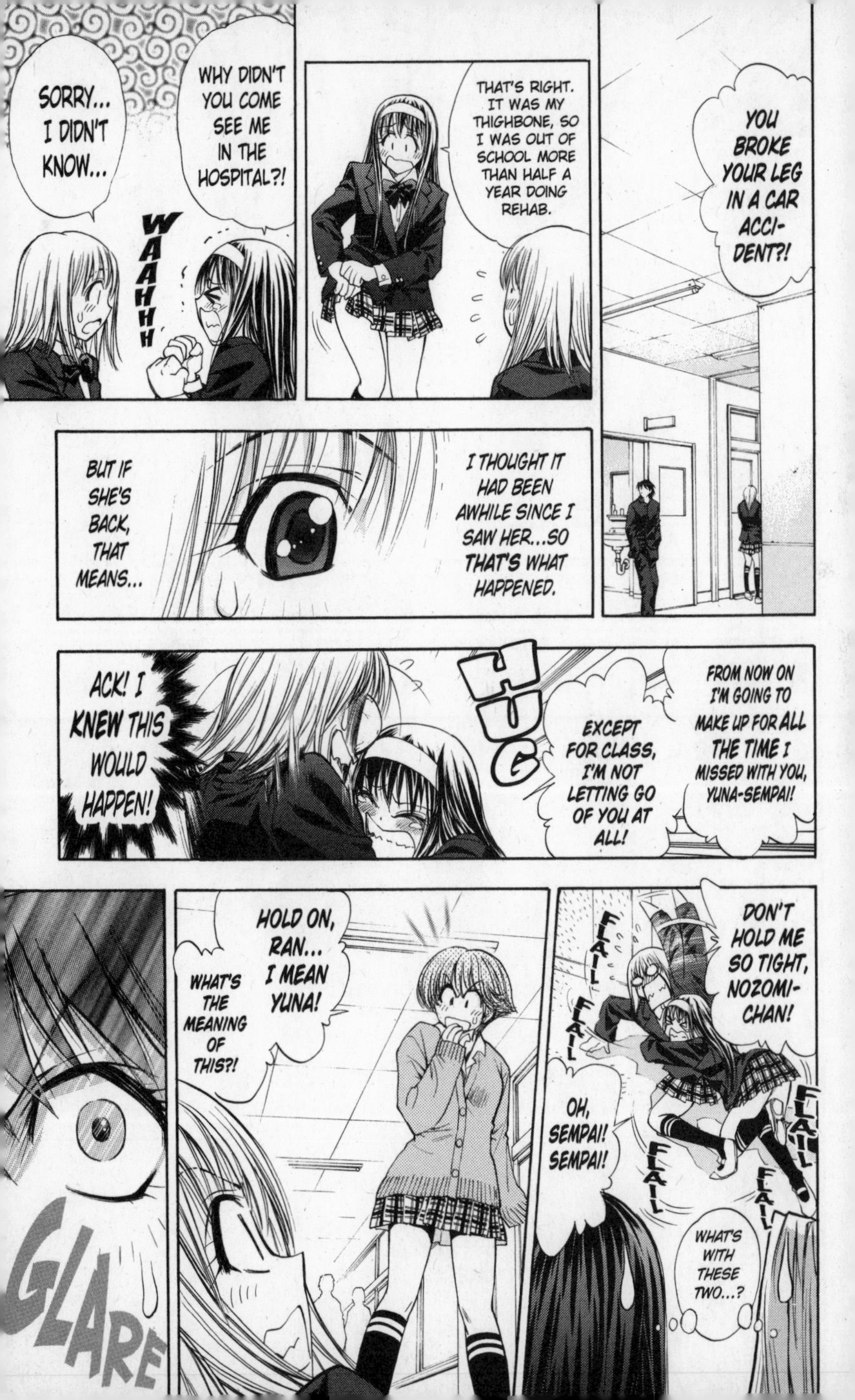
YOU BROKE YOUR LEG IN A CAR ACCI-DENT?!
THAT'S RIGHT. IT WAS MY THIGHBONE, SO I WAS OUT OF SCHOOL MORE THAN HALF A YEAR DOING REHAB.
WHY DIDN'T YOU COME SEE ME IN THE HOSPITAL?!
WAAAHHH
SORRY... I DIDN'T KNOW...
I THOUGHT IT HAD BEEN AWHILE SINCE I SAW HER...SO THAT'S WHAT HAPPENED.
BUT IF SHE'S BACK, THAT MEANS...
FROM NOW ON I'M GOING TO MAKE UP FOR ALL THE TIME I MISSED WITH YOU, YUNA-SEMPAI!
EXCEPT FOR CLASS, I'M NOT LETTING GO OF YOU AT ALL!
HUG
ACK! I KNEW THIS WOULD HAPPEN!
DON'T HOLD ME SO TIGHT, NOZOMI-CHAN!
FLAIL
FLAIL
OH, SEMPAI! SEMPAI!
FLAIL
FLAIL
FLAIL
WHAT'S WITH THESE TWO...?
HOLD ON, RAN... I MEAN YUNA!
WHAT'S THE MEANING OF THIS?!
GLARE

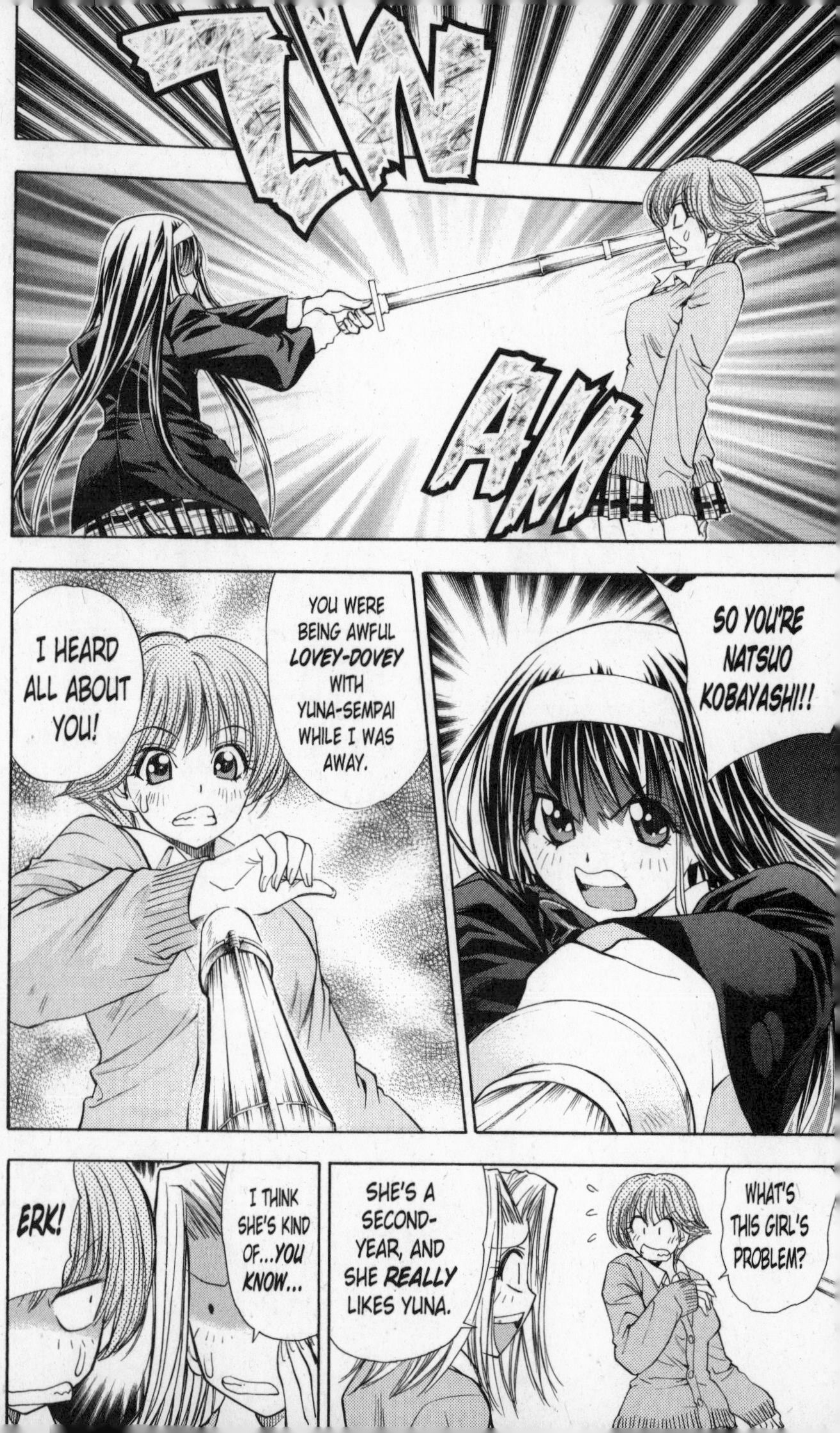
TW
AN
SO YOU'RE NATSUO KOBAYASHI!!
YOU WERE BEING AWFUL *LOVEY-DOVEY* WITH YUNA-SEMPAI WHILE I WAS AWAY.
I HEARD ALL ABOUT YOU!
WHAT'S THIS GIRL'S PROBLEM?
SHE'S A SECOND-YEAR, AND SHE *REALLY* LIKES YUNA.
I THINK SHE'S KIND OF...*YOU KNOW*...
ERK!

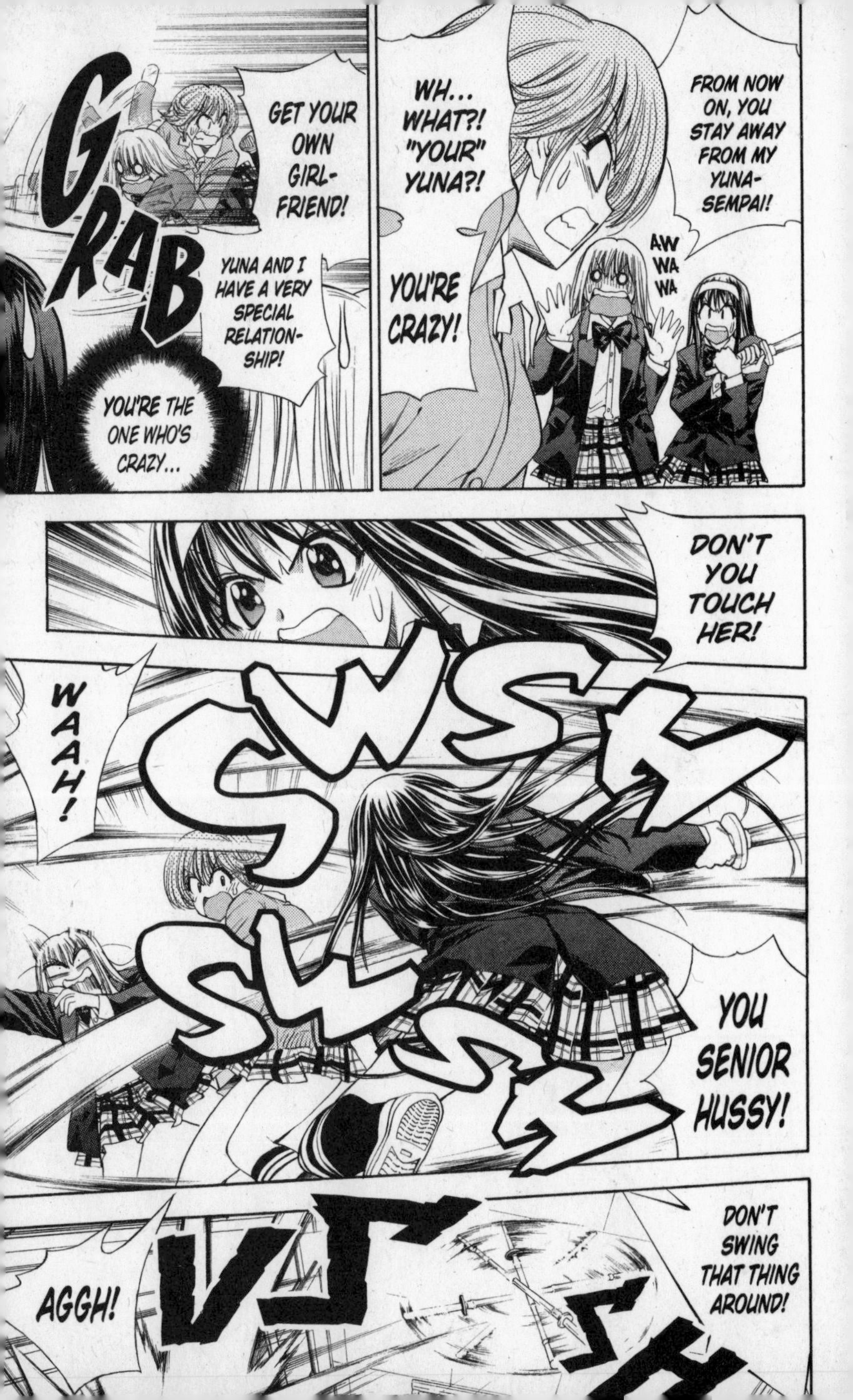
FROM NOW ON, YOU STAY AWAY FROM MY YUNA-SEMPAI!
AW WA WA
WH... WHAT?! "YOUR" YUNA?!
YOU'RE CRAZY!
GET YOUR OWN GIRL-FRIEND!
GRAB
YUNA AND I HAVE A VERY SPECIAL RELATION-SHIP!
YOU'RE THE ONE WHO'S CRAZY...
DON'T YOU TOUCH HER!
SWSH
SWSH
YOU SENIOR HUSSY!
WAAAH!
DON'T SWING THAT THING AROUND!
AGGH!

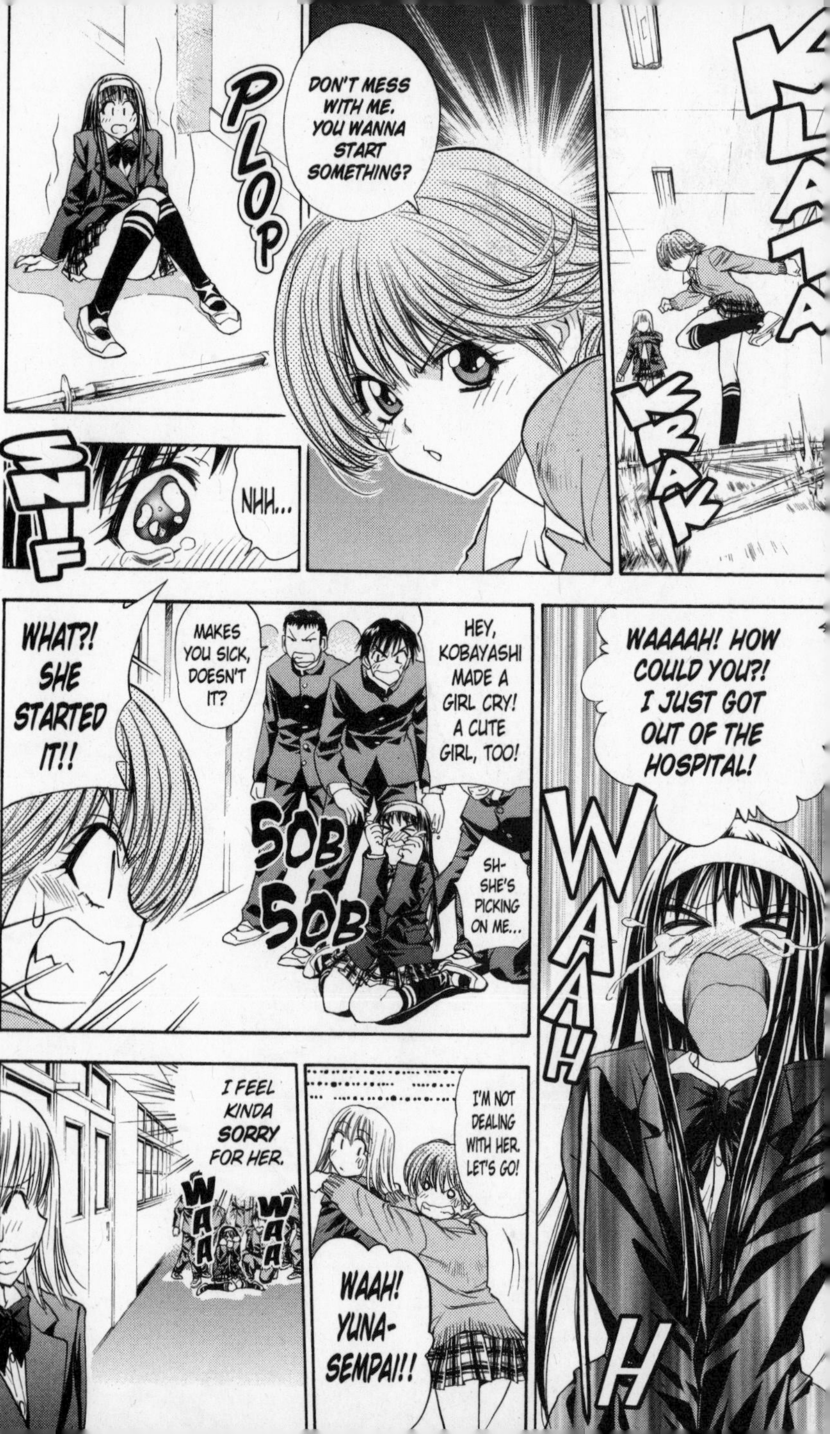
KRAK
DON'T MESS WITH ME. YOU WANNA START SOMETHING?
PLOP
SNIF
NHH...
WAAAAH! HOW COULD YOU?! I JUST GOT OUT OF THE HOSPITAL!
WAAAHH
HEY, KOBAYASHI MADE A GIRL CRY! A CUTE GIRL, TOO!
MAKES YOU SICK, DOESN'T IT?
SH-SHE'S PICKING ON ME...
SOB SOB
WHAT?! SHE STARTED IT!!
I'M NOT DEALING WITH HER. LET'S GO!
WAAH! YUNA-SEMPAI!!
I FEEL KINDA SORRY FOR HER.
WAA WAA

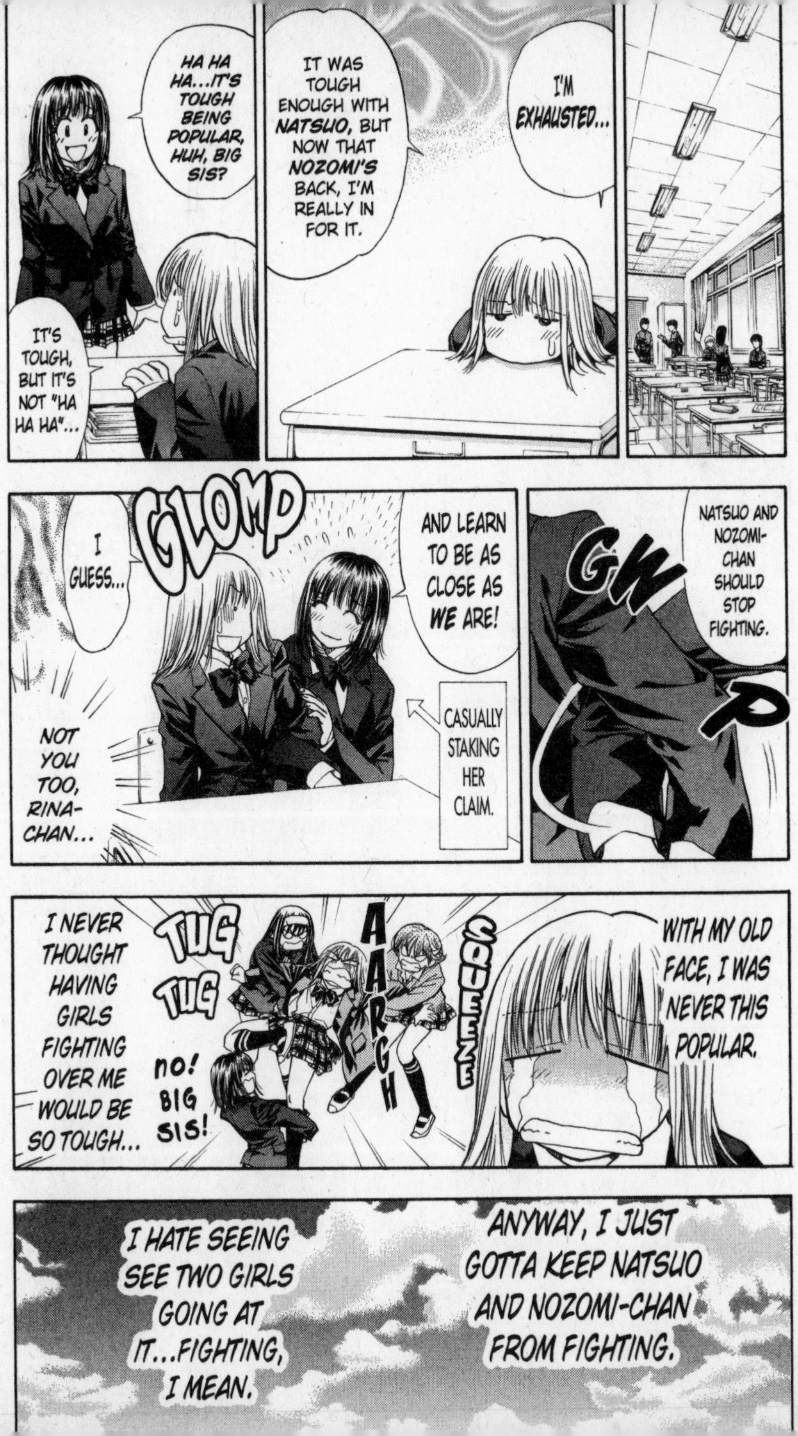
I'M EXHAUSTED...
IT WAS TOUGH ENOUGH WITH NATSUO, BUT NOW THAT NOZOMI'S BACK, I'M REALLY IN FOR IT.
HA HA HA...IT'S TOUGH BEING POPULAR, HUH, BIG SIS?
IT'S TOUGH, BUT IT'S NOT "HA HA HA"...
NATSUO AND NOZOMI-CHAN SHOULD STOP FIGHTING.
GWP
AND LEARN TO BE AS CLOSE AS WE ARE!
GLOMP
CASUALLY STAKING HER CLAIM.
I GUESS...
NOT YOU TOO, RINA-CHAN...
WITH MY OLD FACE, I WAS NEVER THIS POPULAR.
SQUEEZE
AARGH
TUG TUG
no! BIG SIS!
I NEVER THOUGHT HAVING GIRLS FIGHTING OVER ME WOULD BE SO TOUGH...
ANYWAY, I JUST GOTTA KEEP NATSUO AND NOZOMI-CHAN FROM FIGHTING.
I HATE SEEING SEE TWO GIRLS GOING AT IT...FIGHTING, I MEAN.

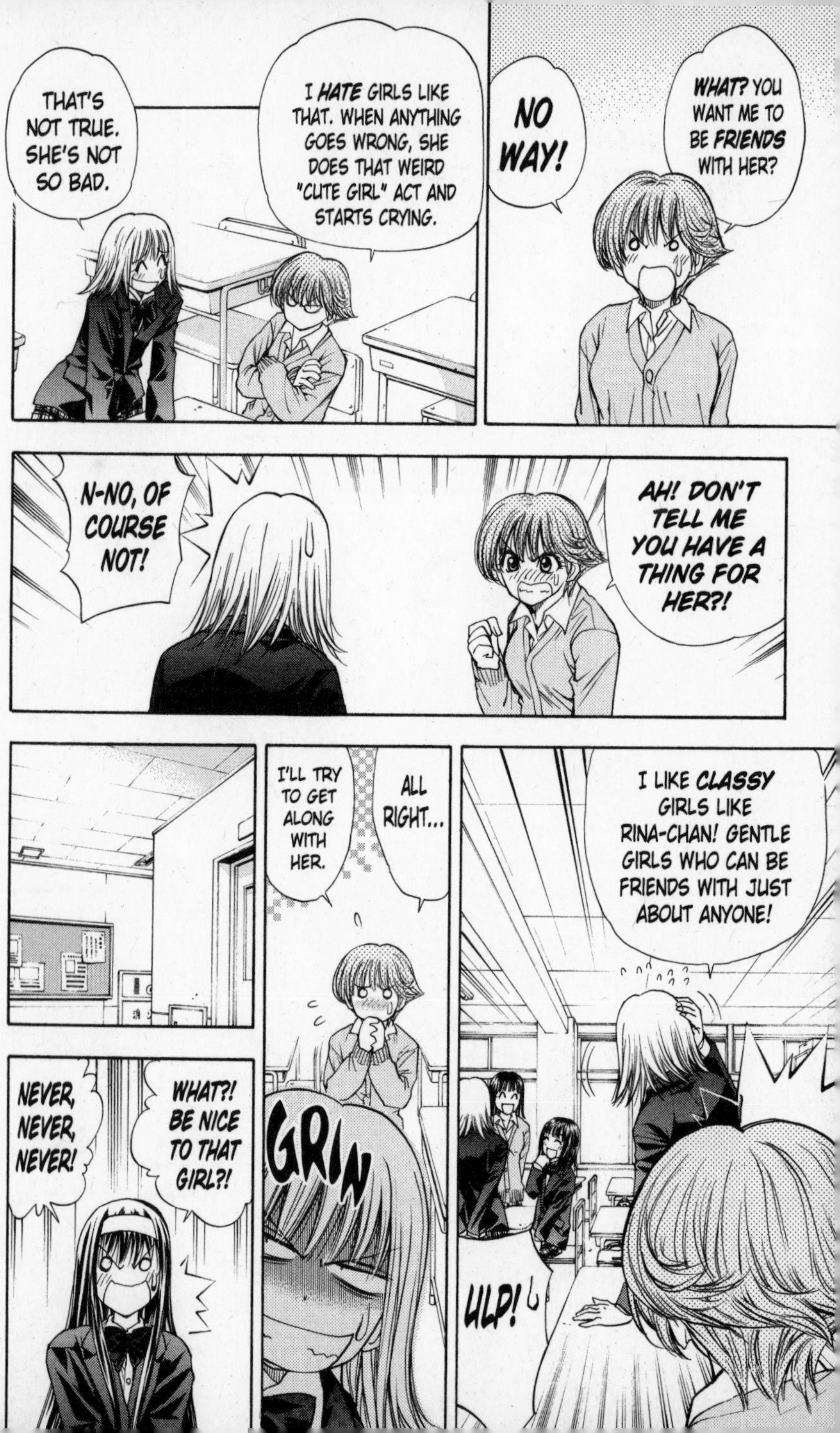
WHAT? YOU WANT ME TO BE FRIENDS WITH HER?
NO WAY!
I HATE GIRLS LIKE THAT. WHEN ANYTHING GOES WRONG, SHE DOES THAT WEIRD "CUTE GIRL" ACT AND STARTS CRYING.
THAT'S NOT TRUE. SHE'S NOT SO BAD.
AH! DON'T TELL ME YOU HAVE A THING FOR HER?!
N-NO, OF COURSE NOT!
I LIKE CLASSY GIRLS LIKE RINA-CHAN! GENTLE GIRLS WHO CAN BE FRIENDS WITH JUST ABOUT ANYONE!
ULP!
ALL RIGHT...
I'LL TRY TO GET ALONG WITH HER.
GRIN
WHAT?! BE NICE TO THAT GIRL?!
NEVER, NEVER, NEVER!

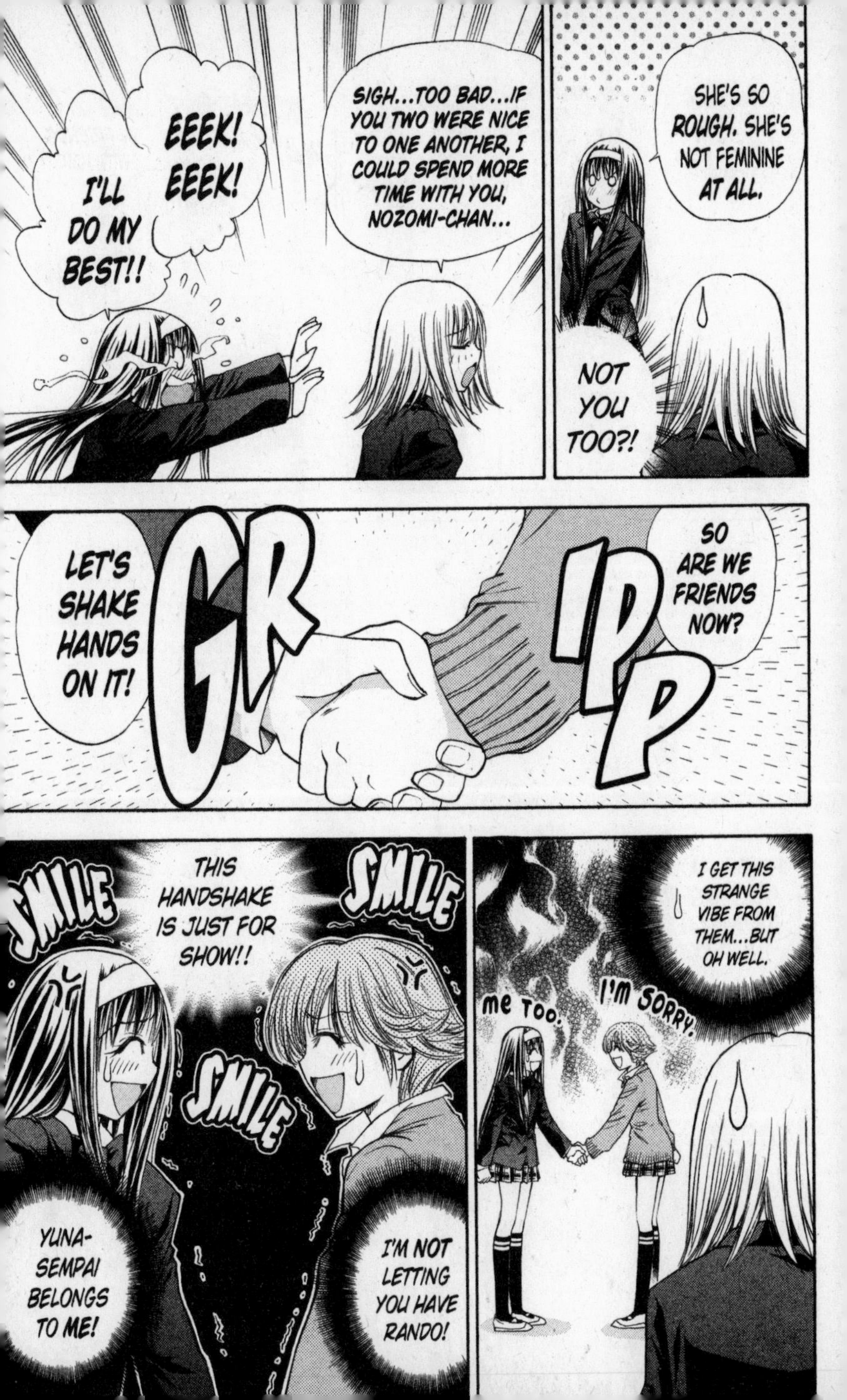
SHE'S SO ROUGH. SHE'S NOT FEMININE AT ALL.
NOT YOU TOO?!
SIGH...TOO BAD...IF YOU TWO WERE NICE TO ONE ANOTHER, I COULD SPEND MORE TIME WITH YOU, NOZOMI-CHAN...
EEEK! EEEK!
I'LL DO MY BEST!!
SO ARE WE FRIENDS NOW?
GRIPP
LET'S SHAKE HANDS ON IT!
I GET THIS STRANGE VIBE FROM THEM...BUT OH WELL.
I'M SORRY.
me Too.
SMILE
THIS HANDSHAKE IS JUST FOR SHOW!!
SMILE
SMILE
I'M NOT LETTING YOU HAVE RANDO!
YUNA-SEMPAI BELONGS TO ME!

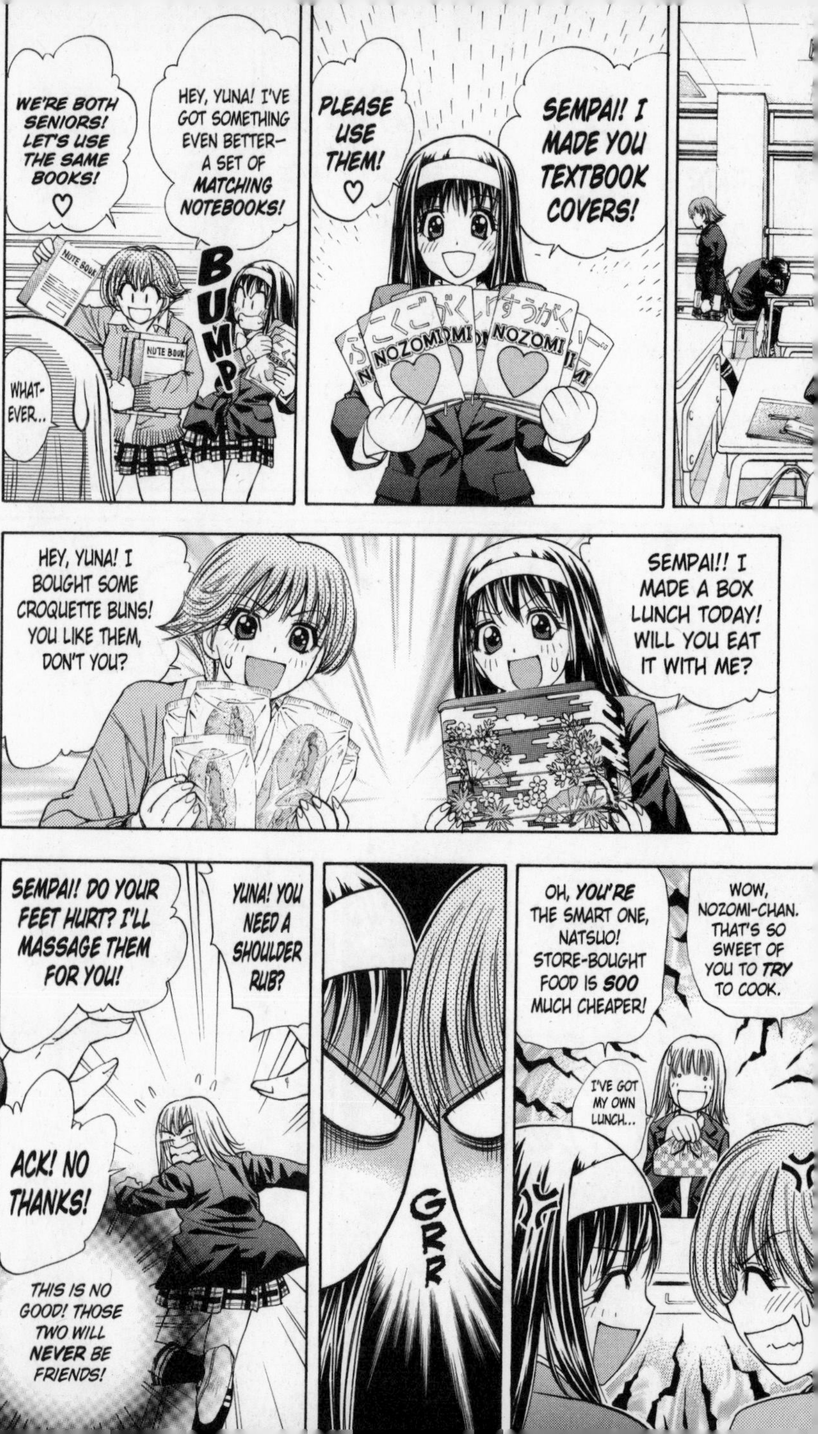
SEMPAI! I MADE YOU TEXTBOOK COVERS!
PLEASE USE THEM! ♡
こくごがく
すうがく
NOZOMI
NOZOMI
HEY, YUNA! I'VE GOT SOMETHING EVEN BETTER— A SET OF MATCHING NOTEBOOKS!
WE'RE BOTH SENIORS! LET'S USE THE SAME BOOKS! ♡
NUTE BOOK
BUMP
NUTE BOOK
WHAT-EVER...
SEMPAI!! I MADE A BOX LUNCH TODAY! WILL YOU EAT IT WITH ME?
HEY, YUNA! I BOUGHT SOME CROQUETTE BUNS! YOU LIKE THEM, DON'T YOU?
WOW, NOZOMI-CHAN. THAT'S SO SWEET OF YOU TO TRY TO COOK.
OH, YOU'RE THE SMART ONE, NATSUO! STORE-BOUGHT FOOD IS SOO MUCH CHEAPER!
I'VE GOT MY OWN LUNCH...
GRR
YUNA! YOU NEED A SHOULDER RUB?
SEMPAI! DO YOUR FEET HURT? I'LL MASSAGE THEM FOR YOU!
ACK! NO THANKS!
THIS IS NO GOOD! THOSE TWO WILL NEVER BE FRIENDS!

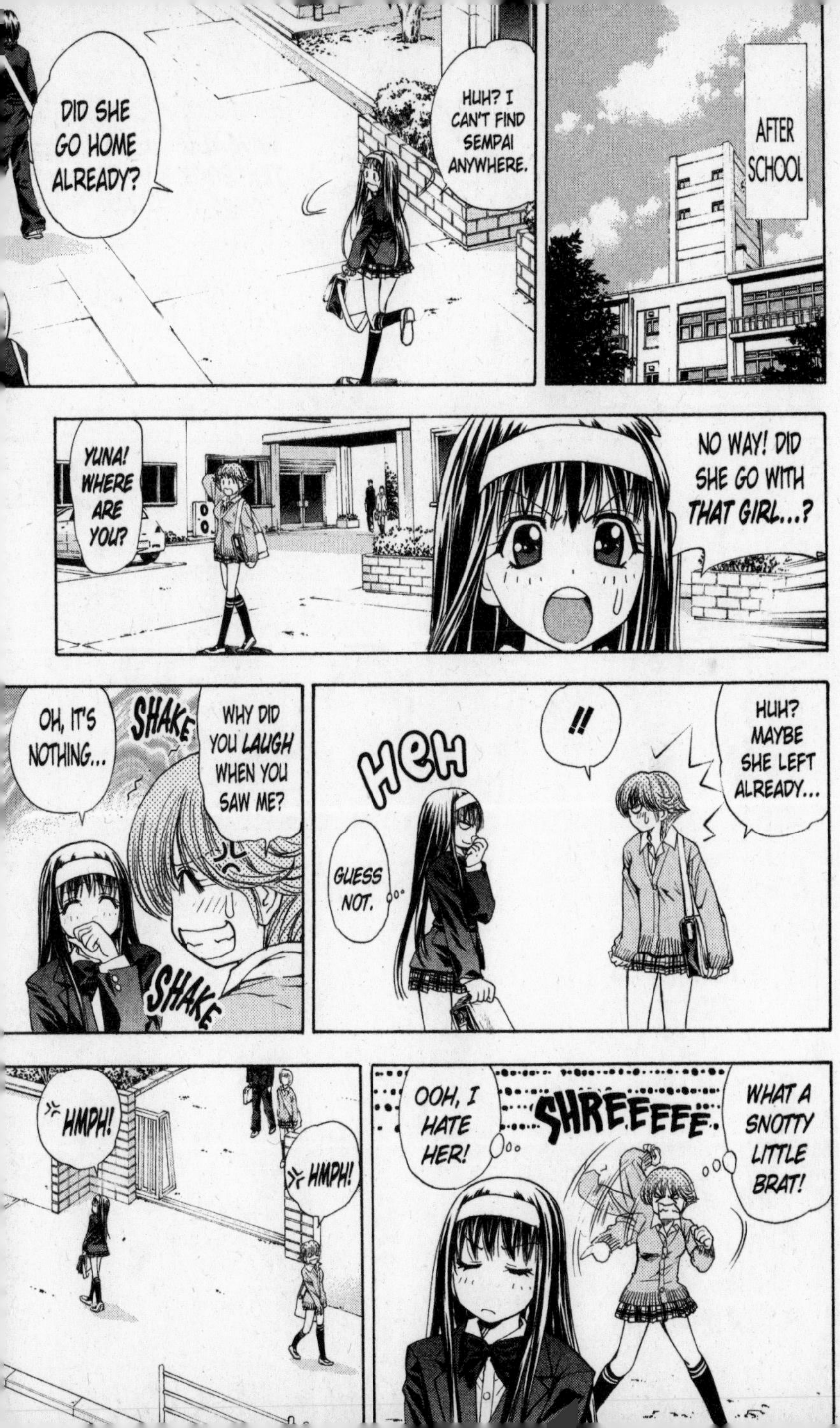
AFTER SCHOOL
HUH? I CAN'T FIND SEMPAI ANYWHERE.
DID SHE GO HOME ALREADY?
NO WAY! DID SHE GO WITH THAT GIRL...?
YUNA! WHERE ARE YOU?
HUH? MAYBE SHE LEFT ALREADY...
!!
HEH
GUESS NOT.
WHY DID YOU LAUGH WHEN YOU SAW ME?
SHAKE
OH, IT'S NOTHING...
SHAKE
WHAT A SNOTTY LITTLE BRAT!
SHREEEEEE
OOH, I HATE HER!
HMPH!
HMPH!

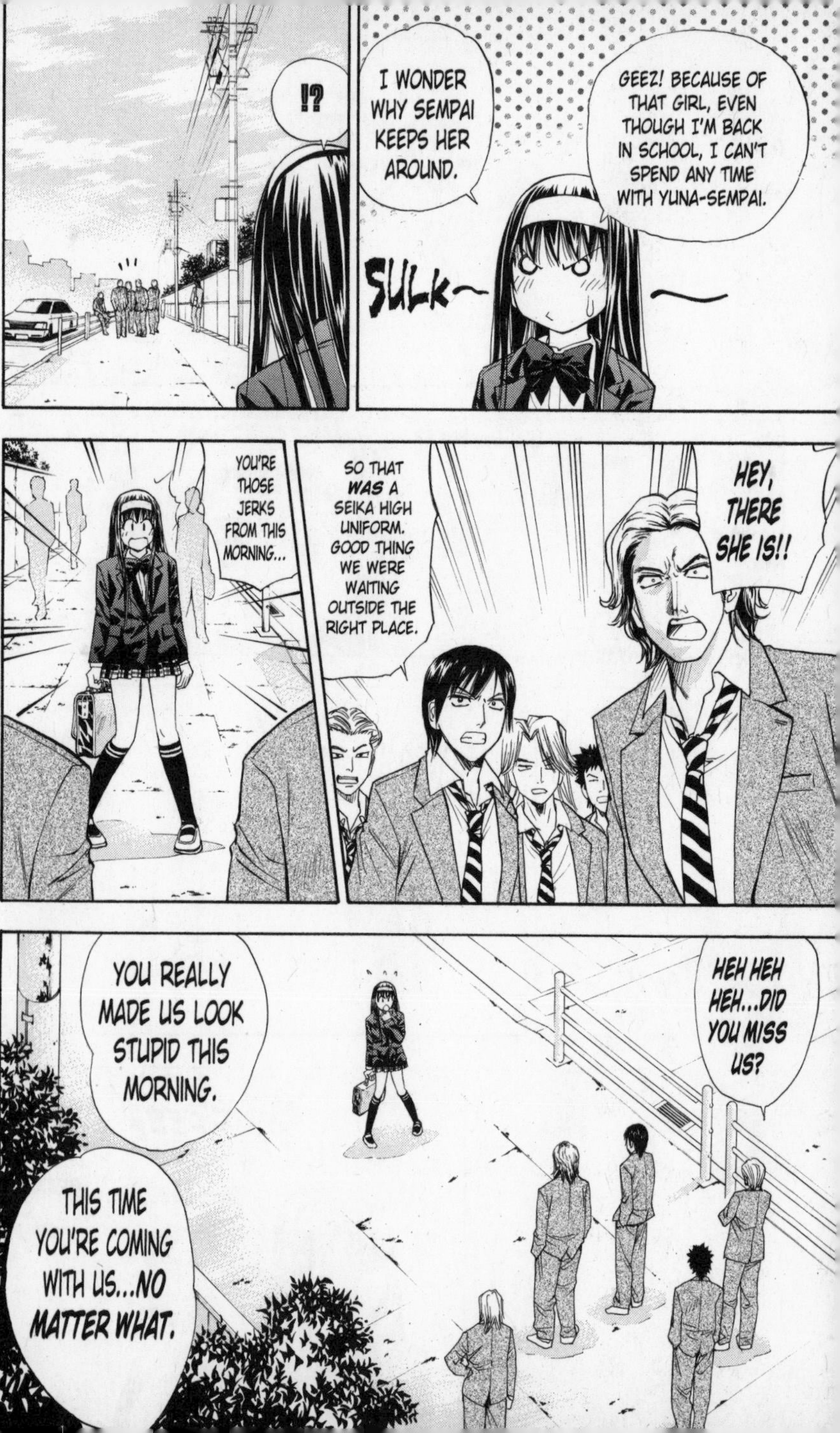
GEEZ! BECAUSE OF THAT GIRL, EVEN THOUGH I'M BACK IN SCHOOL, I CAN'T SPEND ANY TIME WITH YUNA-SEMPAI.
I WONDER WHY SEMPAI KEEPS HER AROUND.
SULK~ ~
!?
HEY, THERE SHE IS!!
SO THAT WAS A SEIKA HIGH UNIFORM. GOOD THING WE WERE WAITING OUTSIDE THE RIGHT PLACE.
YOU'RE THOSE JERKS FROM THIS MORNING...
HEH HEH HEH...DID YOU MISS US?
YOU REALLY MADE US LOOK STUPID THIS MORNING.
THIS TIME YOU'RE COMING WITH US...NO MATTER WHAT.

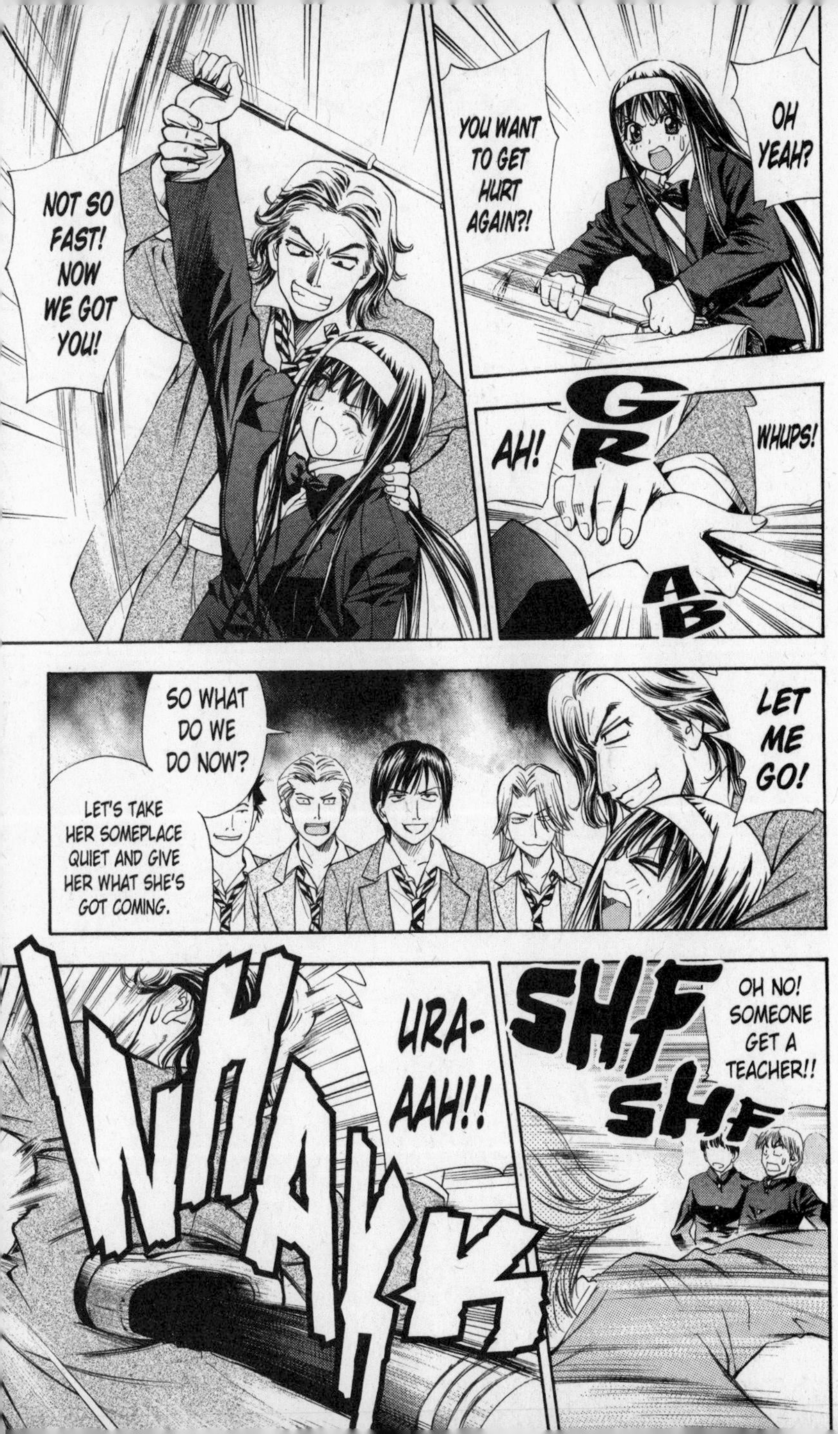
OH YEAH?
YOU WANT TO GET HURT AGAIN?!
WHUPS!
GR
AH!
AB
NOT SO FAST! NOW WE GOT YOU!
LET ME GO!
SO WHAT DO WE DO NOW?
LET'S TAKE HER SOMEPLACE QUIET AND GIVE HER WHAT SHE'S GOT COMING.
OH NO! SOMEONE GET A TEACHER!!
SHF
SHF
URA-AAH!!
WHAK

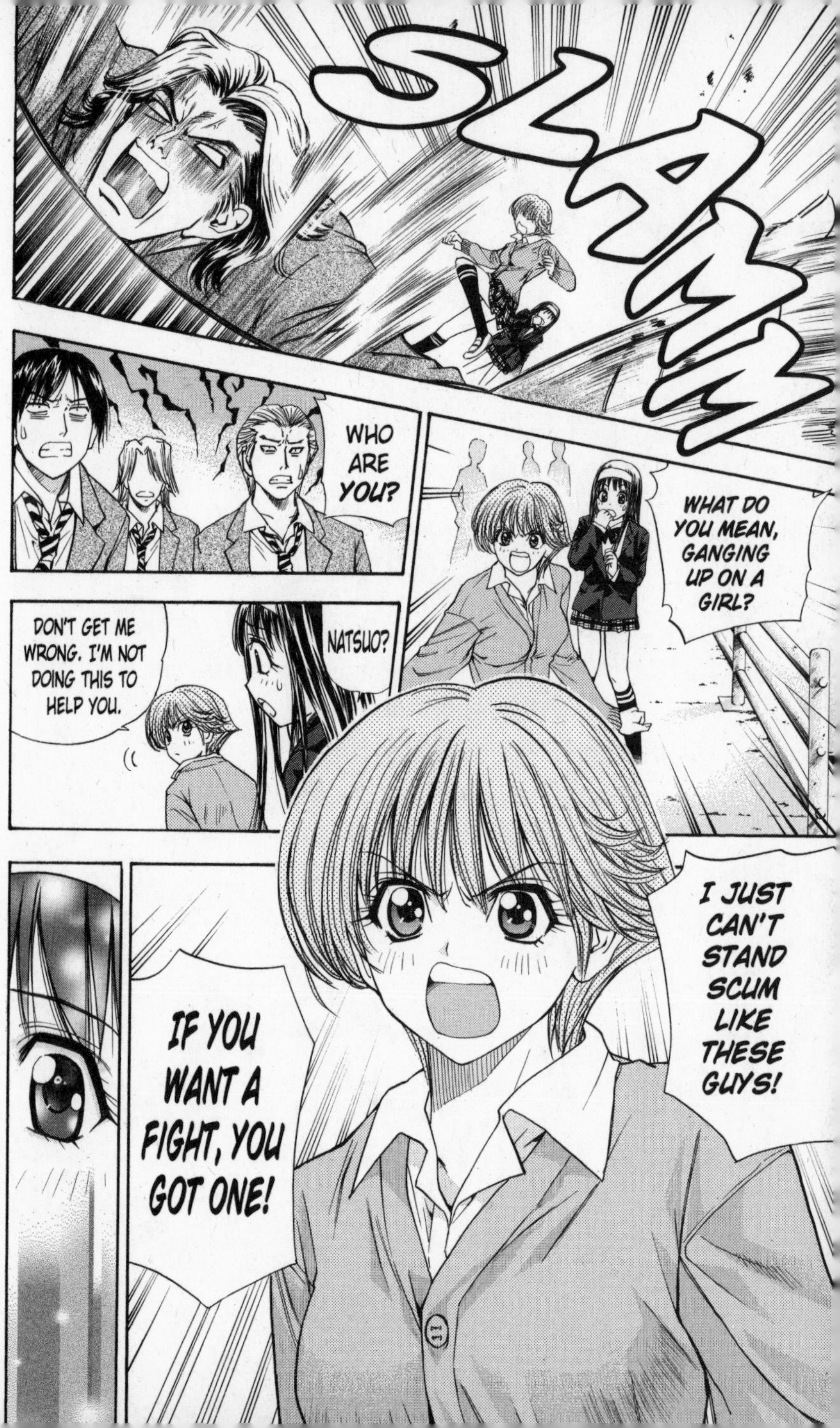
SLAMM
WHAT DO YOU MEAN, GANGING UP ON A GIRL?
WHO ARE YOU?
NATSUO?
DON'T GET ME WRONG. I'M NOT DOING THIS TO HELP YOU.
I JUST CAN'T STAND SCUM LIKE THESE GUYS!
IF YOU WANT A FIGHT, YOU GOT ONE!

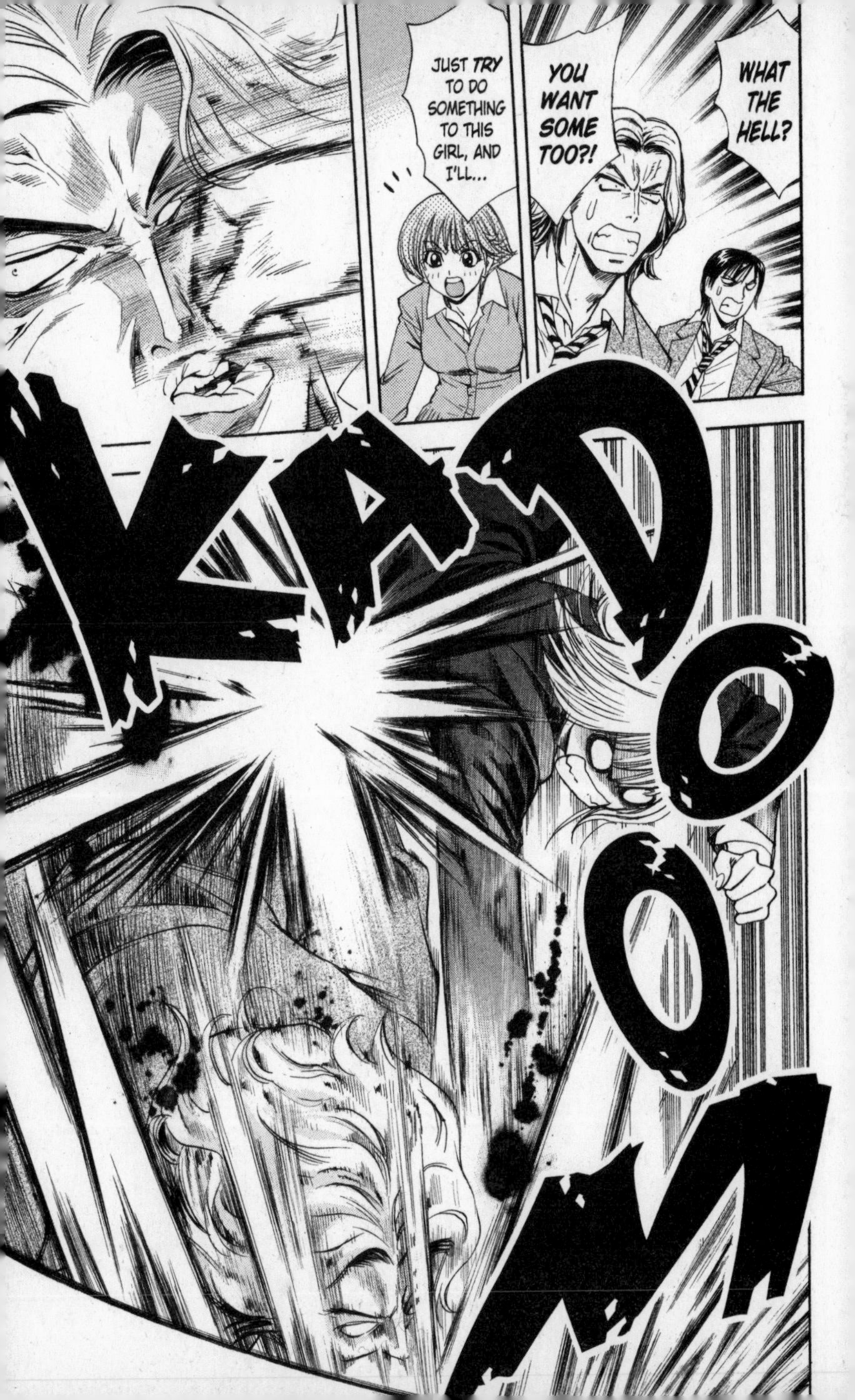
WHAT THE HELL?
YOU WANT SOME TOO?!
JUST TRY TO DO SOMETHING TO THIS GIRL, AND I'LL...
KADOOM

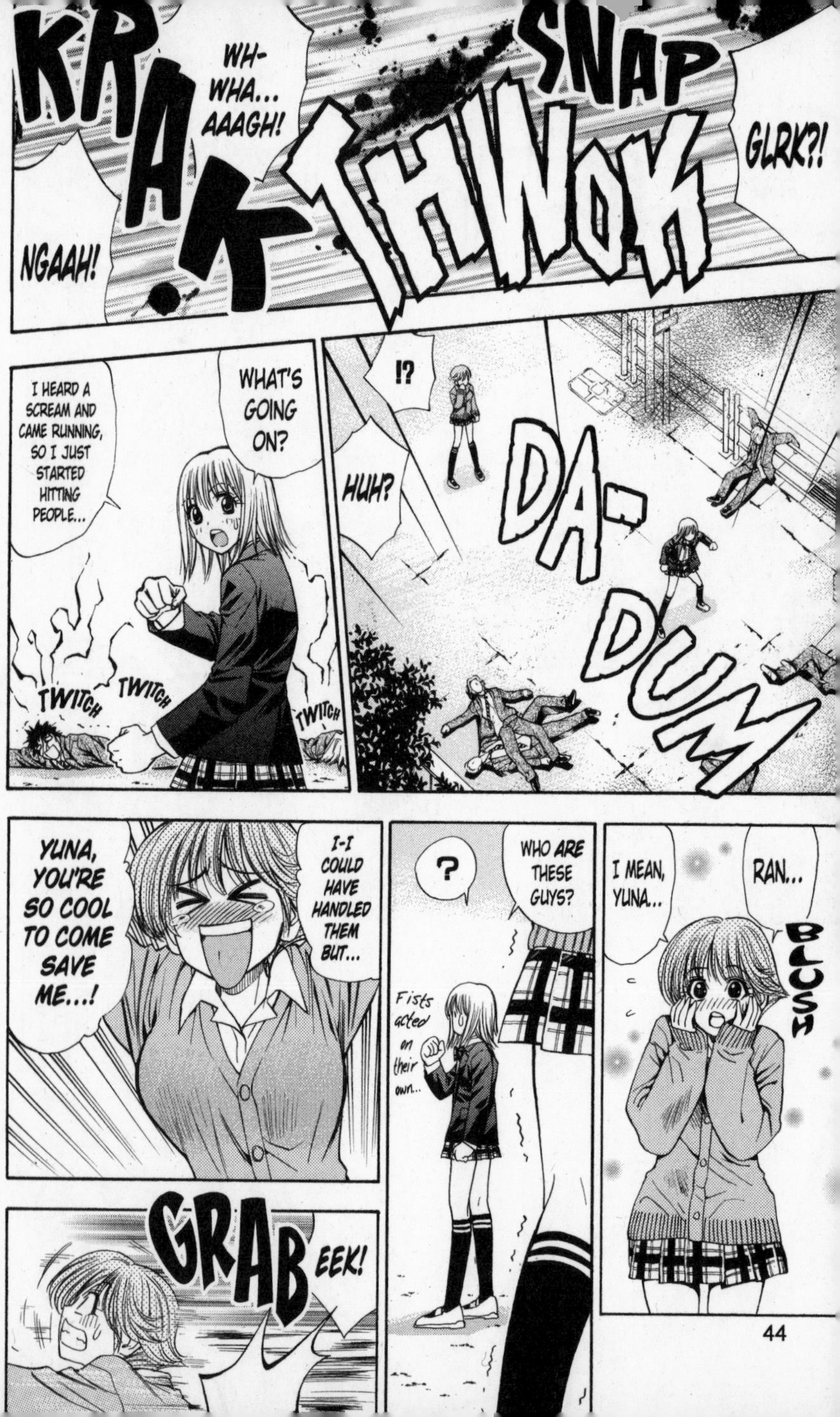

GLRK?!
SNAP
THWOK
WH- WHA... AAAGH!
KRAAK
NGAAH!
!?
HUH?
DA-DUM
WHAT'S GOING ON?
I HEARD A SCREAM AND CAME RUNNING, SO I JUST STARTED HITTING PEOPLE...
TWITCH
TWITCH
TWITCH
RAN...
I MEAN, YUNA...
BLUSH
WHO ARE THESE GUYS?
?
Fists acted on their own...
I-I COULD HAVE HANDLED THEM BUT...
YUNA, YOU'RE SO COOL TO COME SAVE ME...!
GRAB
EEK!

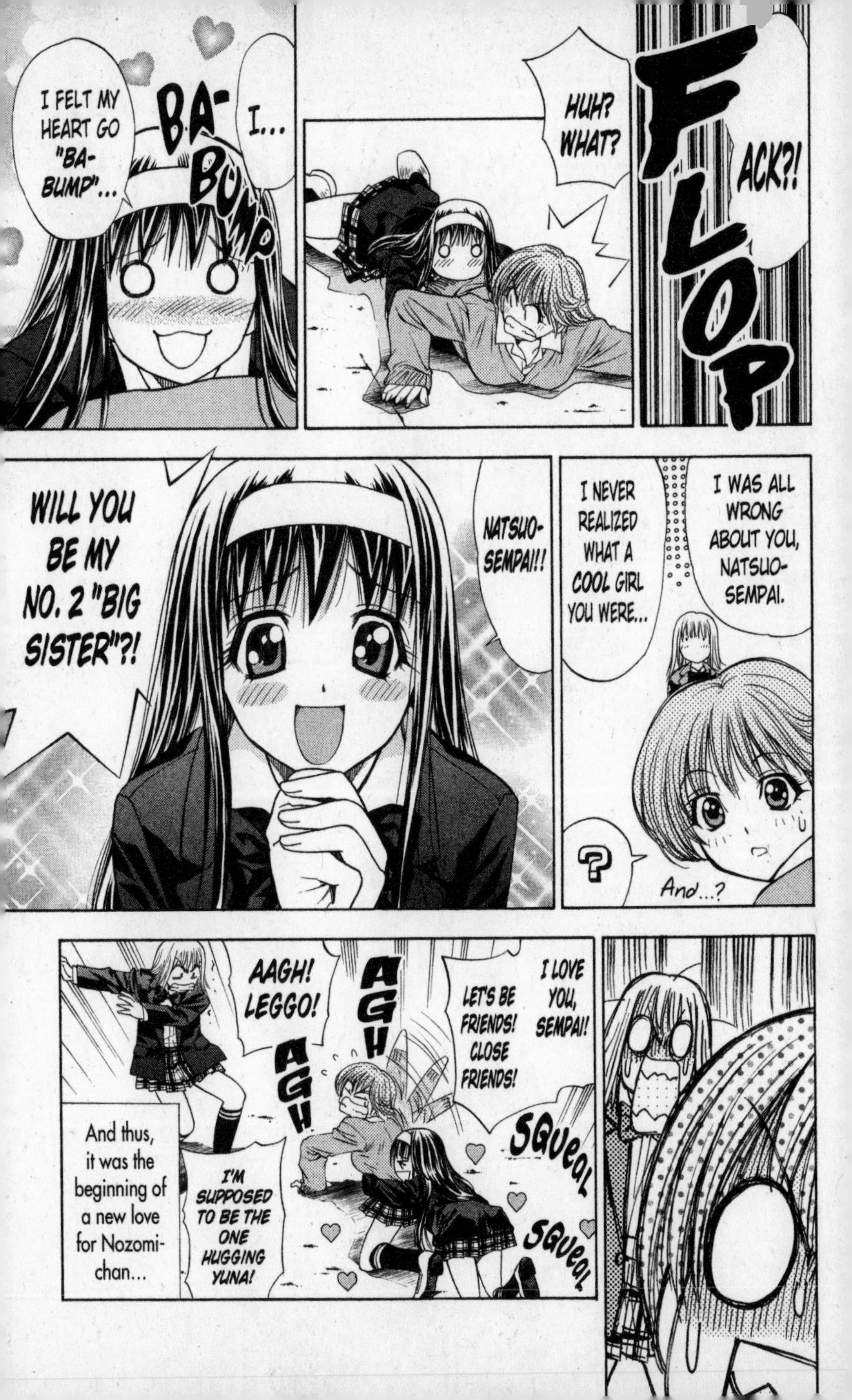
ACK?!
FLOP
HUH? WHAT?
I...
I FELT MY HEART GO "BA-BUMP"...
BA-BUMP
I WAS ALL WRONG ABOUT YOU, NATSUO-SEMPAI.
I NEVER REALIZED WHAT A COOL GIRL YOU WERE...
?
And...?
NATSUO-SEMPAI!!
WILL YOU BE MY NO. 2 "BIG SISTER"?!
I LOVE YOU, SEMPAI!
LET'S BE FRIENDS! CLOSE FRIENDS!
SQUEAL SQUEAL
AGH AGH
AAGH! LEGGO!
I'M SUPPOSED TO BE THE ONE HUGGING YUNA!
And thus, it was the beginning of a new love for Nozomi-chan...

# CHAPTER 48: NOZOMI'S FUNHOUSE

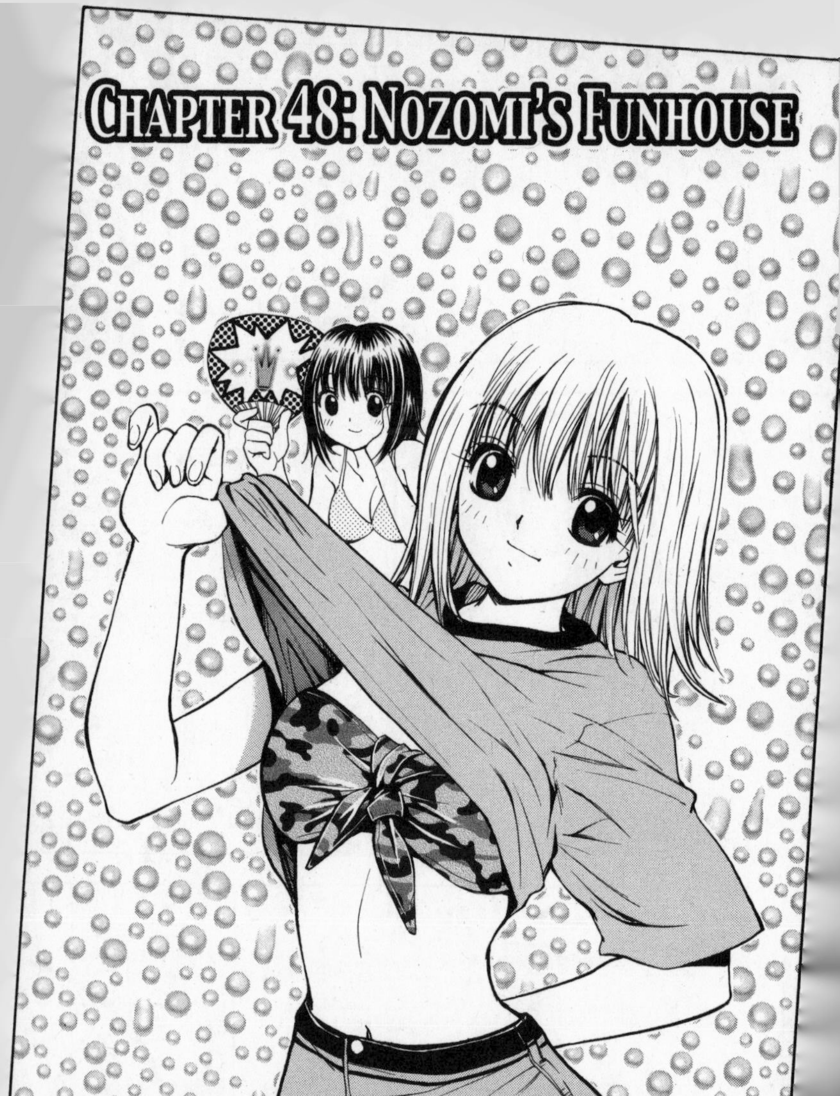

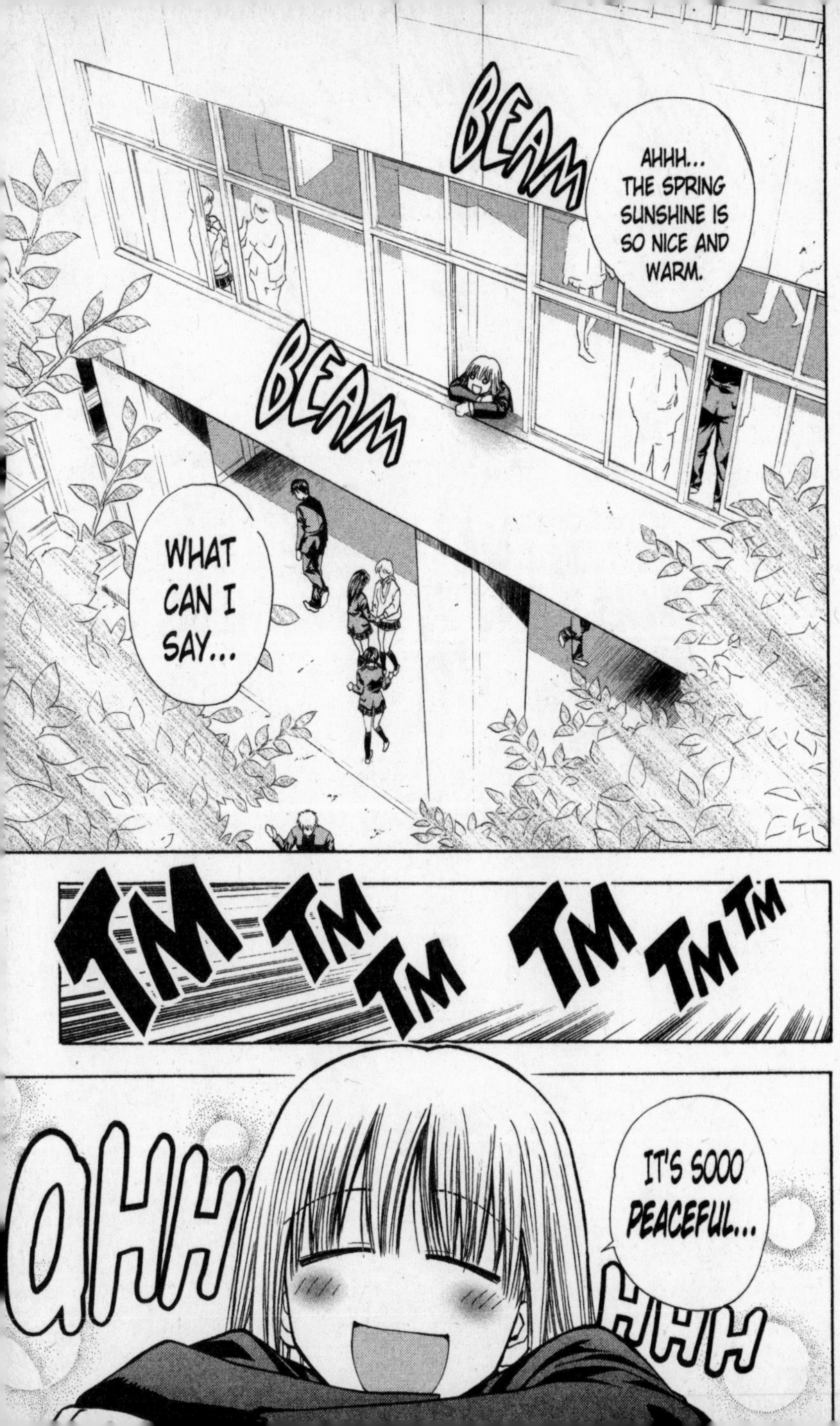
AHHH... THE SPRING SUNSHINE IS SO NICE AND WARM.
BEAM
BEAM
WHAT CAN I SAY...
TM TM TM TM TM TM
IT'S SOOO PEACEFUL...
AHH
HHH

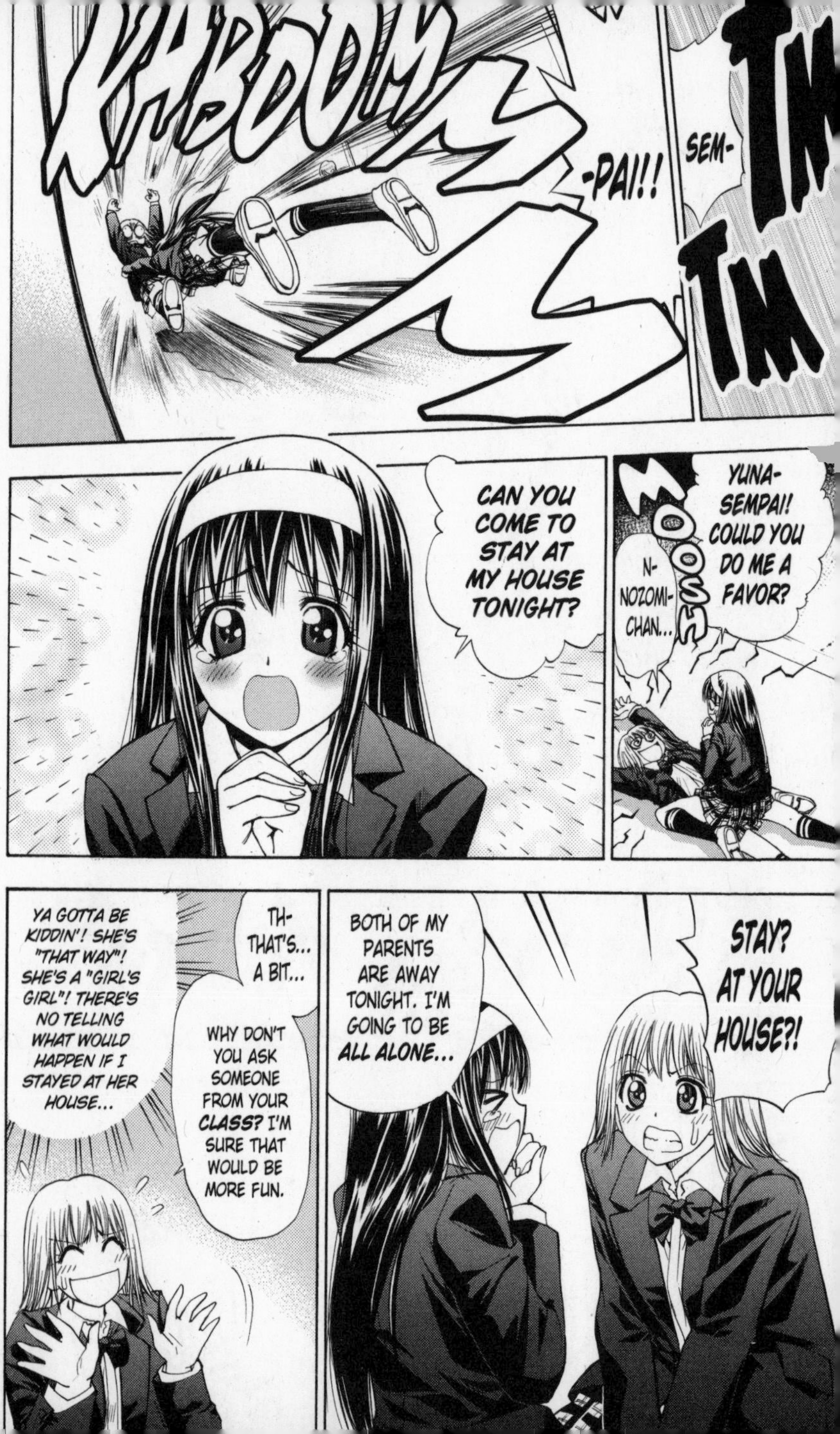
SEM-
TM
TM
-PAI!!
KABOOM
YUNA-SEMPAI! COULD YOU DO ME A FAVOR?
WOOSH
N-NOZOMI-CHAN...
CAN YOU COME TO STAY AT MY HOUSE TONIGHT?
STAY? AT YOUR HOUSE?!
BOTH OF MY PARENTS ARE AWAY TONIGHT. I'M GOING TO BE ALL ALONE...
TH-THAT'S... A BIT...
WHY DON'T YOU ASK SOMEONE FROM YOUR CLASS? I'M SURE THAT WOULD BE MORE FUN.
YA GOTTA BE KIDDIN'! SHE'S "THAT WAY"! SHE'S A "GIRL'S GIRL"! THERE'S NO TELLING WHAT WOULD HAPPEN IF I STAYED AT HER HOUSE...

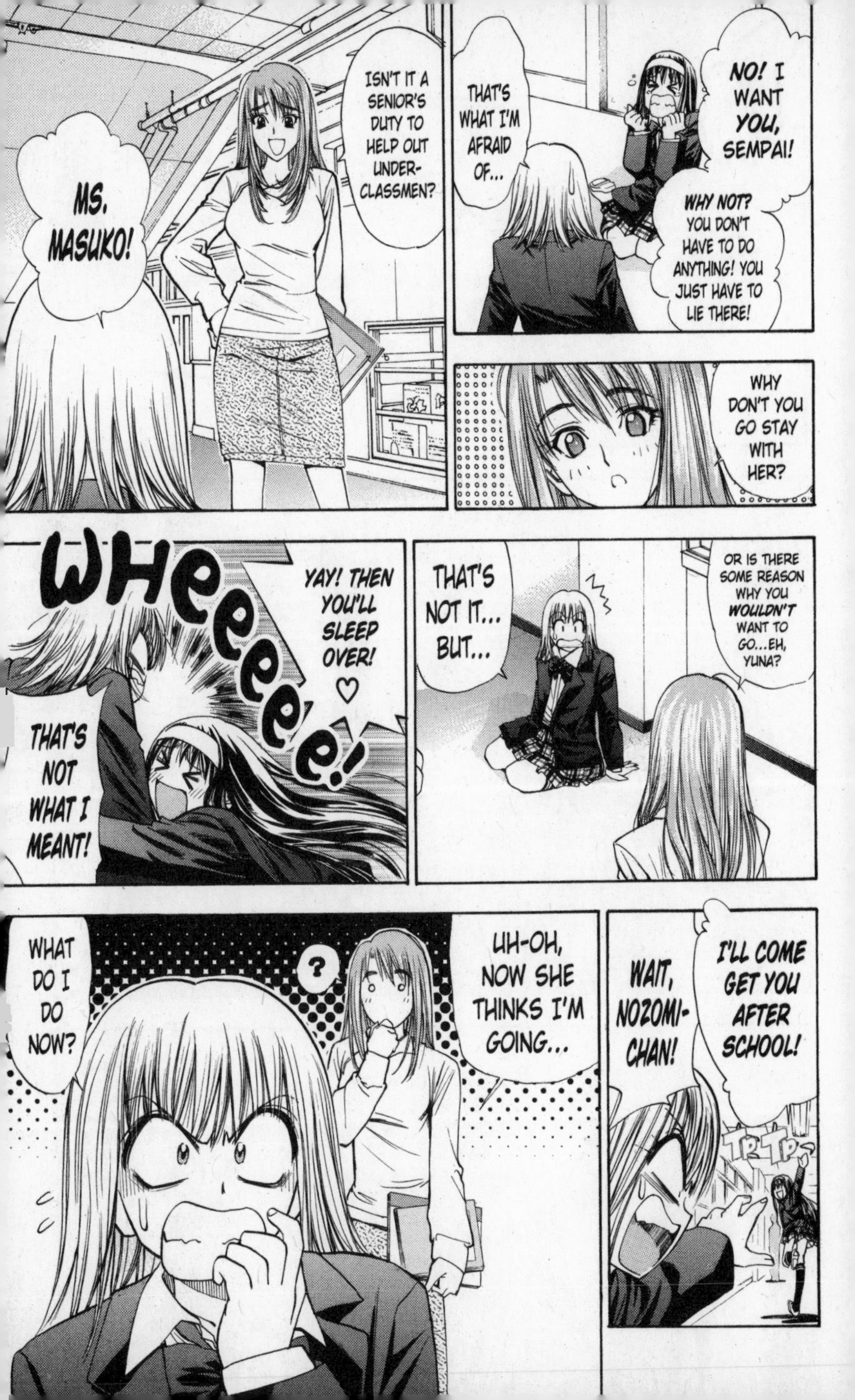
NO! I WANT YOU, SEMPAI!
WHY NOT? YOU DON'T HAVE TO DO ANYTHING! YOU JUST HAVE TO LIE THERE!
THAT'S WHAT I'M AFRAID OF...
WHY DON'T YOU GO STAY WITH HER?
ISN'T IT A SENIOR'S DUTY TO HELP OUT UNDER-CLASSMEN?
MS. MASUKO!
OR IS THERE SOME REASON WHY YOU WOULDN'T WANT TO GO...EH, YUNA?
THAT'S NOT IT... BUT...
YAY! THEN YOU'LL SLEEP OVER! ♡
WHEEEEE!
THAT'S NOT WHAT I MEANT!
I'LL COME GET YOU AFTER SCHOOL!
WAIT, NOZOMI-CHAN!
TP TP
UH-OH, NOW SHE THINKS I'M GOING...
?
WHAT DO I DO NOW?

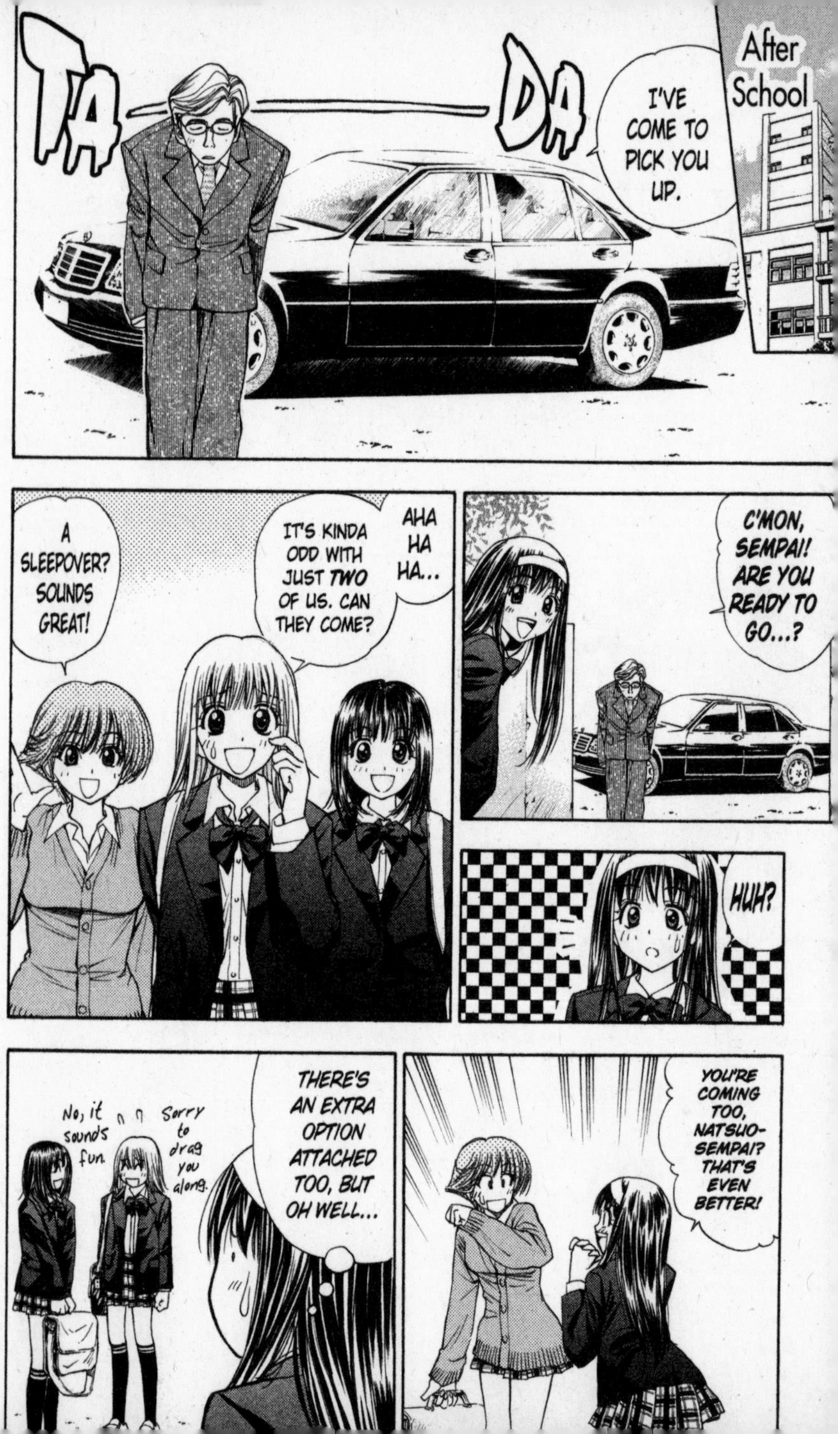
After School
I'VE COME TO PICK YOU UP.
TA——DA
C'MON, SEMPAI! ARE YOU READY TO GO...?
HUH?
AHA HA HA...
IT'S KINDA ODD WITH JUST TWO OF US. CAN THEY COME?
A SLEEPOVER? SOUNDS GREAT!
YOU'RE COMING TOO, NATSUO-SEMPAI? THAT'S EVEN BETTER!
THERE'S AN EXTRA OPTION ATTACHED TOO, BUT OH WELL...
Sorry to drag you along.
No, it sounds fun.

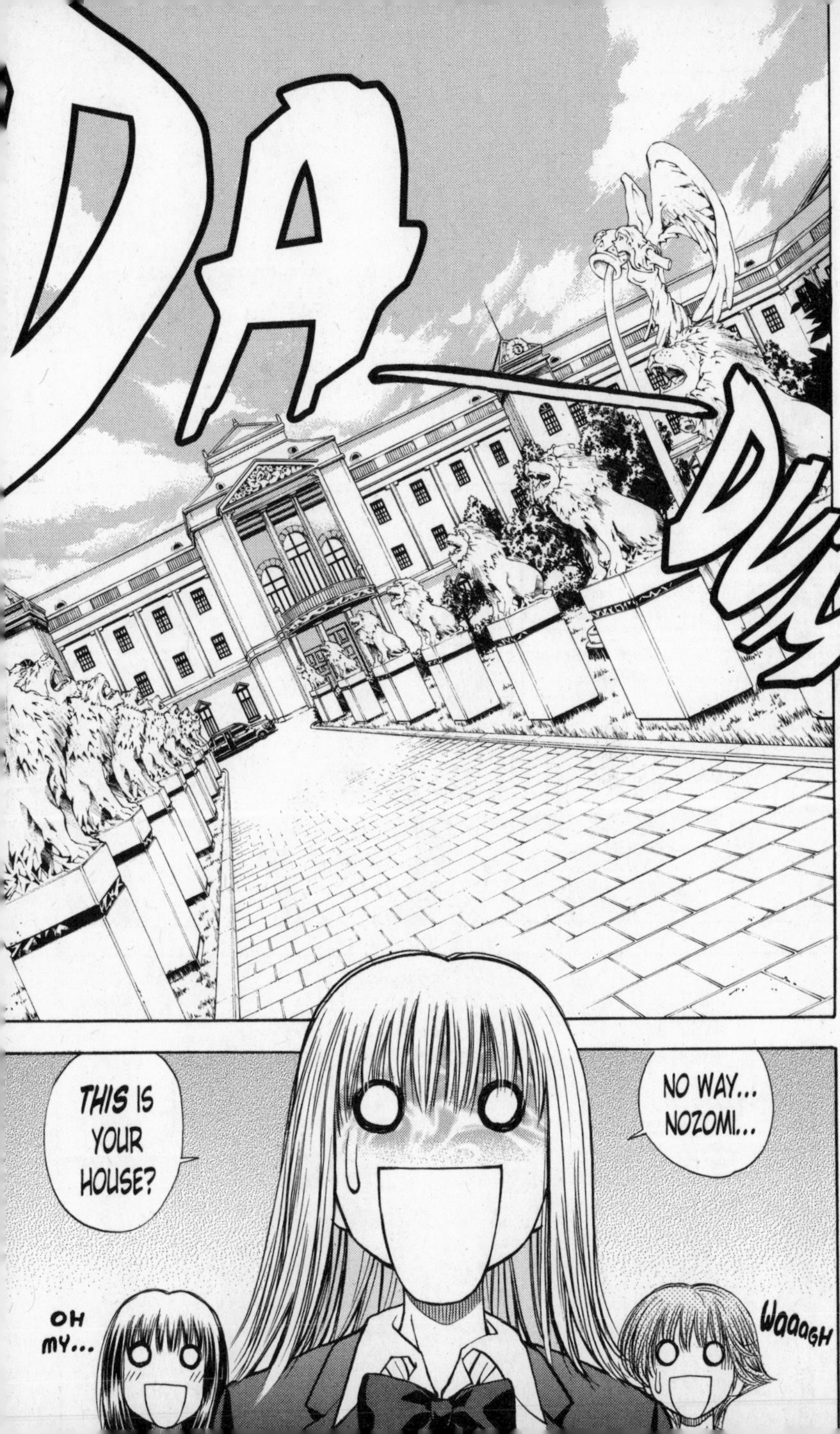
DA
DUM
NO WAY... NOZOMI...
THIS IS YOUR HOUSE?
Waaagh
OH MY...

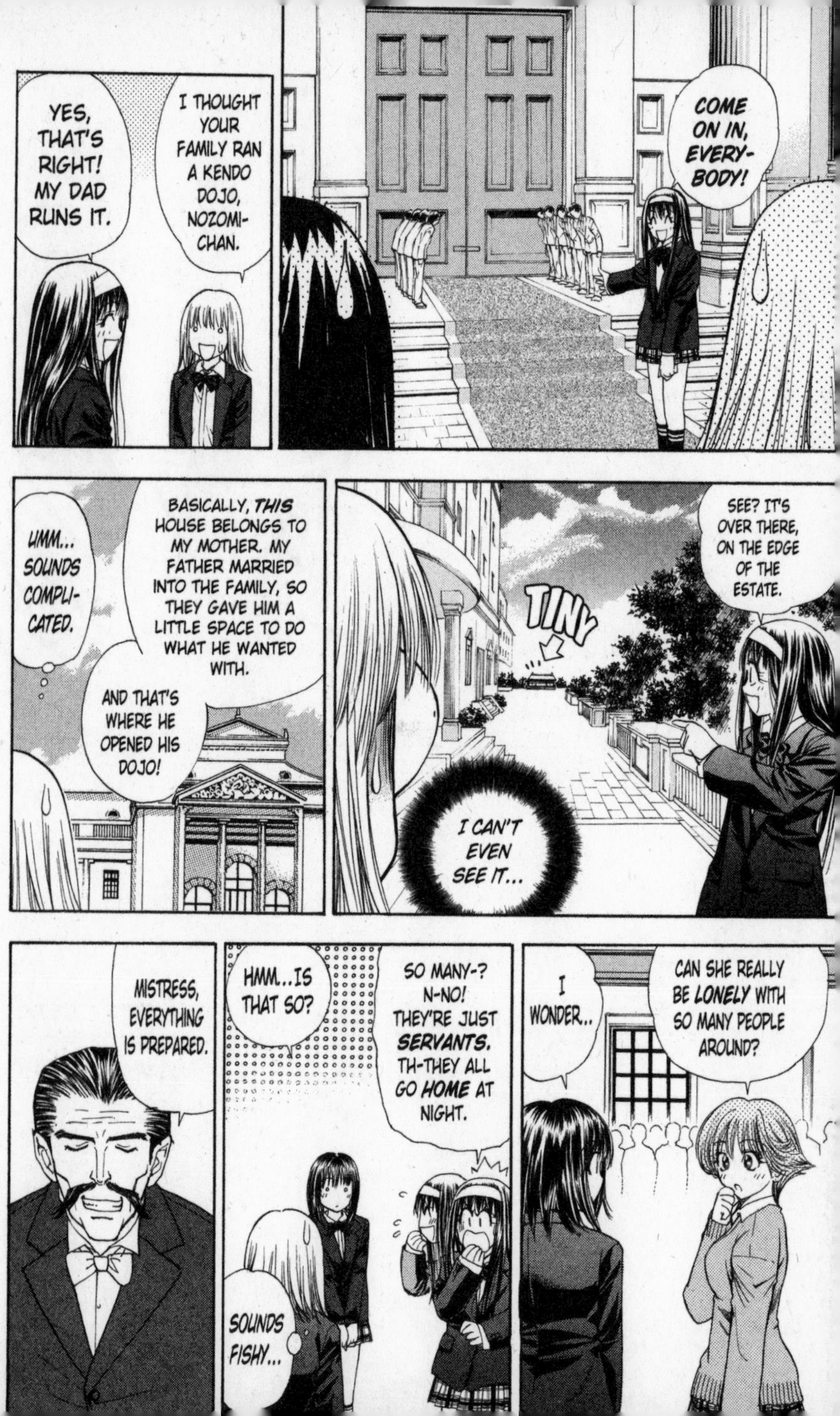
COME ON IN, EVERYBODY!
I THOUGHT YOUR FAMILY RAN A KENDO DOJO, NOZOMI-CHAN.
YES, THAT'S RIGHT! MY DAD RUNS IT.
SEE? IT'S OVER THERE, ON THE EDGE OF THE ESTATE.
TINY
I CAN'T EVEN SEE IT...
BASICALLY, THIS HOUSE BELONGS TO MY MOTHER. MY FATHER MARRIED INTO THE FAMILY, SO THEY GAVE HIM A LITTLE SPACE TO DO WHAT HE WANTED WITH.
UMM... SOUNDS COMPLICATED.
AND THAT'S WHERE HE OPENED HIS DOJO!
CAN SHE REALLY BE LONELY WITH SO MANY PEOPLE AROUND?
I WONDER...
SO MANY-? N-NO! THEY'RE JUST SERVANTS. TH-THEY ALL GO HOME AT NIGHT.
HMM...IS THAT SO?
SOUNDS FISHY...
MISTRESS, EVERYTHING IS PREPARED.

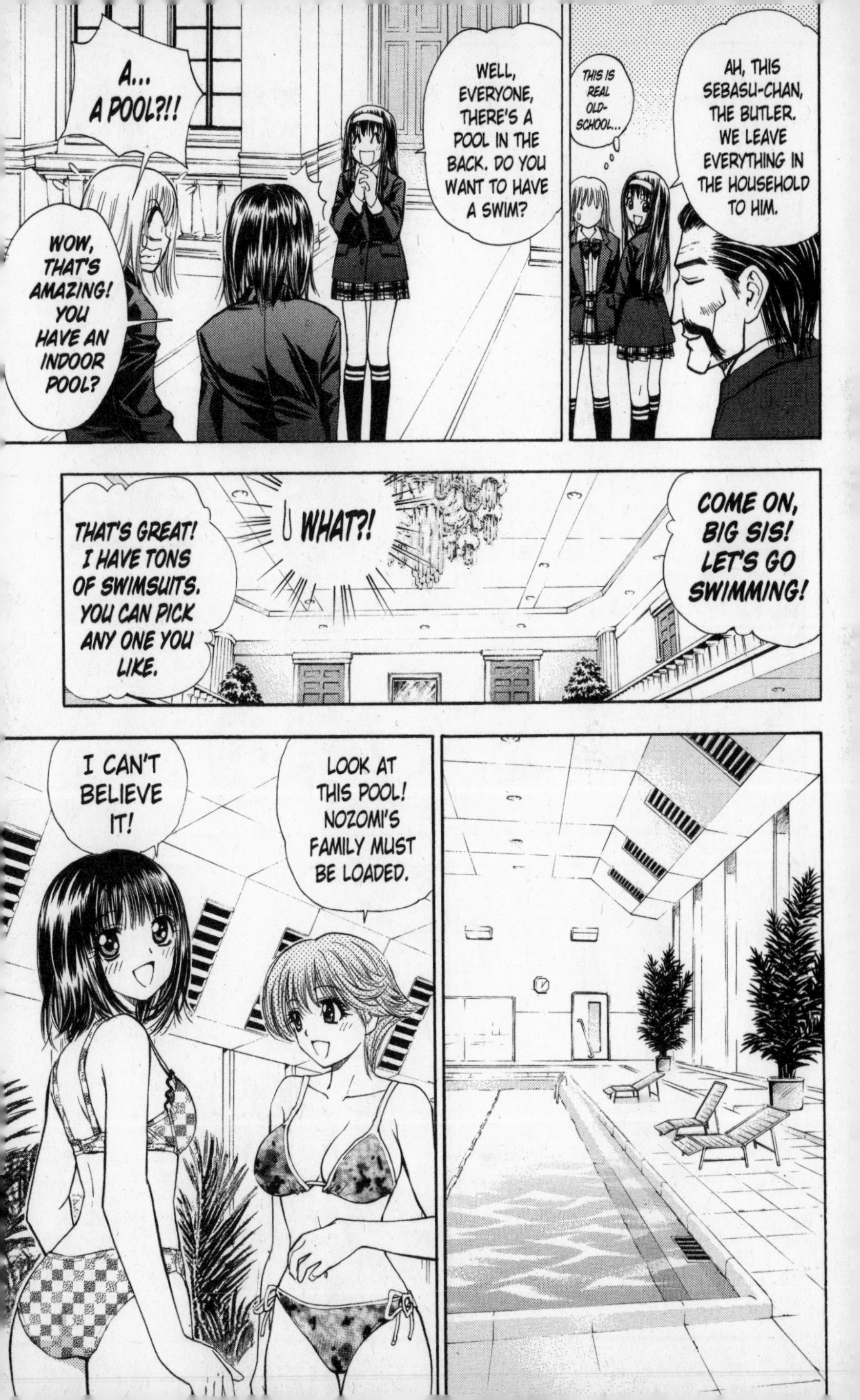
AH, THIS SEBASU-CHAN, THE BUTLER. WE LEAVE EVERYTHING IN THE HOUSEHOLD TO HIM.
THIS IS REAL OLD-SCHOOL...
WELL, EVERYONE, THERE'S A POOL IN THE BACK. DO YOU WANT TO HAVE A SWIM?
A... A POOL?!!
WOW, THAT'S AMAZING! YOU HAVE AN INDOOR POOL?
COME ON, BIG SIS! LET'S GO SWIMMING!
WHAT?!
THAT'S GREAT! I HAVE TONS OF SWIMSUITS. YOU CAN PICK ANY ONE YOU LIKE.
LOOK AT THIS POOL! NOZOMI'S FAMILY MUST BE LOADED.
I CAN'T BELIEVE IT!

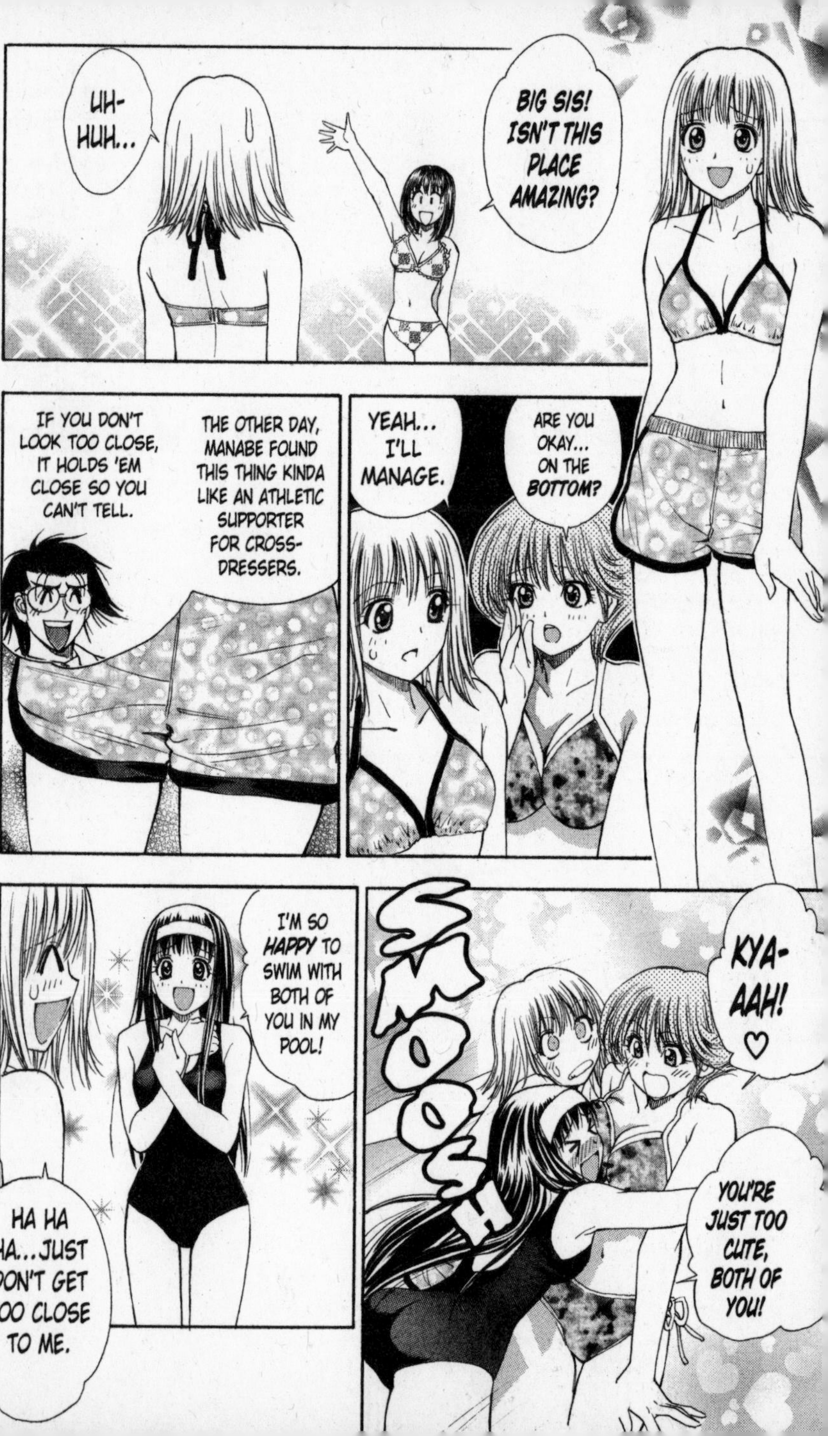
BIG SIS! ISN'T THIS PLACE AMAZING?
UH-HUH...
ARE YOU OKAY... ON THE BOTTOM?
YEAH... I'LL MANAGE.
THE OTHER DAY, MANABE FOUND THIS THING KINDA LIKE AN ATHLETIC SUPPORTER FOR CROSS-DRESSERS.
IF YOU DON'T LOOK TOO CLOSE, IT HOLDS 'EM CLOSE SO YOU CAN'T TELL.
KYA-AAH! ♡
SMOOSH
YOU'RE JUST TOO CUTE, BOTH OF YOU!
I'M SO HAPPY TO SWIM WITH BOTH OF YOU IN MY POOL!
HA HA HA...JUST DON'T GET TOO CLOSE TO ME.

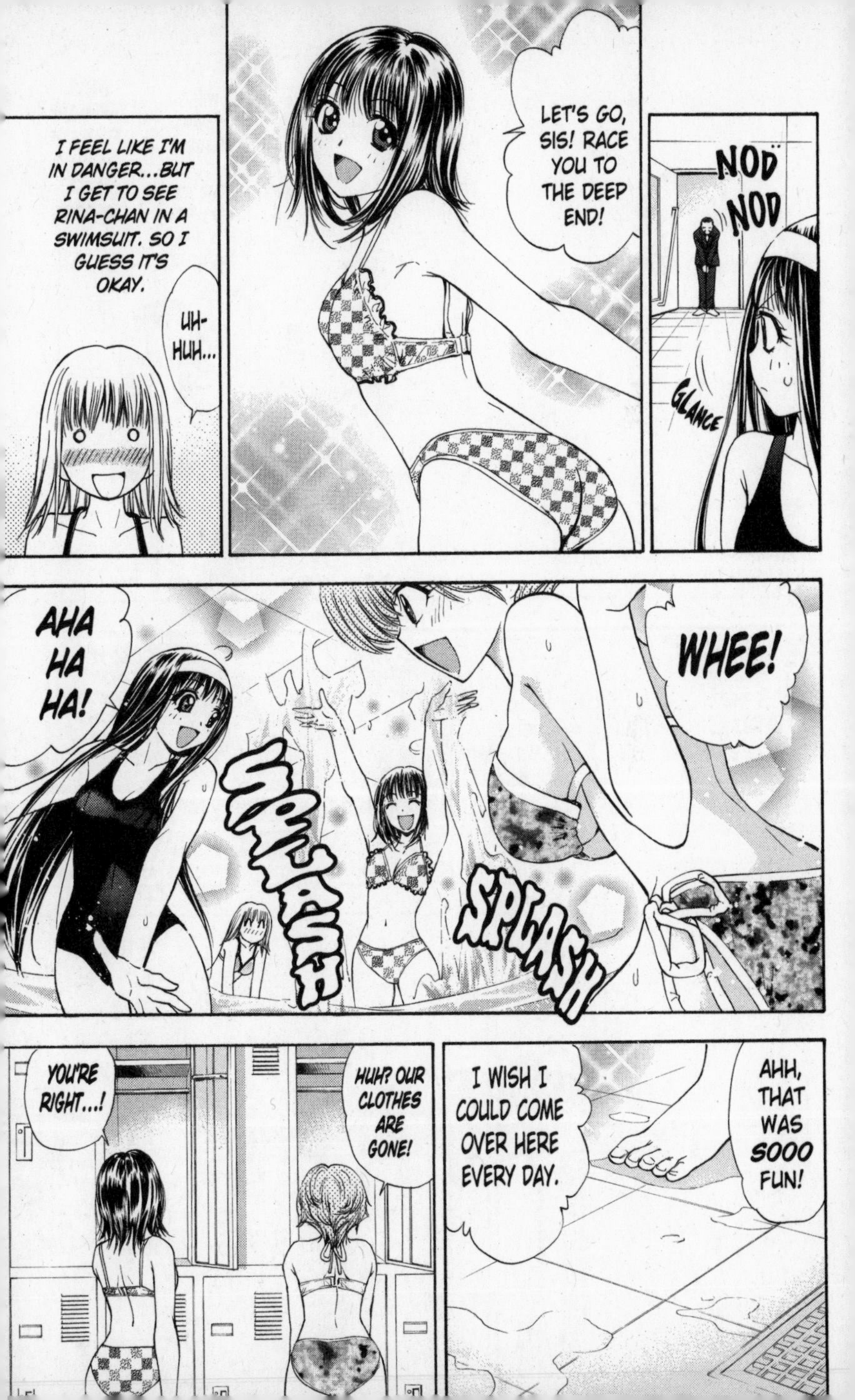
NOD NOD
GLANCE
LET'S GO, SIS! RACE YOU TO THE DEEP END!
I FEEL LIKE I'M IN DANGER...BUT I GET TO SEE RINA-CHAN IN A SWIMSUIT. SO I GUESS IT'S OKAY.
UH-HUH...
WHEE!
AHA HA HA!
SPLASH
SPLASH
AHH, THAT WAS SOOO FUN!
I WISH I COULD COME OVER HERE EVERY DAY.
HUH? OUR CLOTHES ARE GONE!
YOU'RE RIGHT...!

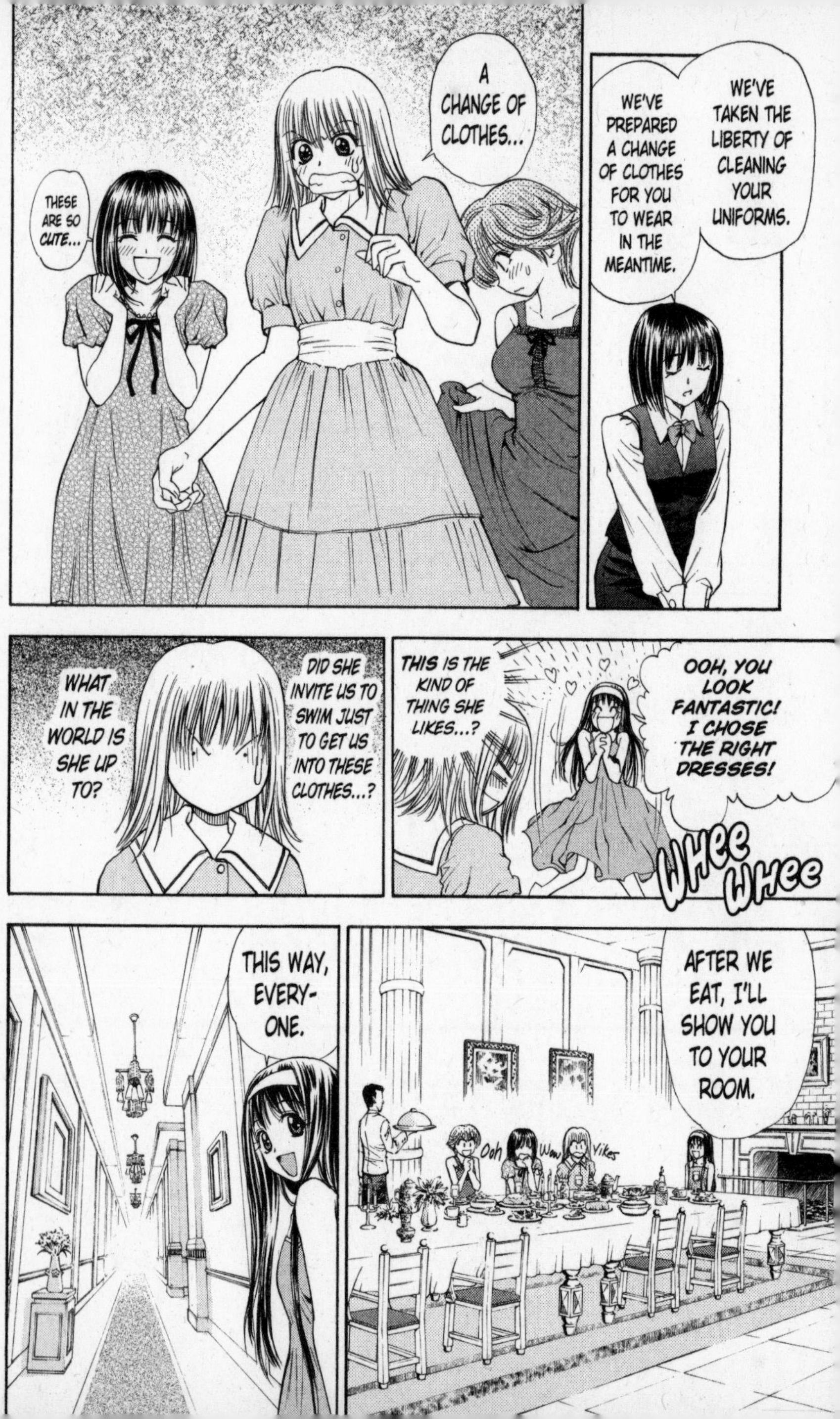
WE'VE TAKEN THE LIBERTY OF CLEANING YOUR UNIFORMS.
WE'VE PREPARED A CHANGE OF CLOTHES FOR YOU TO WEAR IN THE MEANTIME.
A CHANGE OF CLOTHES...
THESE ARE SO CUTE...
OOH, YOU LOOK FANTASTIC! I CHOSE THE RIGHT DRESSES!
WHEE WHEE
THIS IS THE KIND OF THING SHE LIKES...?
DID SHE INVITE US TO SWIM JUST TO GET US INTO THESE CLOTHES...?
WHAT IN THE WORLD IS SHE UP TO?
AFTER WE EAT, I'LL SHOW YOU TO YOUR ROOM.
Yikes
Wow
Ooh
THIS WAY, EVERY-ONE.

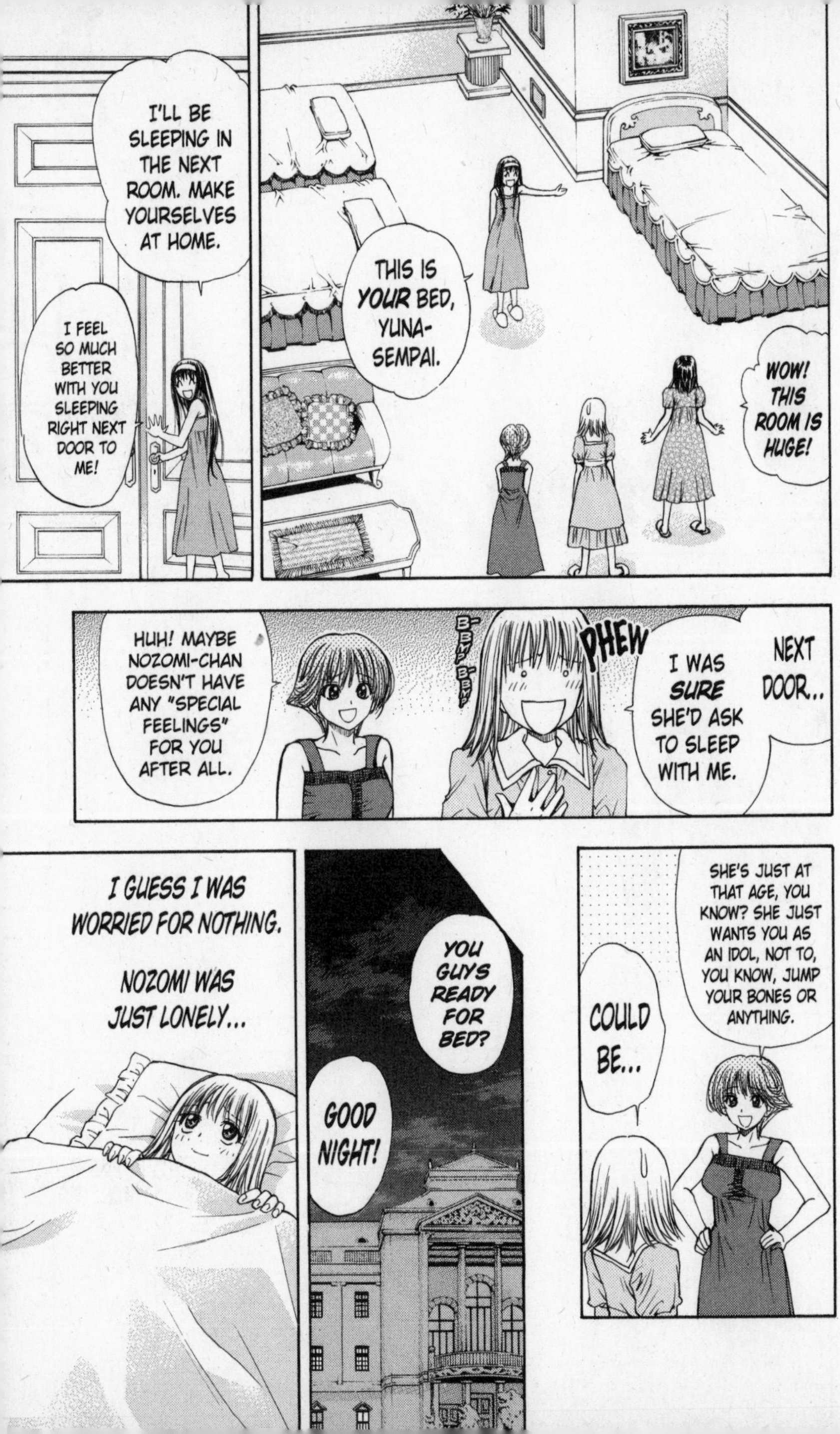
WOW! THIS ROOM IS HUGE!
THIS IS YOUR BED, YUNA-SEMPAI.
I'LL BE SLEEPING IN THE NEXT ROOM. MAKE YOURSELVES AT HOME.
I FEEL SO MUCH BETTER WITH YOU SLEEPING RIGHT NEXT DOOR TO ME!
NEXT DOOR...
PHEW
I WAS SURE SHE'D ASK TO SLEEP WITH ME.
B-BMP B-BMP
HUH! MAYBE NOZOMI-CHAN DOESN'T HAVE ANY "SPECIAL FEELINGS" FOR YOU AFTER ALL.
SHE'S JUST AT THAT AGE, YOU KNOW? SHE JUST WANTS YOU AS AN IDOL, NOT TO, YOU KNOW, JUMP YOUR BONES OR ANYTHING.
COULD BE...
YOU GUYS READY FOR BED?
GOOD NIGHT!
I GUESS I WAS WORRIED FOR NOTHING.
NOZOMI WAS JUST LONELY...

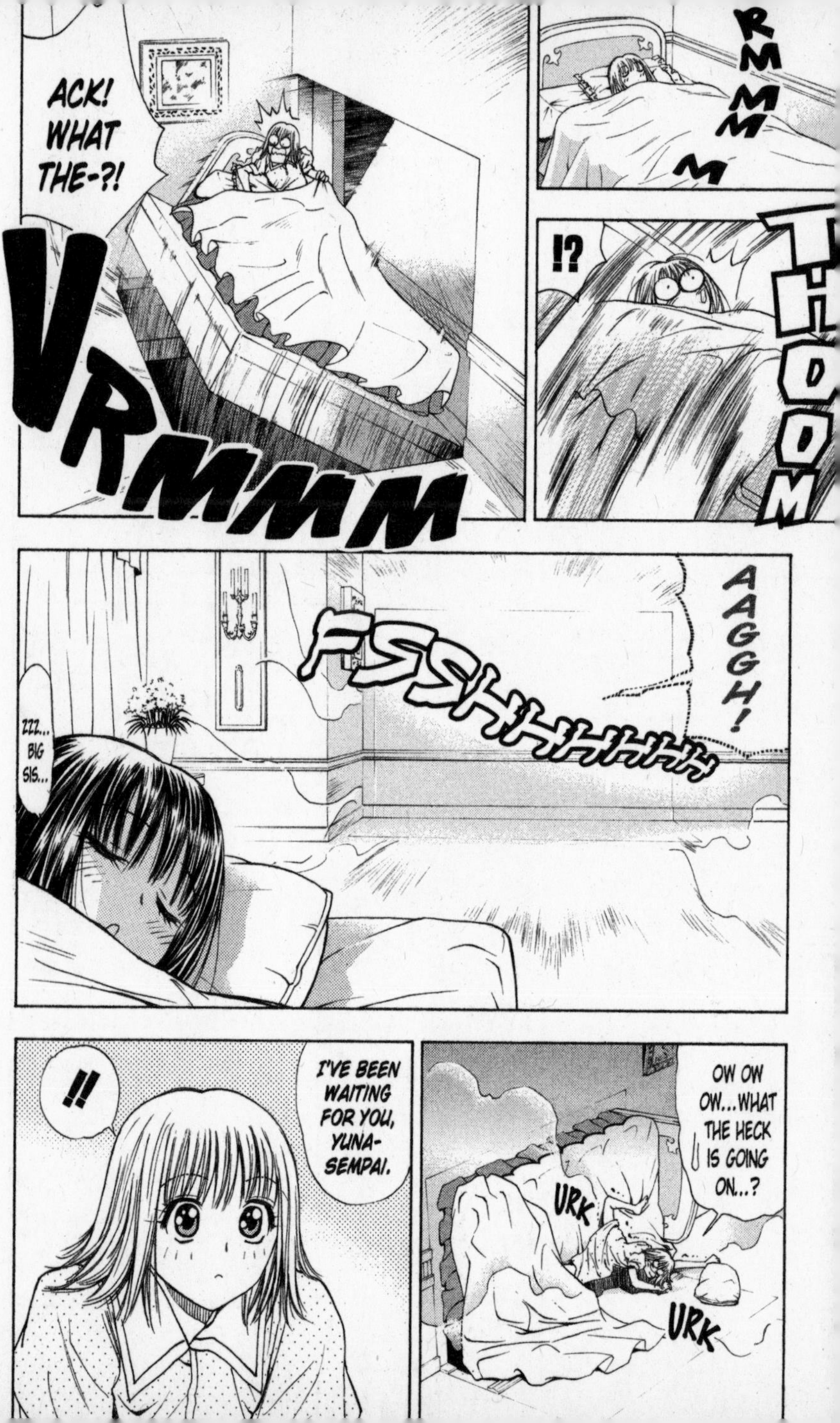
RMMMMM
!?
THOOM
ACK! WHAT THE-?!
VRMMMM
AAGGH!
FSSHHHHHH
ZZZ... BIG SIS...
OW OW OW...WHAT THE HECK IS GOING ON...?
URK
URK
I'VE BEEN WAITING FOR YOU, YUNA-SEMPAI.
!!

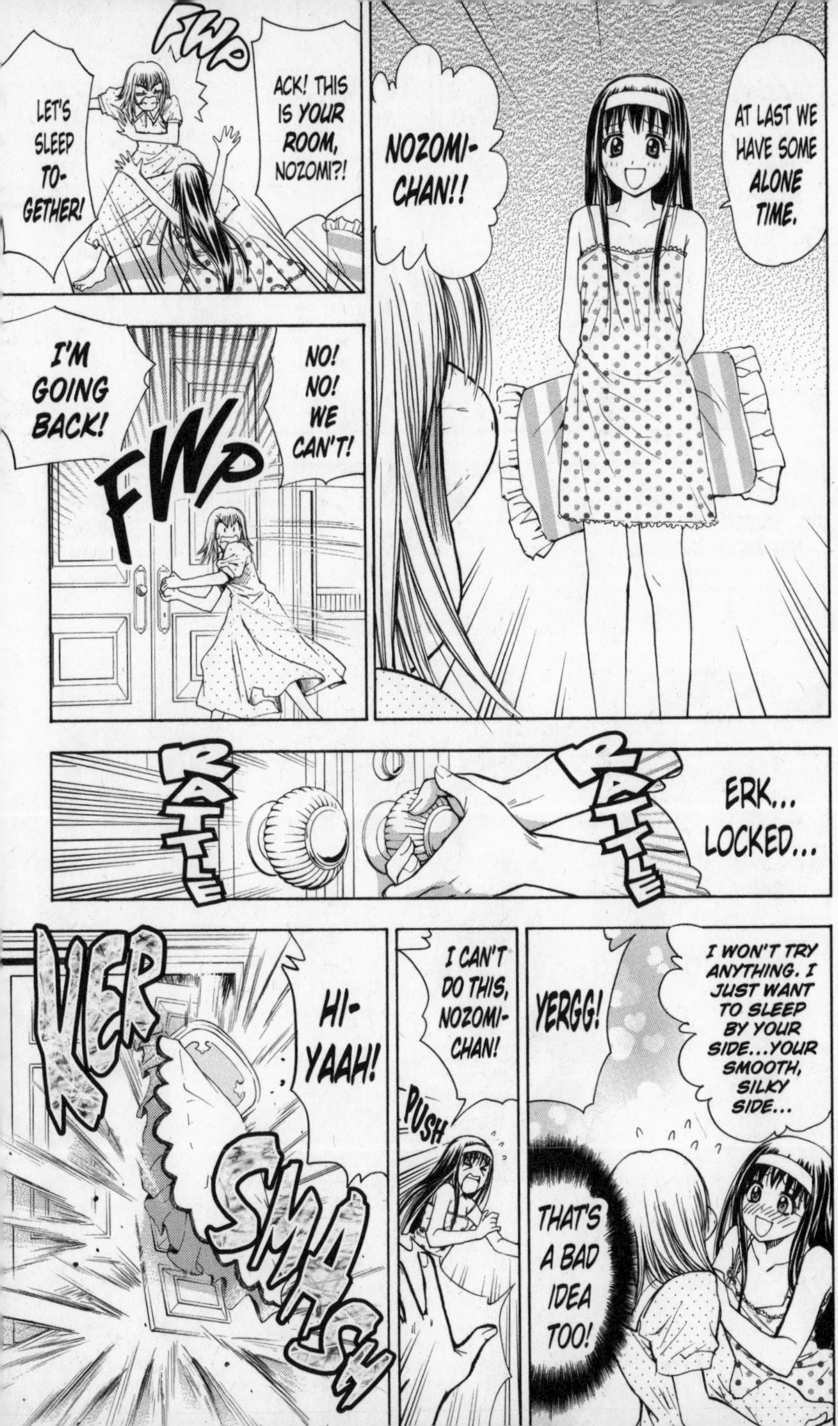
AT LAST WE HAVE SOME ALONE TIME.
NOZOMI-CHAN!!
FWP
ACK! THIS IS YOUR ROOM, NOZOMI?!
LET'S SLEEP TO-GETHER!
NO! NO! WE CAN'T!
I'M GOING BACK!
FWP
ERK... LOCKED...
RATTLE
RATTLE
I WON'T TRY ANYTHING. I JUST WANT TO SLEEP BY YOUR SIDE...YOUR SMOOTH, SILKY SIDE...
YERGG!
THAT'S A BAD IDEA TOO!
I CAN'T DO THIS, NOZOMI-CHAN!
PUSH
HI-YAAH!
KER
SMASH

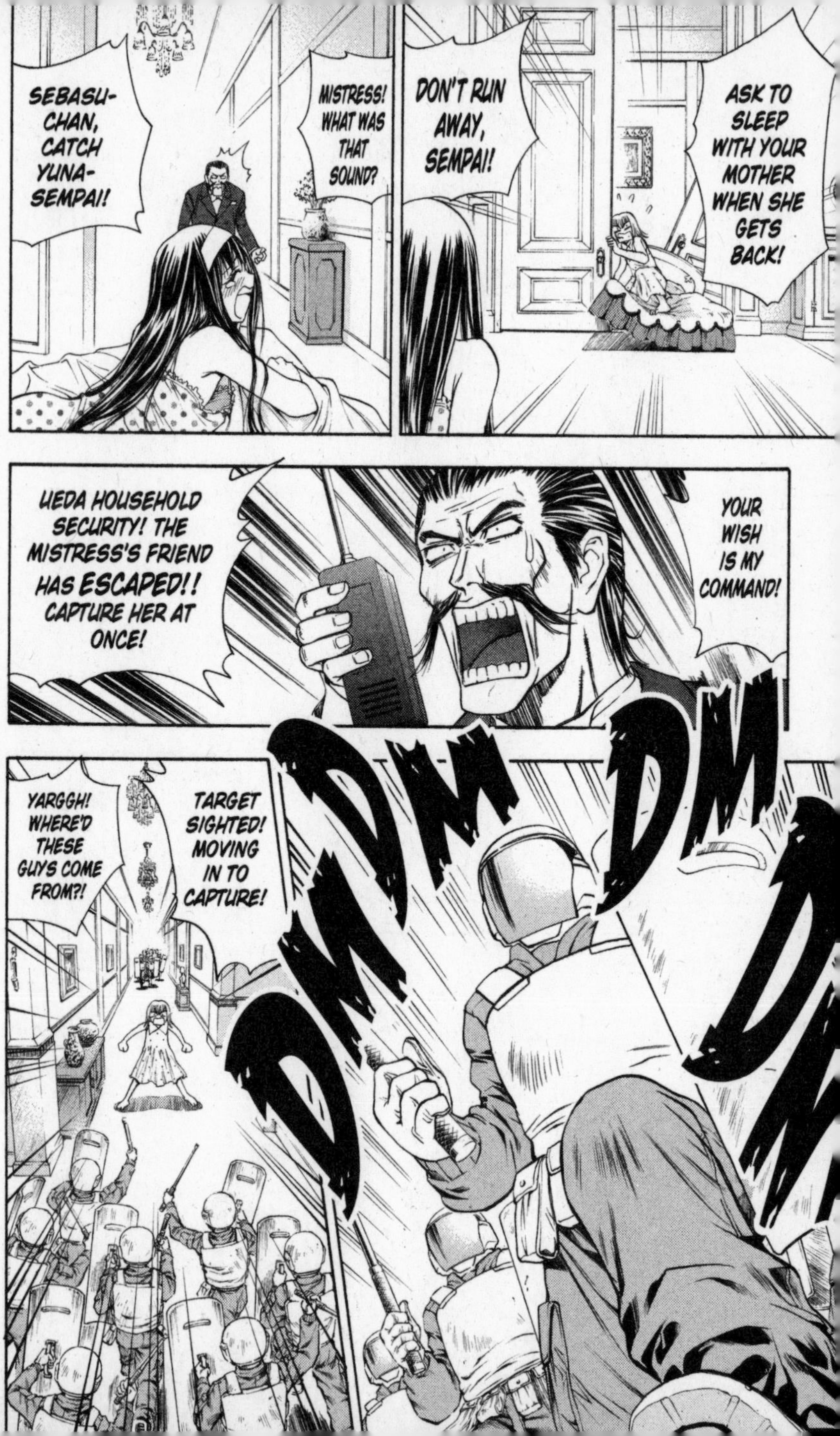
ASK TO SLEEP WITH YOUR MOTHER WHEN SHE GETS BACK!
DON'T RUN AWAY, SEMPAI!
MISTRESS! WHAT WAS THAT SOUND?
SEBASU-CHAN, CATCH YUNA-SEMPAI!
YOUR WISH IS MY COMMAND!
UEDA HOUSEHOLD SECURITY! THE MISTRESS'S FRIEND HAS ESCAPED!! CAPTURE HER AT ONCE!
DM DM DM
TARGET SIGHTED! MOVING IN TO CAPTURE!
YARGGH! WHERE'D THESE GUYS COME FROM?!

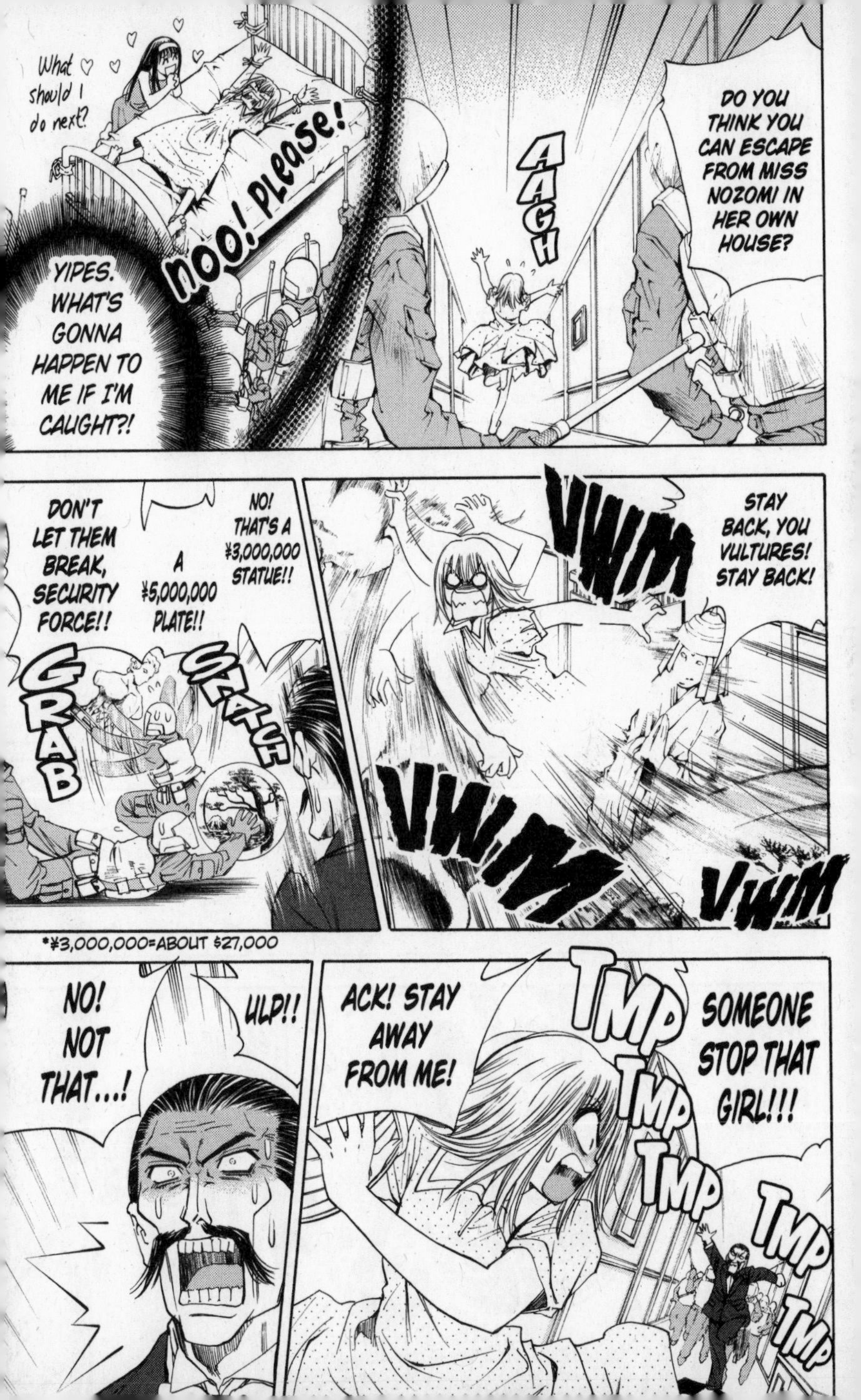
DO YOU THINK YOU CAN ESCAPE FROM MISS NOZOMI IN HER OWN HOUSE?
AAGH
What should I do next?
noo! PLEASE!
YIPES. WHAT'S GONNA HAPPEN TO ME IF I'M CAUGHT?!
STAY BACK, YOU VULTURES! STAY BACK!
VWM
VWM
VWM
NO! THAT'S A ¥3,000,000 STATUE!!
A ¥5,000,000 PLATE!!
DON'T LET THEM BREAK, SECURITY FORCE!!
SNATCH
GRAB
SOMEONE STOP THAT GIRL!!!
TMP
TMP
TMP
TMP
TMP
ACK! STAY AWAY FROM ME!
ULP!!
NO! NOT THAT...!
*¥3,000,000=ABOUT $27,000

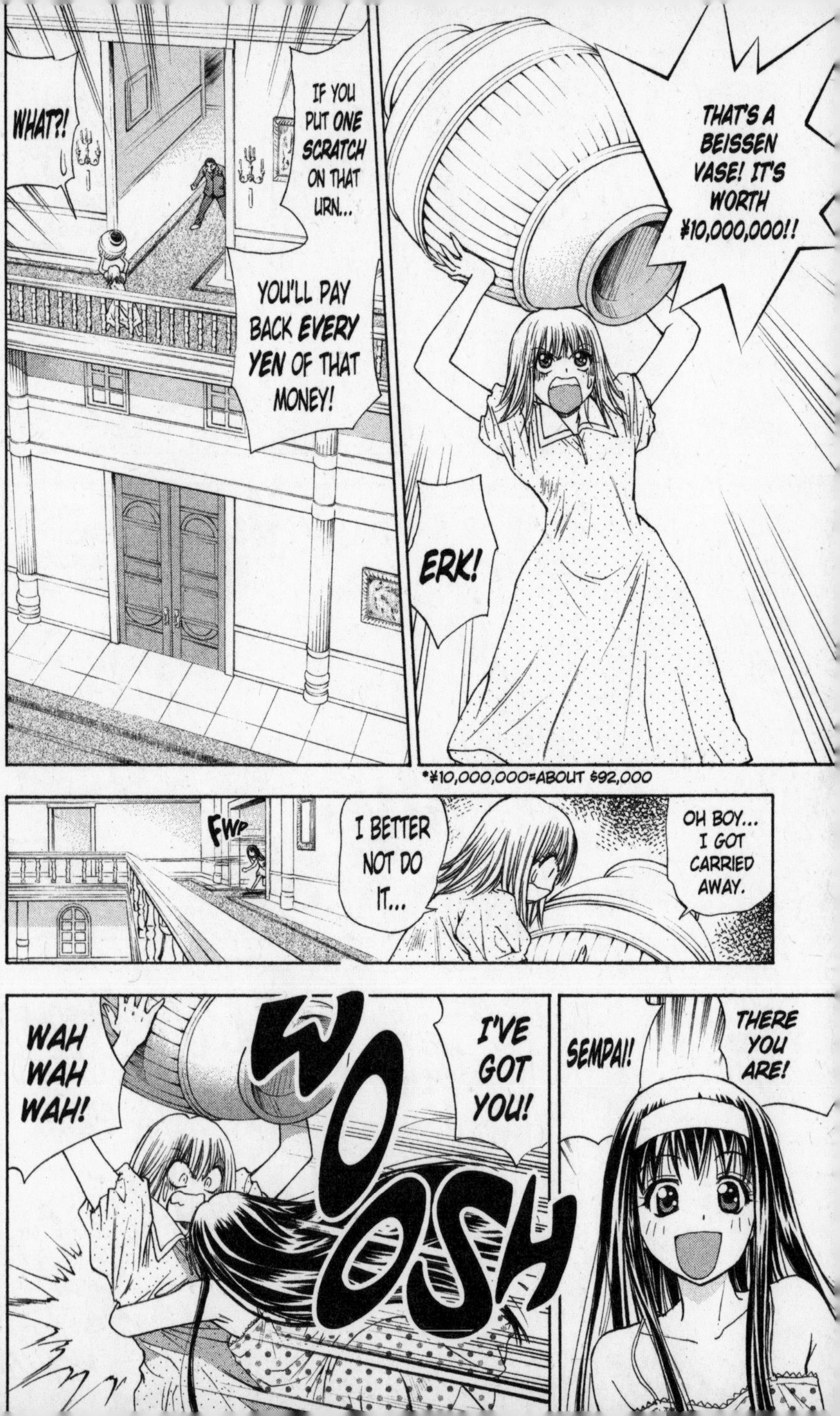
THAT'S A BEISSEN VASE! IT'S WORTH ¥10,000,000!!
ERK!
IF YOU PUT ONE SCRATCH ON THAT URN...
YOU'LL PAY BACK EVERY YEN OF THAT MONEY!
WHAT?!
*¥10,000,000=ABOUT $92,000
OH BOY... I GOT CARRIED AWAY.
I BETTER NOT DO IT...
FWP
THERE YOU ARE!
SEMPAI!
I'VE GOT YOU!
WOOSH
WAH WAH WAH!

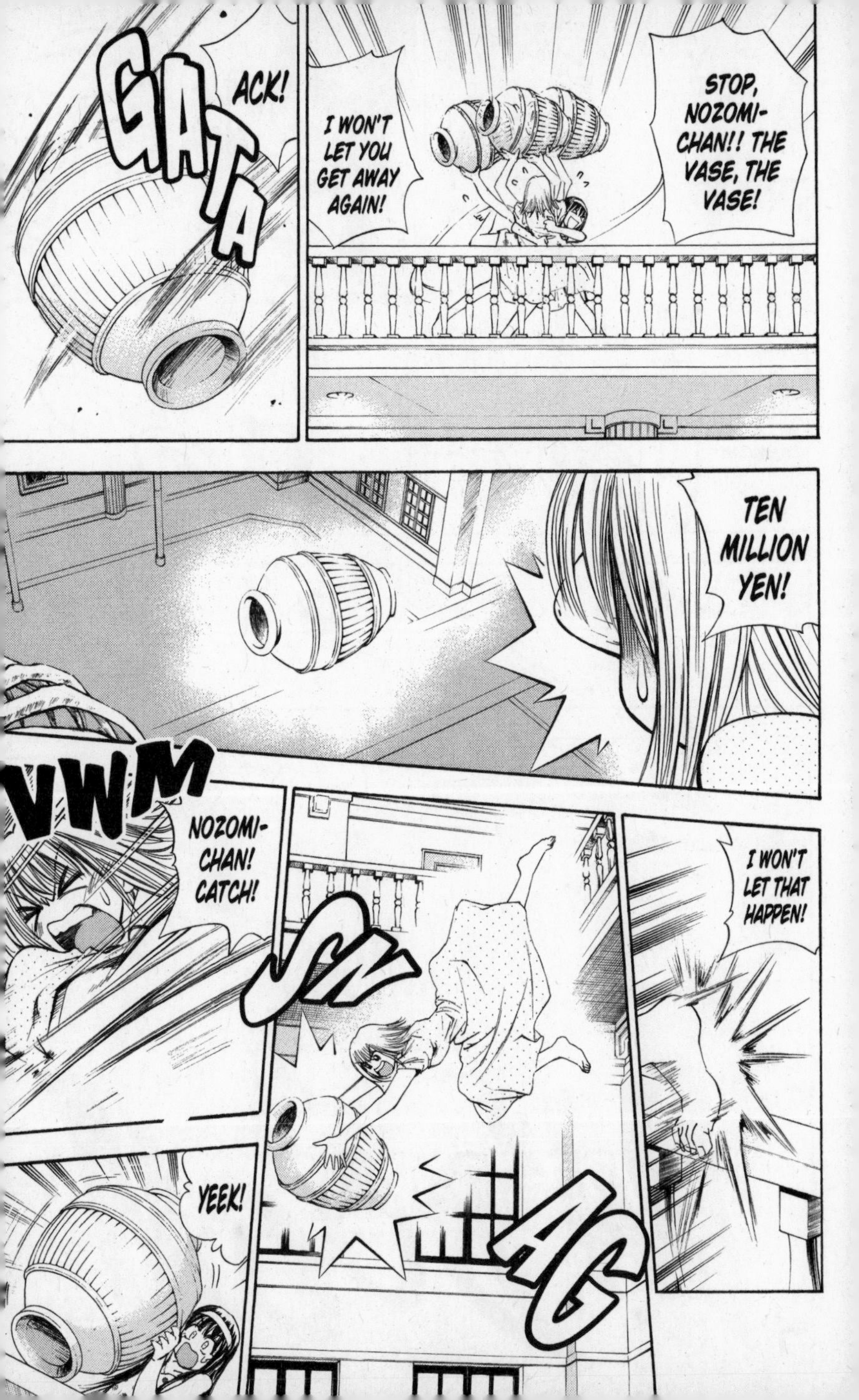
STOP, NOZOMI-CHAN!! THE VASE, THE VASE!
I WON'T LET YOU GET AWAY AGAIN!
GATA
ACK!
TEN MILLION YEN!
I WON'T LET THAT HAPPEN!
SN
AG
VWM
NOZOMI-CHAN! CATCH!
YEEK!

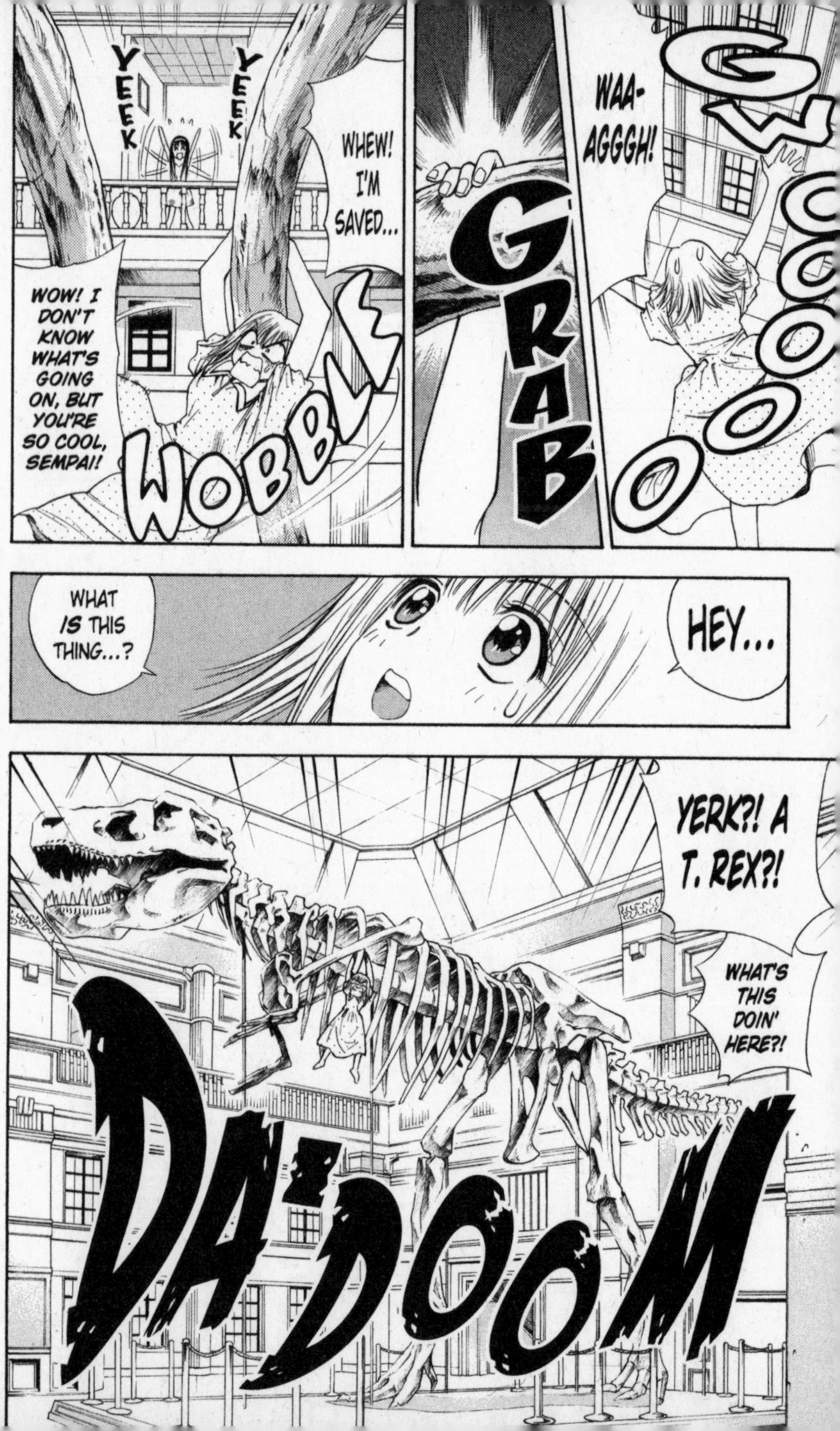
GWOOOOO
WAA-AGGGH!
GRAB
YEEK
YEEK
WHEW! I'M SAVED...
WOW! I DON'T KNOW WHAT'S GOING ON, BUT YOU'RE SO COOL, SEMPAI!
WOBBLE
HEY...
WHAT IS THIS THING...?
YERK?! A T. REX?!
WHAT'S THIS DOIN' HERE?!
DADOOM

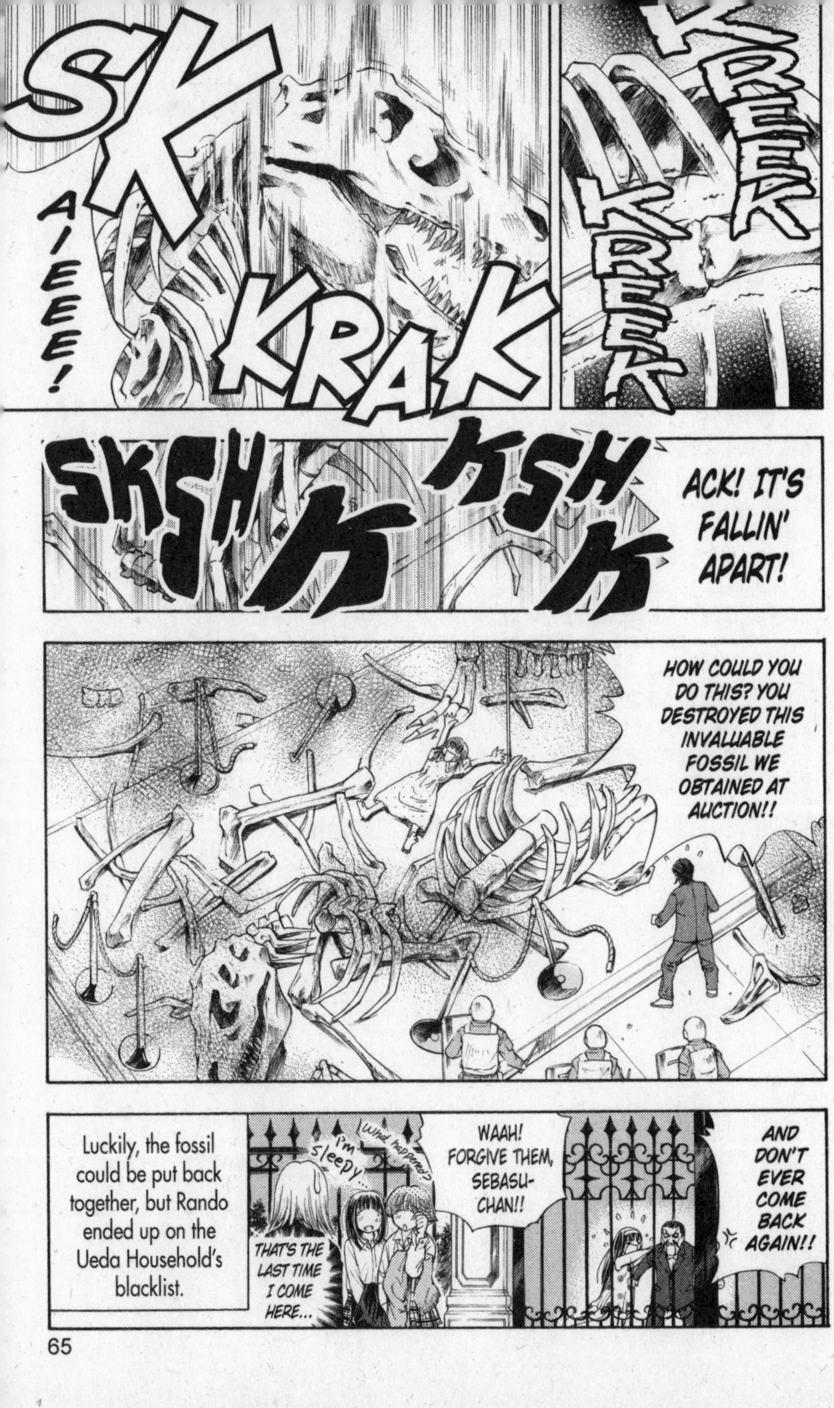
KREEK
KREEK
SK
KRAK
AIEEEE!
ACK! IT'S FALLIN' APART!
KSH
K
SKSH
K
HOW COULD YOU DO THIS? YOU DESTROYED THIS INVALUABLE FOSSIL WE OBTAINED AT AUCTION!!
AND DON'T EVER COME BACK AGAIN!!
WAAH! FORGIVE THEM, SEBASU-CHAN!!
What happened?
I'm sleepy...
THAT'S THE LAST TIME I COME HERE...
Luckily, the fossil could be put back together, but Rando ended up on the Ueda Household's blacklist.

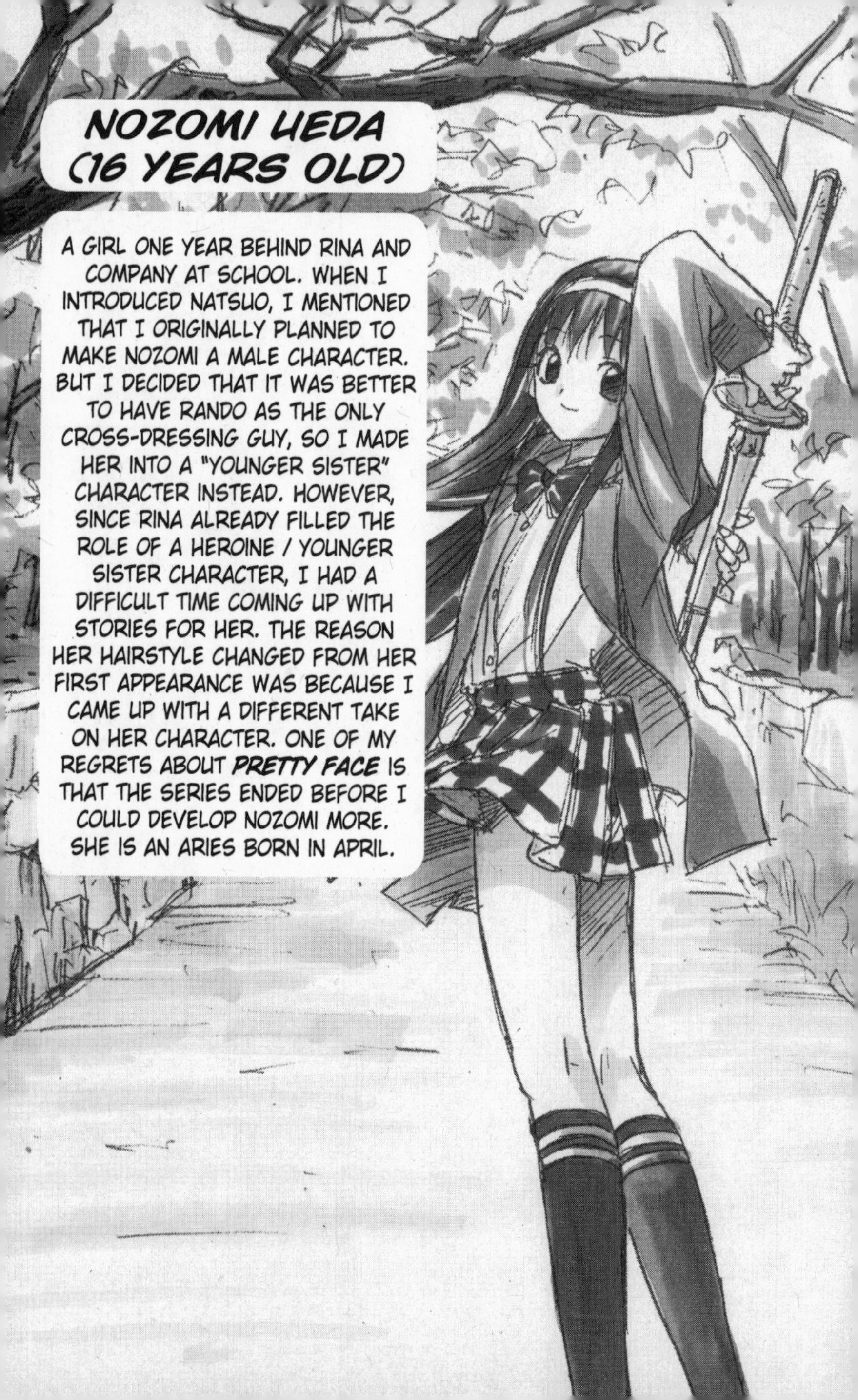
NOZOMI UEDA (16 YEARS OLD)
A GIRL ONE YEAR BEHIND RINA AND COMPANY AT SCHOOL. WHEN I INTRODUCED NATSUO, I MENTIONED THAT I ORIGINALLY PLANNED TO MAKE NOZOMI A MALE CHARACTER. BUT I DECIDED THAT IT WAS BETTER TO HAVE RANDO AS THE ONLY CROSS-DRESSING GUY, SO I MADE HER INTO A "YOUNGER SISTER" CHARACTER INSTEAD. HOWEVER, SINCE RINA ALREADY FILLED THE ROLE OF A HEROINE / YOUNGER SISTER CHARACTER, I HAD A DIFFICULT TIME COMING UP WITH STORIES FOR HER. THE REASON HER HAIRSTYLE CHANGED FROM HER FIRST APPEARANCE WAS BECAUSE I CAME UP WITH A DIFFERENT TAKE ON HER CHARACTER. ONE OF MY REGRETS ABOUT *PRETTY FACE* IS THAT THE SERIES ENDED BEFORE I COULD DEVELOP NOZOMI MORE. SHE IS AN ARIES BORN IN APRIL.

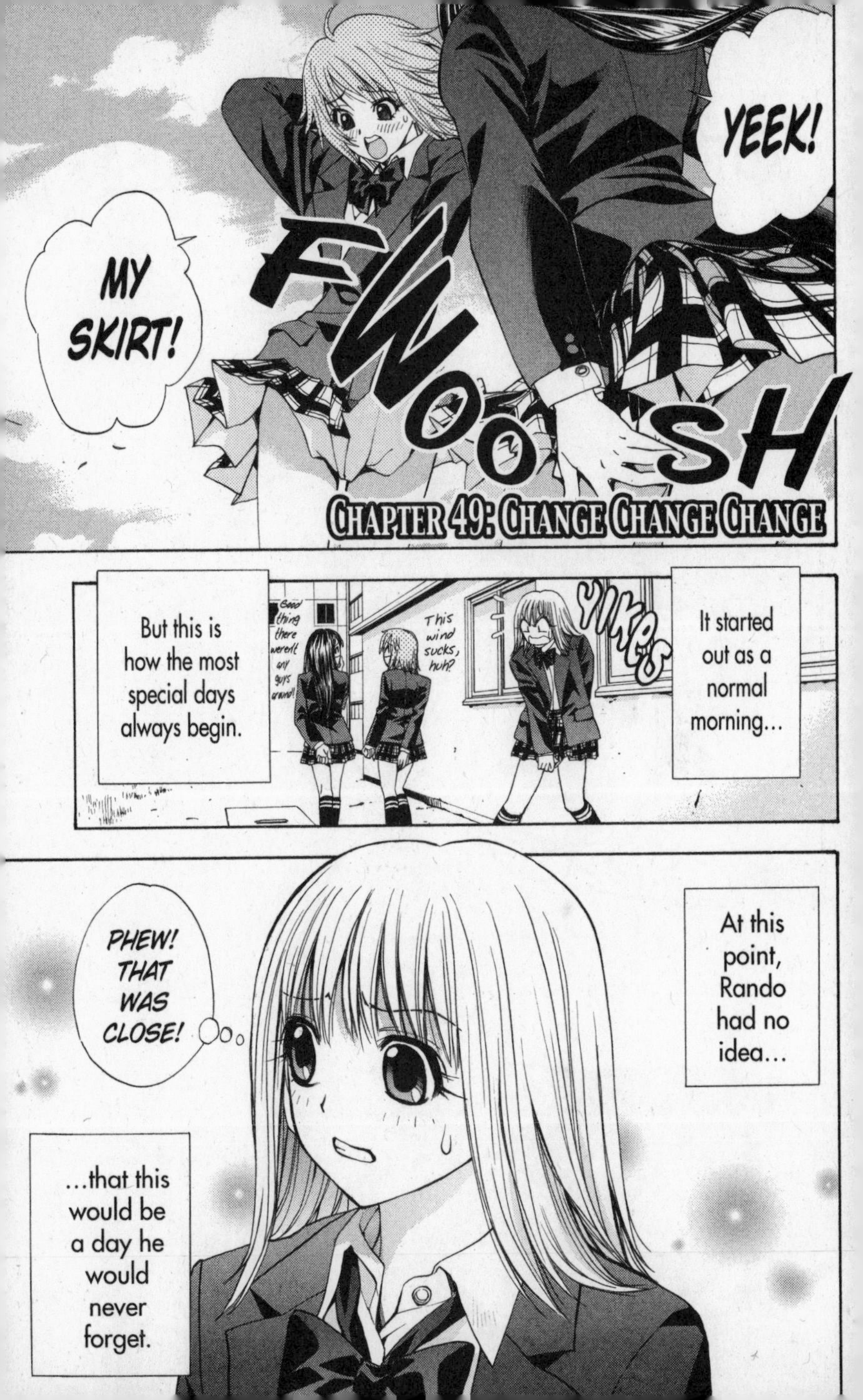
YEEK!
FWOOSH
MY SKIRT!
CHAPTER 49: CHANGE CHANGE CHANGE
It started out as a normal morning...
YIKES
This wind sucks, huh?
Good thing there weren't any guys around!
But this is how the most special days always begin.
At this point, Rando had no idea...
PHEW! THAT WAS CLOSE!
...that this would be a day he would never forget.

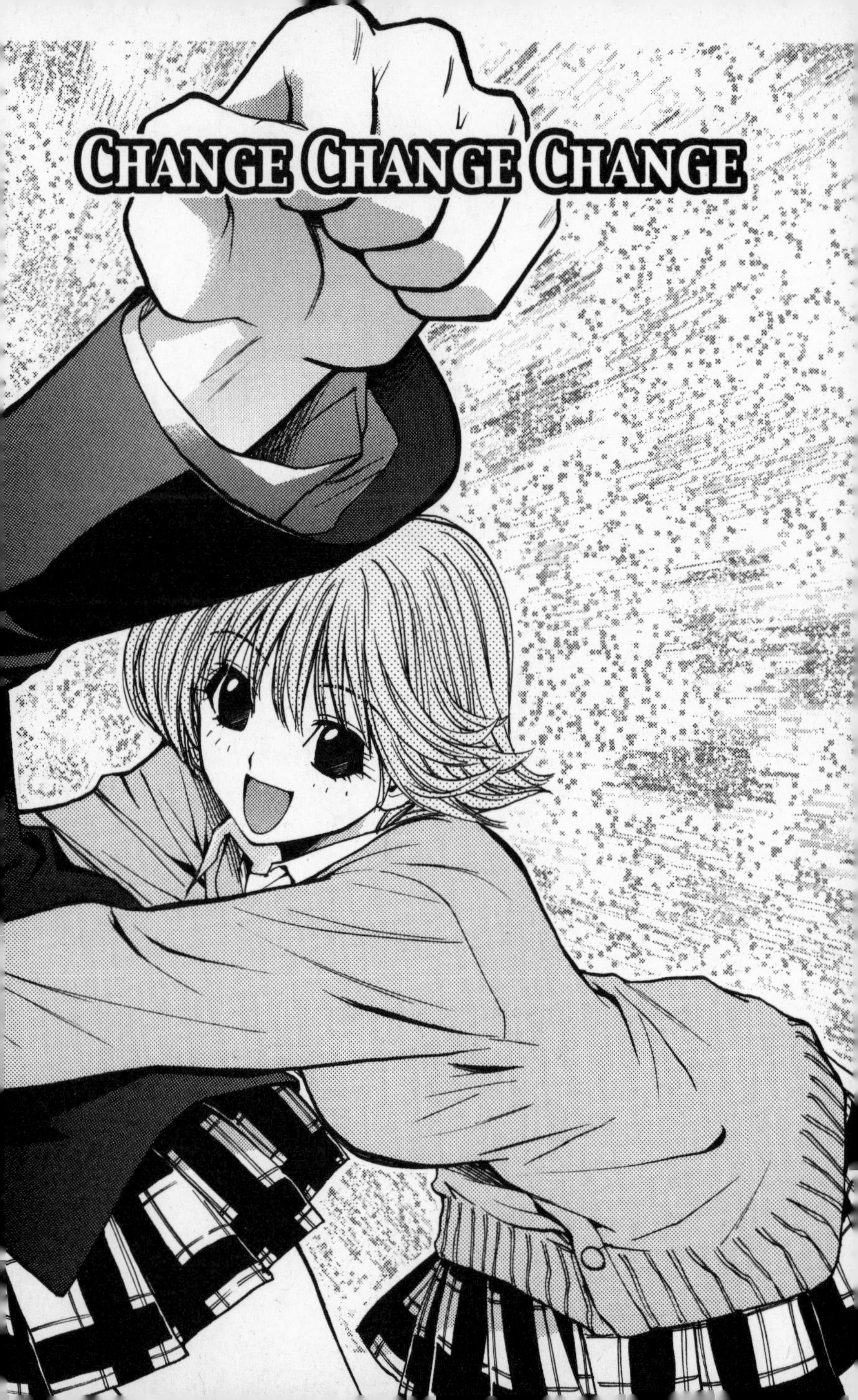
CHANGE CHANGE CHANGE

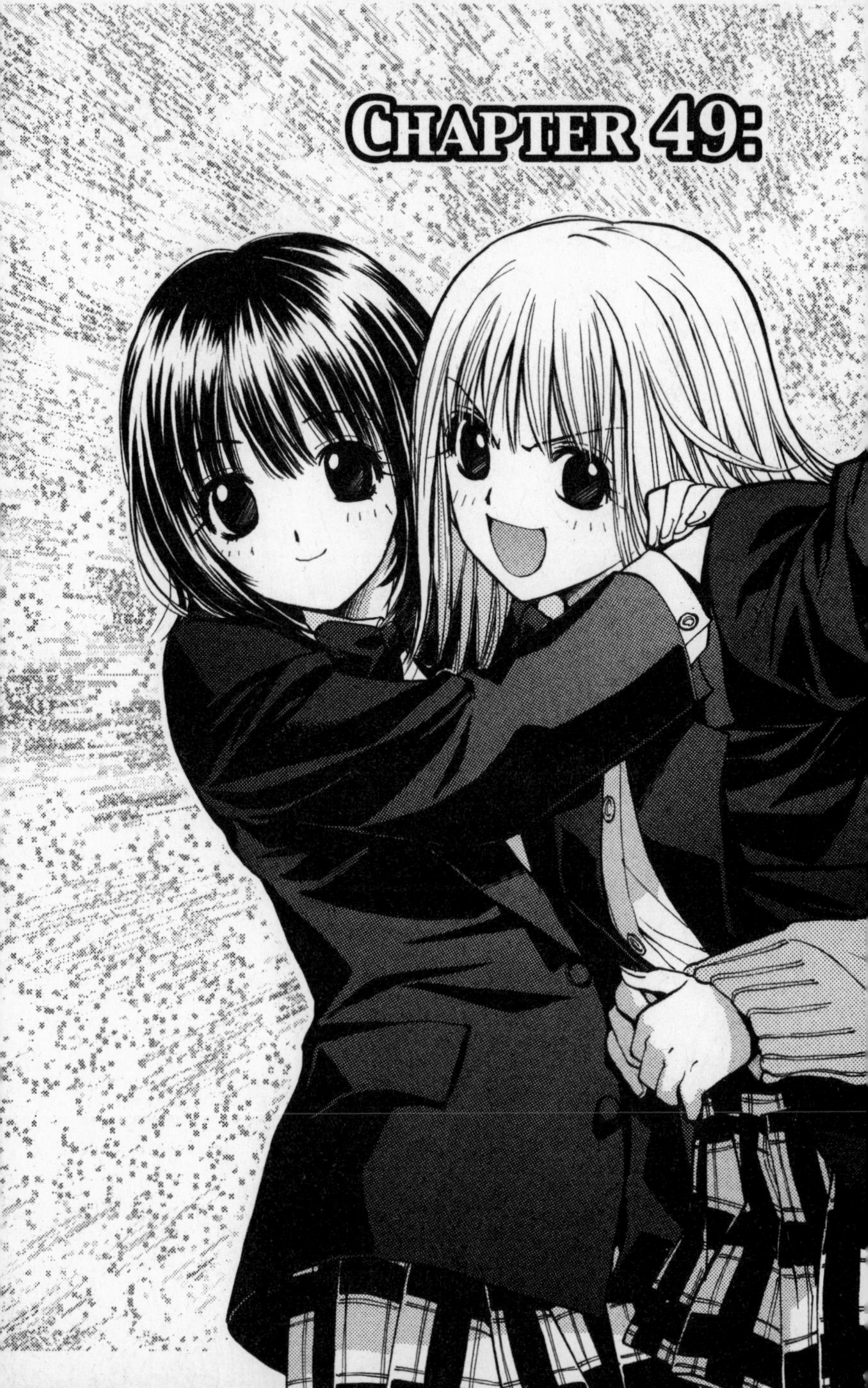
CHAPTER 49:

Rough sketch for the Akamaru Jump Summer Edition

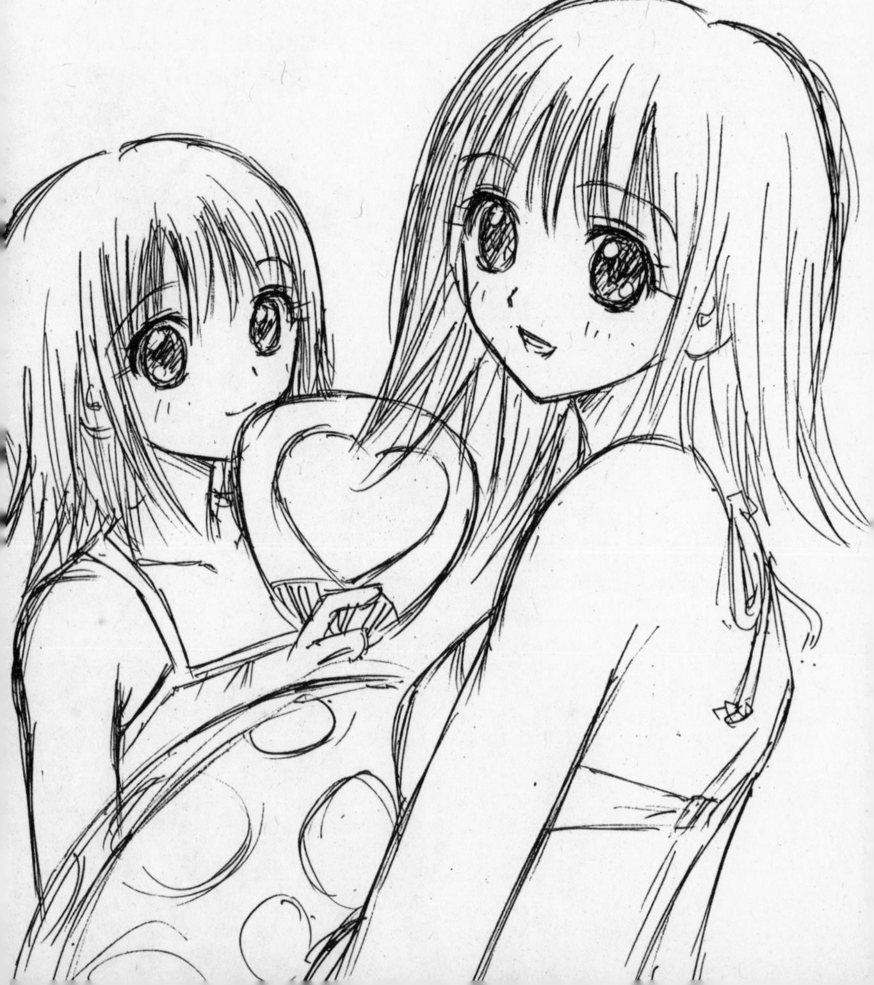

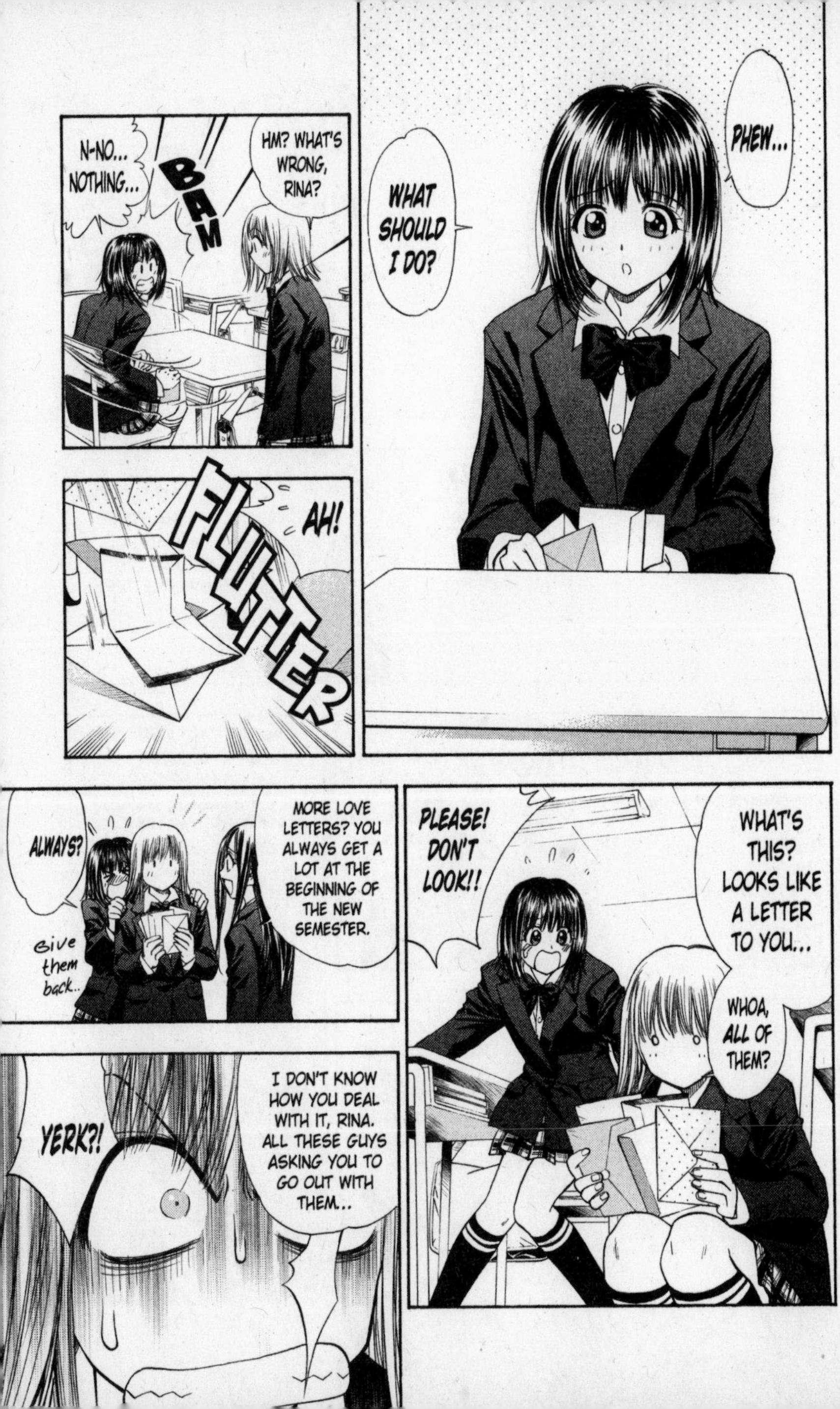
PHEW...
WHAT SHOULD I DO?
HM? WHAT'S WRONG, RINA?
N-NO... NOTHING...
BAM
AH!
FLUTTER
WHAT'S THIS? LOOKS LIKE A LETTER TO YOU...
PLEASE! DON'T LOOK!!
WHOA, ALL OF THEM?
MORE LOVE LETTERS? YOU ALWAYS GET A LOT AT THE BEGINNING OF THE NEW SEMESTER.
ALWAYS?
Give them back..
I DON'T KNOW HOW YOU DEAL WITH IT, RINA. ALL THESE GUYS ASKING YOU TO GO OUT WITH THEM...
YERK?!

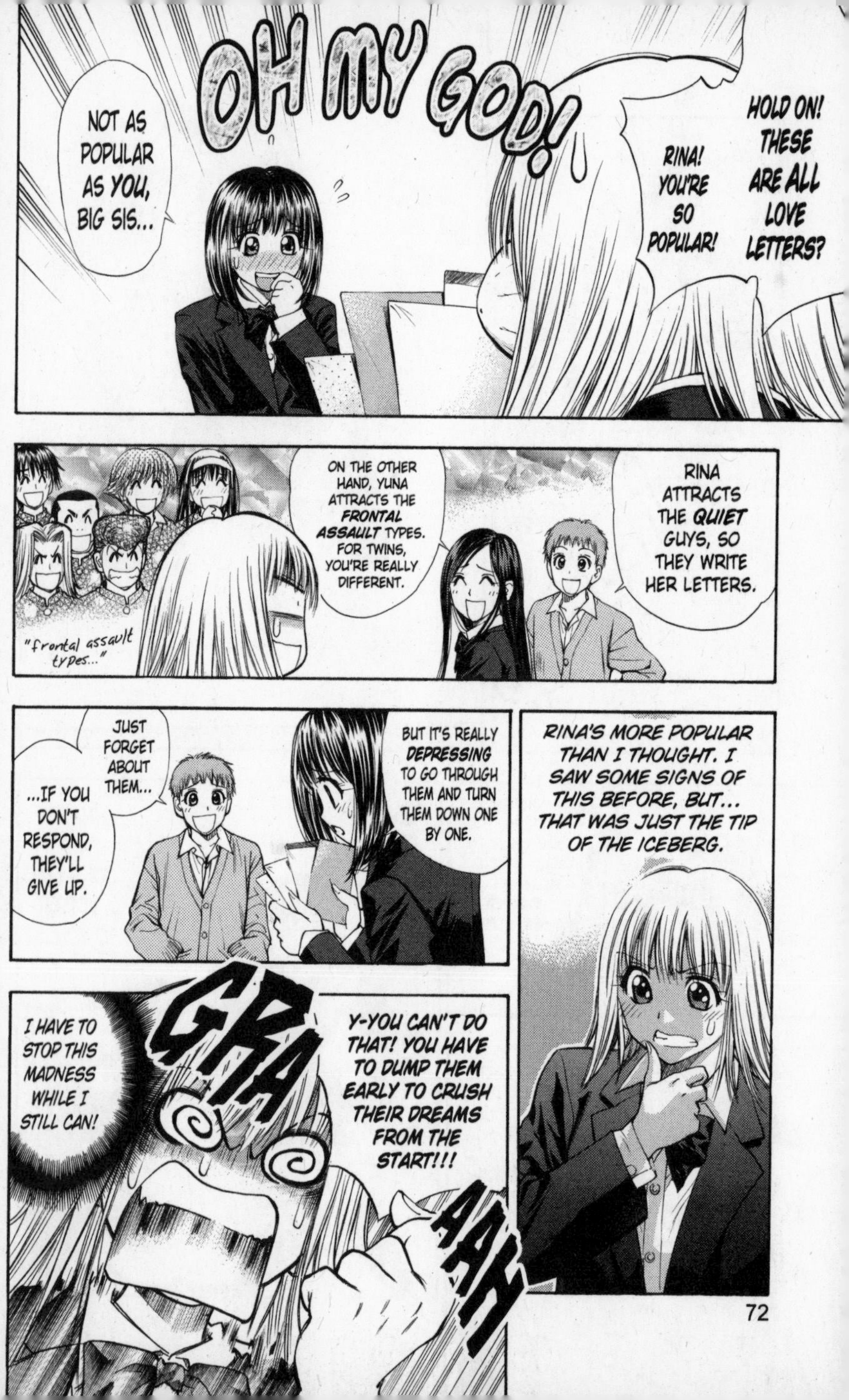
HOLD ON! THESE ARE ALL LOVE LETTERS?
RINA! YOU'RE SO POPULAR!
OH MY GOD!
NOT AS POPULAR AS YOU, BIG SIS...
RINA ATTRACTS THE QUIET GUYS, SO THEY WRITE HER LETTERS.
ON THE OTHER HAND, YUNA ATTRACTS THE FRONTAL ASSAULT TYPES. FOR TWINS, YOU'RE REALLY DIFFERENT.
"frontal assault types..."
RINA'S MORE POPULAR THAN I THOUGHT. I SAW SOME SIGNS OF THIS BEFORE, BUT... THAT WAS JUST THE TIP OF THE ICEBERG.
BUT IT'S REALLY DEPRESSING TO GO THROUGH THEM AND TURN THEM DOWN ONE BY ONE.
JUST FORGET ABOUT THEM...
...IF YOU DON'T RESPOND, THEY'LL GIVE UP.
Y-YOU CAN'T DO THAT! YOU HAVE TO DUMP THEM EARLY TO CRUSH THEIR DREAMS FROM THE START!!!
GRAAAH
I HAVE TO STOP THIS MADNESS WHILE I STILL CAN!

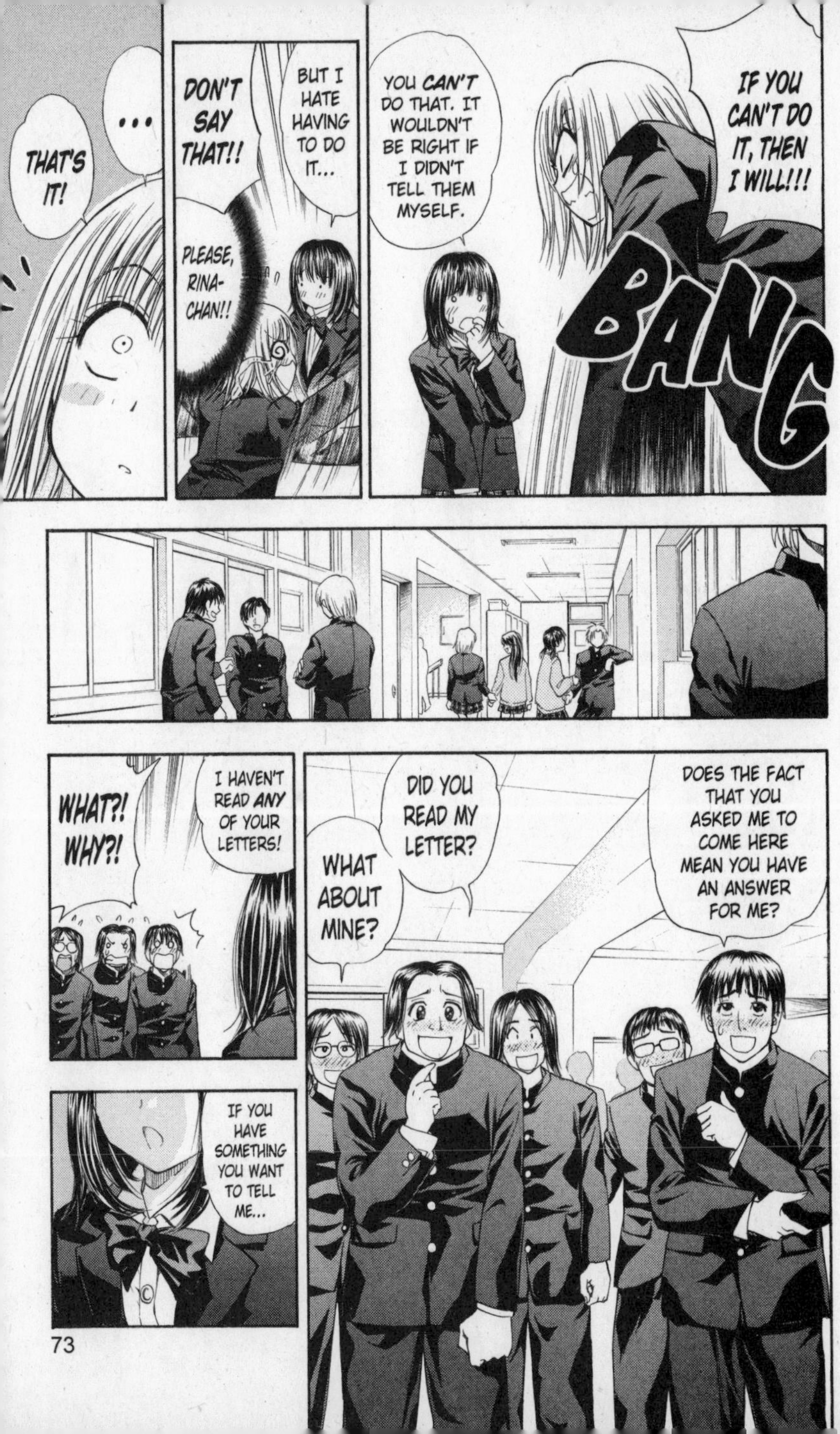
IF YOU CAN'T DO IT, THEN I WILL!!!
BANG
YOU CAN'T DO THAT. IT WOULDN'T BE RIGHT IF I DIDN'T TELL THEM MYSELF.
BUT I HATE HAVING TO DO IT...
DON'T SAY THAT!!
PLEASE, RINA-CHAN!!
...
THAT'S IT!
DOES THE FACT THAT YOU ASKED ME TO COME HERE MEAN YOU HAVE AN ANSWER FOR ME?
DID YOU READ MY LETTER?
WHAT ABOUT MINE?
I HAVEN'T READ ANY OF YOUR LETTERS!
WHAT?! WHY?!
IF YOU HAVE SOMETHING YOU WANT TO TELL ME...

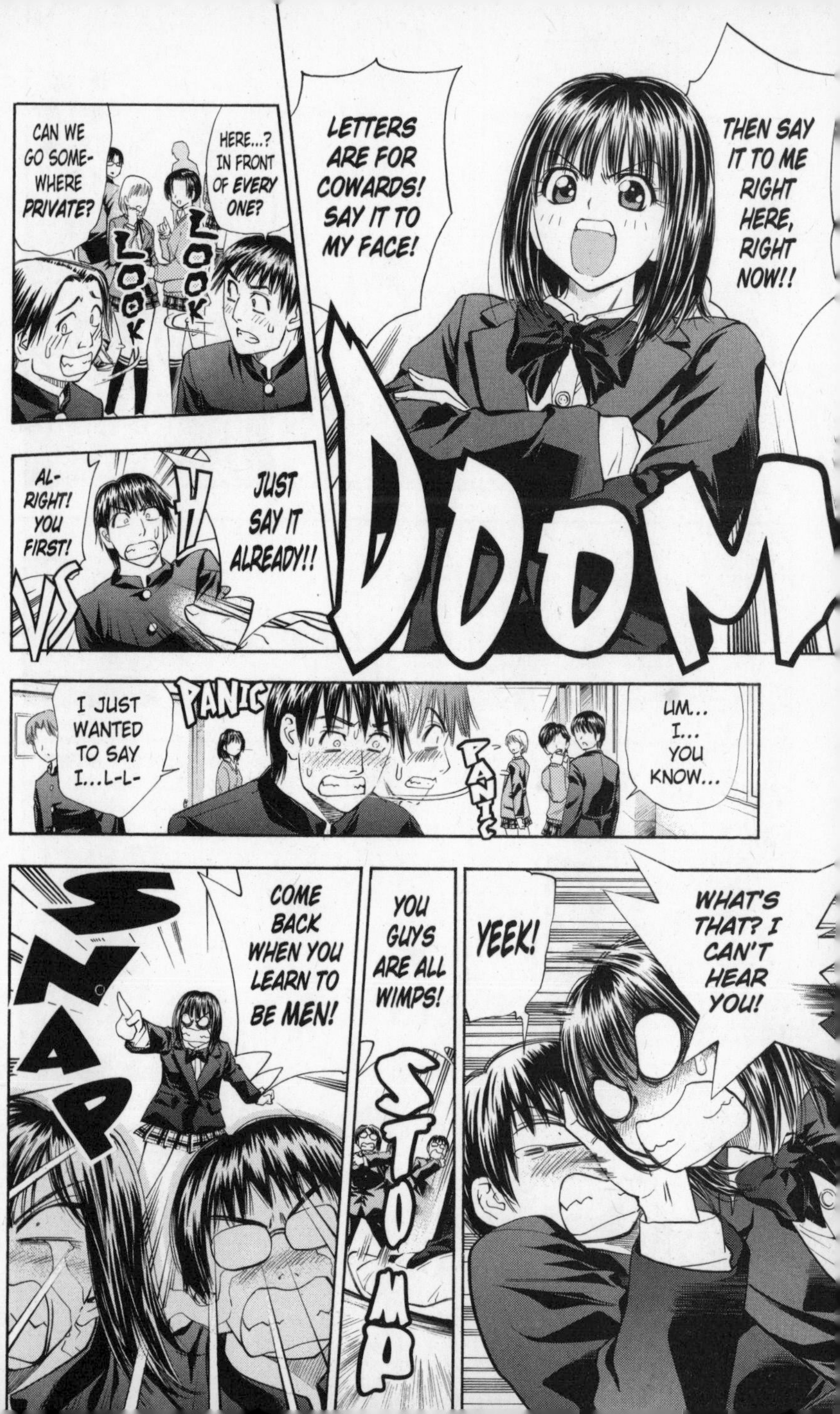
THEN SAY IT TO ME RIGHT HERE, RIGHT NOW!!
LETTERS ARE FOR COWARDS! SAY IT TO MY FACE!
DOOM
HERE...? IN FRONT OF EVERY ONE?
LOOK
LOOK
CAN WE GO SOME-WHERE PRIVATE?
JUST SAY IT ALREADY!!
AL-RIGHT! YOU FIRST!
UM... I... YOU KNOW...
PANIC
PANIC
I JUST WANTED TO SAY I...L-L-
WHAT'S THAT? I CAN'T HEAR YOU!
YEEK!
YOU GUYS ARE ALL WIMPS!
STOMP
COME BACK WHEN YOU LEARN TO BE MEN!
SNAP

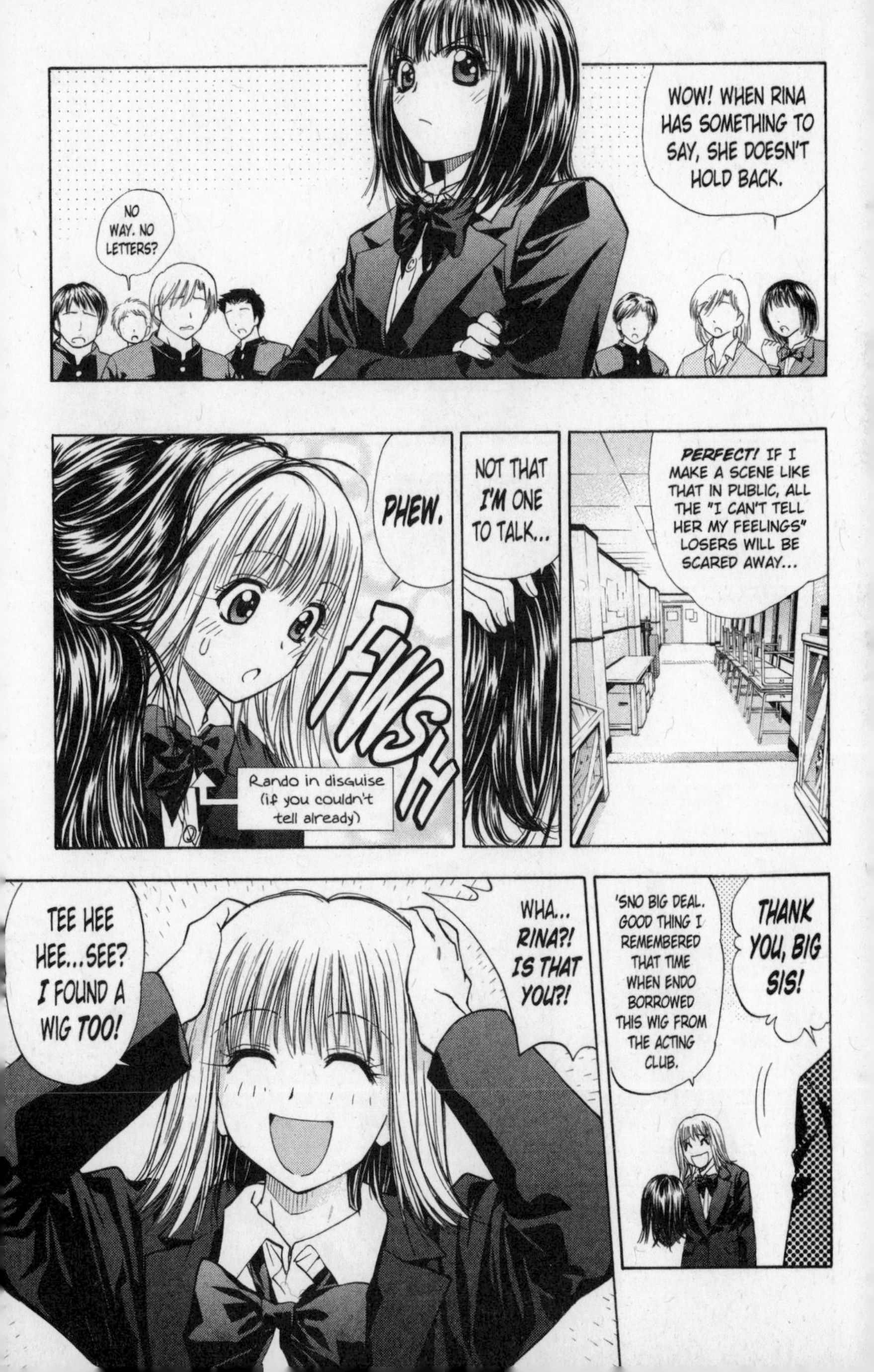
WOW! WHEN RINA HAS SOMETHING TO SAY, SHE DOESN'T HOLD BACK.
NO WAY. NO LETTERS?
*PERFECT!* IF I MAKE A SCENE LIKE THAT IN PUBLIC, ALL THE "I CAN'T TELL HER MY FEELINGS" LOSERS WILL BE SCARED AWAY...
NOT THAT *I'M* ONE TO TALK...
PHEW.
FWISH
Rando in disguise (if you couldn't tell already)
THANK YOU, BIG SIS!
'SNO BIG DEAL. GOOD THING I REMEMBERED THAT TIME WHEN ENDO BORROWED THIS WIG FROM THE ACTING CLUB.
WHA... *RINA?!* *IS THAT YOU?!*
TEE HEE HEE...SEE? *I* FOUND A WIG TOO!

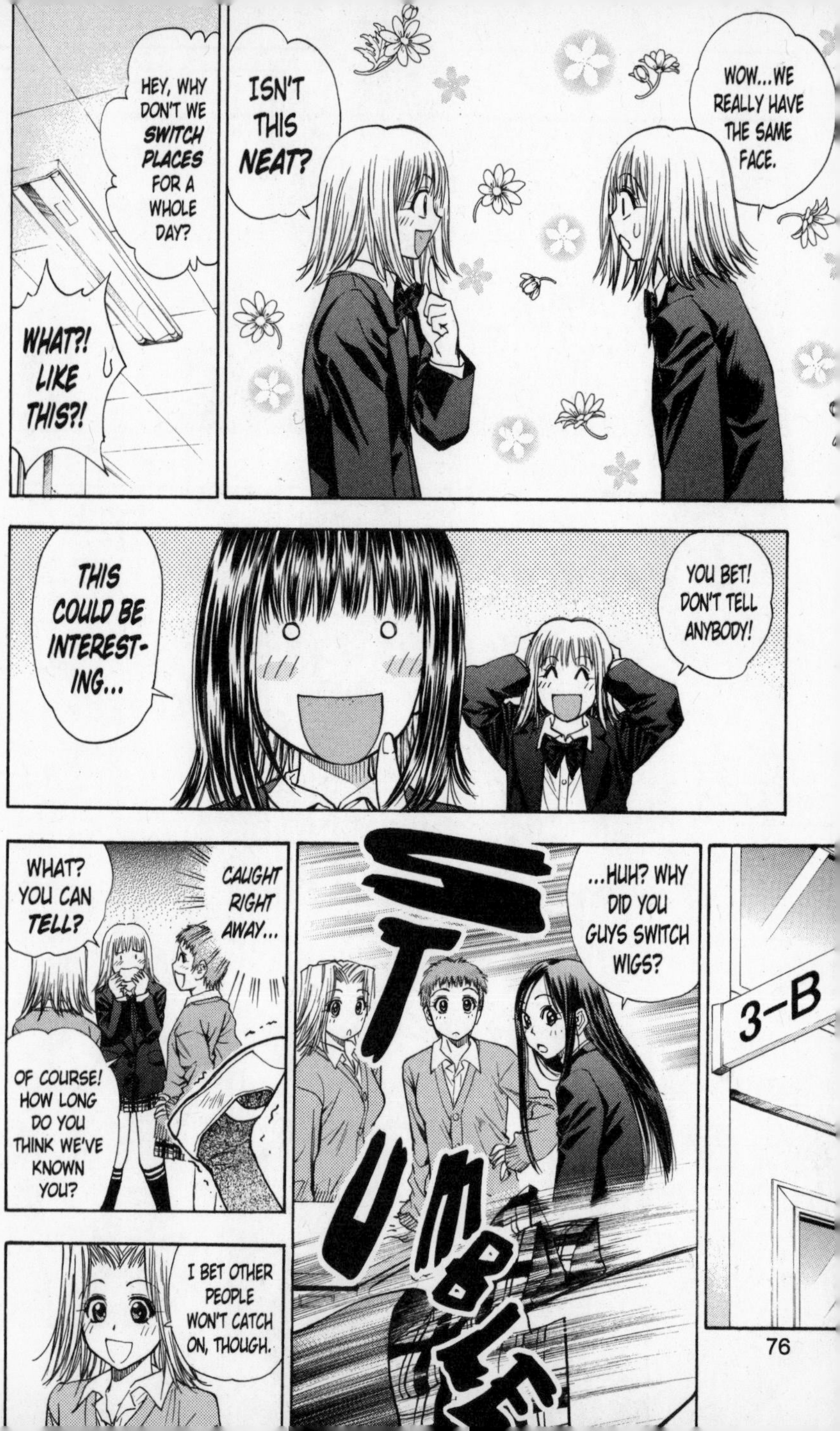
WOW...WE REALLY HAVE THE SAME FACE.
ISN'T THIS NEAT?
HEY, WHY DON'T WE SWITCH PLACES FOR A WHOLE DAY?
WHAT?! LIKE THIS?!
YOU BET! DON'T TELL ANYBODY!
THIS COULD BE INTERESTING...
3-B
...HUH? WHY DID YOU GUYS SWITCH WIGS?
CAUGHT RIGHT AWAY...
WHAT? YOU CAN TELL?
OF COURSE! HOW LONG DO YOU THINK WE'VE KNOWN YOU?
I BET OTHER PEOPLE WON'T CATCH ON, THOUGH.

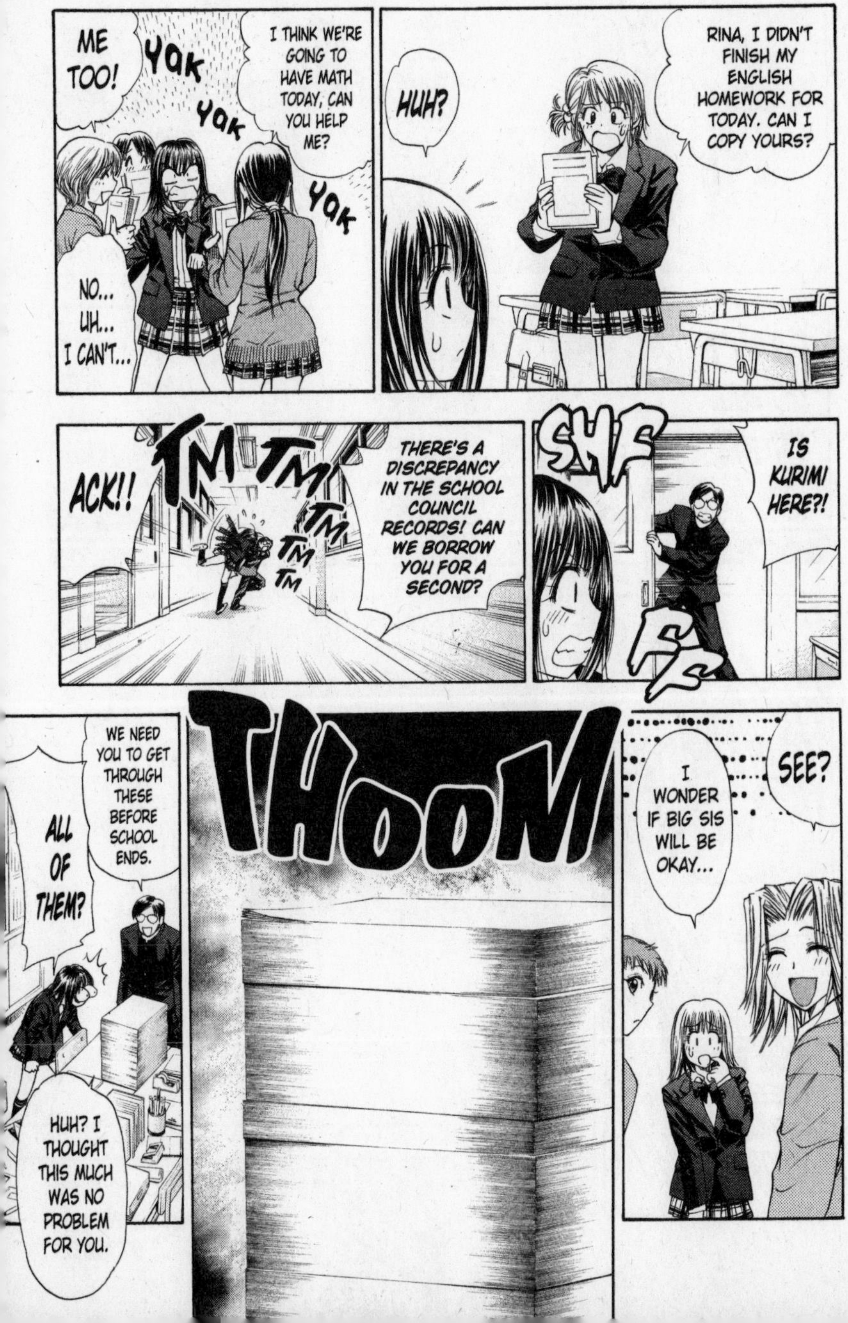
RINA, I DIDN'T FINISH MY ENGLISH HOMEWORK FOR TODAY. CAN I COPY YOURS?
HUH?
I THINK WE'RE GOING TO HAVE MATH TODAY, CAN YOU HELP ME?
YAK YAK YAK
ME TOO!
NO... UH... I CAN'T...
SHF
IS KURIMI HERE?!
FF
THERE'S A DISCREPANCY IN THE SCHOOL COUNCIL RECORDS! CAN WE BORROW YOU FOR A SECOND?
TM TM TM TM TM
ACK!!
SEE?
I WONDER IF BIG SIS WILL BE OKAY...
THOOM
WE NEED YOU TO GET THROUGH THESE BEFORE SCHOOL ENDS.
ALL OF THEM?
HUH? I THOUGHT THIS MUCH WAS NO PROBLEM FOR YOU.

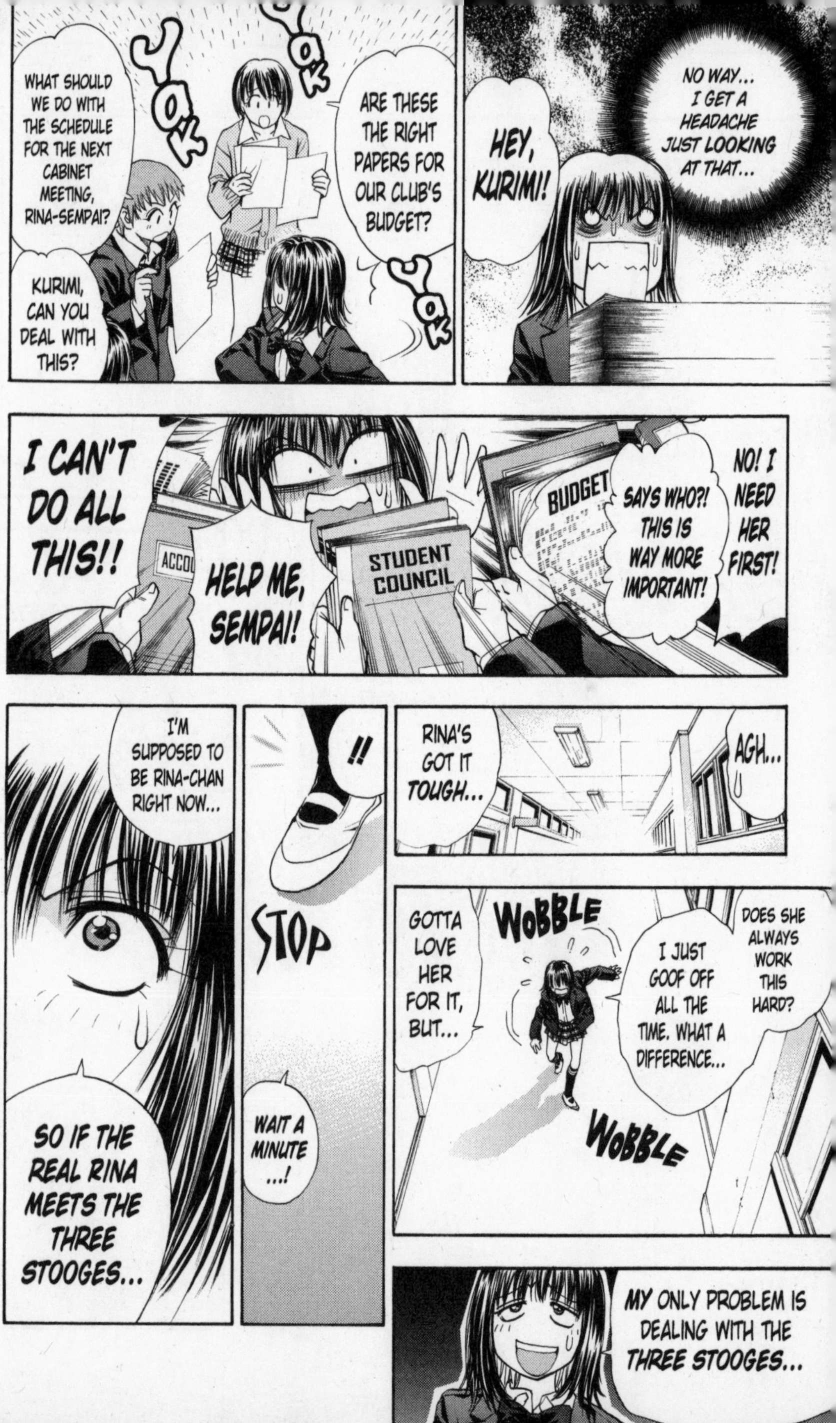
NO WAY... I GET A HEADACHE JUST LOOKING AT THAT...
HEY, KURIMI!
YOK
ARE THESE THE RIGHT PAPERS FOR OUR CLUB'S BUDGET?
YOK
WHAT SHOULD WE DO WITH THE SCHEDULE FOR THE NEXT CABINET MEETING, RINA-SEMPAI?
YOK
KURIMI, CAN YOU DEAL WITH THIS?
NO! I NEED HER FIRST!
SAYS WHO?! THIS IS WAY MORE IMPORTANT!
BUDGET
STUDENT COUNCIL
HELP ME, SEMPAI!
ACCOU
I CAN'T DO ALL THIS!!
AGH...
RINA'S GOT IT TOUGH...
DOES SHE ALWAYS WORK THIS HARD?
I JUST GOOF OFF ALL THE TIME. WHAT A DIFFERENCE...
WOBBLE
GOTTA LOVE HER FOR IT, BUT...
WOBBLE
MY ONLY PROBLEM IS DEALING WITH THE THREE STOOGES...
!!
STOP
WAIT A MINUTE ...!
I'M SUPPOSED TO BE RINA-CHAN RIGHT NOW...
SO IF THE REAL RINA MEETS THE THREE STOOGES...

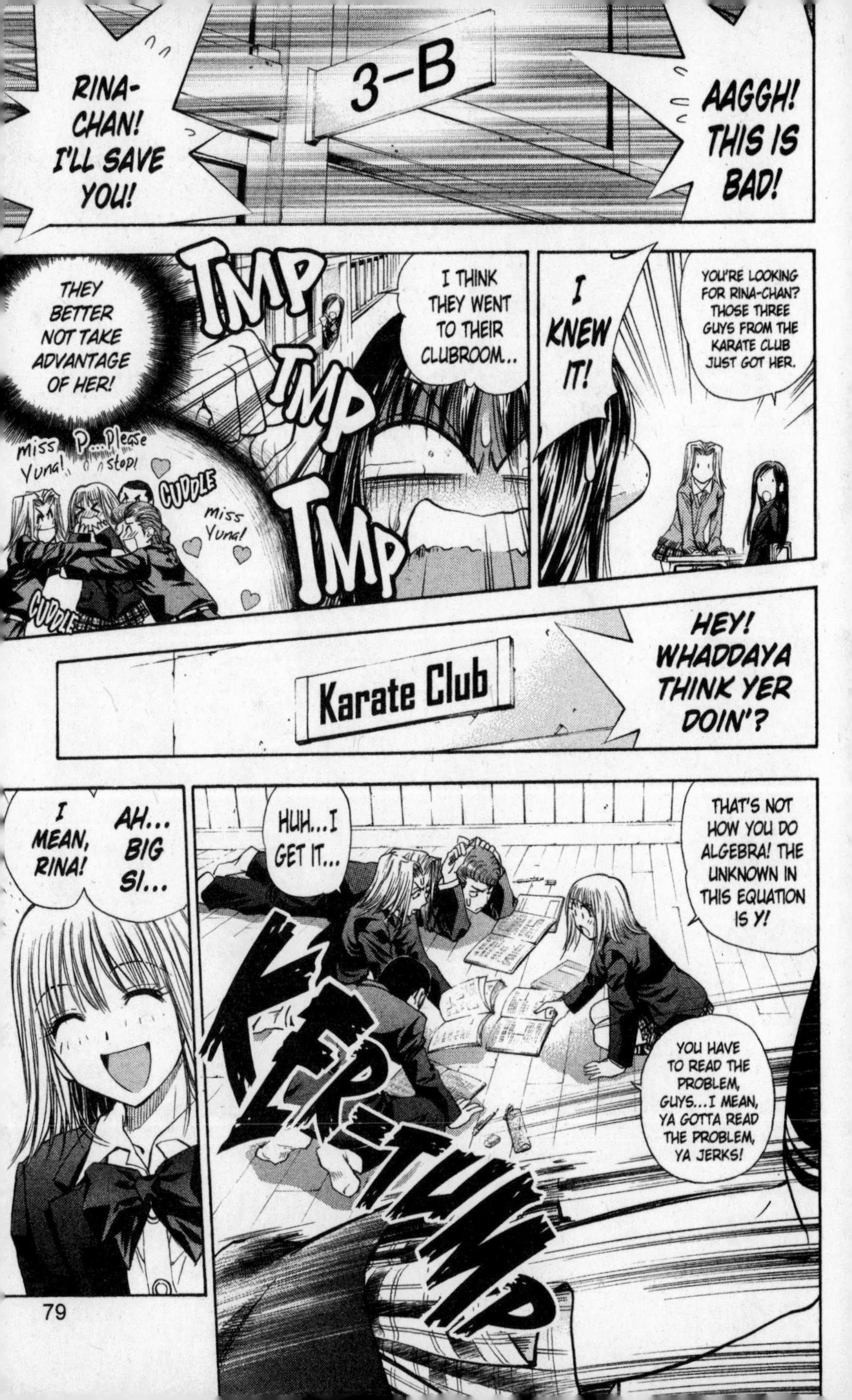
AAGGH! THIS IS BAD!
3-B
RINA-CHAN! I'LL SAVE YOU!
YOU'RE LOOKING FOR RINA-CHAN? THOSE THREE GUYS FROM THE KARATE CLUB JUST GOT HER.
I KNEW IT!
I THINK THEY WENT TO THEIR CLUBROOM...
TMP TMP TMP
THEY BETTER NOT TAKE ADVANTAGE OF HER!
P...Please stop!
miss Yuna!
CUDDLE
miss Yuna!
CUDDLE
HEY! WHADDAYA THINK YER DOIN'?
Karate Club
THAT'S NOT HOW YOU DO ALGEBRA! THE UNKNOWN IN THIS EQUATION IS Y!
YOU HAVE TO READ THE PROBLEM, GUYS...I MEAN, YA GOTTA READ THE PROBLEM, YA JERKS!
HUH...I GET IT...
KER-THUMP
AH... BIG SI...
I MEAN, RINA!

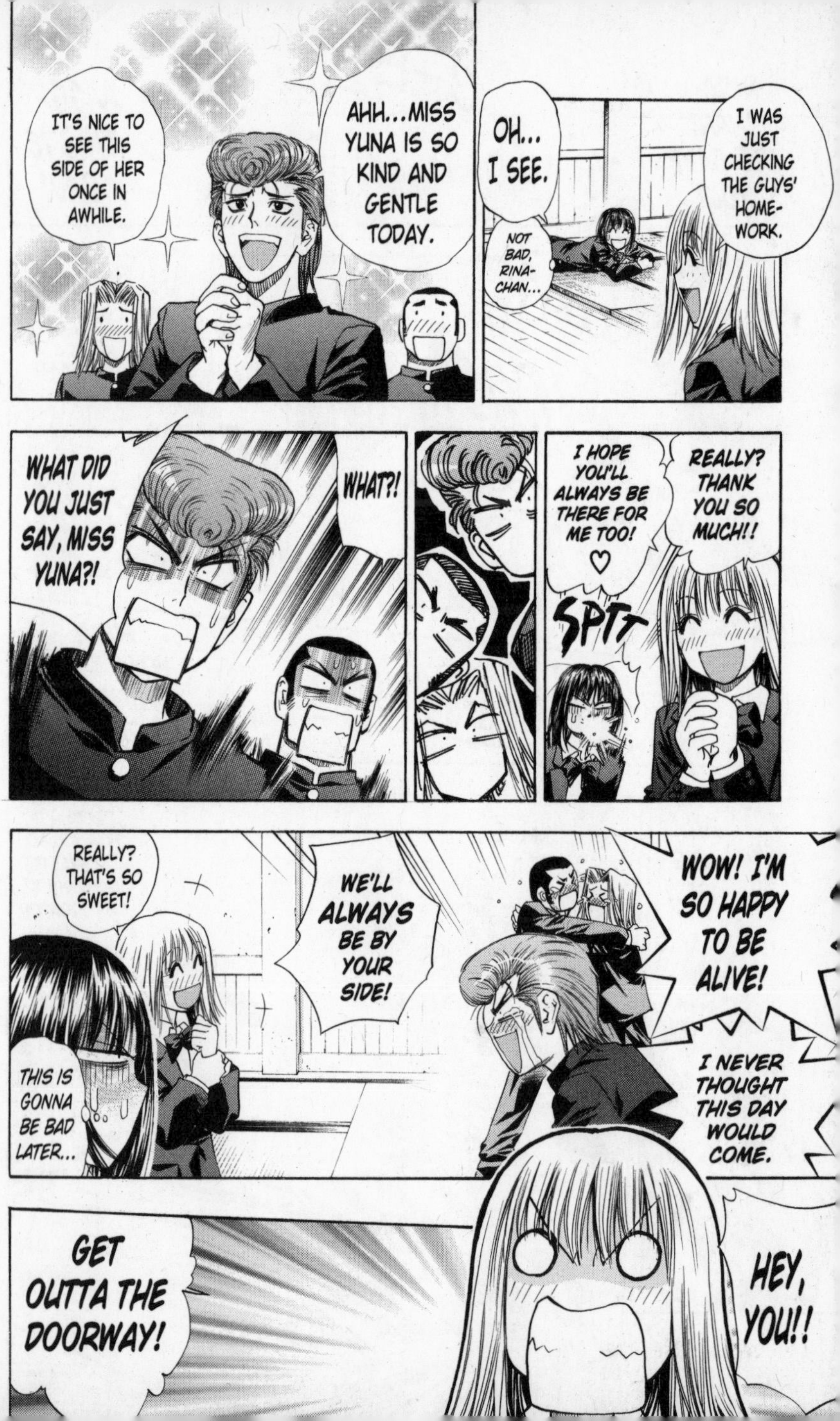
I WAS JUST CHECKING THE GUYS' HOME-WORK.
OH... I SEE.
NOT BAD, RINA-CHAN...
AHH...MISS YUNA IS SO KIND AND GENTLE TODAY.
IT'S NICE TO SEE THIS SIDE OF HER ONCE IN AWHILE.
REALLY? THANK YOU SO MUCH!!
I HOPE YOU'LL ALWAYS BE THERE FOR ME TOO! ♡
SPTT
WHAT?!
WHAT DID YOU JUST SAY, MISS YUNA?!
WOW! I'M SO HAPPY TO BE ALIVE!
I NEVER THOUGHT THIS DAY WOULD COME.
WE'LL ALWAYS BE BY YOUR SIDE!
REALLY? THAT'S SO SWEET!
THIS IS GONNA BE BAD LATER...
HEY, YOU!!
GET OUTTA THE DOORWAY!

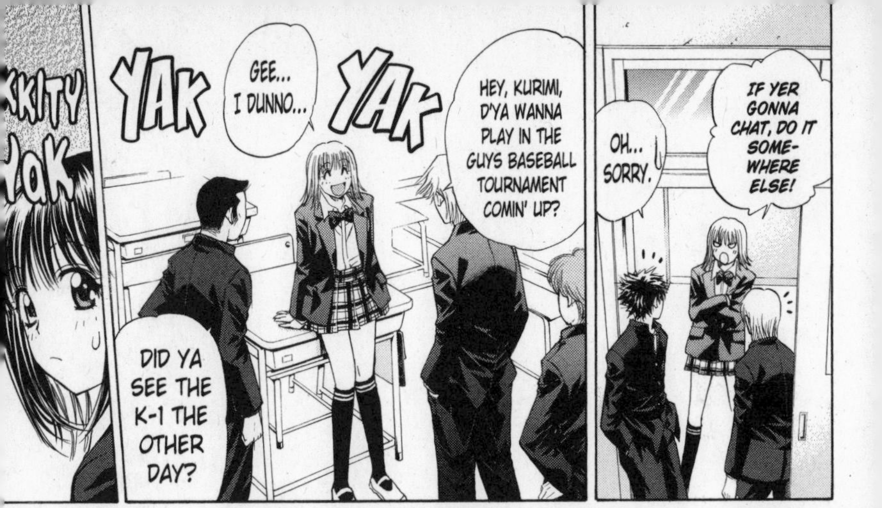
IF YER GONNA CHAT, DO IT SOMEWHERE ELSE!
OH... SORRY.
HEY, KURIMI, D'YA WANNA PLAY IN THE GUYS BASEBALL TOURNAMENT COMIN' UP?
YAK
GEE... I DUNNO...
YAK
DID YA SEE THE K-1 THE OTHER DAY?
YAK

And so, the day passed…

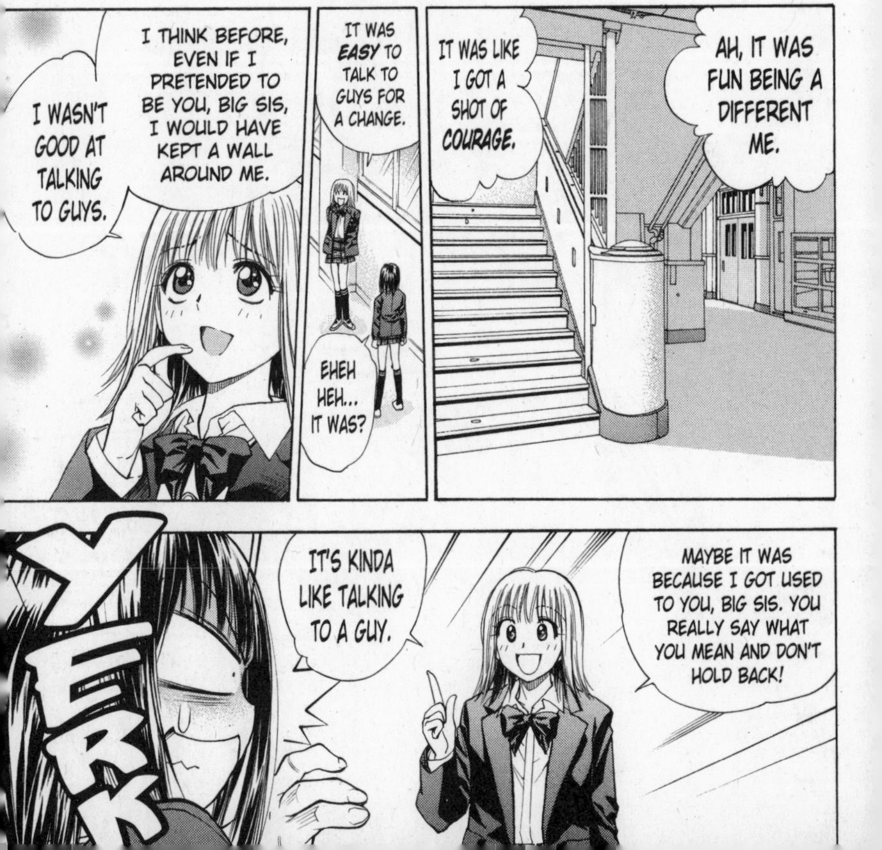
AH, IT WAS FUN BEING A DIFFERENT ME.
IT WAS LIKE I GOT A SHOT OF COURAGE.
IT WAS EASY TO TALK TO GUYS FOR A CHANGE.
EHEH HEH... IT WAS?
I THINK BEFORE, EVEN IF I PRETENDED TO BE YOU, BIG SIS, I WOULD HAVE KEPT A WALL AROUND ME.
I WASN'T GOOD AT TALKING TO GUYS.
MAYBE IT WAS BECAUSE I GOT USED TO YOU, BIG SIS. YOU REALLY SAY WHAT YOU MEAN AND DON'T HOLD BACK!
IT'S KINDA LIKE TALKING TO A GUY.
YERK

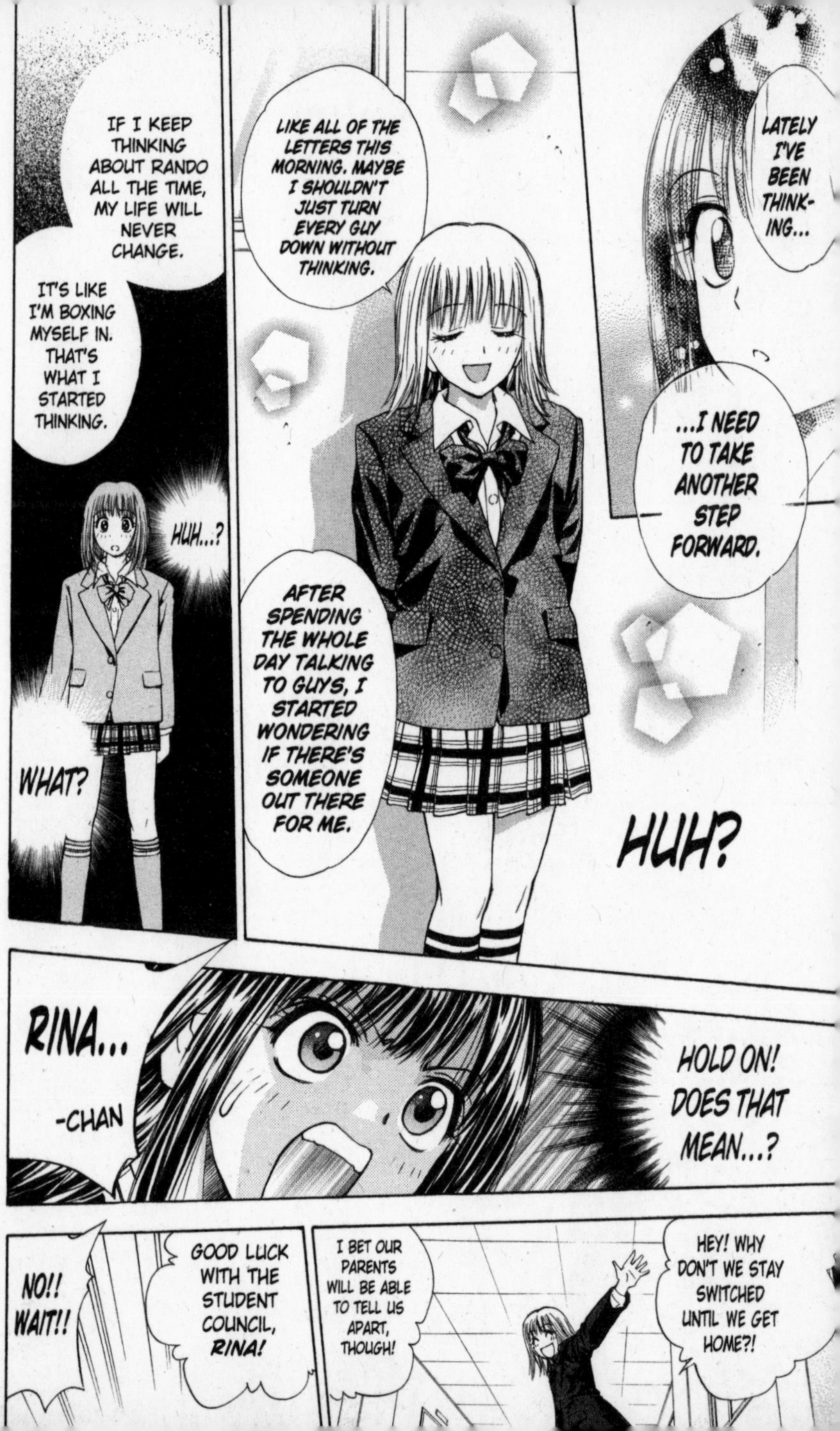
LATELY I'VE BEEN THINK-ING...
...I NEED TO TAKE ANOTHER STEP FORWARD.
HUH?
LIKE ALL OF THE LETTERS THIS MORNING. MAYBE I SHOULDN'T JUST TURN EVERY GUY DOWN WITHOUT THINKING.
AFTER SPENDING THE WHOLE DAY TALKING TO GUYS, I STARTED WONDERING IF THERE'S SOMEONE OUT THERE FOR ME.
IF I KEEP THINKING ABOUT RANDO ALL THE TIME, MY LIFE WILL NEVER CHANGE.
IT'S LIKE I'M BOXING MYSELF IN. THAT'S WHAT I STARTED THINKING.
HUH...?
WHAT?
HOLD ON! DOES THAT MEAN...?
RINA... -CHAN
HEY! WHY DON'T WE STAY SWITCHED UNTIL WE GET HOME?!
I BET OUR PARENTS WILL BE ABLE TO TELL US APART, THOUGH!
GOOD LUCK WITH THE STUDENT COUNCIL, RINA!
NO!! WAIT!!

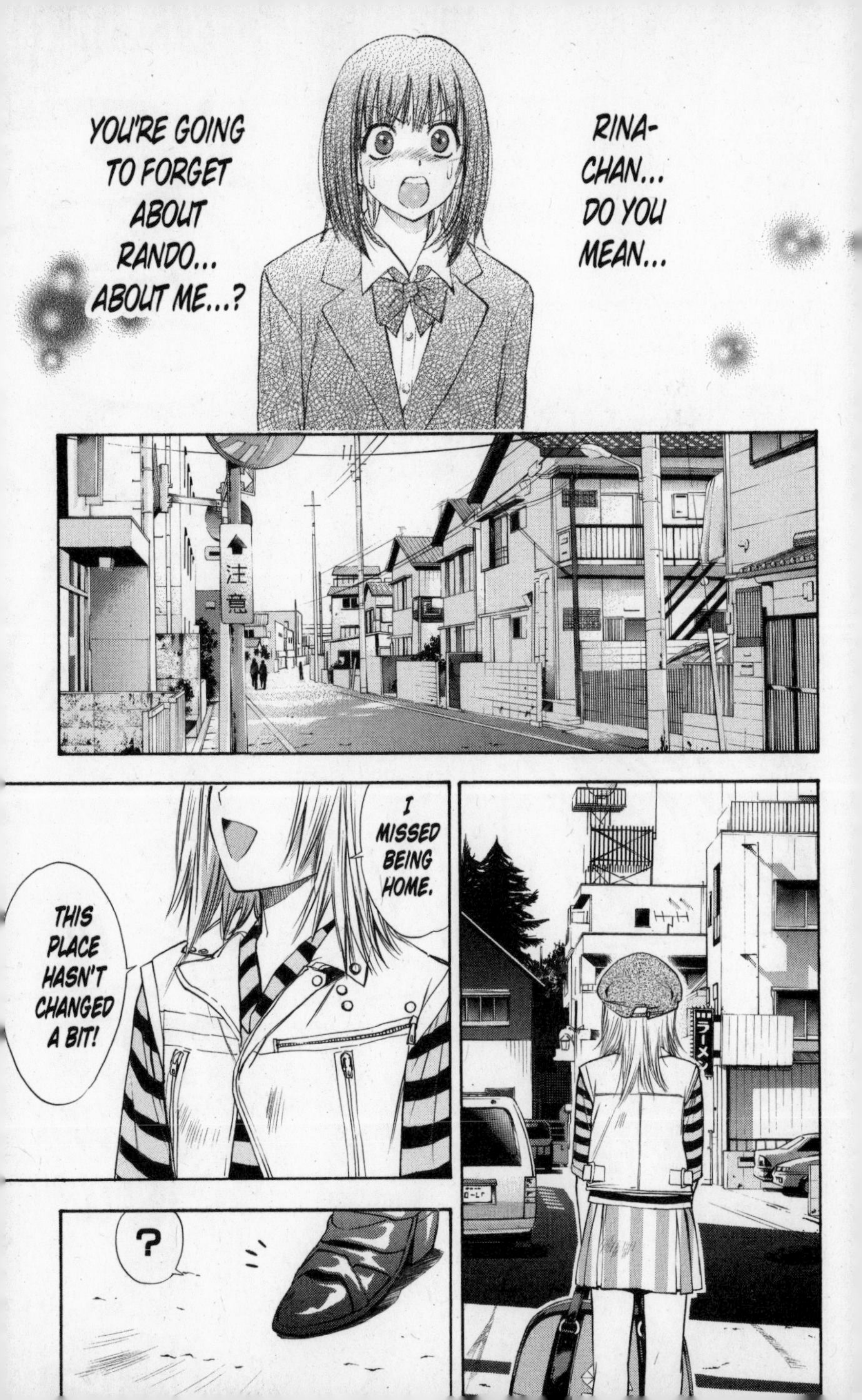
RINA-CHAN... DO YOU MEAN...
YOU'RE GOING TO FORGET ABOUT RANDO... ABOUT ME...?
注意
ラーメン
I MISSED BEING HOME.
THIS PLACE HASN'T CHANGED A BIT!
?

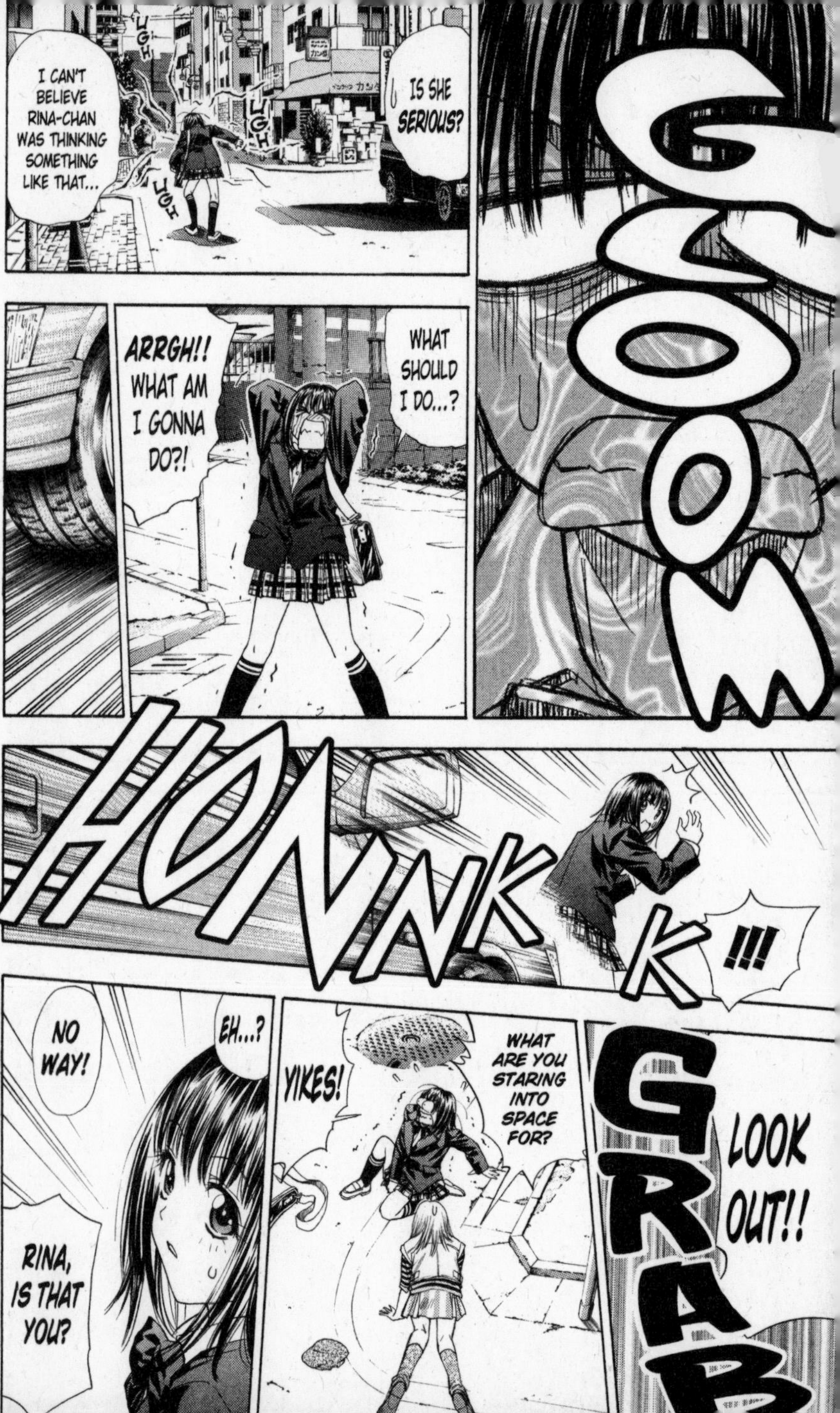
GLOOM
IS SHE SERIOUS?
UGH
UGH
UGH
UGH
I CAN'T BELIEVE RINA-CHAN WAS THINKING SOMETHING LIKE THAT...
WHAT SHOULD I DO...?
ARRGH!! WHAT AM I GONNA DO?!
HONNKK!!!
GRAB
LOOK OUT!!
WHAT ARE YOU STARING INTO SPACE FOR?
YIKES!
EH...?
NO WAY!
RINA, IS THAT YOU?

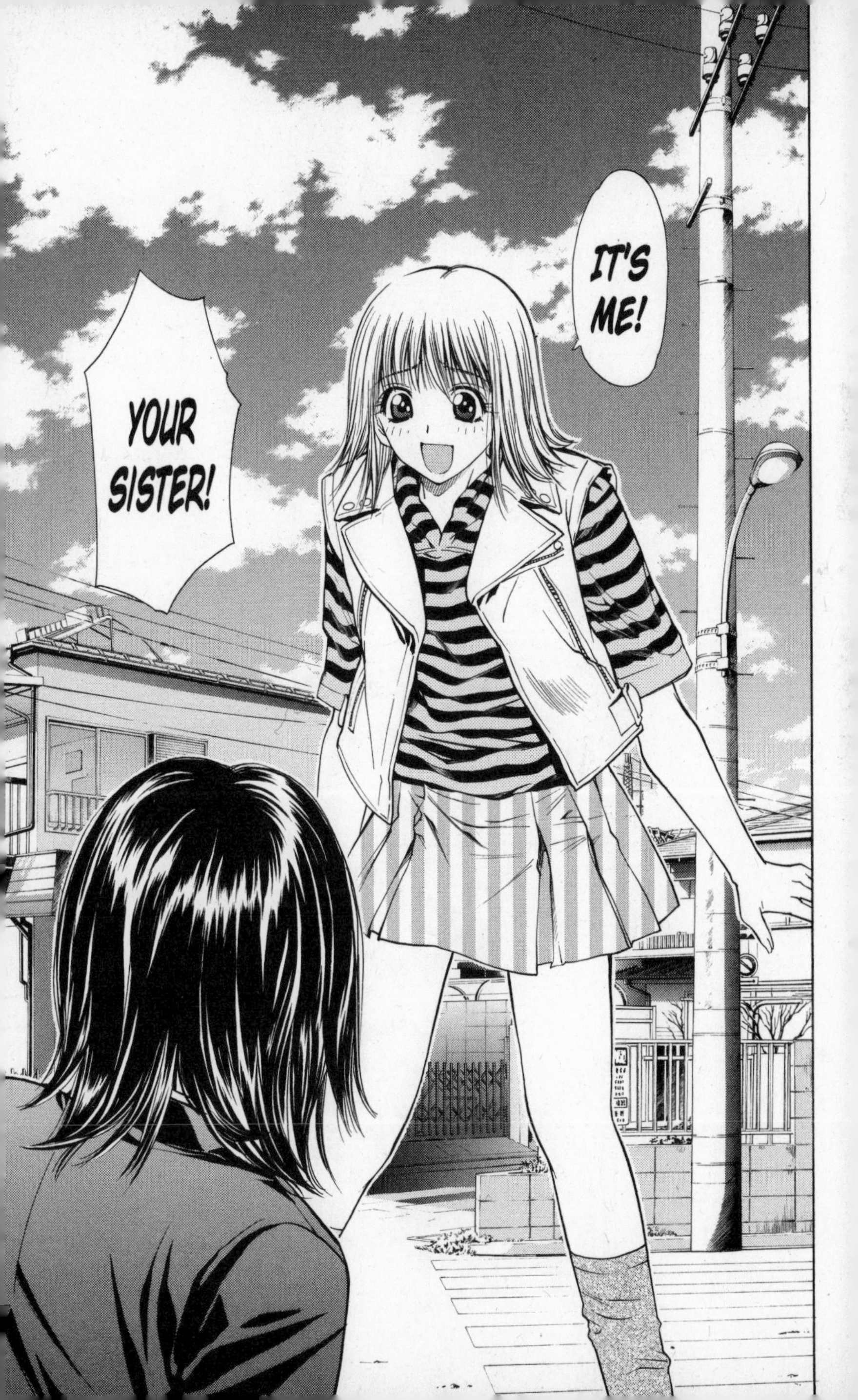
IT'S ME!
YOUR SISTER!

A planned scene from a
*Weekly Shonen Jump* manga

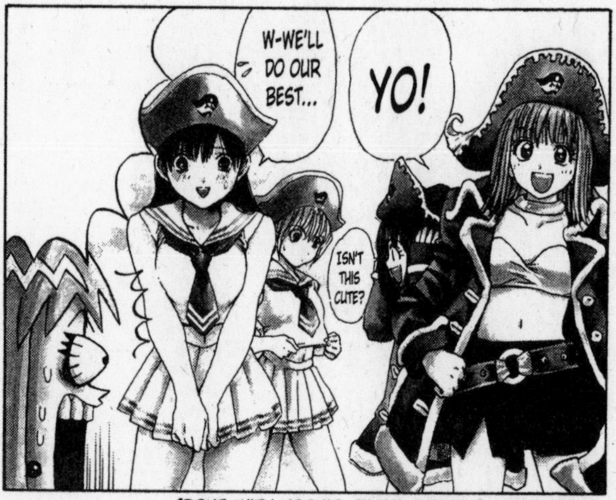
YO!
W-WE'LL DO OUR BEST...
ISN'T THIS CUTE?

(DONE WITH YOSHIO SAWAI AND MIKI KAWASHITA.)

# Chapter 50: Pretty Face

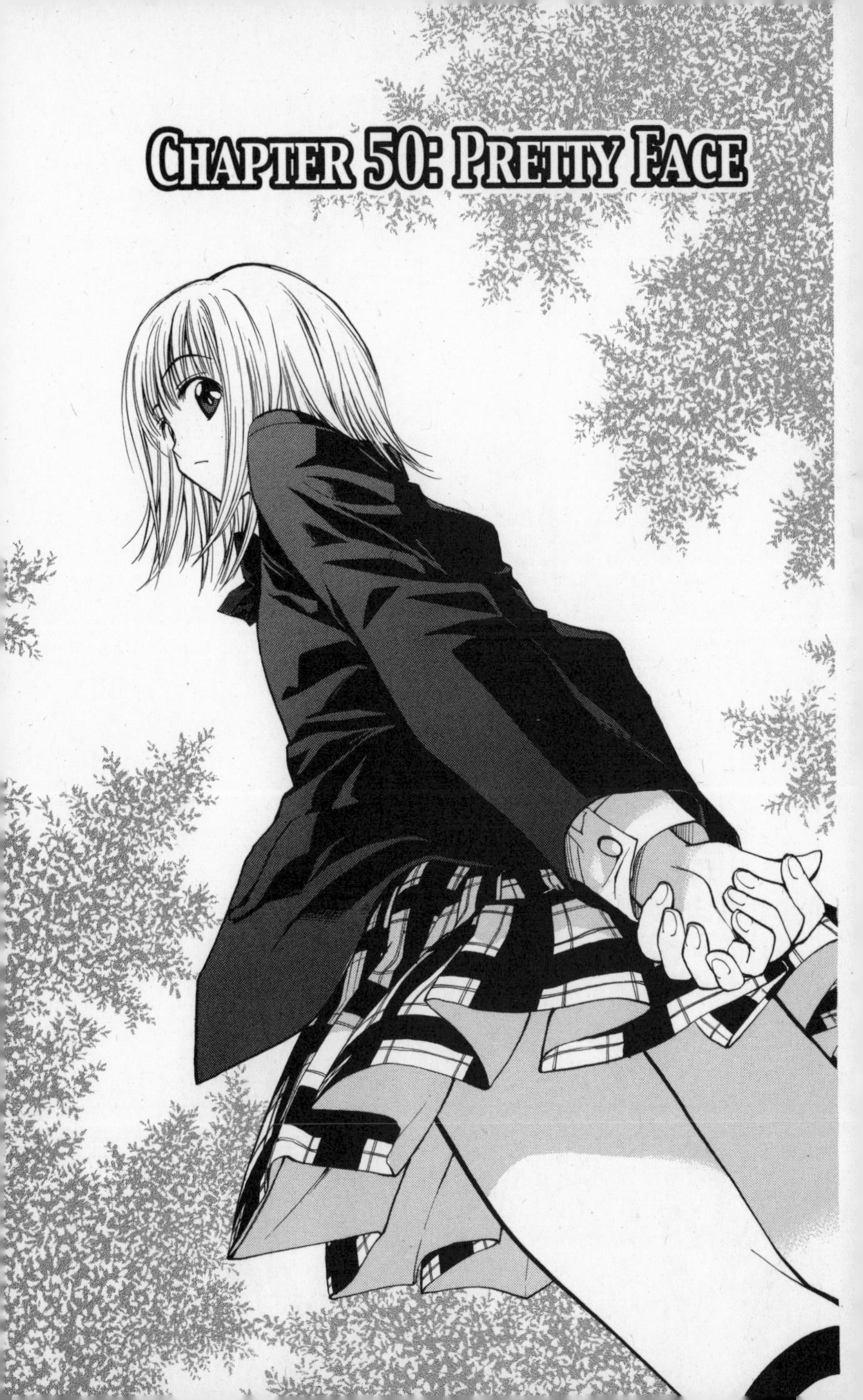

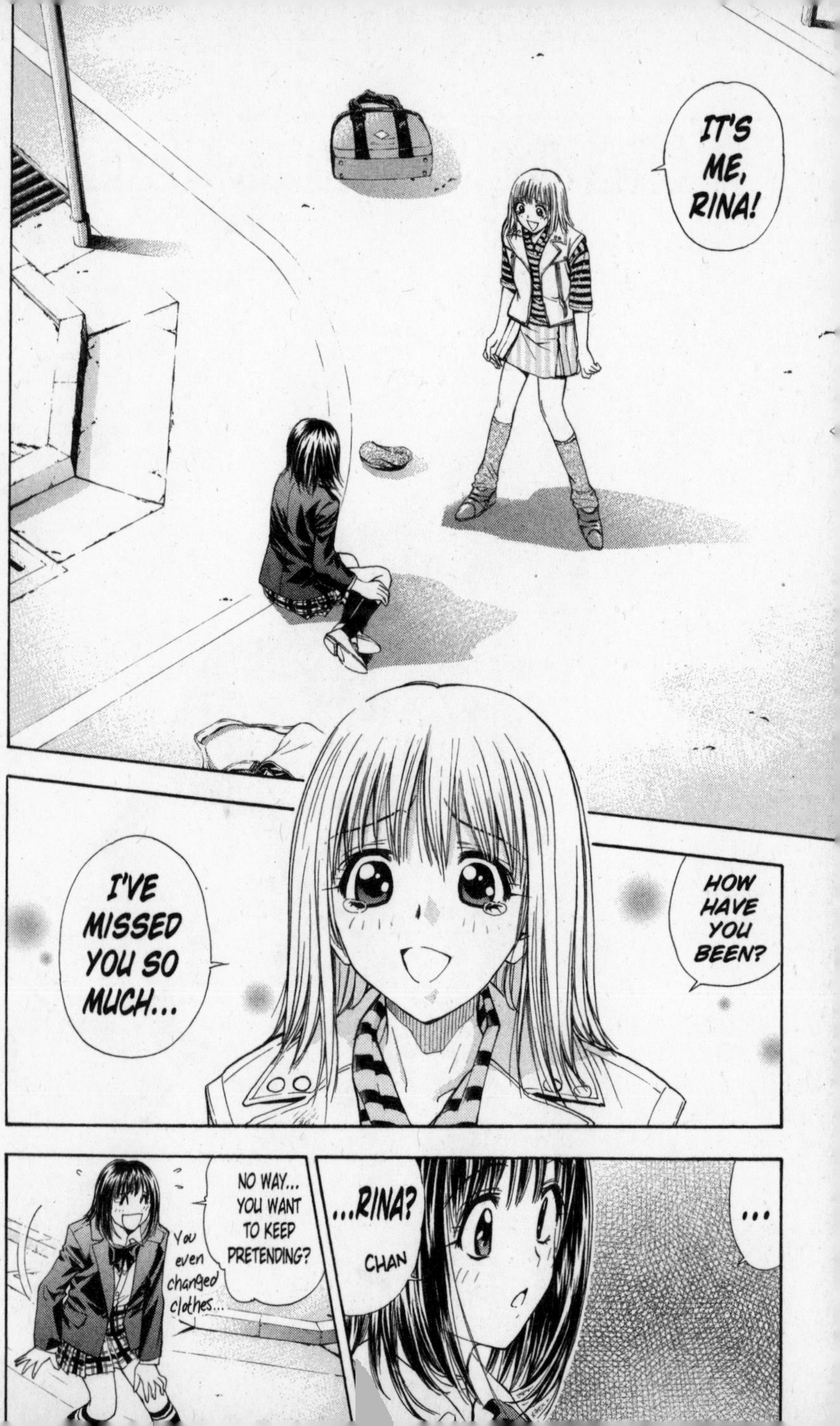
IT'S ME, RINA!
HOW HAVE YOU BEEN?
I'VE MISSED YOU SO MUCH...
...
...RINA? CHAN
NO WAY... YOU WANT TO KEEP PRETENDING?
You even changed clothes...

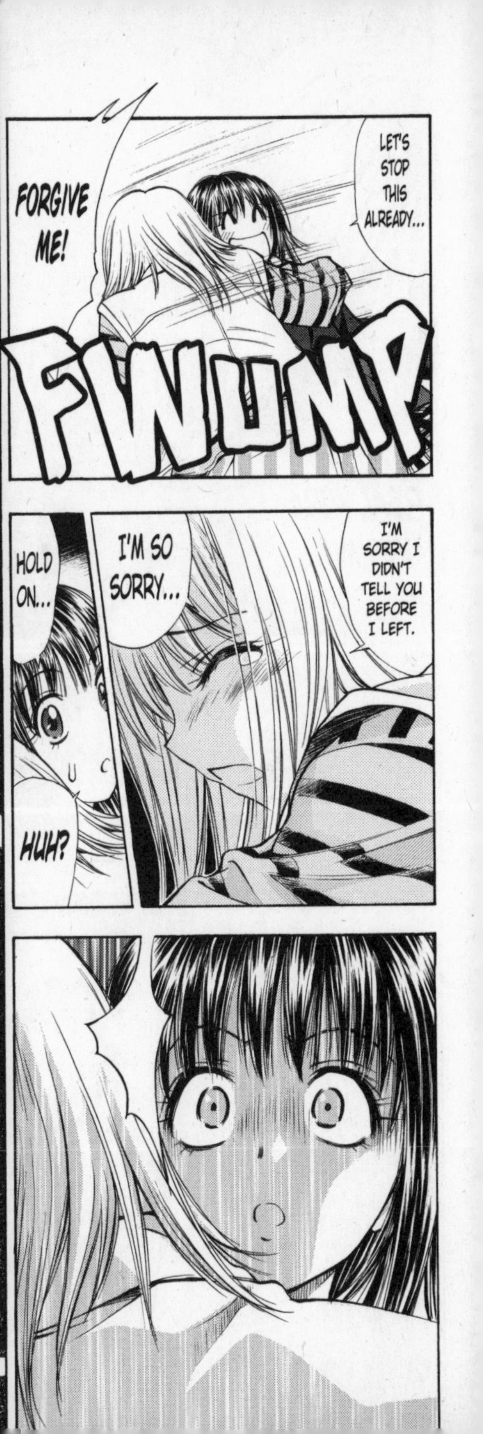
LET'S STOP THIS ALREADY...
FORGIVE ME!
FWUMP
I'M SORRY I DIDN'T TELL YOU BEFORE I LEFT.
I'M SO SORRY...
HOLD ON...
HUH?

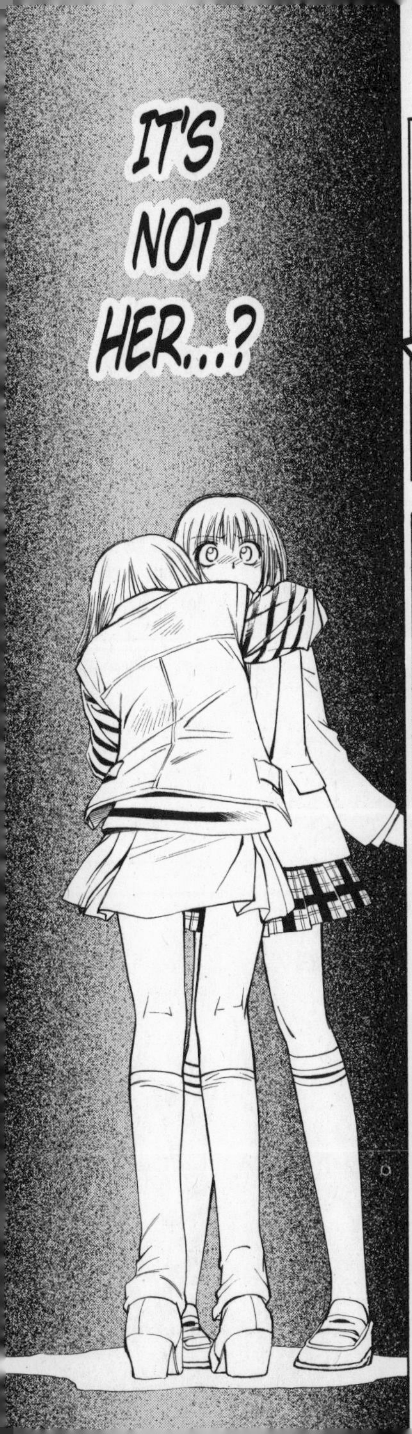
IT'S NOT HER...?

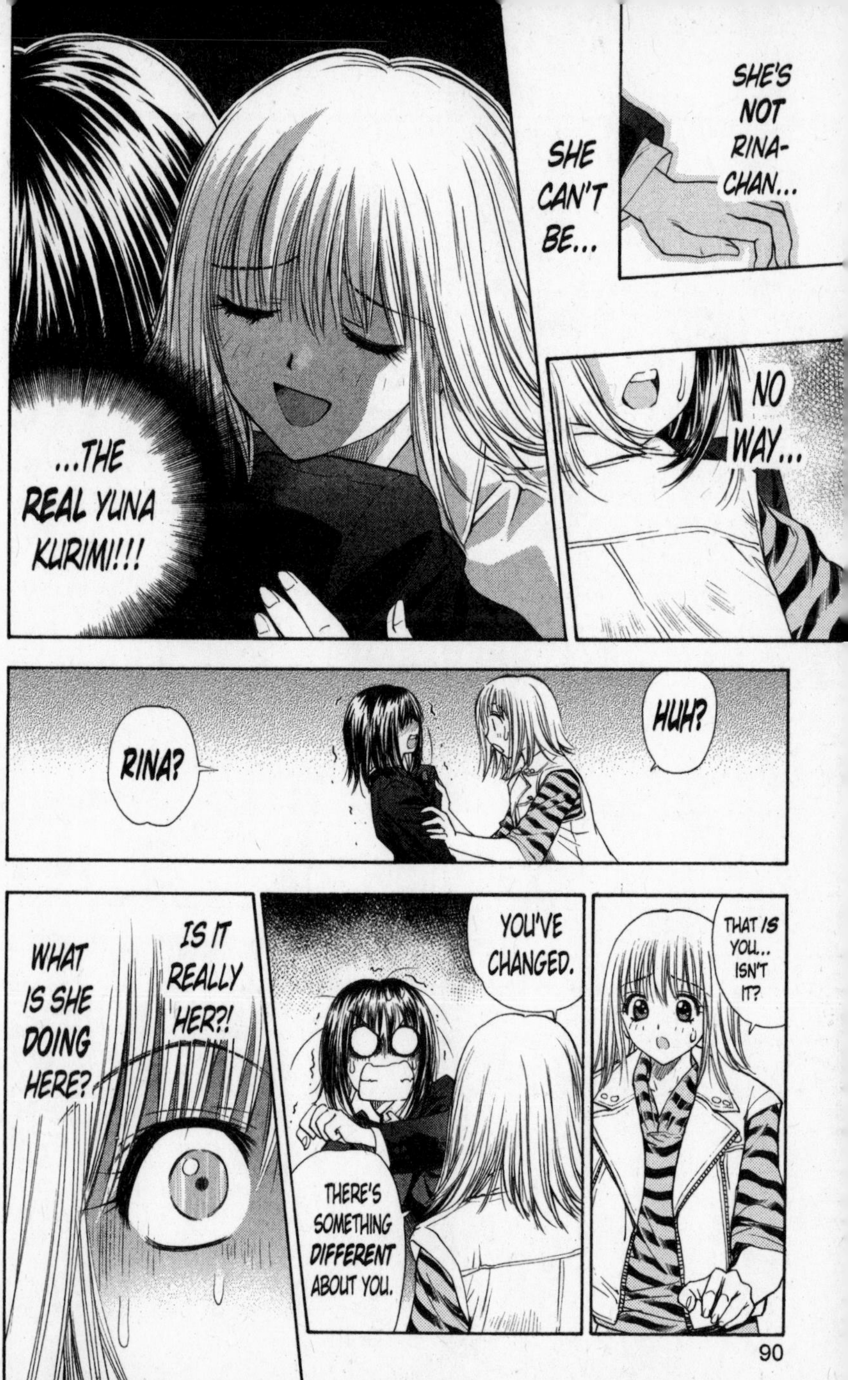
SHE'S NOT RINA-CHAN...
SHE CAN'T BE...
NO WAY...
...THE REAL YUNA KURIMI!!!
HUH?
RINA?
THAT *IS* YOU... ISN'T IT?
YOU'VE CHANGED.
THERE'S SOMETHING *DIFFERENT* ABOUT YOU.
IS IT REALLY HER?!
WHAT IS SHE DOING HERE?

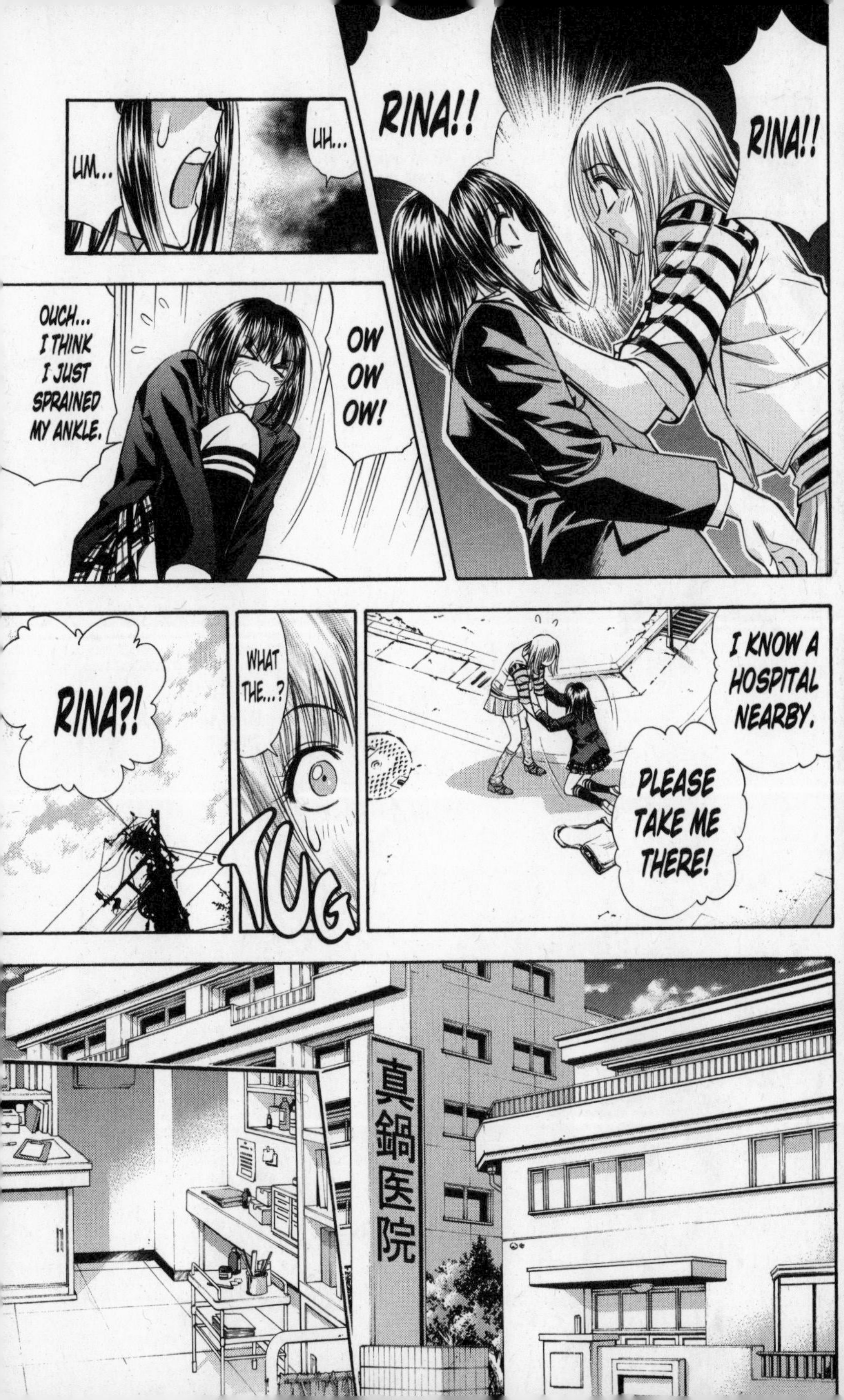
RINA!!
RINA!!
UH...
UM...
OW OW OW!
OUCH... I THINK I JUST SPRAINED MY ANKLE.
I KNOW A HOSPITAL NEARBY.
PLEASE TAKE ME THERE!
WHAT THE...?
TUG
RINA?!
真鍋医院

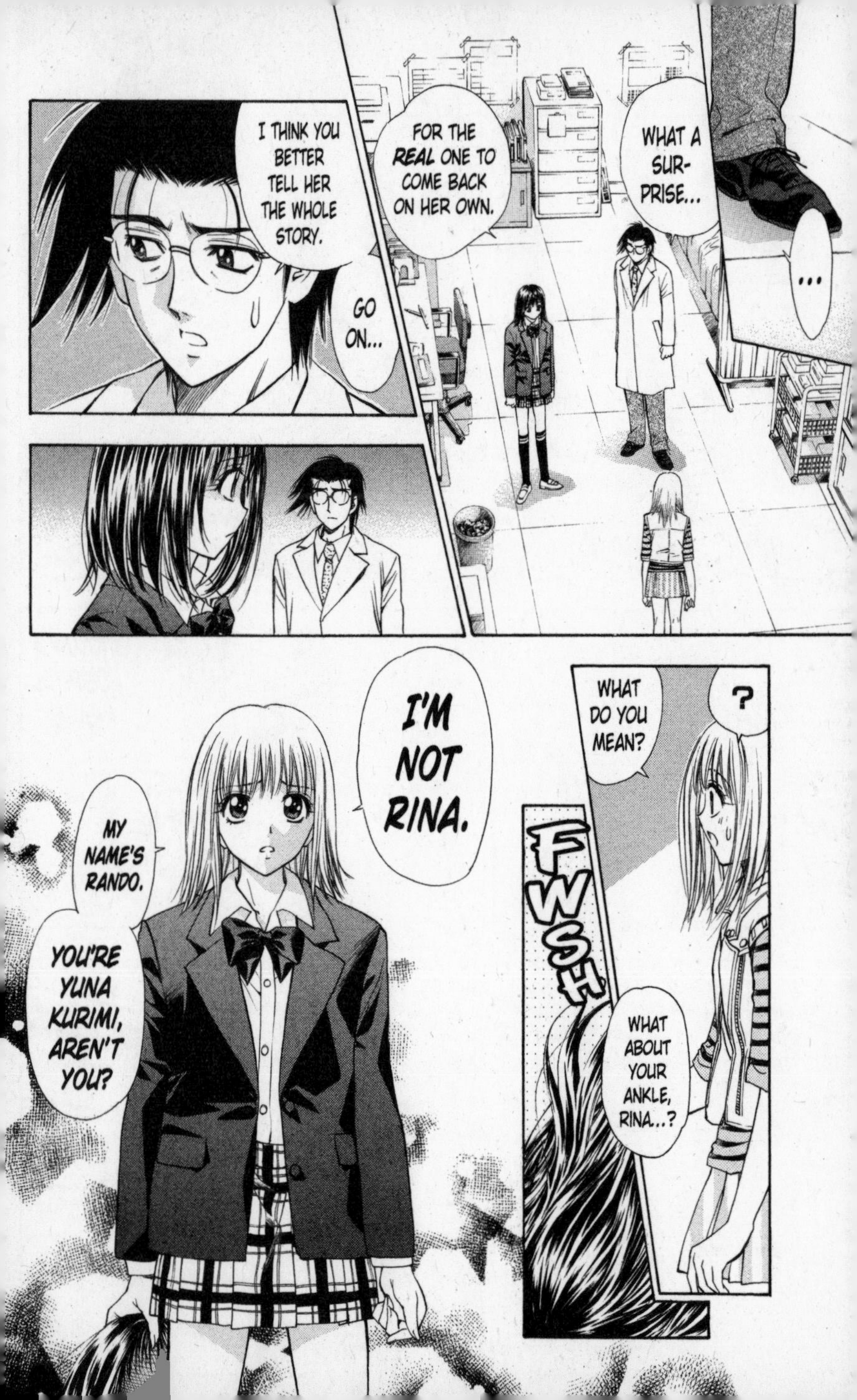
WHAT A SUR-PRISE...
...
FOR THE REAL ONE TO COME BACK ON HER OWN.
I THINK YOU BETTER TELL HER THE WHOLE STORY.
GO ON...
?
WHAT DO YOU MEAN?
FWSH
WHAT ABOUT YOUR ANKLE, RINA...?
I'M NOT RINA.
MY NAME'S RANDO.
YOU'RE YUNA KURIMI, AREN'T YOU?

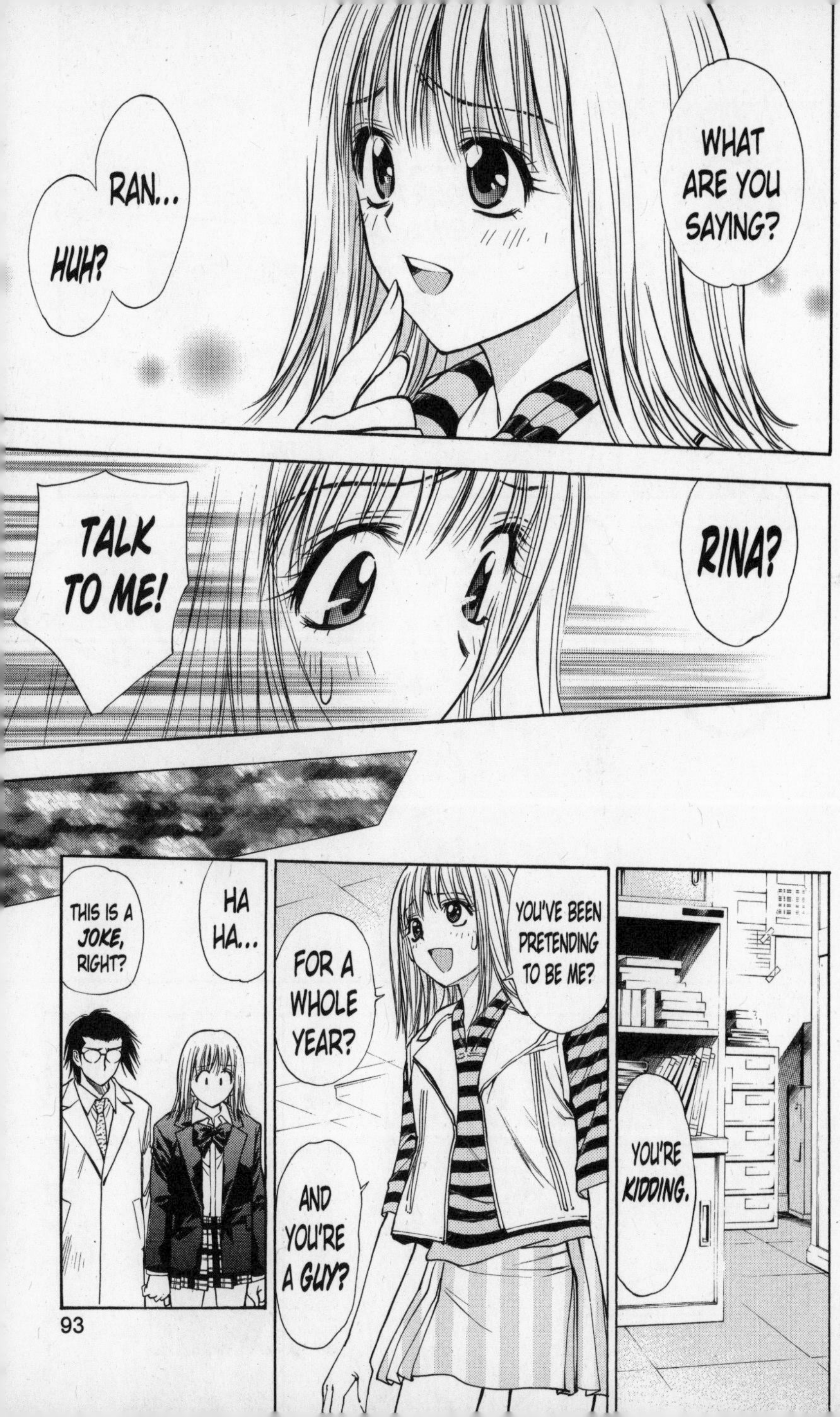
WHAT ARE YOU SAYING?
RAN... HUH?
RINA?
TALK TO ME!
YOU'RE KIDDING.
YOU'VE BEEN PRETENDING TO BE ME?
FOR A WHOLE YEAR?
AND YOU'RE A GUY?
HA HA...
THIS IS A JOKE, RIGHT?

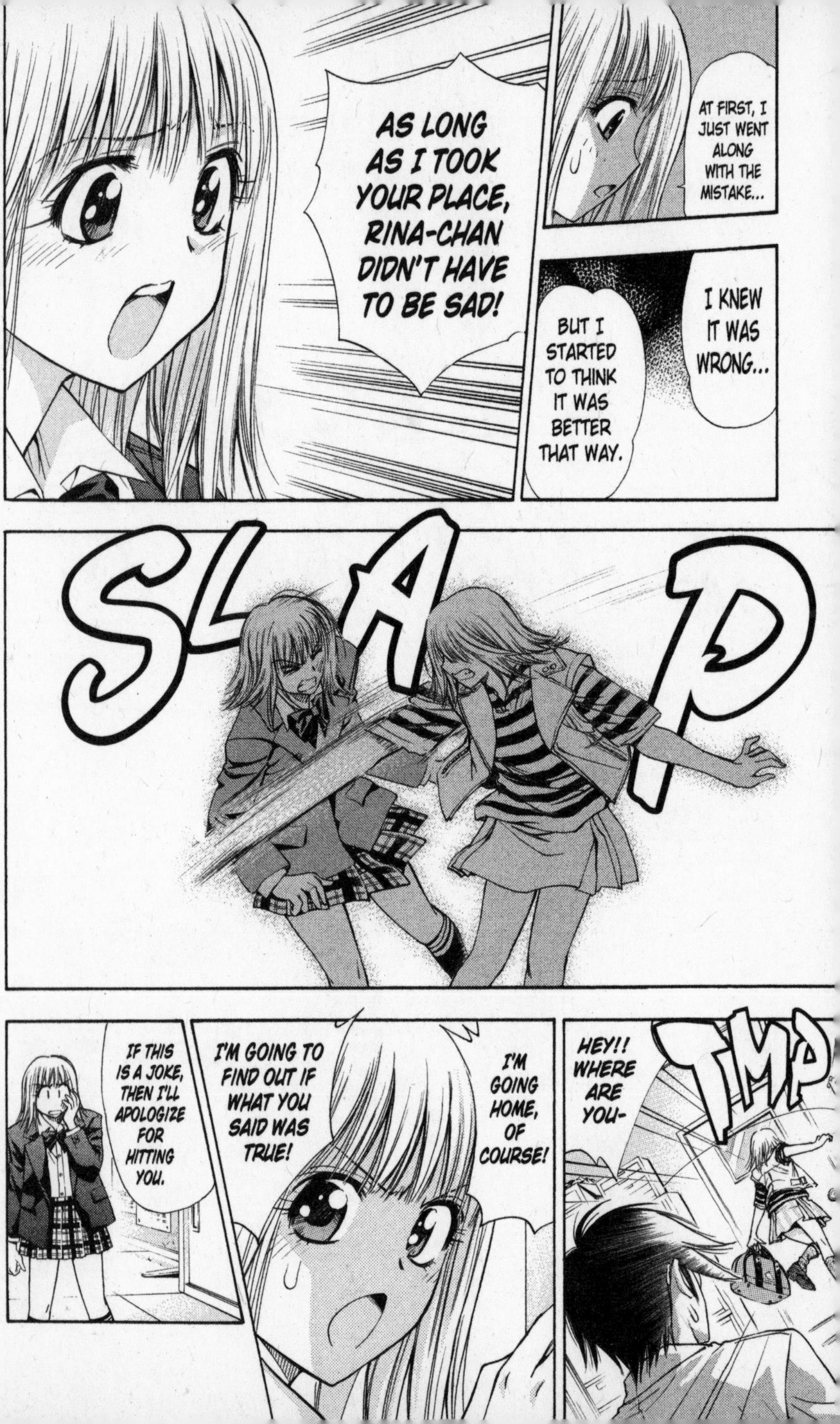
AT FIRST, I JUST WENT ALONG WITH THE MISTAKE...
I KNEW IT WAS WRONG...
BUT I STARTED TO THINK IT WAS BETTER THAT WAY.
AS LONG AS I TOOK YOUR PLACE, RINA-CHAN DIDN'T HAVE TO BE SAD!
SLAP
TMP
HEY!! WHERE ARE YOU-
I'M GOING HOME, OF COURSE!
I'M GOING TO FIND OUT IF WHAT YOU SAID WAS TRUE!
IF THIS IS A JOKE, THEN I'LL APOLOGIZE FOR HITTING YOU.

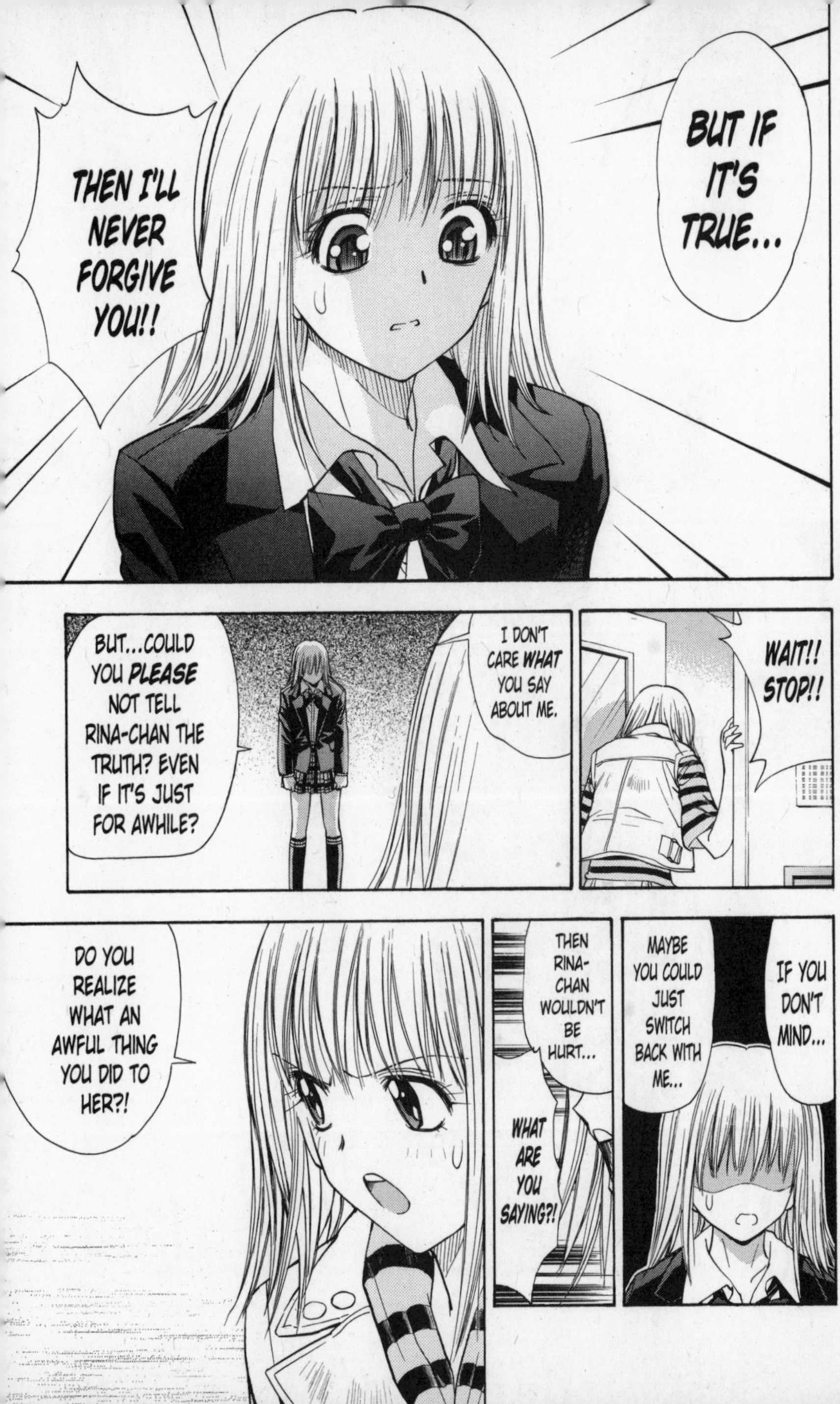
BUT IF IT'S TRUE...
THEN I'LL NEVER FORGIVE YOU!!
WAIT!! STOP!!
I DON'T CARE WHAT YOU SAY ABOUT ME.
BUT...COULD YOU PLEASE NOT TELL RINA-CHAN THE TRUTH? EVEN IF IT'S JUST FOR AWHILE?
IF YOU DON'T MIND...
MAYBE YOU COULD JUST SWITCH BACK WITH ME...
THEN RINA-CHAN WOULDN'T BE HURT...
WHAT ARE YOU SAYING?!
DO YOU REALIZE WHAT AN AWFUL THING YOU DID TO HER?!

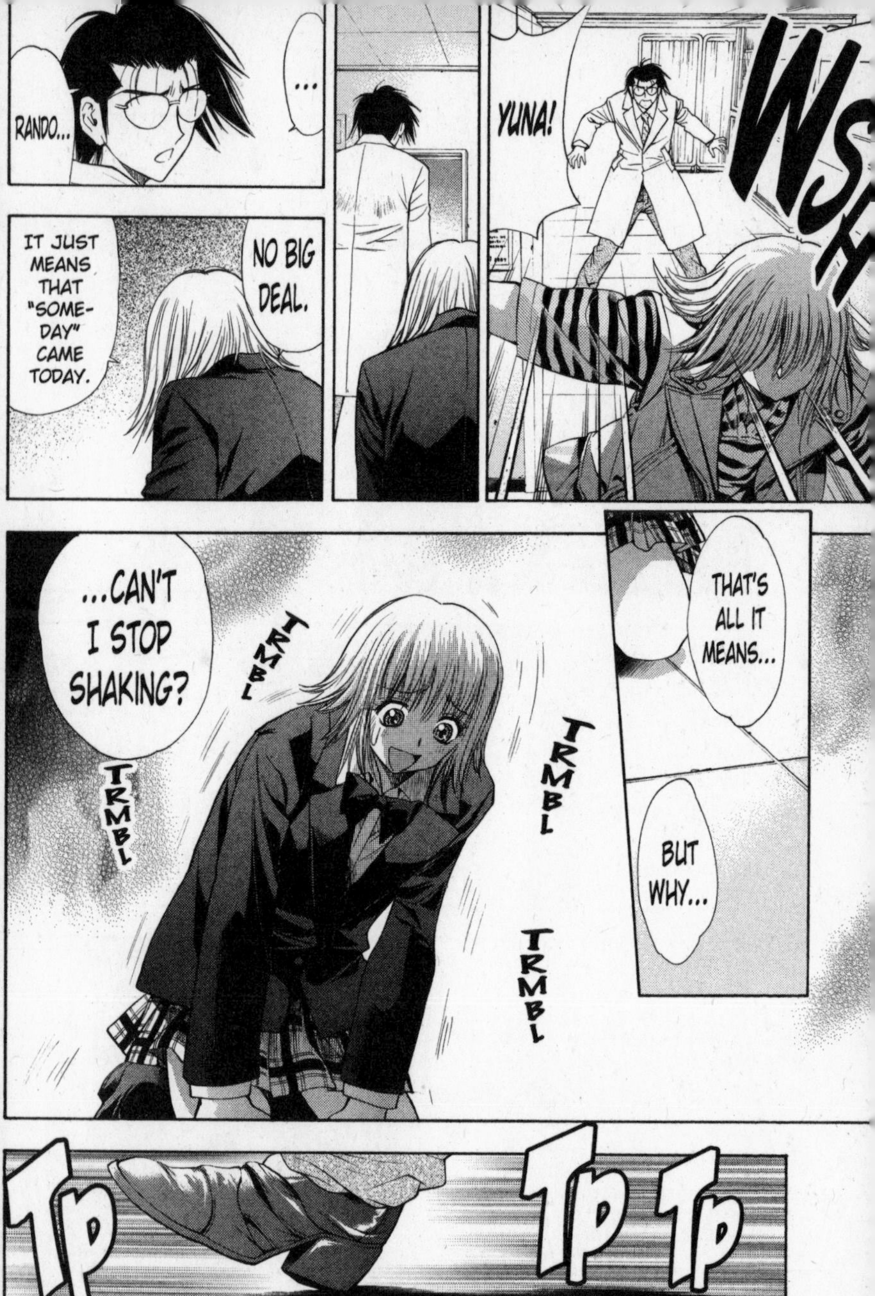
YUNA!
WSH
...
NO BIG DEAL.
RANDO...
IT JUST MEANS THAT "SOME-DAY" CAME TODAY.
THAT'S ALL IT MEANS...
BUT WHY...
TRMBL
TRMBL
...CAN'T I STOP SHAKING?
TRMBL
TRMBL
Tp Tp
Tp

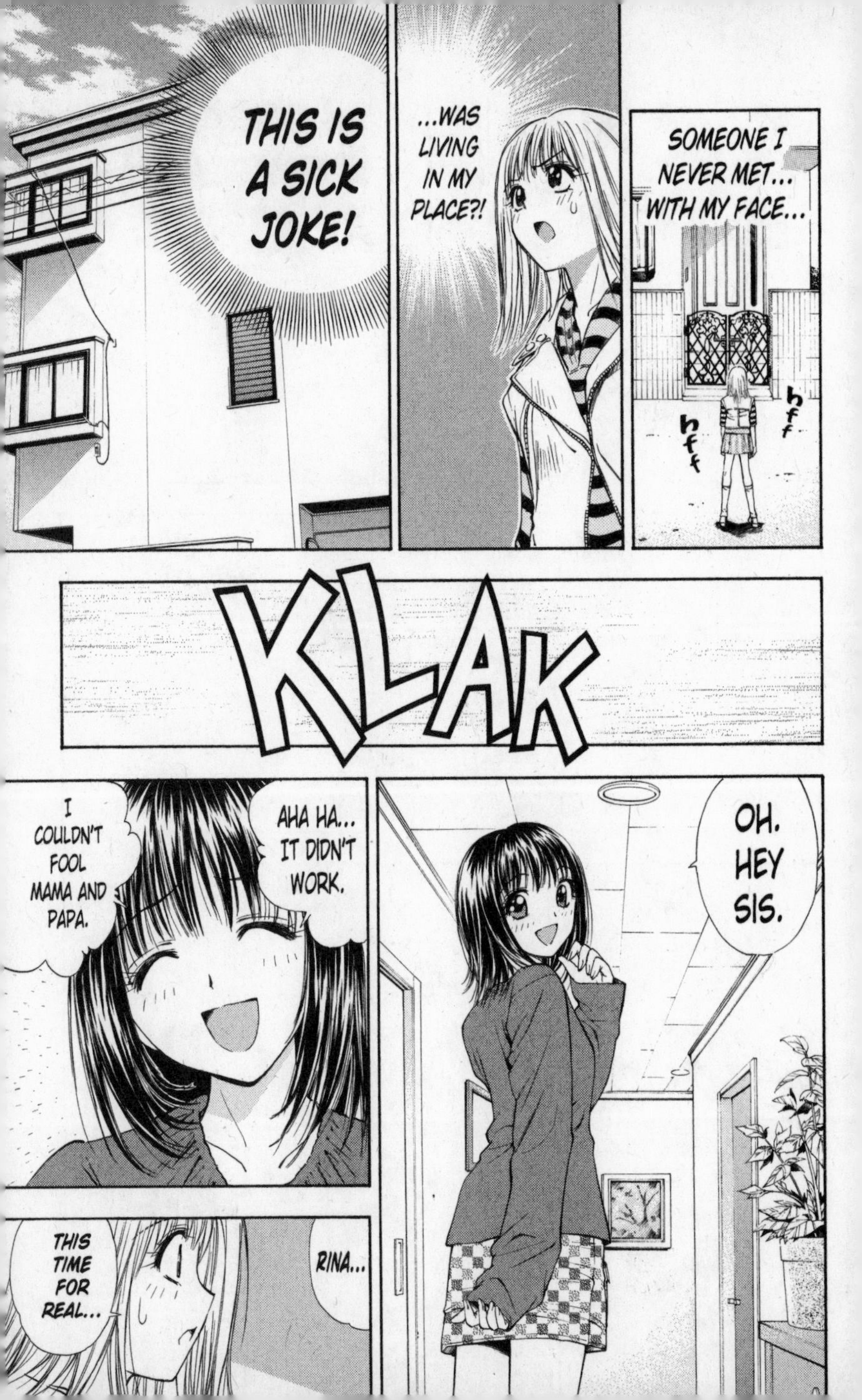
SOMEONE I NEVER MET... WITH MY FACE...
hff
hff
...WAS LIVING IN MY PLACE?!
THIS IS A SICK JOKE!
KLAK
OH. HEY SIS.
AHA HA... IT DIDN'T WORK.
I COULDN'T FOOL MAMA AND PAPA.
RINA...
THIS TIME FOR REAL...

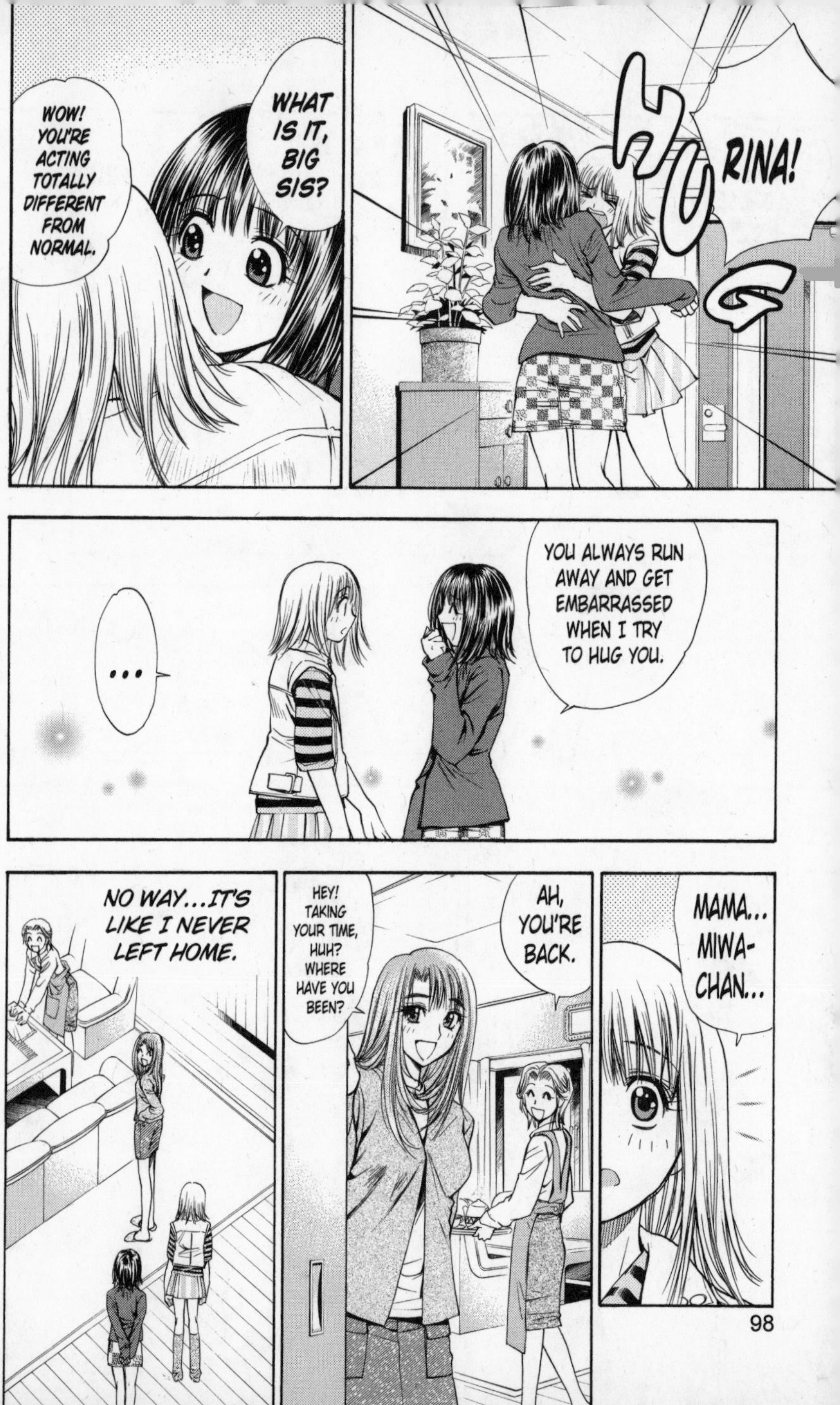
HUG
RINA!
WHAT IS IT, BIG SIS?
WOW! YOU'RE ACTING TOTALLY DIFFERENT FROM NORMAL.
YOU ALWAYS RUN AWAY AND GET EMBARRASSED WHEN I TRY TO HUG YOU.
...
MAMA... MIWA-CHAN...
AH, YOU'RE BACK.
HEY! TAKING YOUR TIME, HUH? WHERE HAVE YOU BEEN?
NO WAY...IT'S LIKE I NEVER LEFT HOME.

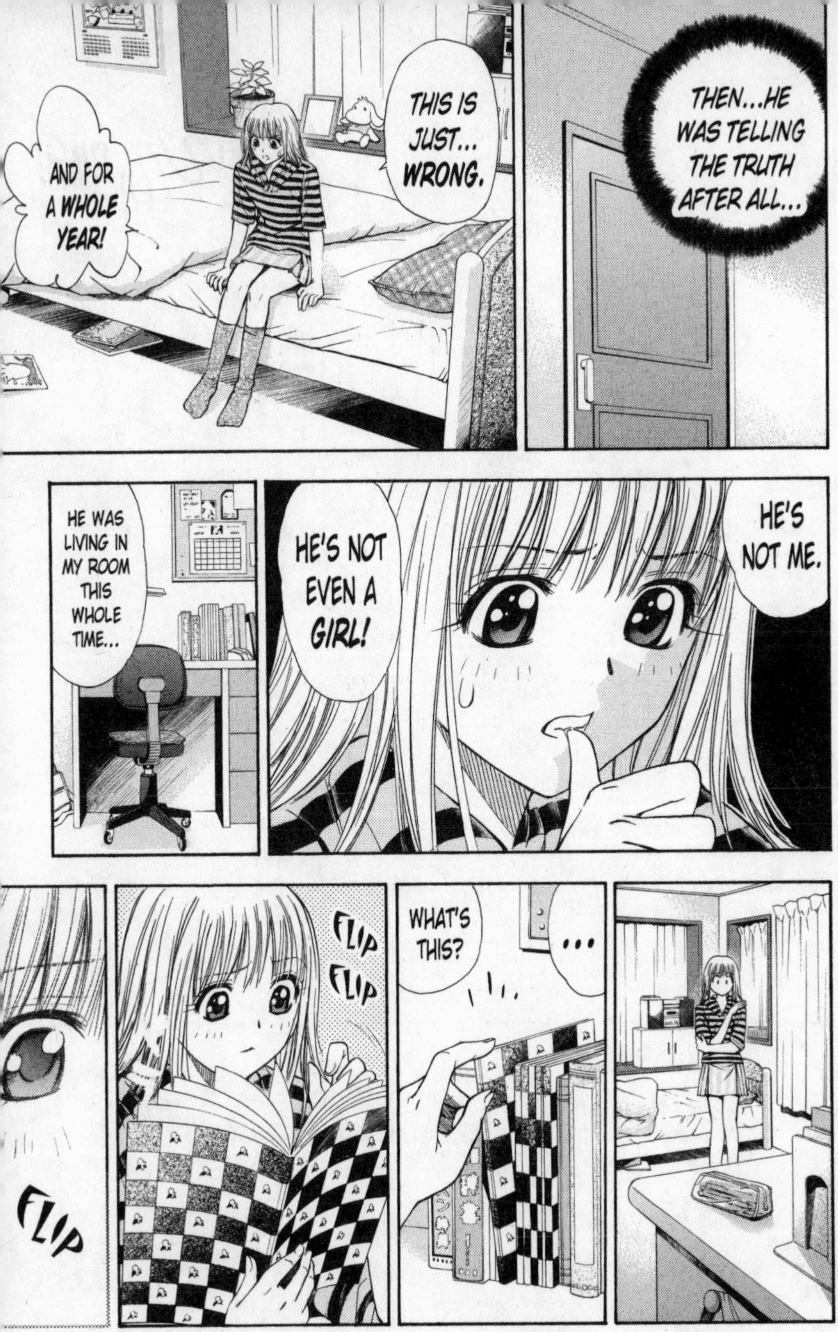
THEN...HE WAS TELLING THE TRUTH AFTER ALL...
THIS IS JUST... WRONG.
AND FOR A WHOLE YEAR!
HE'S NOT ME.
HE'S NOT EVEN A GIRL!
HE WAS LIVING IN MY ROOM THIS WHOLE TIME...
...
WHAT'S THIS?
FLIP
FLIP
FLIP

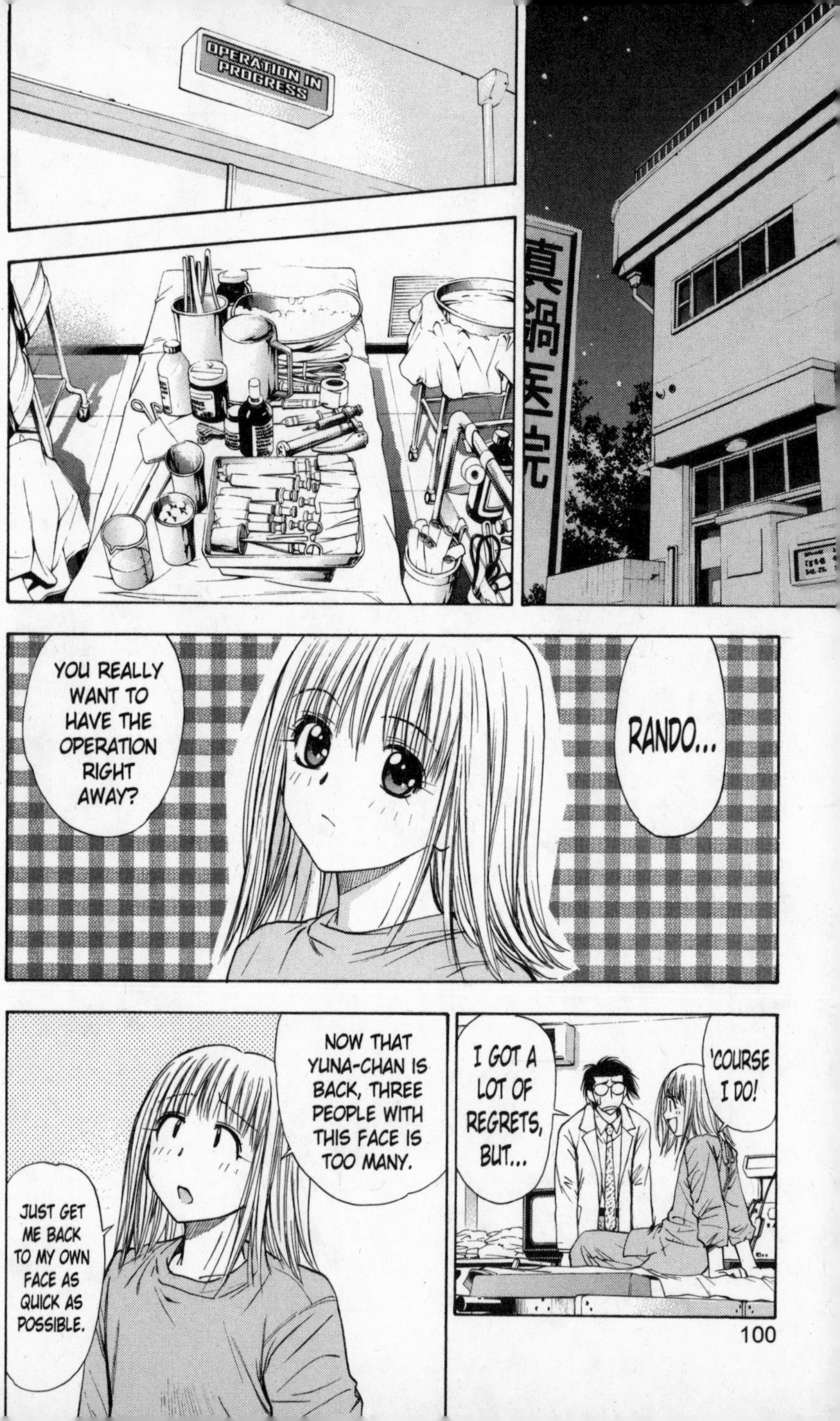
真鍋医院
OPERATION IN PROGRESS
RANDO...
YOU REALLY WANT TO HAVE THE OPERATION RIGHT AWAY?
'COURSE I DO!
I GOT A LOT OF REGRETS, BUT...
NOW THAT YUNA-CHAN IS BACK, THREE PEOPLE WITH THIS FACE IS TOO MANY.
JUST GET ME BACK TO MY OWN FACE AS QUICK AS POSSIBLE.

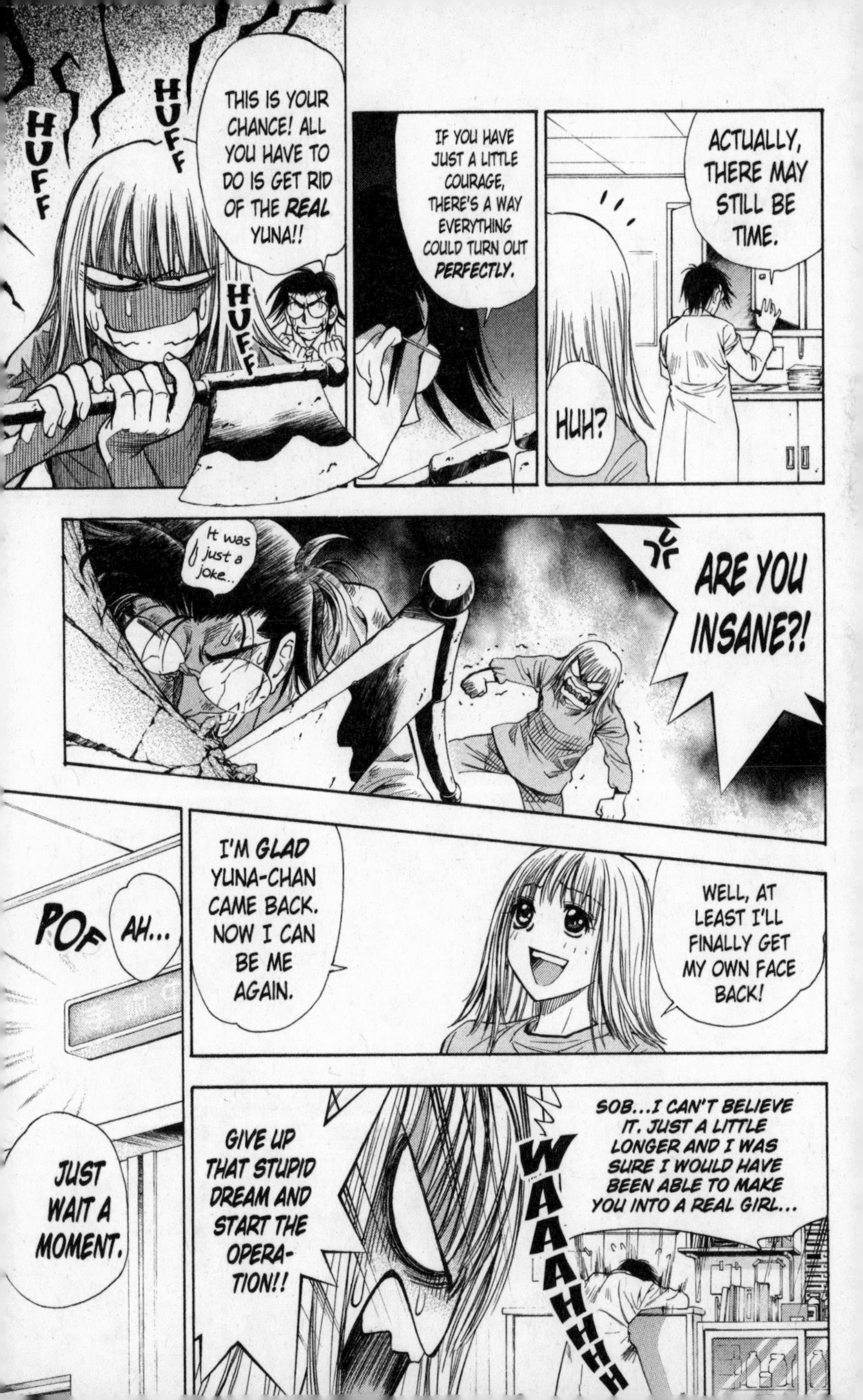
ACTUALLY, THERE MAY STILL BE TIME.
HUH?
IF YOU HAVE JUST A LITTLE COURAGE, THERE'S A WAY EVERYTHING COULD TURN OUT PERFECTLY.
THIS IS YOUR CHANCE! ALL YOU HAVE TO DO IS GET RID OF THE REAL YUNA!!
HUFF
HUFF
HUFF
ARE YOU INSANE?!
It was just a joke...
WELL, AT LEAST I'LL FINALLY GET MY OWN FACE BACK!
I'M GLAD YUNA-CHAN CAME BACK. NOW I CAN BE ME AGAIN.
SOB...I CAN'T BELIEVE IT. JUST A LITTLE LONGER AND I WAS SURE I WOULD HAVE BEEN ABLE TO MAKE YOU INTO A REAL GIRL...
WAAAHHHH
GIVE UP THAT STUPID DREAM AND START THE OPERA-TION!!
AH...
POF
JUST WAIT A MOMENT.

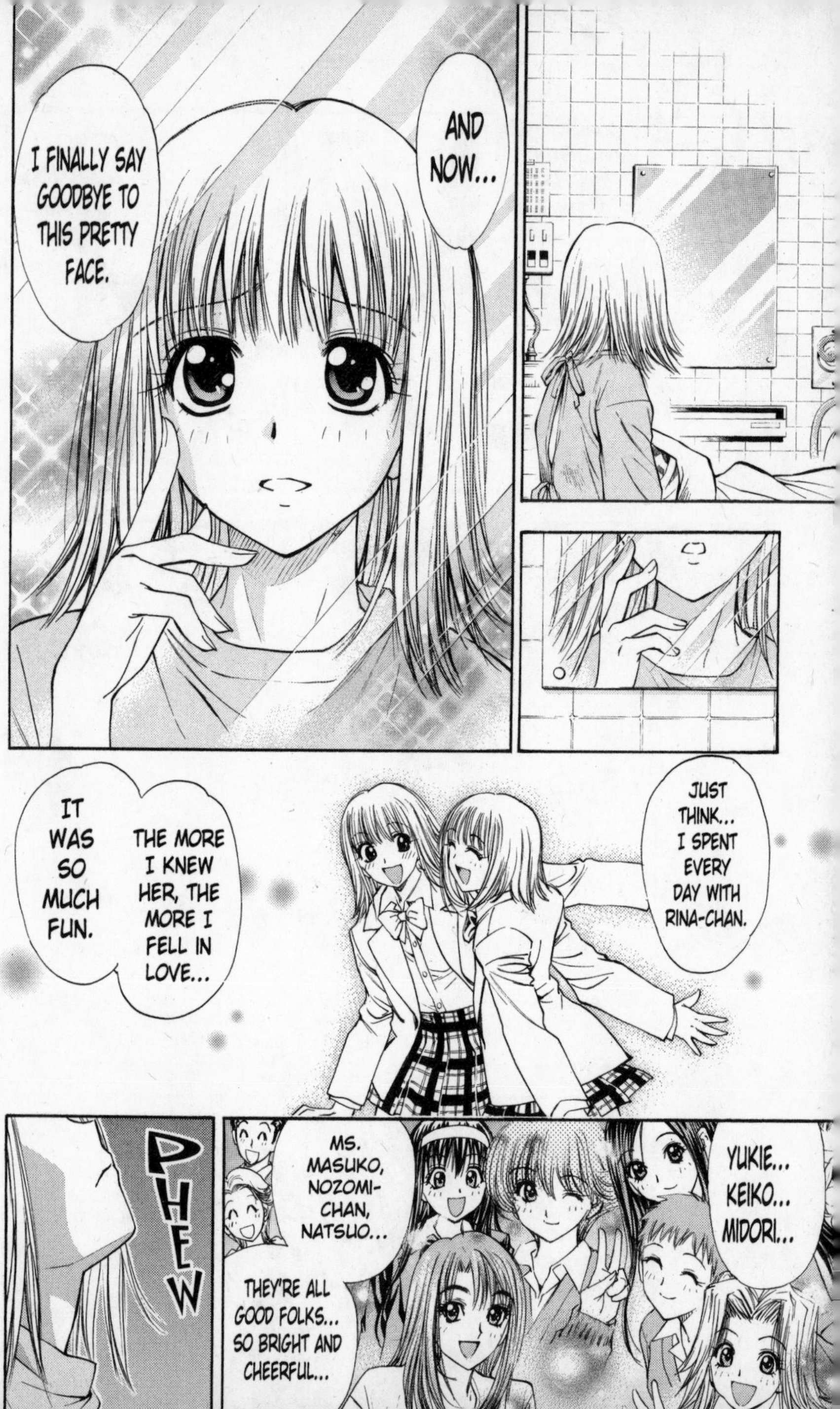
AND NOW...
I FINALLY SAY GOODBYE TO THIS PRETTY FACE.
JUST THINK... I SPENT EVERY DAY WITH RINA-CHAN.
THE MORE I KNEW HER, THE MORE I FELL IN LOVE...
IT WAS SO MUCH FUN.
YUKIE... KEIKO... MIDORI...
MS. MASUKO, NOZOMI-CHAN, NATSUO...
THEY'RE ALL GOOD FOLKS... SO BRIGHT AND CHEERFUL...
PHEW

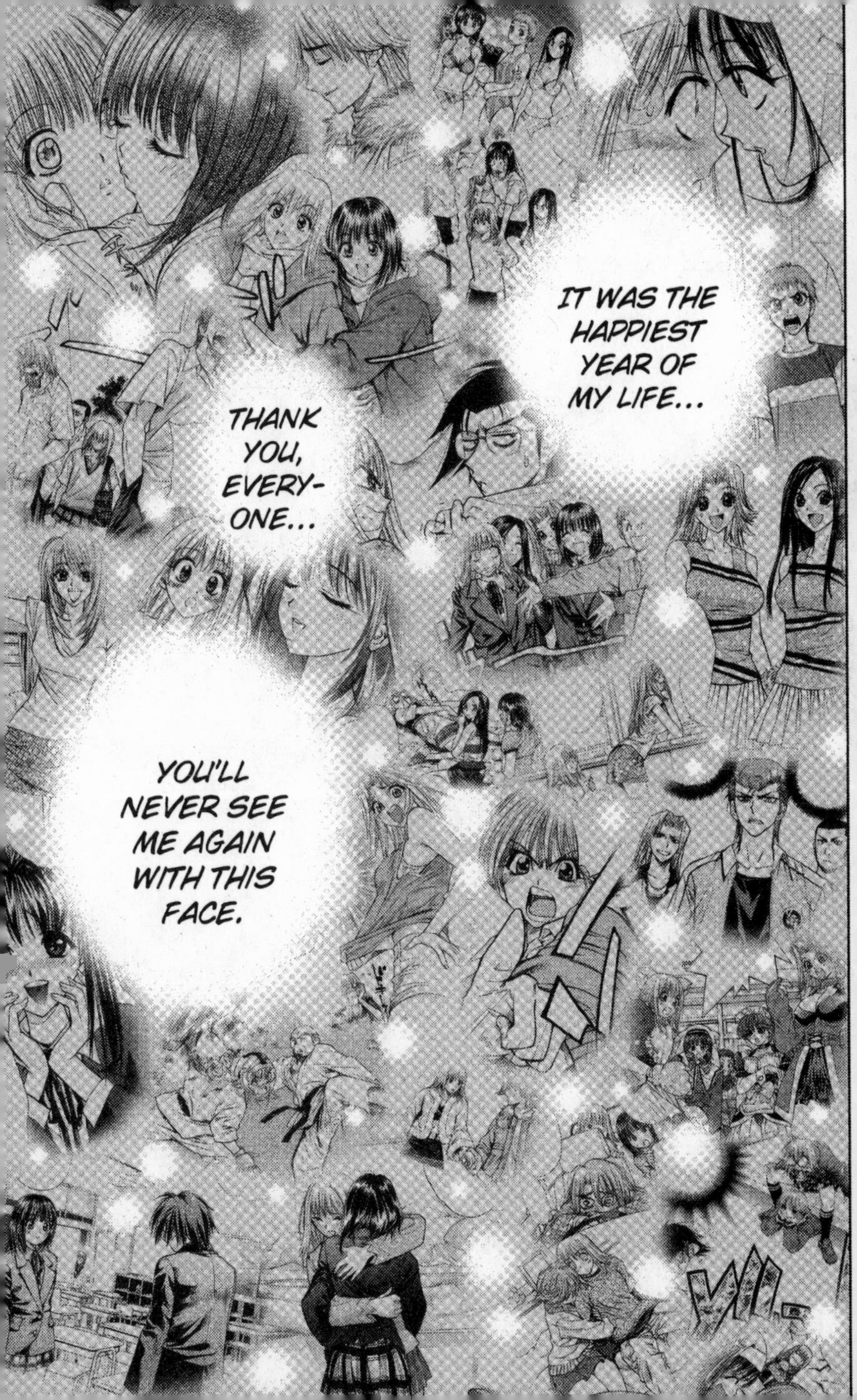
IT WAS THE HAPPIEST YEAR OF MY LIFE...
THANK YOU, EVERY-ONE...
YOU'LL NEVER SEE ME AGAIN WITH THIS FACE.

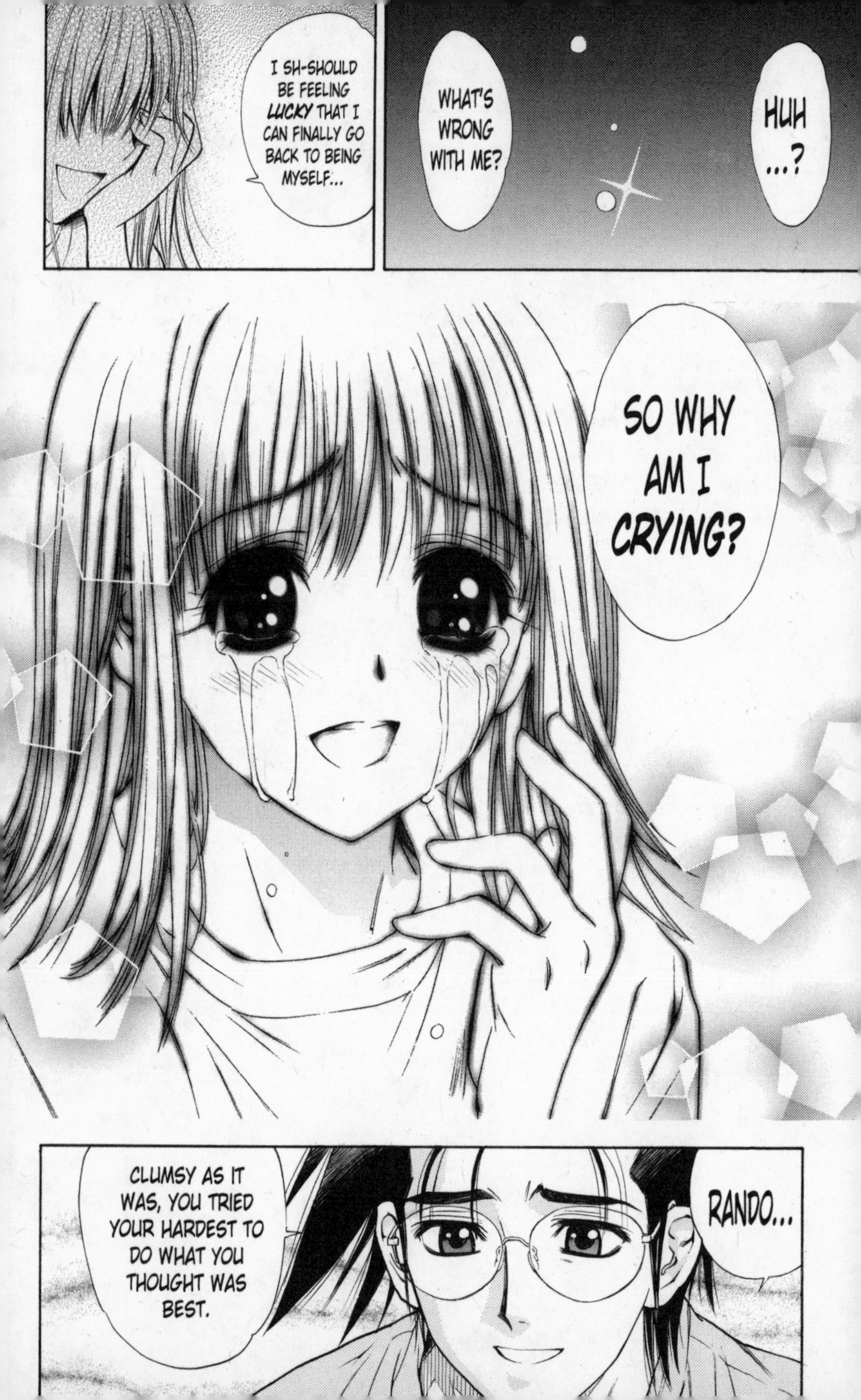
HUH ...?
WHAT'S WRONG WITH ME?
I SH-SHOULD BE FEELING *LUCKY* THAT I CAN FINALLY GO BACK TO BEING MYSELF...
SO WHY AM I CRYING?
RANDO...
CLUMSY AS IT WAS, YOU TRIED YOUR HARDEST TO DO WHAT YOU THOUGHT WAS BEST.

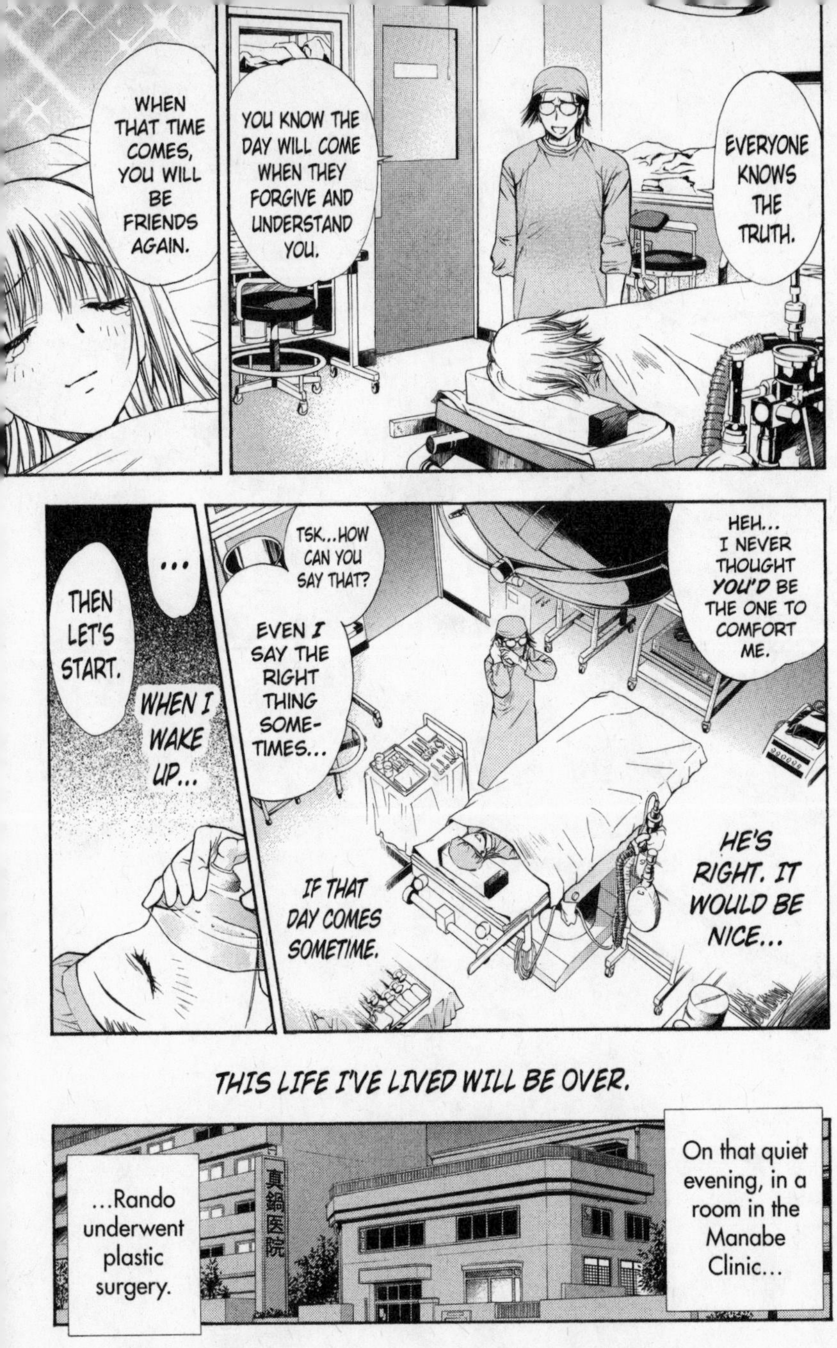
EVERYONE KNOWS THE TRUTH.
YOU KNOW THE DAY WILL COME WHEN THEY FORGIVE AND UNDERSTAND YOU.
WHEN THAT TIME COMES, YOU WILL BE FRIENDS AGAIN.
HEH... I NEVER THOUGHT YOU'D BE THE ONE TO COMFORT ME.
TSK...HOW CAN YOU SAY THAT?
EVEN I SAY THE RIGHT THING SOME-TIMES...
HE'S RIGHT. IT WOULD BE NICE...
IF THAT DAY COMES SOMETIME.
...
THEN LET'S START.
WHEN I WAKE UP...
THIS LIFE I'VE LIVED WILL BE OVER.
On that quiet evening, in a room in the Manabe Clinic...
真鍋医院
...Rando underwent plastic surgery.

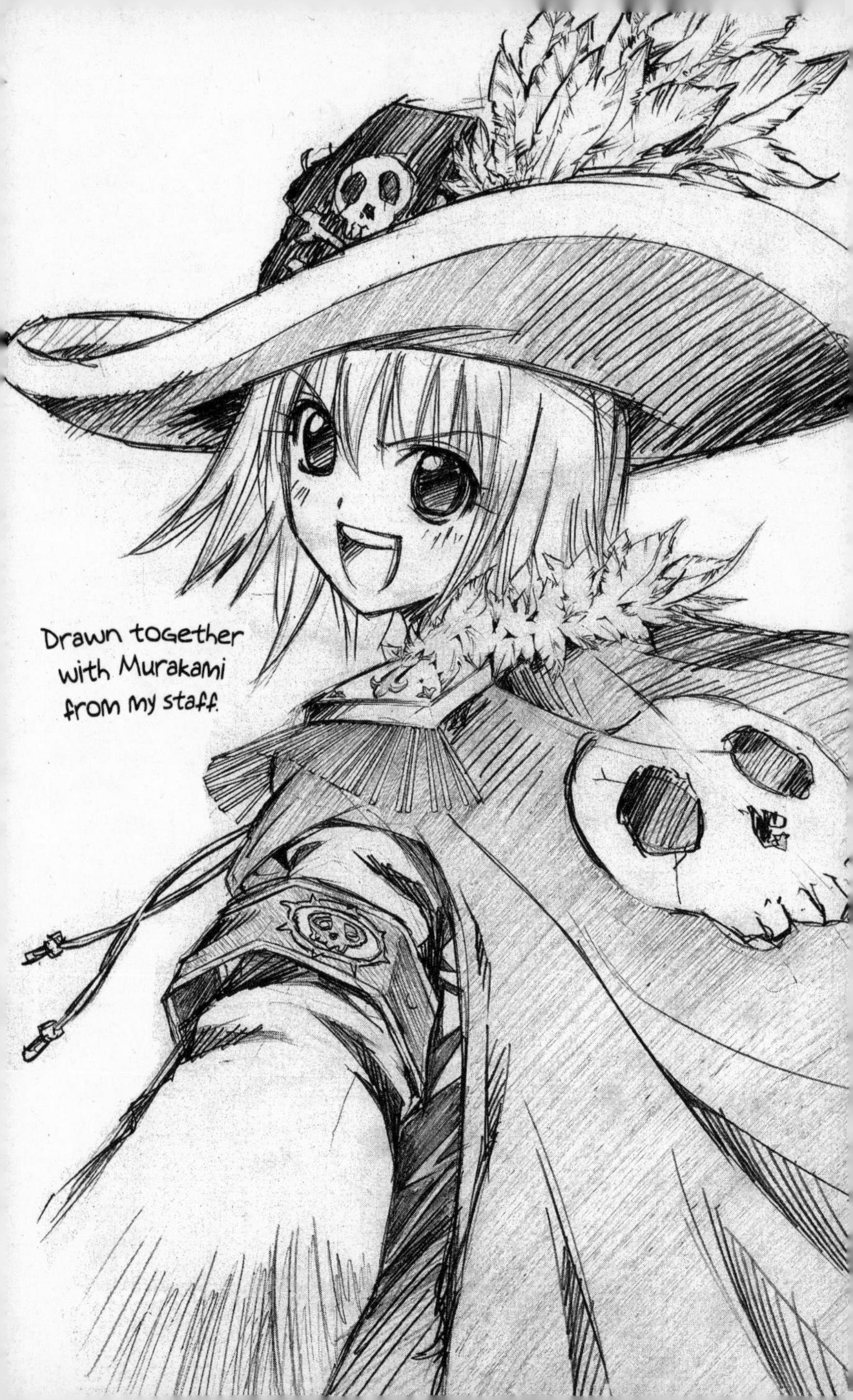
Drawn together with Murakami from my staff.

# CHAPTER 51: AT LAST I CAN TELL YOU

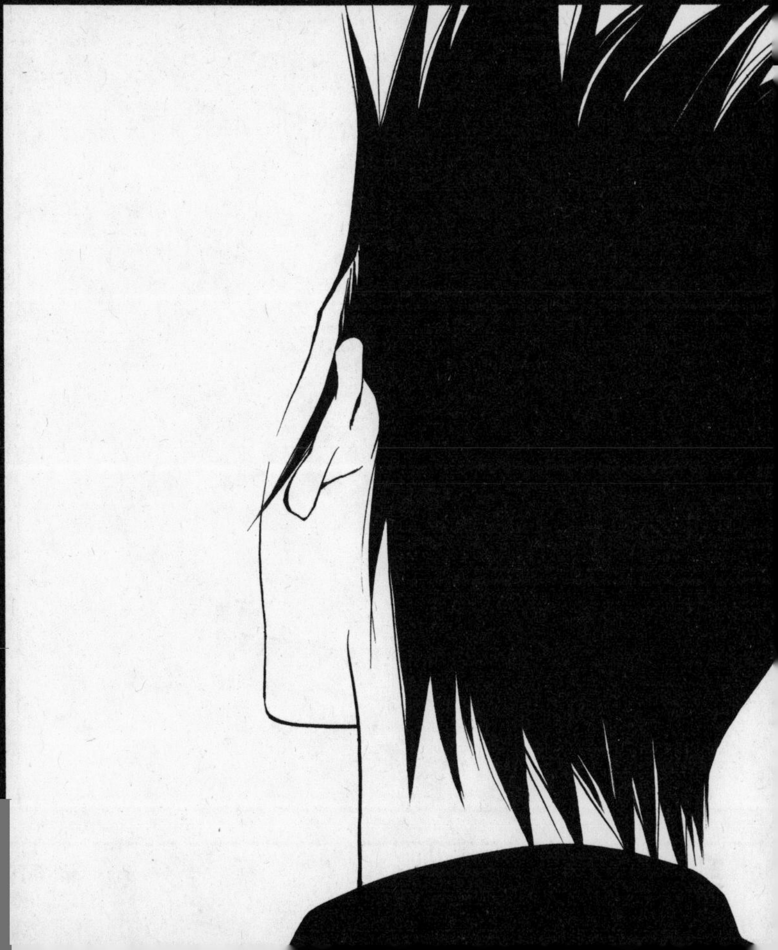

Two weeks after the operation…

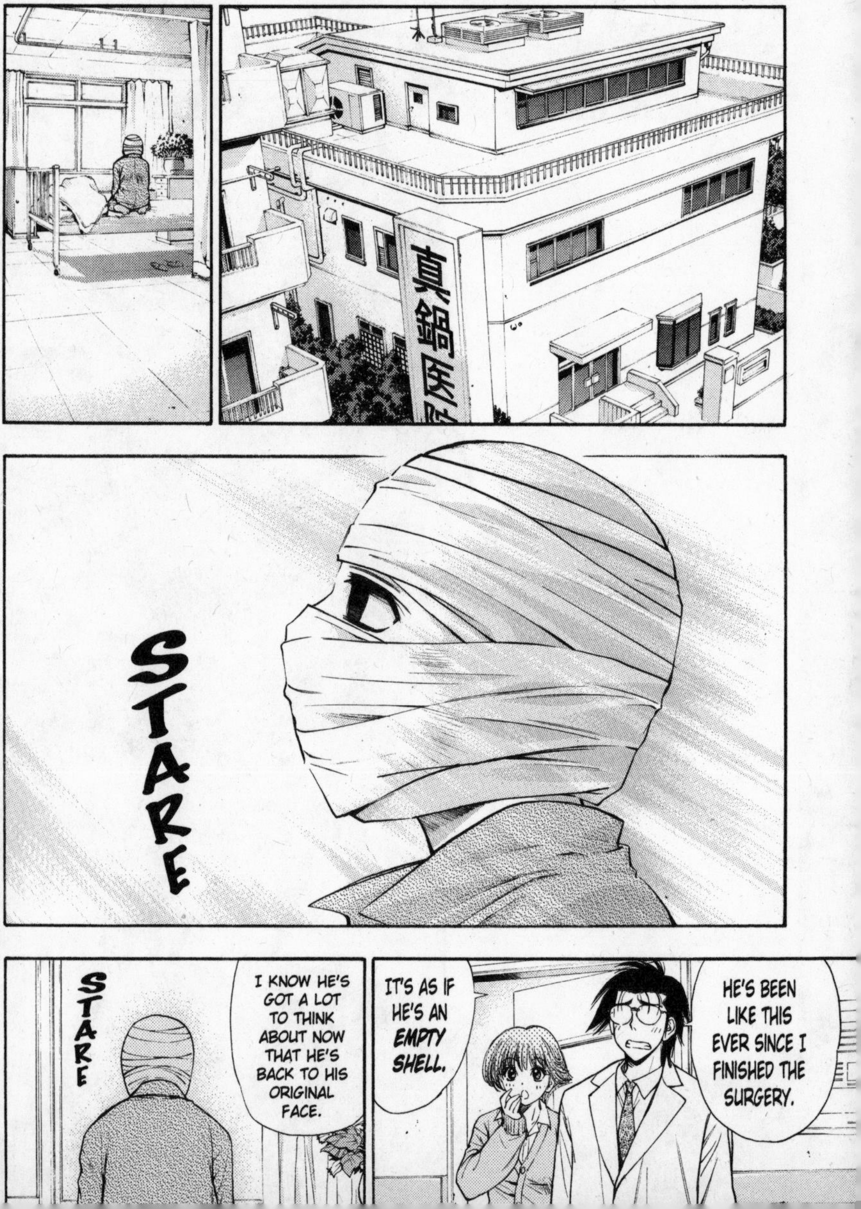

真鍋医
STARE
HE'S BEEN LIKE THIS EVER SINCE I FINISHED THE SURGERY.
IT'S AS IF HE'S AN *EMPTY SHELL*.
I KNOW HE'S GOT A LOT TO THINK ABOUT NOW THAT HE'S BACK TO HIS ORIGINAL FACE.
STARE

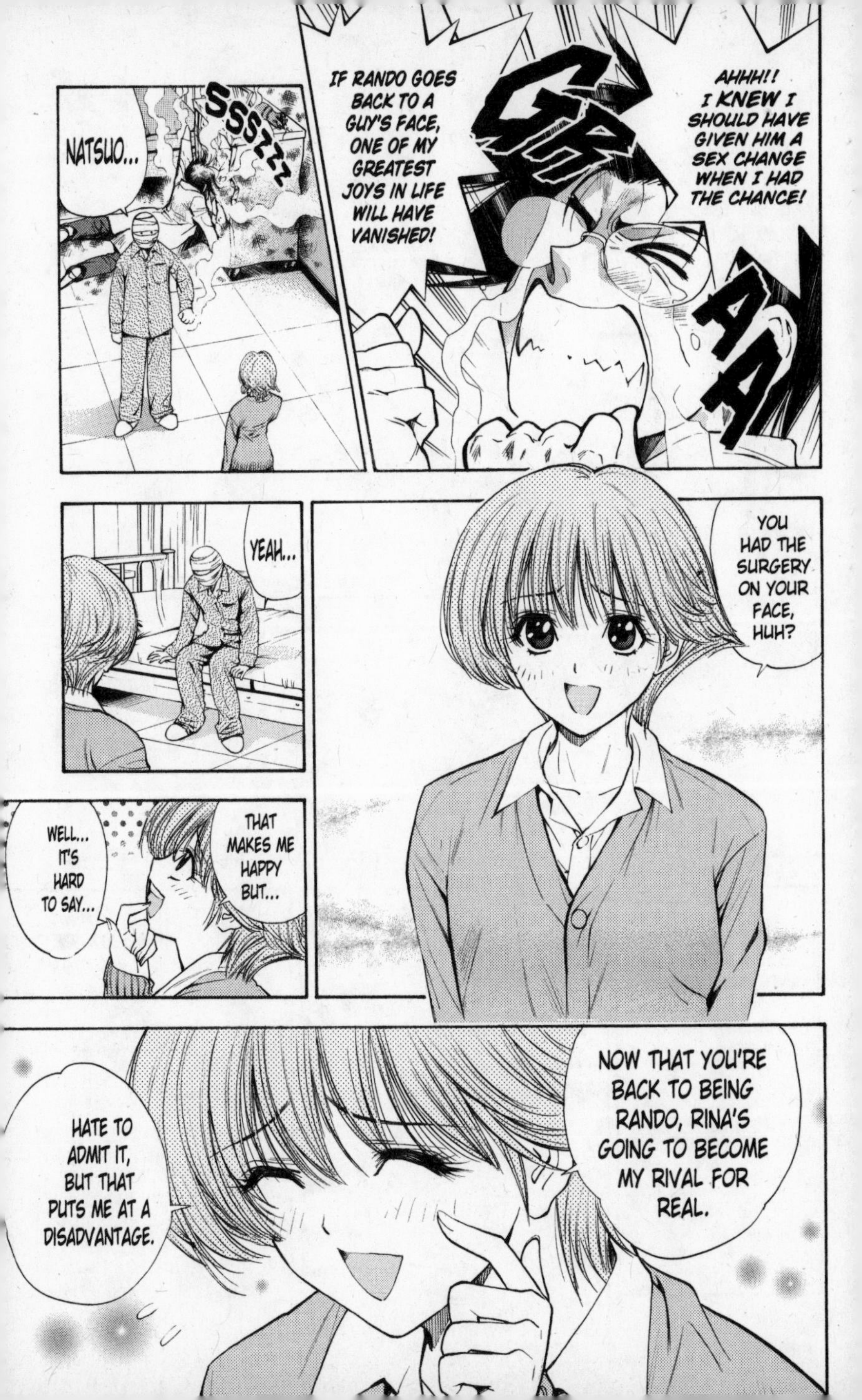
AHHH!! I KNEW I SHOULD HAVE GIVEN HIM A SEX CHANGE WHEN I HAD THE CHANCE!
GAAA
IF RANDO GOES BACK TO A GUY'S FACE, ONE OF MY GREATEST JOYS IN LIFE WILL HAVE VANISHED!
SSSZZZ
NATSUO...
YOU HAD THE SURGERY ON YOUR FACE, HUH?
YEAH...
THAT MAKES ME HAPPY BUT...
WELL... IT'S HARD TO SAY...
NOW THAT YOU'RE BACK TO BEING RANDO, RINA'S GOING TO BECOME MY RIVAL FOR REAL.
HATE TO ADMIT IT, BUT THAT PUTS ME AT A DISADVANTAGE.

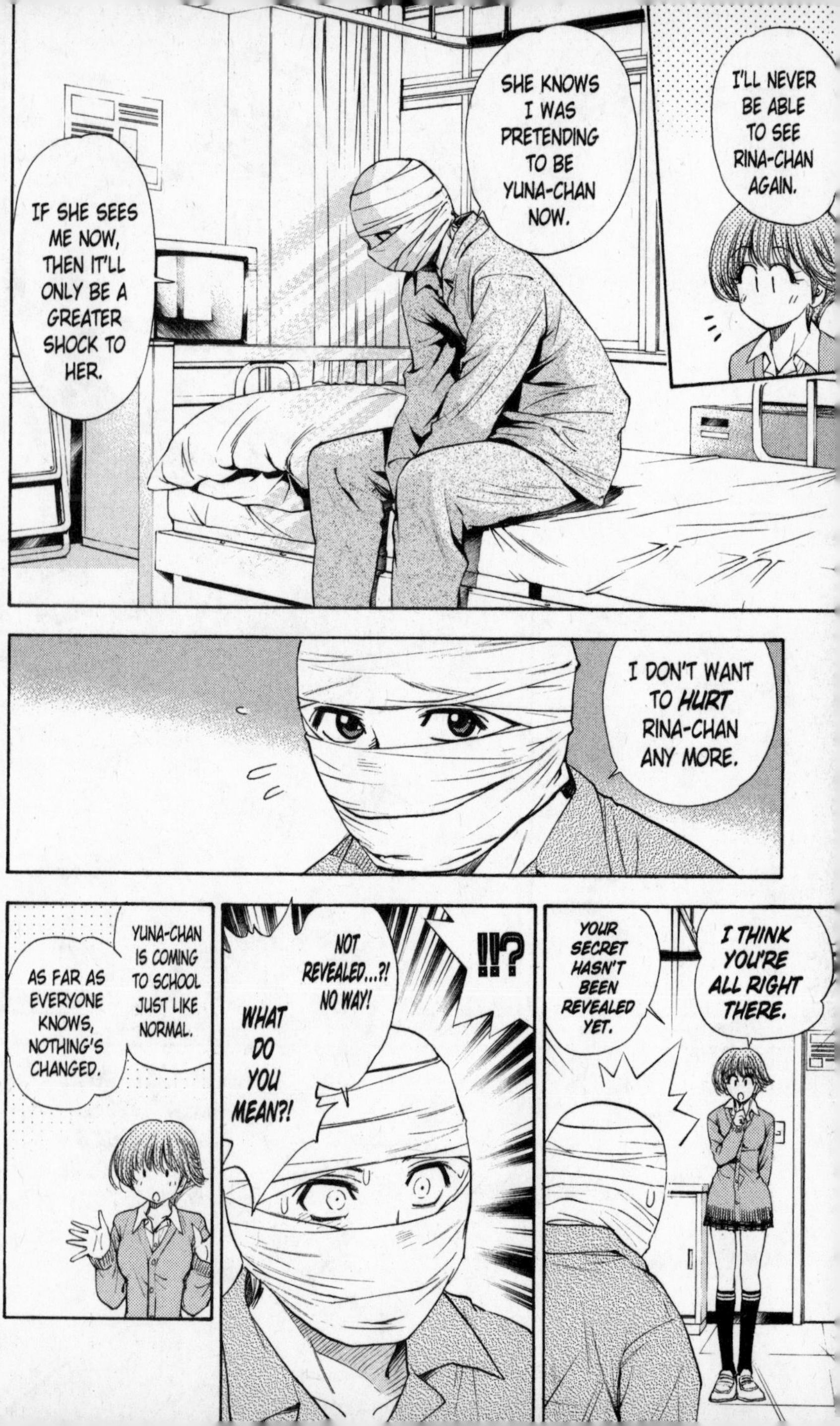
I'LL NEVER BE ABLE TO SEE RINA-CHAN AGAIN.
SHE KNOWS I WAS PRETENDING TO BE YUNA-CHAN NOW.
IF SHE SEES ME NOW, THEN IT'LL ONLY BE A GREATER SHOCK TO HER.
I DON'T WANT TO *HURT* RINA-CHAN ANY MORE.
I THINK YOU'RE ALL RIGHT THERE.
YOUR SECRET HASN'T BEEN REVEALED YET.
!!?
NOT REVEALED...?! NO WAY!
WHAT DO YOU MEAN?!
YUNA-CHAN IS COMING TO SCHOOL JUST LIKE NORMAL.
AS FAR AS EVERYONE KNOWS, NOTHING'S CHANGED.

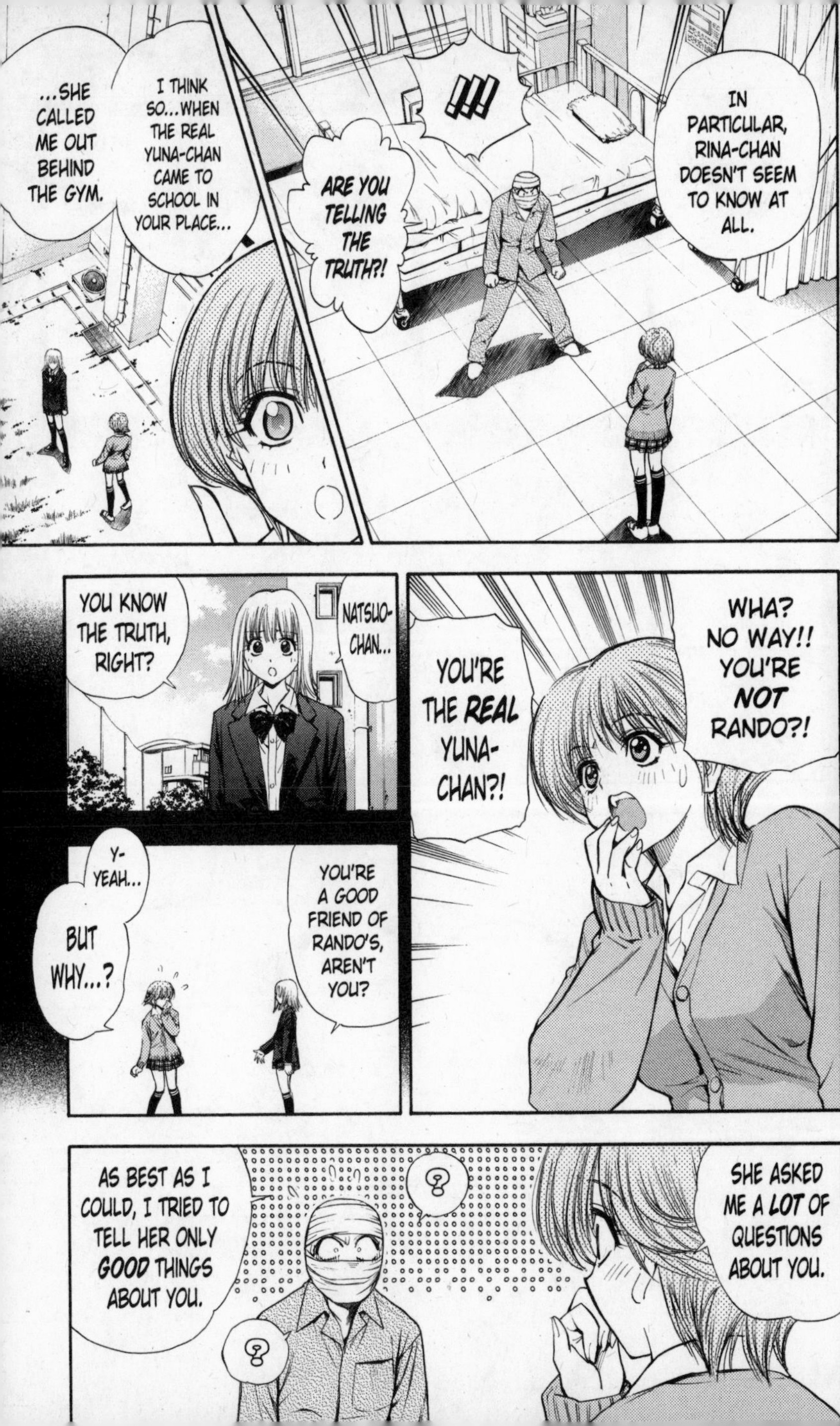
IN PARTICULAR, RINA-CHAN DOESN'T SEEM TO KNOW AT ALL.
!!!
ARE YOU TELLING THE TRUTH?!
I THINK SO...WHEN THE REAL YUNA-CHAN CAME TO SCHOOL IN YOUR PLACE...
...SHE CALLED ME OUT BEHIND THE GYM.
WHA? NO WAY!! YOU'RE NOT RANDO?!
YOU'RE THE REAL YUNA-CHAN?!
NATSUO-CHAN...
YOU KNOW THE TRUTH, RIGHT?
YOU'RE A GOOD FRIEND OF RANDO'S, AREN'T YOU?
Y-YEAH...
BUT WHY...?
SHE ASKED ME A LOT OF QUESTIONS ABOUT YOU.
?
?
AS BEST AS I COULD, I TRIED TO TELL HER ONLY GOOD THINGS ABOUT YOU.

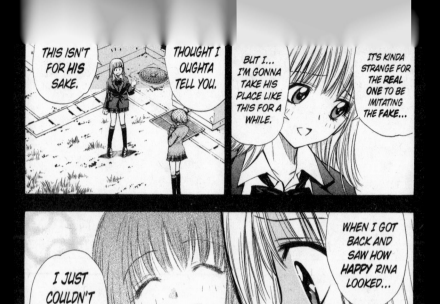

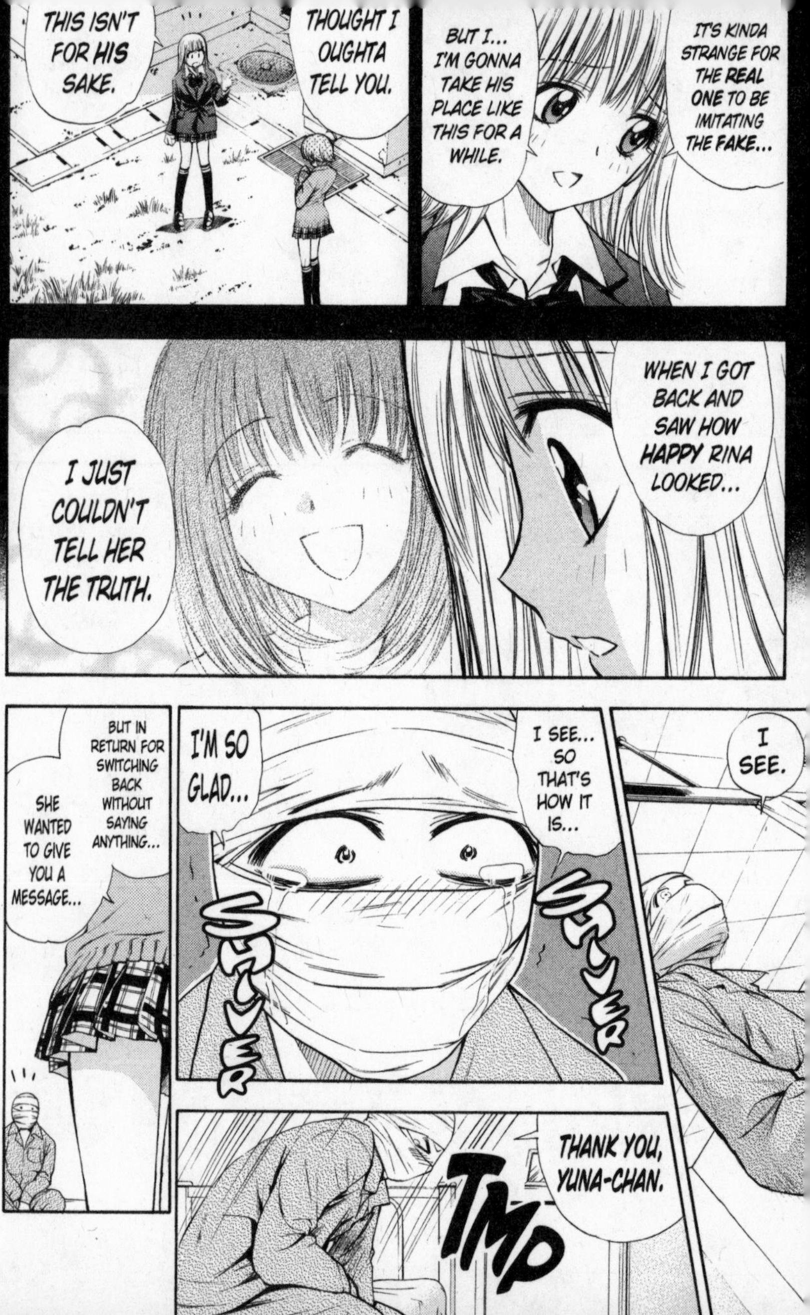
IT'S KINDA STRANGE FOR THE REAL ONE TO BE IMITATING THE FAKE...
BUT I... I'M GONNA TAKE HIS PLACE LIKE THIS FOR A WHILE.
THOUGHT I OUGHTA TELL YOU.
THIS ISN'T FOR HIS SAKE.
WHEN I GOT BACK AND SAW HOW HAPPY RINA LOOKED...
I JUST COULDN'T TELL HER THE TRUTH.
I SEE.
I SEE... SO THAT'S HOW IT IS...
SHIVER
I'M SO GLAD...
SHIVER
THANK YOU, YUNA-CHAN.
TMP
BUT IN RETURN FOR SWITCHING BACK WITHOUT SAYING ANYTHING...
SHE WANTED TO GIVE YOU A MESSAGE...

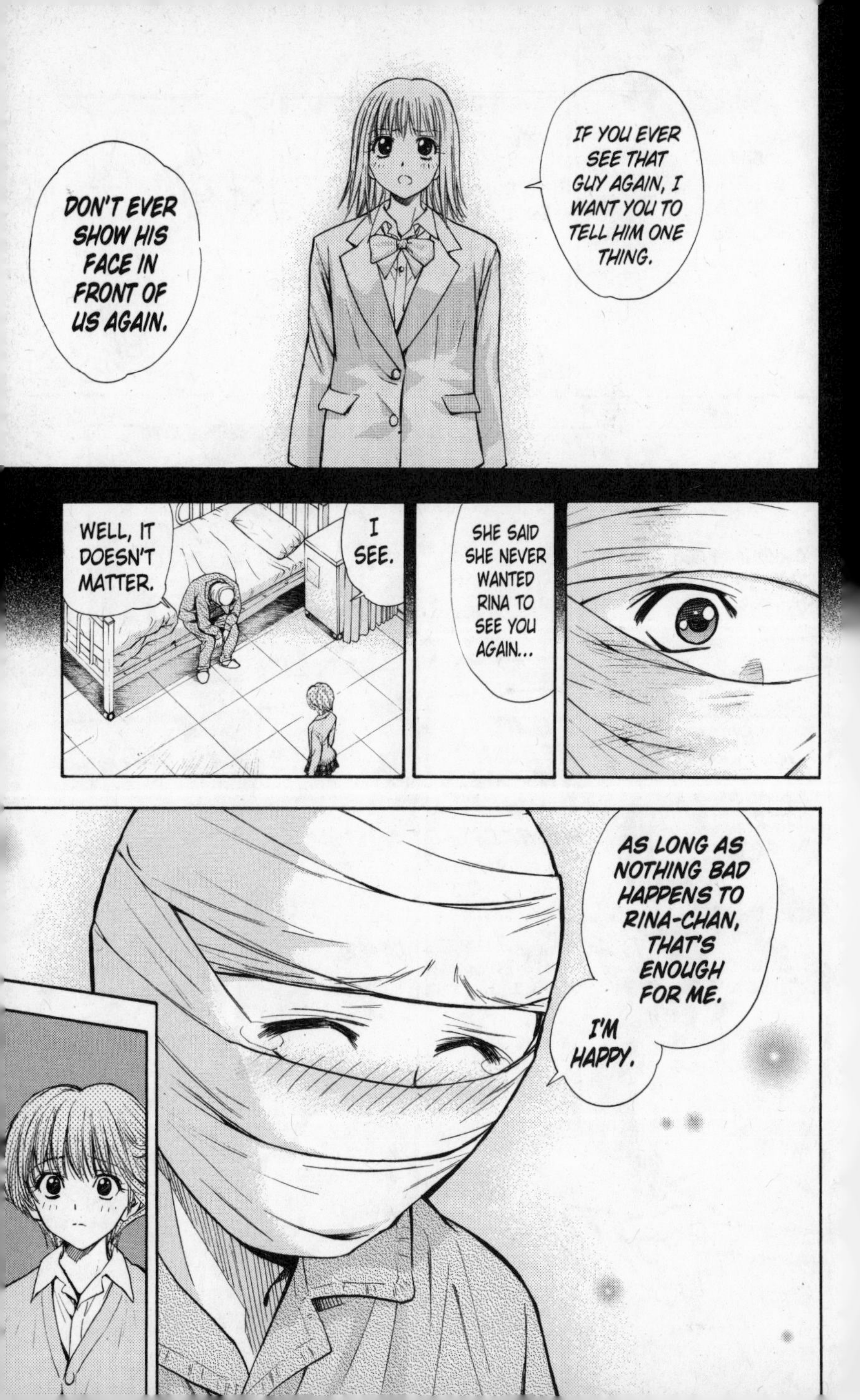
IF YOU EVER SEE THAT GUY AGAIN, I WANT YOU TO TELL HIM ONE THING.
DON'T EVER SHOW HIS FACE IN FRONT OF US AGAIN.
SHE SAID SHE NEVER WANTED RINA TO SEE YOU AGAIN...
I SEE.
WELL, IT DOESN'T MATTER.
AS LONG AS NOTHING BAD HAPPENS TO RINA-CHAN, THAT'S ENOUGH FOR ME.
I'M HAPPY.

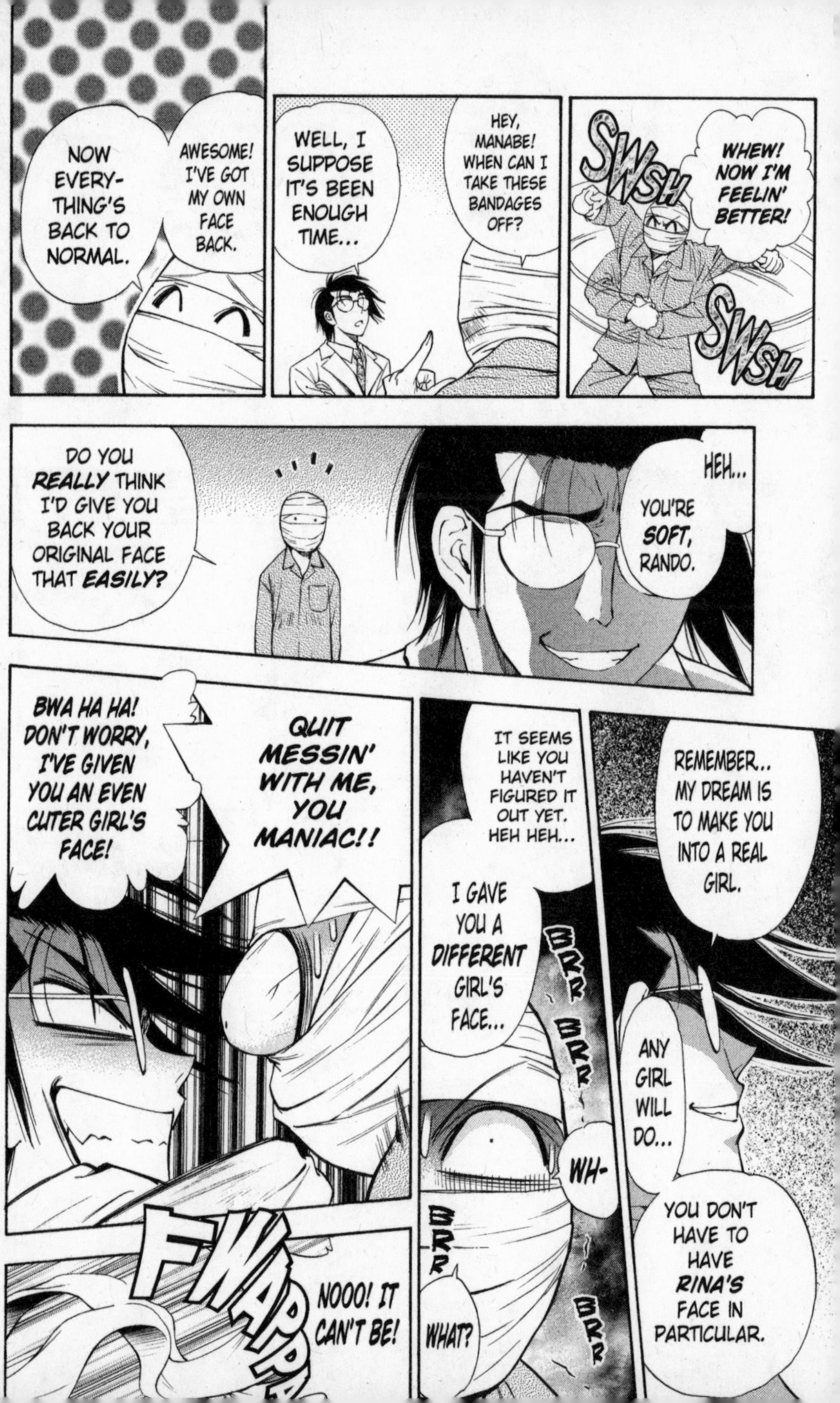
SWSH
WHEW! NOW I'M FEELIN' BETTER!
SWSH
HEY, MANABE! WHEN CAN I TAKE THESE BANDAGES OFF?
WELL, I SUPPOSE IT'S BEEN ENOUGH TIME...
AWESOME! I'VE GOT MY OWN FACE BACK.
NOW EVERYTHING'S BACK TO NORMAL.
HEH...
YOU'RE SOFT, RANDO.
DO YOU REALLY THINK I'D GIVE YOU BACK YOUR ORIGINAL FACE THAT EASILY?
REMEMBER... MY DREAM IS TO MAKE YOU INTO A REAL GIRL.
ANY GIRL WILL DO...
YOU DON'T HAVE TO HAVE RINA'S FACE IN PARTICULAR.
IT SEEMS LIKE YOU HAVEN'T FIGURED IT OUT YET. HEH HEH...
I GAVE YOU A DIFFERENT GIRL'S FACE...
BRR
BRR
WH-
BRR
WHAT?
BRR
QUIT MESSIN' WITH ME, YOU MANIAC!!
BWA HA HA! DON'T WORRY, I'VE GIVEN YOU AN EVEN CUTER GIRL'S FACE!
FWAPPA
NOOO! IT CAN'T BE!

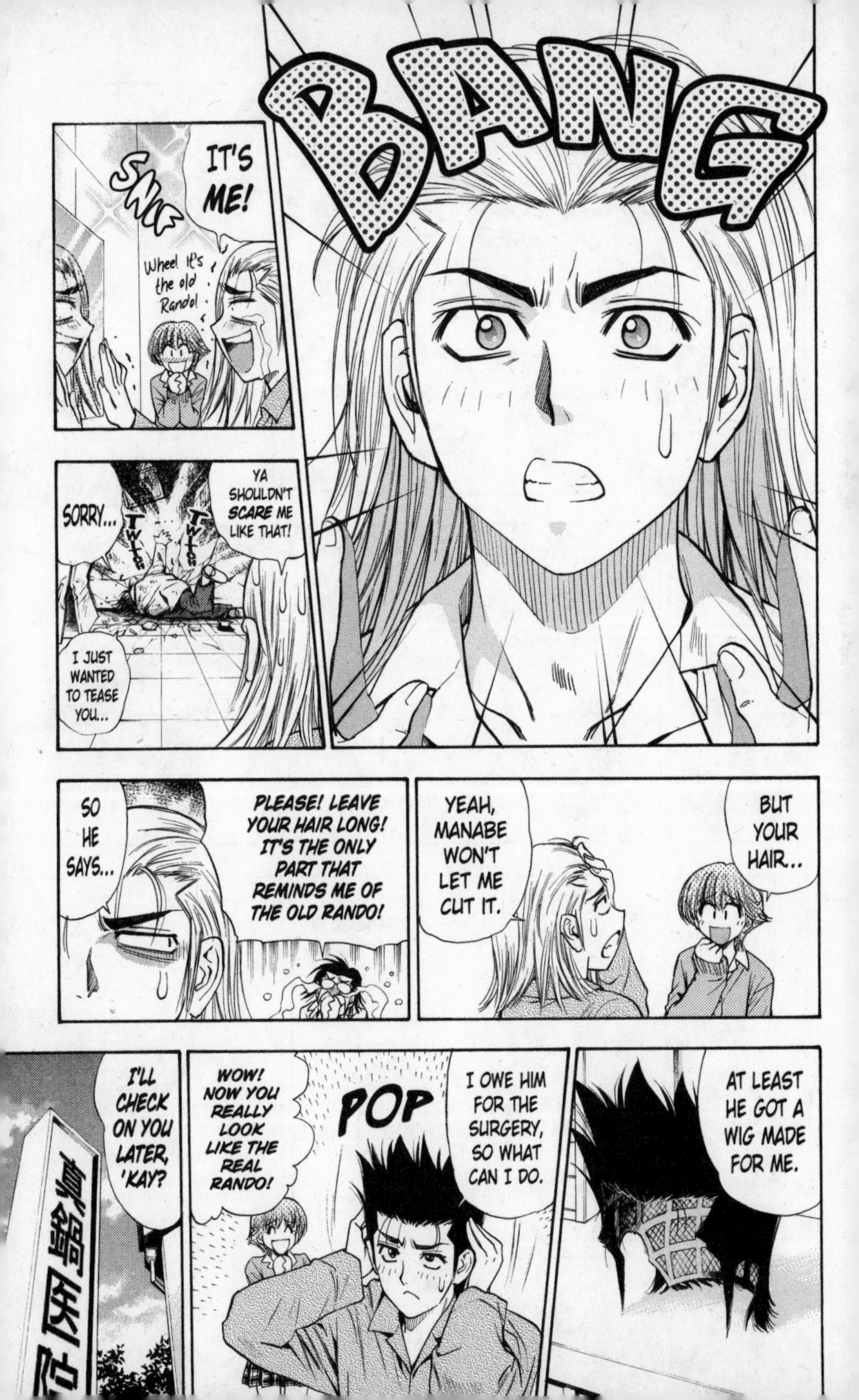
BANG
IT'S ME!
SNICK
Whee! It's the old Rando!
YA SHOULDN'T SCARE ME LIKE THAT!
TWITCH
TWITCH
SORRY...
I JUST WANTED TO TEASE YOU...
BUT YOUR HAIR...
YEAH, MANABE WON'T LET ME CUT IT.
PLEASE! LEAVE YOUR HAIR LONG! IT'S THE ONLY PART THAT REMINDS ME OF THE OLD RANDO!
SO HE SAYS...
AT LEAST HE GOT A WIG MADE FOR ME.
I OWE HIM FOR THE SURGERY, SO WHAT CAN I DO.
POP
WOW! NOW YOU REALLY LOOK LIKE THE REAL RANDO!
I'LL CHECK ON YOU LATER, 'KAY?

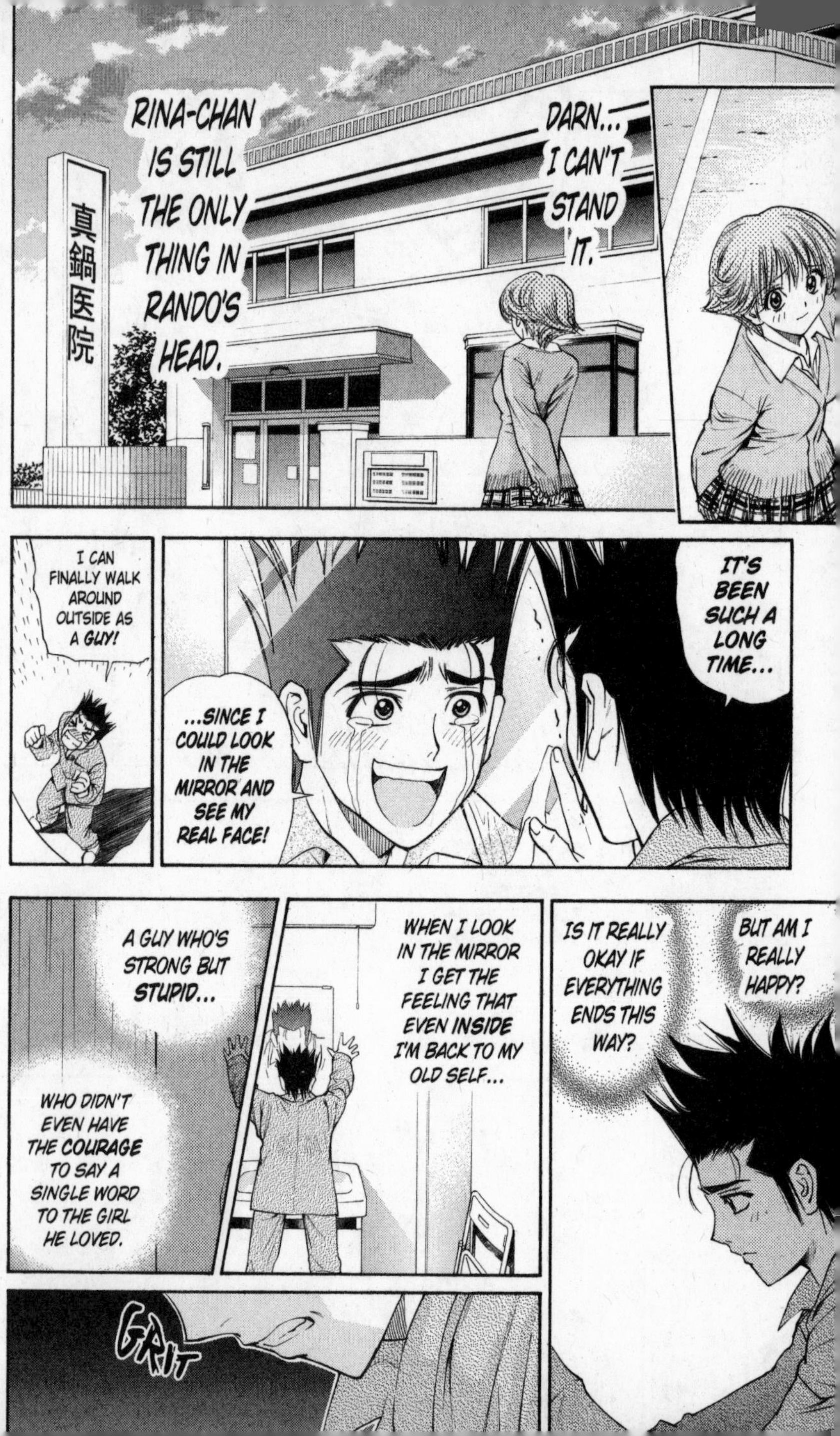
DARN... I CAN'T STAND IT.
RINA-CHAN IS STILL THE ONLY THING IN RANDO'S HEAD.
真鍋医院
IT'S BEEN SUCH A LONG TIME...
...SINCE I COULD LOOK IN THE MIRROR AND SEE MY REAL FACE!
I CAN FINALLY WALK AROUND OUTSIDE AS A GUY!
BUT AM I REALLY HAPPY?
IS IT REALLY OKAY IF EVERYTHING ENDS THIS WAY?
WHEN I LOOK IN THE MIRROR I GET THE FEELING THAT EVEN INSIDE I'M BACK TO MY OLD SELF...
A GUY WHO'S STRONG BUT STUPID...
WHO DIDN'T EVEN HAVE THE COURAGE TO SAY A SINGLE WORD TO THE GIRL HE LOVED.
GRIT

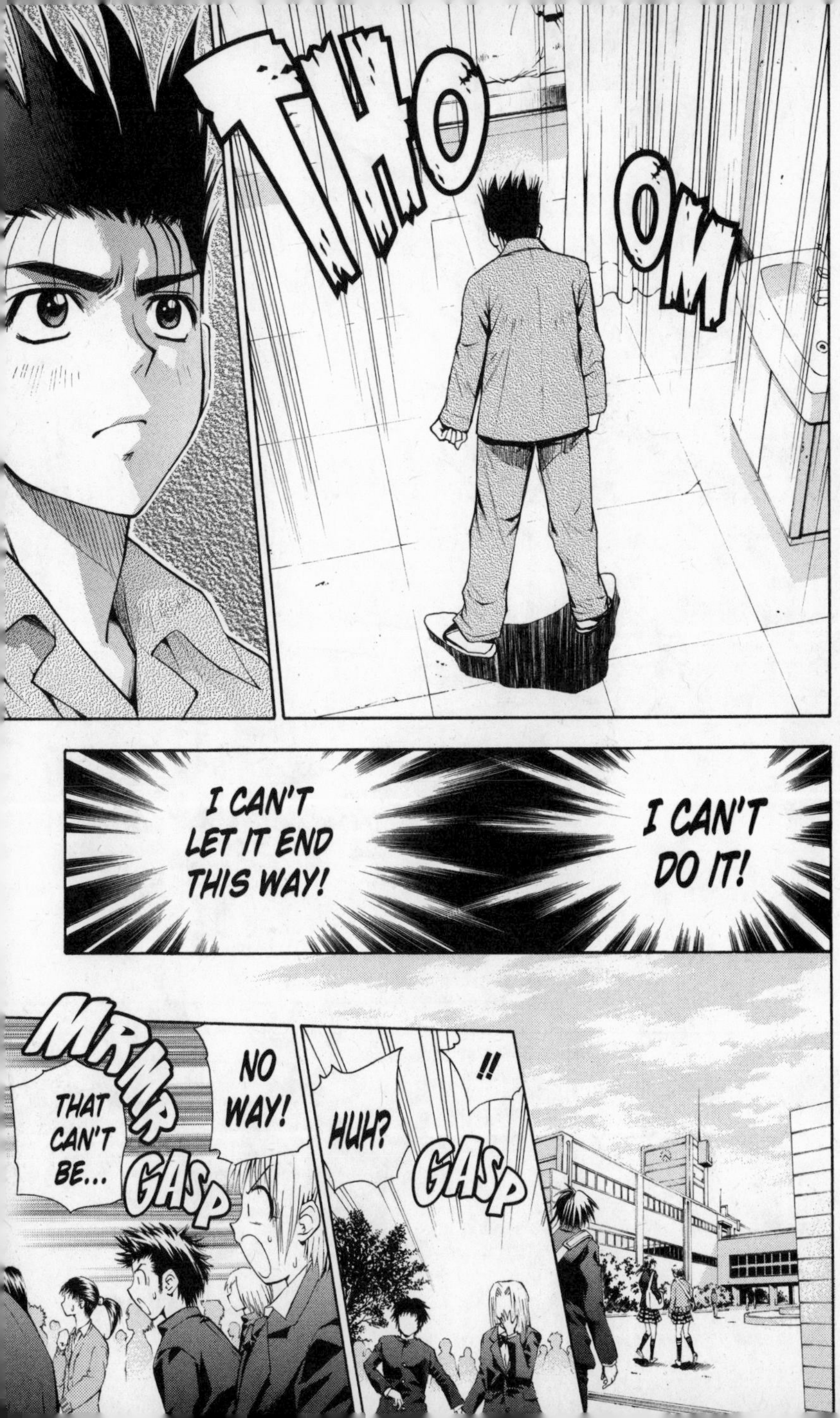
THOOM
I CAN'T DO IT!
I CAN'T LET IT END THIS WAY!
!!
HUH?
GASP
NO WAY!
GASP
MRMR
THAT CAN'T BE...

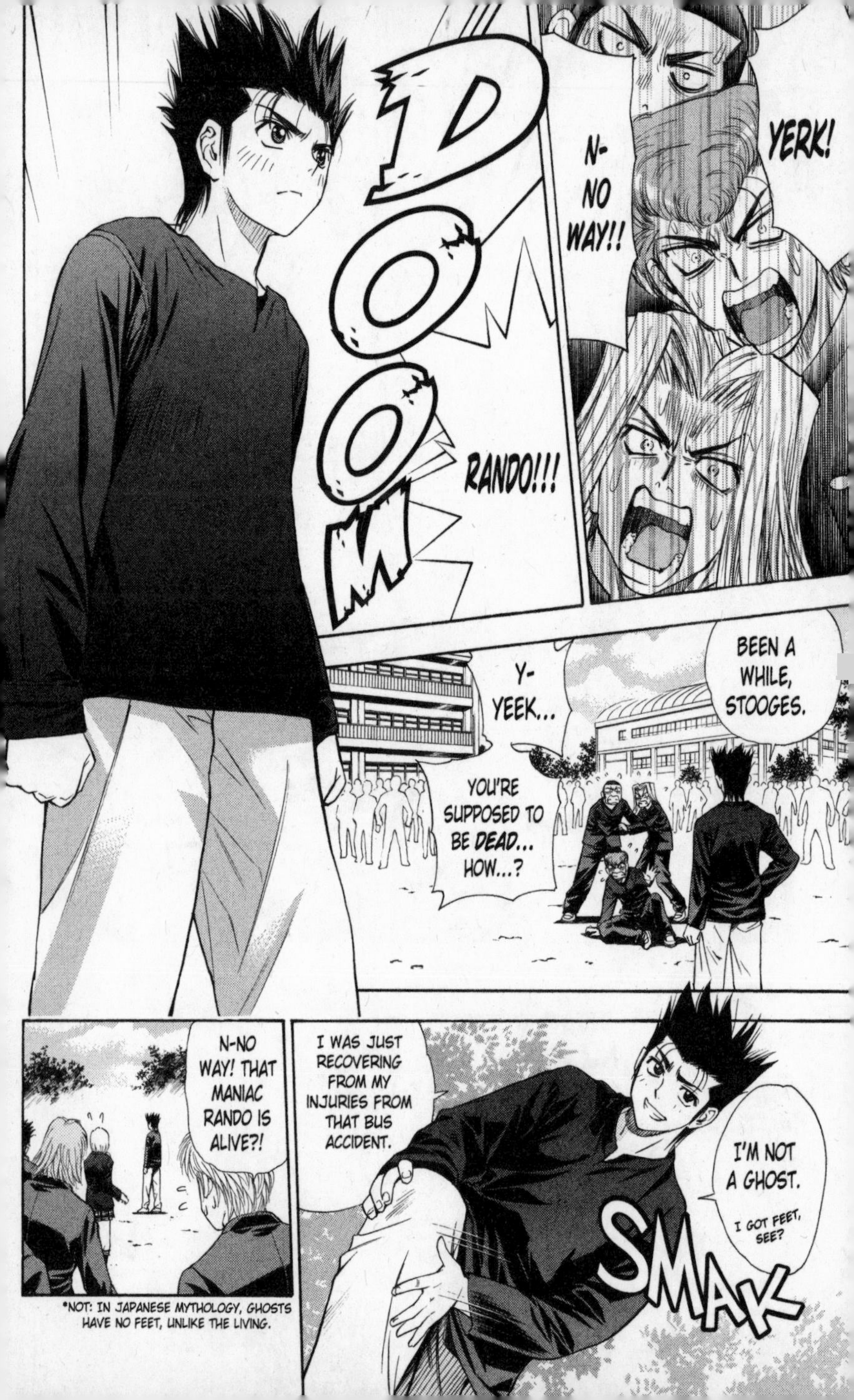
YERK!
N- NO WAY!!
RANDO!!!
DOOOM
BEEN A WHILE, STOOGES.
Y- YEEK...
YOU'RE SUPPOSED TO BE DEAD... HOW...?
I WAS JUST RECOVERING FROM MY INJURIES FROM THAT BUS ACCIDENT.
I'M NOT A GHOST.
I GOT FEET, SEE?
SMAK
N-NO WAY! THAT MANIAC RANDO IS ALIVE?!

*NOT: IN JAPANESE MYTHOLOGY, GHOSTS HAVE NO FEET, UNLIKE THE LIVING.

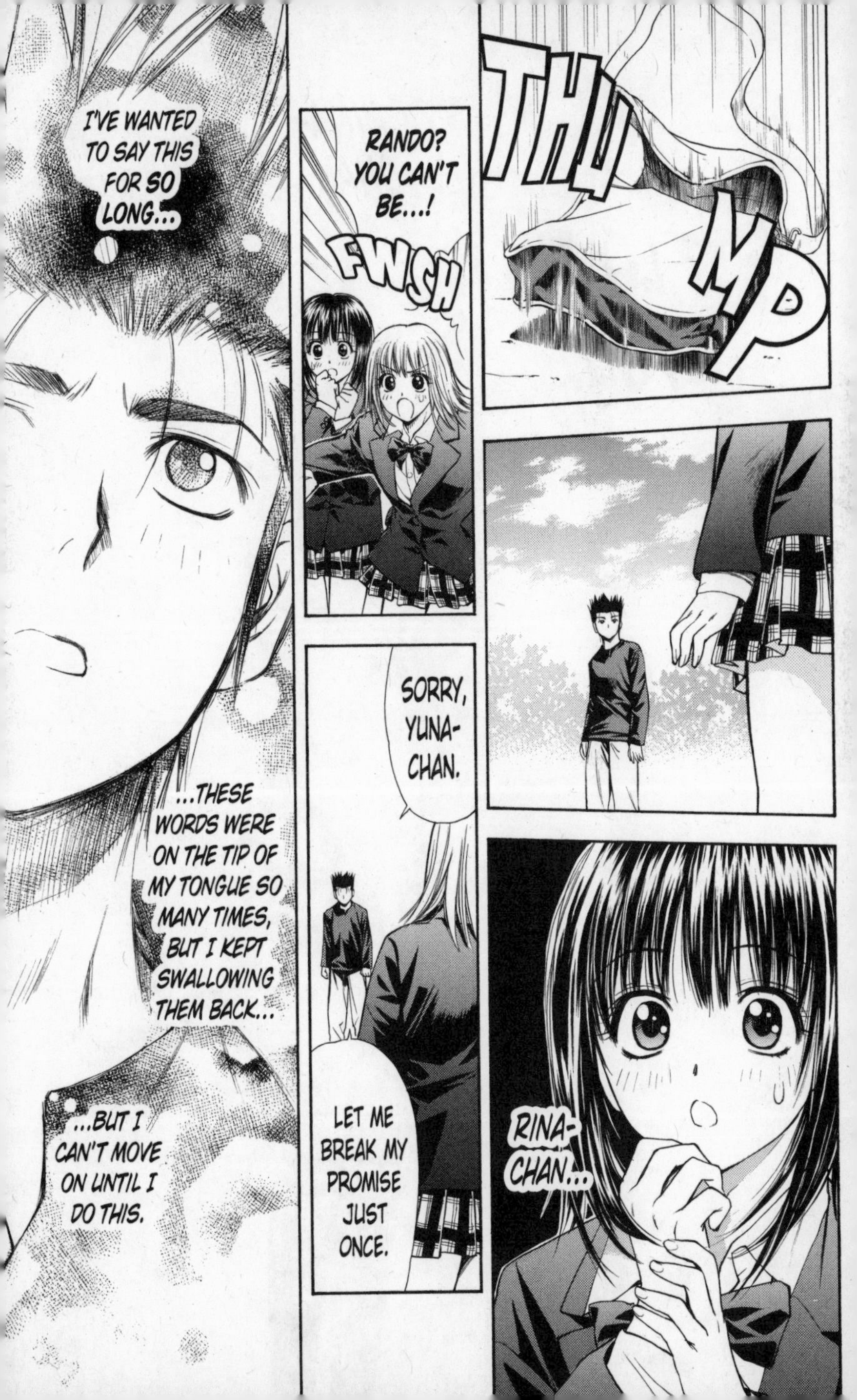
THUMP
RINA-CHAN...
RANDO? YOU CAN'T BE...!
FWISH
SORRY, YUNA-CHAN.
LET ME BREAK MY PROMISE JUST ONCE.
I'VE WANTED TO SAY THIS FOR SO LONG...
...THESE WORDS WERE ON THE TIP OF MY TONGUE SO MANY TIMES, BUT I KEPT SWALLOWING THEM BACK...
...BUT I CAN'T MOVE ON UNTIL I DO THIS.

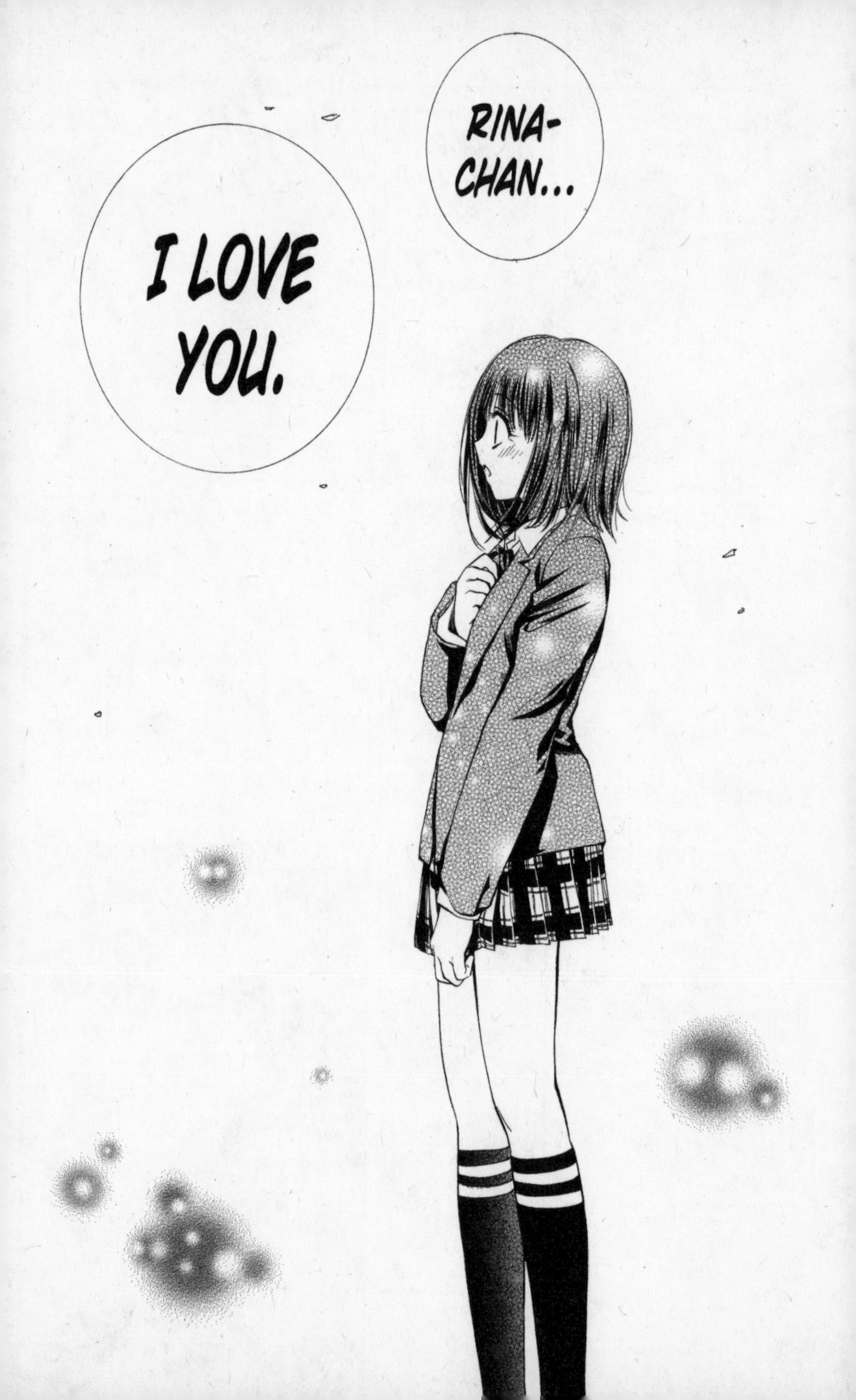
RINA-CHAN...
I LOVE YOU.

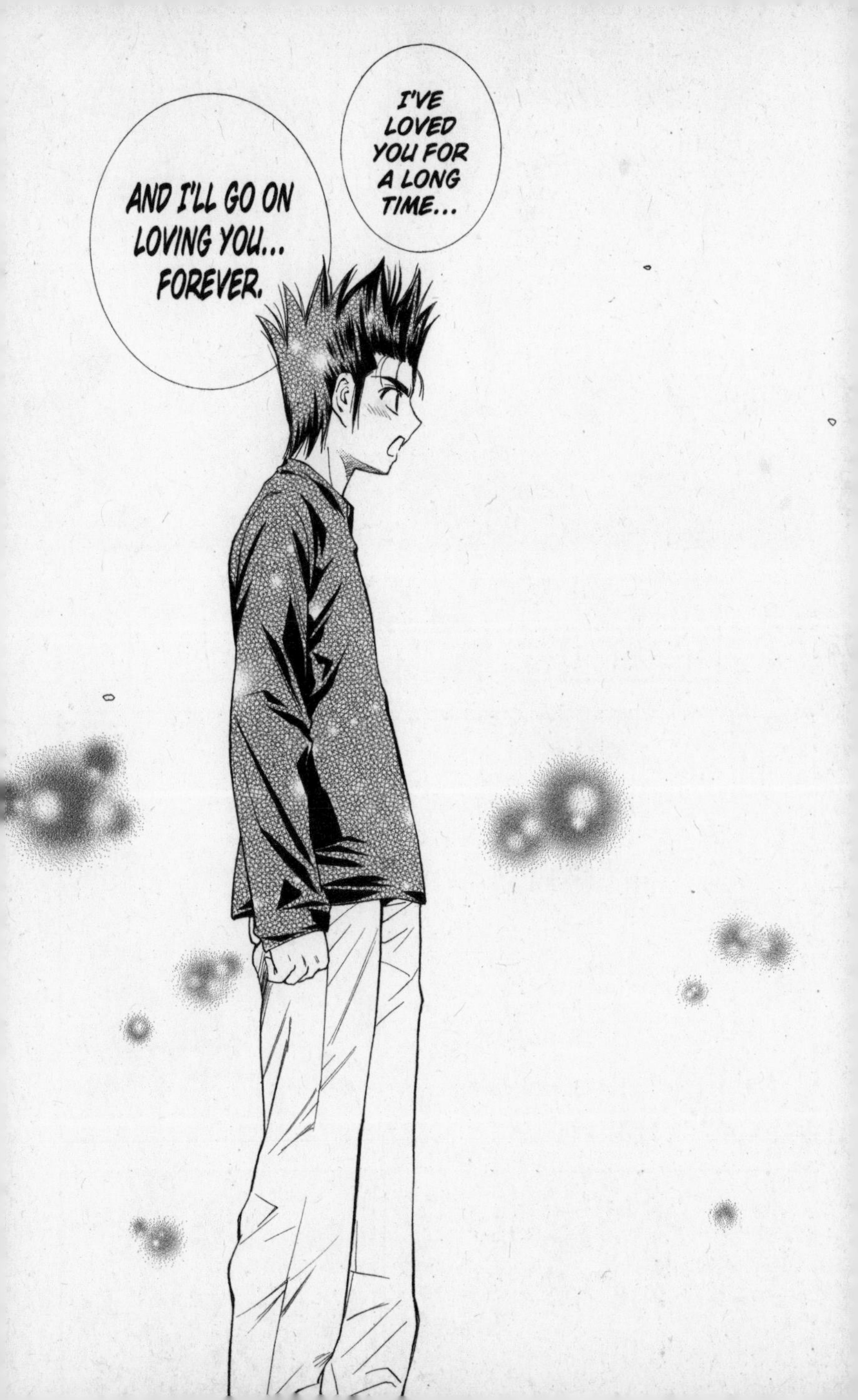
I'VE LOVED YOU FOR A LONG TIME...
AND I'LL GO ON LOVING YOU... FOREVER.

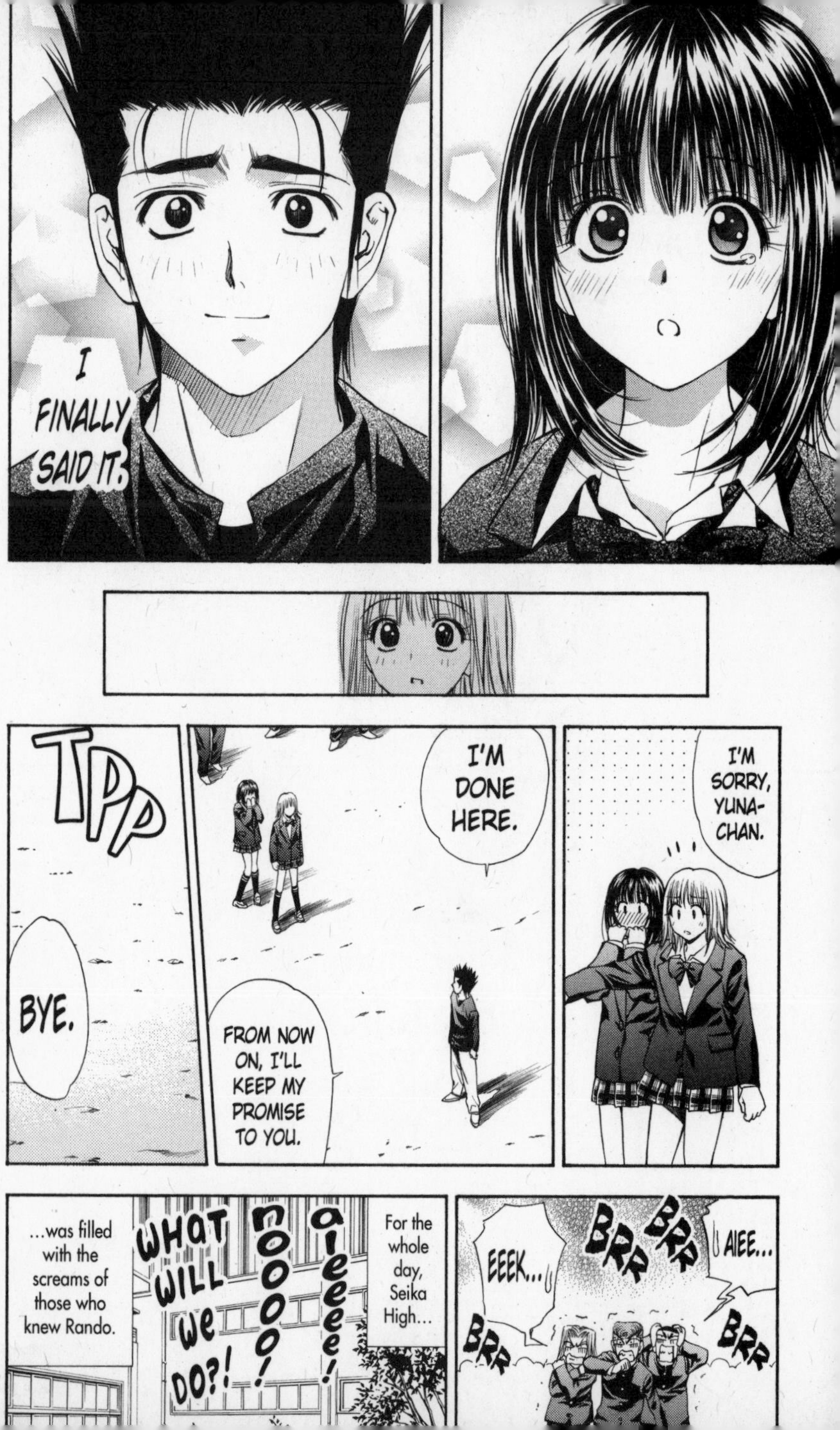
I FINALLY SAID IT.
I'M SORRY, YUNA-CHAN.
I'M DONE HERE.
FROM NOW ON, I'LL KEEP MY PROMISE TO YOU.
TPP
BYE.
AIEE...
BRR
BRR
EEEK...
BRR
BRR
For the whole day, Seika High...
aieeee!
nooooo!
WHAT WILL WE DO?!
...was filled with the screams of those who knew Rando.

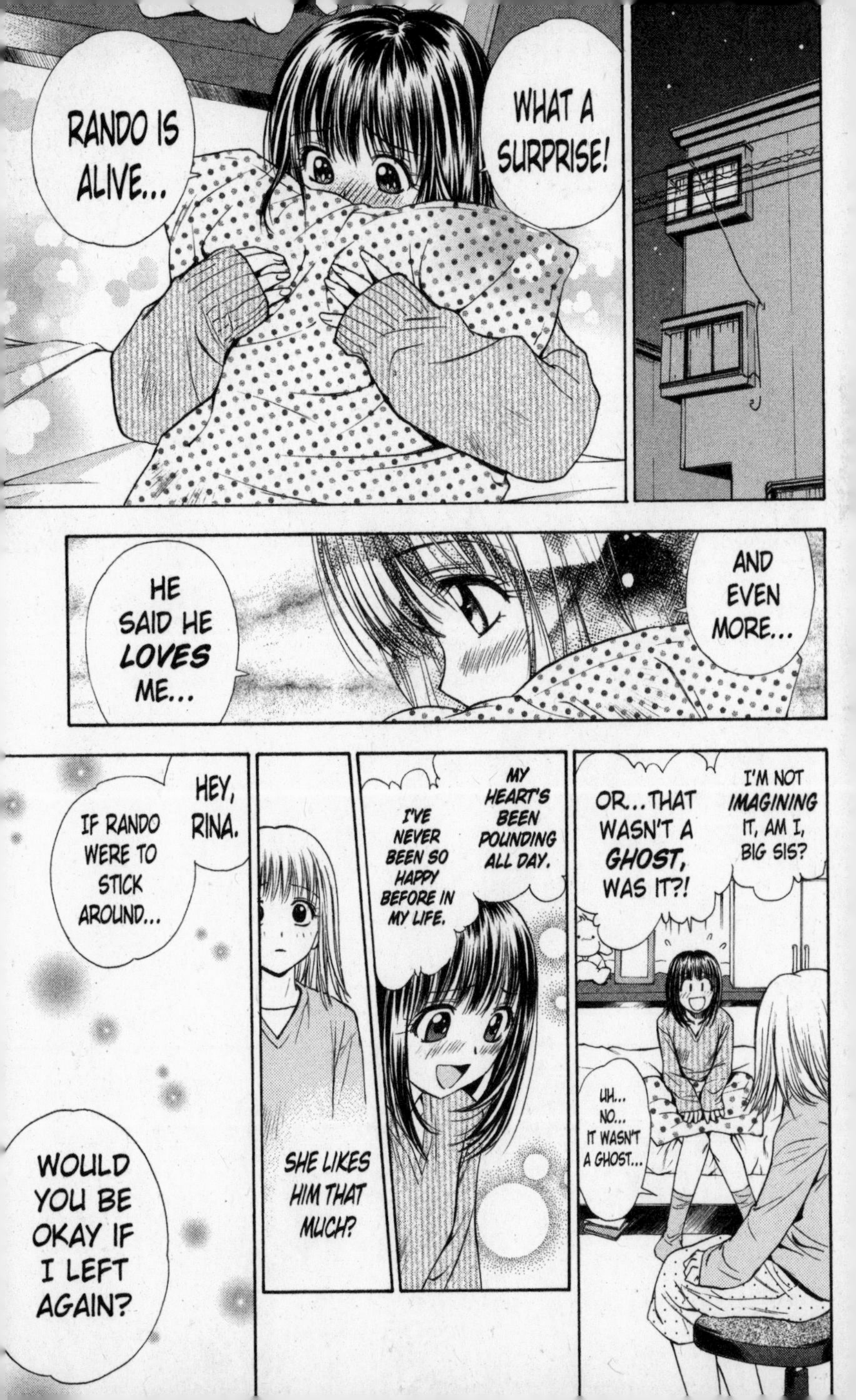
WHAT A SURPRISE!
RANDO IS ALIVE...
AND EVEN MORE...
HE SAID HE *LOVES* ME...
I'M NOT *IMAGINING* IT, AM I, BIG SIS?
OR...THAT WASN'T A *GHOST*, WAS IT?!
UH... NO... IT WASN'T A GHOST...
MY HEART'S BEEN POUNDING ALL DAY.
I'VE NEVER BEEN SO HAPPY BEFORE IN MY LIFE.
SHE LIKES HIM THAT MUCH?
HEY, RINA.
IF RANDO WERE TO STICK AROUND...
WOULD YOU BE OKAY IF I LEFT AGAIN?

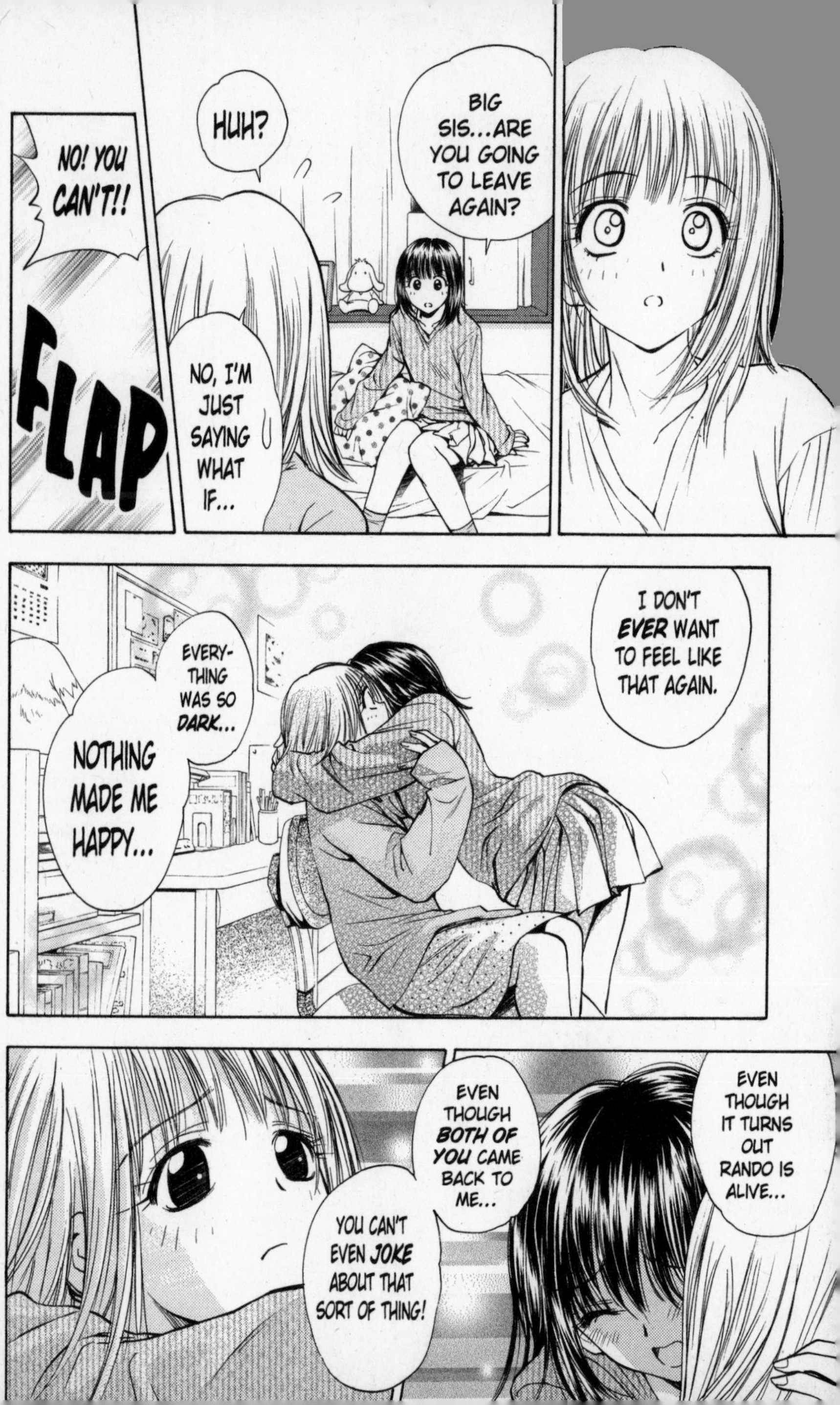
BIG SIS...ARE YOU GOING TO LEAVE AGAIN?
HUH?
NO, I'M JUST SAYING WHAT IF...
NO! YOU CAN'T!!
FLAP
I DON'T EVER WANT TO FEEL LIKE THAT AGAIN.
EVERY-THING WAS SO DARK...
NOTHING MADE ME HAPPY...
EVEN THOUGH IT TURNS OUT RANDO IS ALIVE...
EVEN THOUGH BOTH OF YOU CAME BACK TO ME...
YOU CAN'T EVEN JOKE ABOUT THAT SORT OF THING!

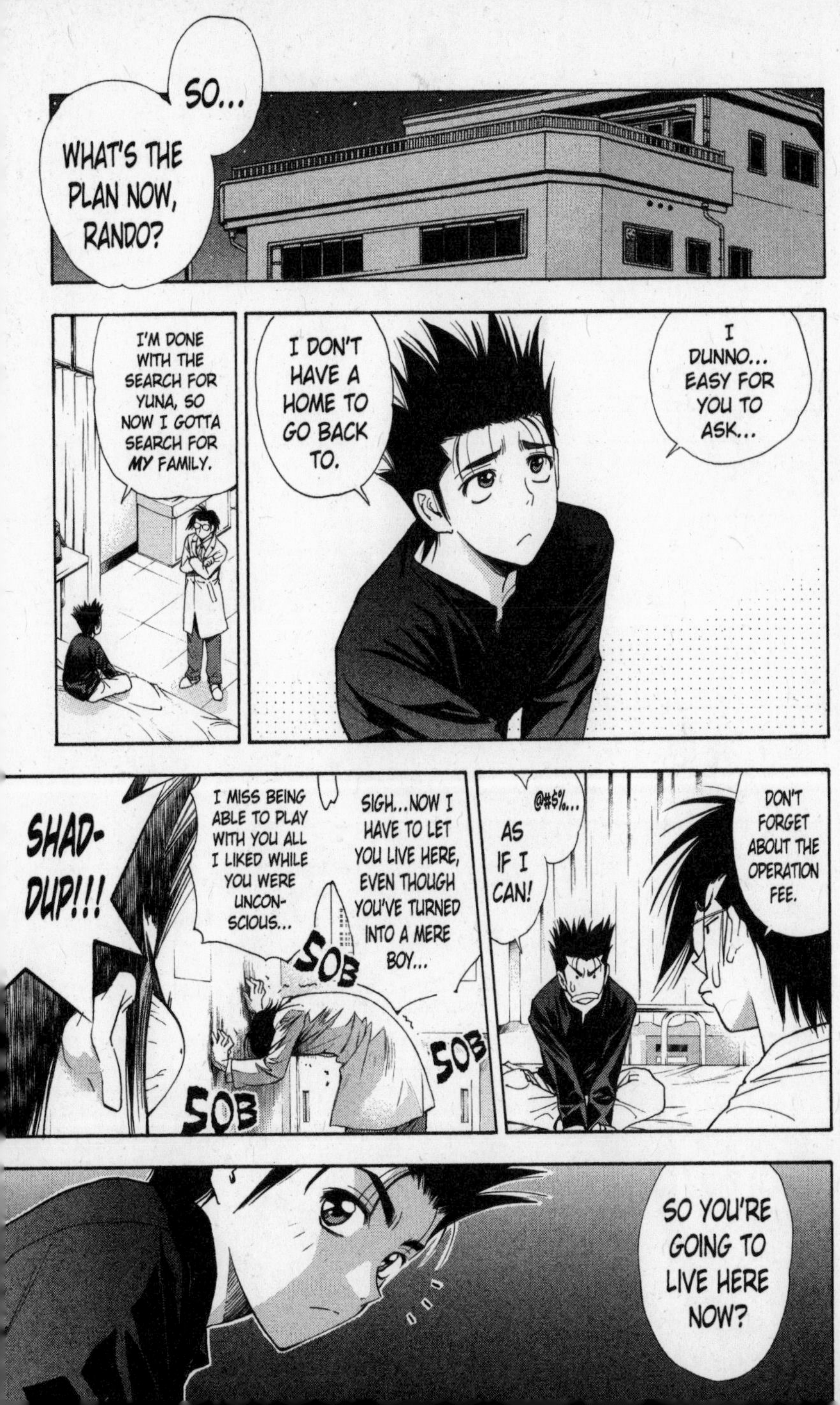
SO...
WHAT'S THE PLAN NOW, RANDO?
I DUNNO... EASY FOR YOU TO ASK...
I DON'T HAVE A HOME TO GO BACK TO.
I'M DONE WITH THE SEARCH FOR YUNA, SO NOW I GOTTA SEARCH FOR MY FAMILY.
DON'T FORGET ABOUT THE OPERATION FEE.
@#$%...
AS IF I CAN!
SIGH...NOW I HAVE TO LET YOU LIVE HERE, EVEN THOUGH YOU'VE TURNED INTO A MERE BOY...
I MISS BEING ABLE TO PLAY WITH YOU ALL I LIKED WHILE YOU WERE UNCONSCIOUS...
SOB
SOB
SOB
SHAD-DUP!!!
SO YOU'RE GOING TO LIVE HERE NOW?

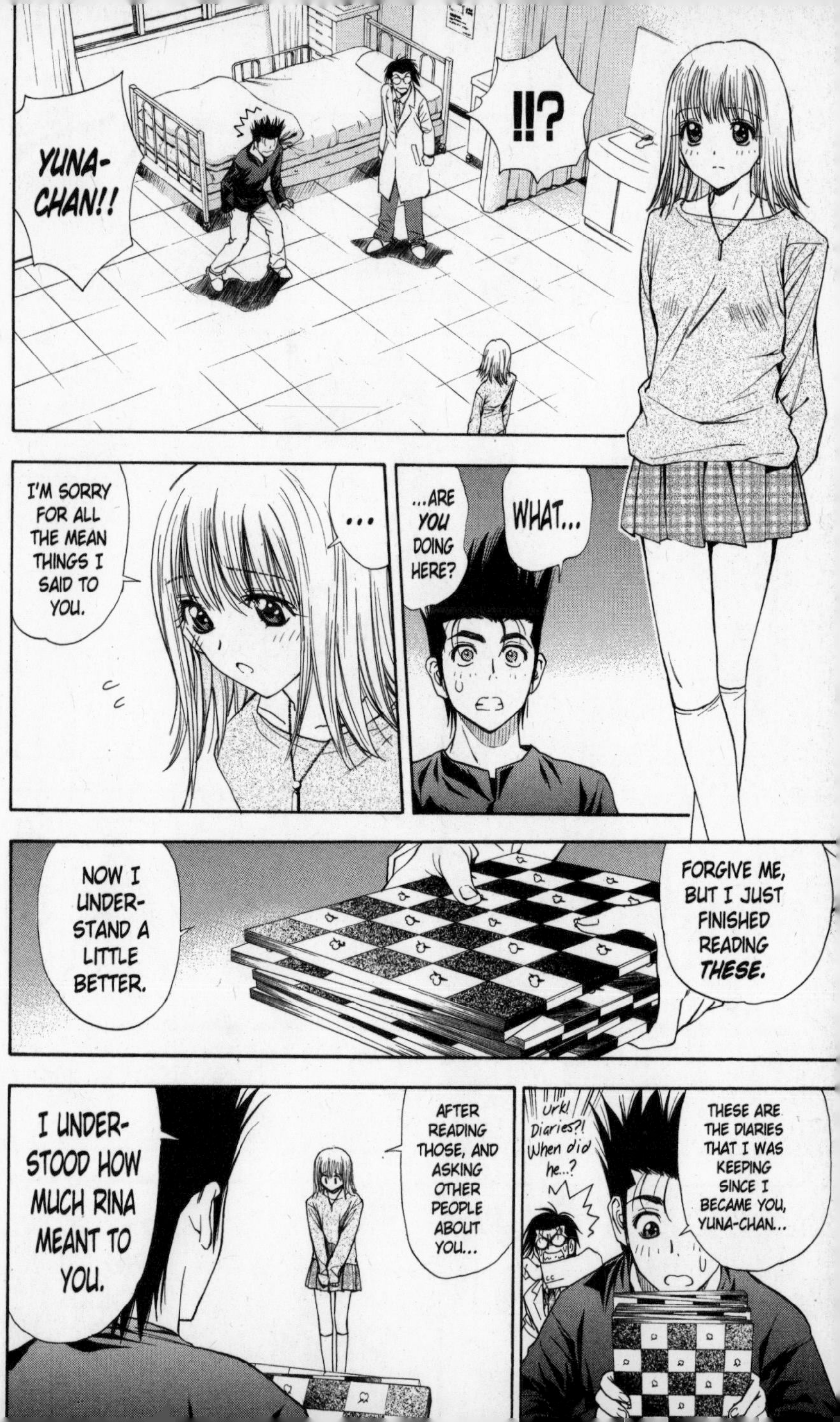
!!?
YUNA-CHAN!!
WHAT...
...ARE YOU DOING HERE?
...
I'M SORRY FOR ALL THE MEAN THINGS I SAID TO YOU.
FORGIVE ME, BUT I JUST FINISHED READING THESE.
NOW I UNDER-STAND A LITTLE BETTER.
THESE ARE THE DIARIES THAT I WAS KEEPING SINCE I BECAME YOU, YUNA-CHAN...
Urk! Diaries?! When did he...?
AFTER READING THOSE, AND ASKING OTHER PEOPLE ABOUT YOU...
I UNDER-STOOD HOW MUCH RINA MEANT TO YOU.

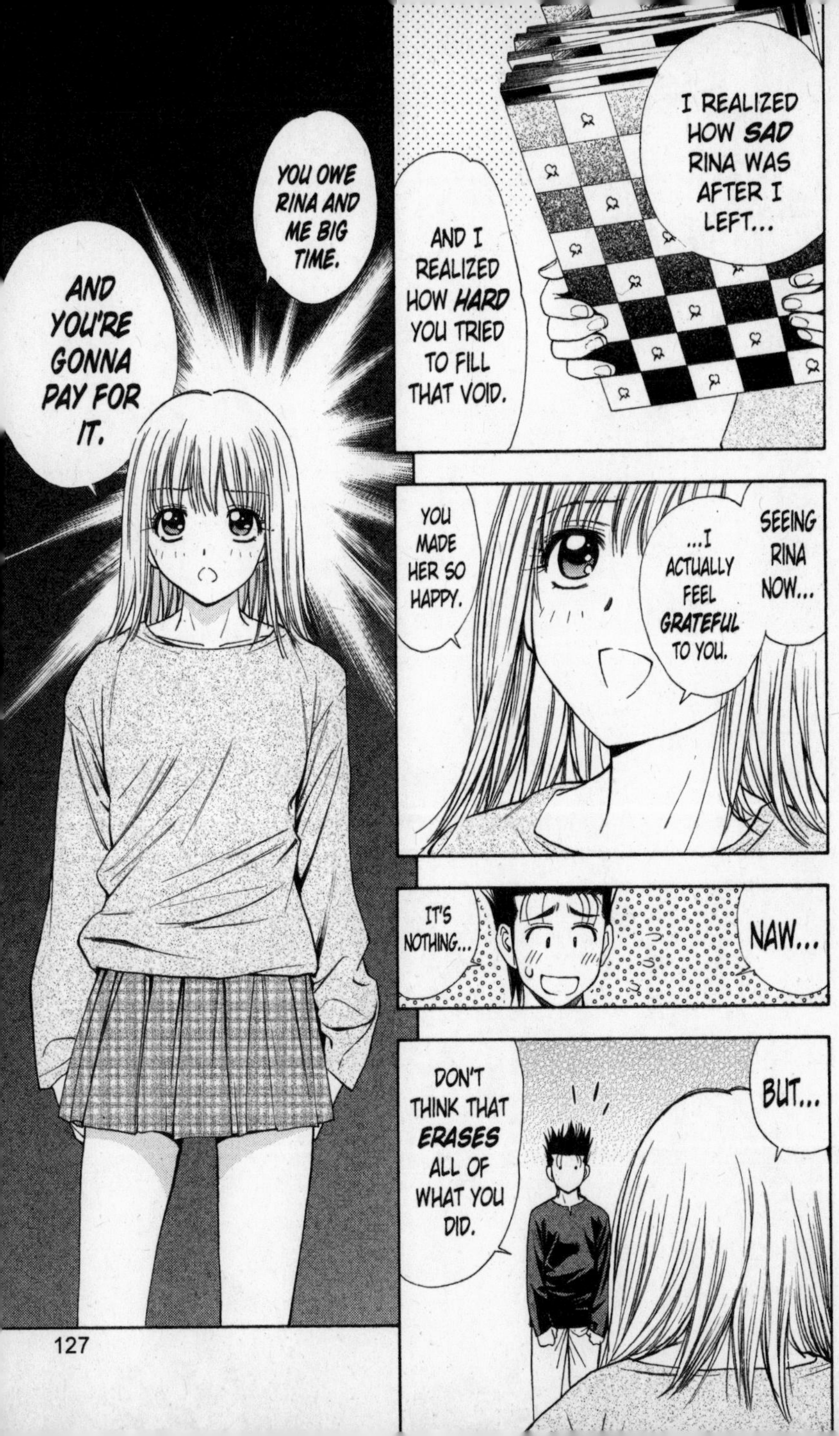
I REALIZED HOW SAD RINA WAS AFTER I LEFT...
AND I REALIZED HOW HARD YOU TRIED TO FILL THAT VOID.
SEEING RINA NOW...
...I ACTUALLY FEEL GRATEFUL TO YOU.
YOU MADE HER SO HAPPY.
NAW...
IT'S NOTHING...
BUT...
DON'T THINK THAT ERASES ALL OF WHAT YOU DID.
YOU OWE RINA AND ME BIG TIME.
AND YOU'RE GONNA PAY FOR IT.

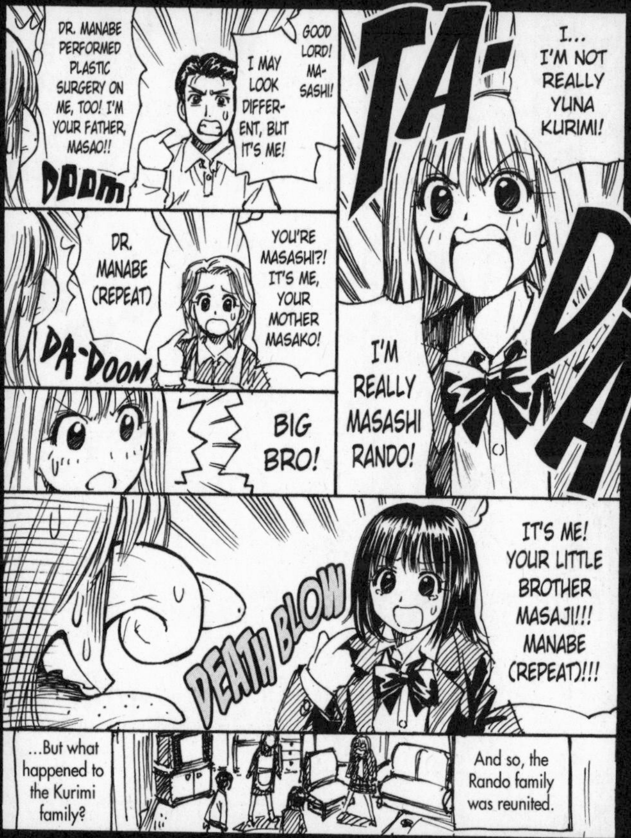
TA-DA
I... I'M NOT REALLY YUNA KURIMI!
I'M REALLY MASASHI RANDO!
GOOD LORD! MA-SASHI!
I MAY LOOK DIFFER-ENT, BUT IT'S ME!
DR. MANABE PERFORMED PLASTIC SURGERY ON ME, TOO! I'M YOUR FATHER, MASAO!!
DOOM
YOU'RE MASASHI?! IT'S ME, YOUR MOTHER MASAKO!
DR. MANABE (REPEAT)
DA-DOOM
BIG BRO!
IT'S ME! YOUR LITTLE BROTHER MASAJI!!! MANABE (REPEAT)!!!
DEATH BLOW
And so, the Rando family was reunited.
...But what happened to the Kurimi family?

# ALTERNATE ENDING #1

THIS IS ONE OF THE MANY ENDINGS I THOUGHT UP FOR THIS SERIES. IT REVEALS THE LOCATION OF THE MISSING RANDO FAMILY, AND I THOUGHT IT WAS A FUNNY TWIST... BUT NATURALLY, OF COURSE, IT GOT REJECTED.

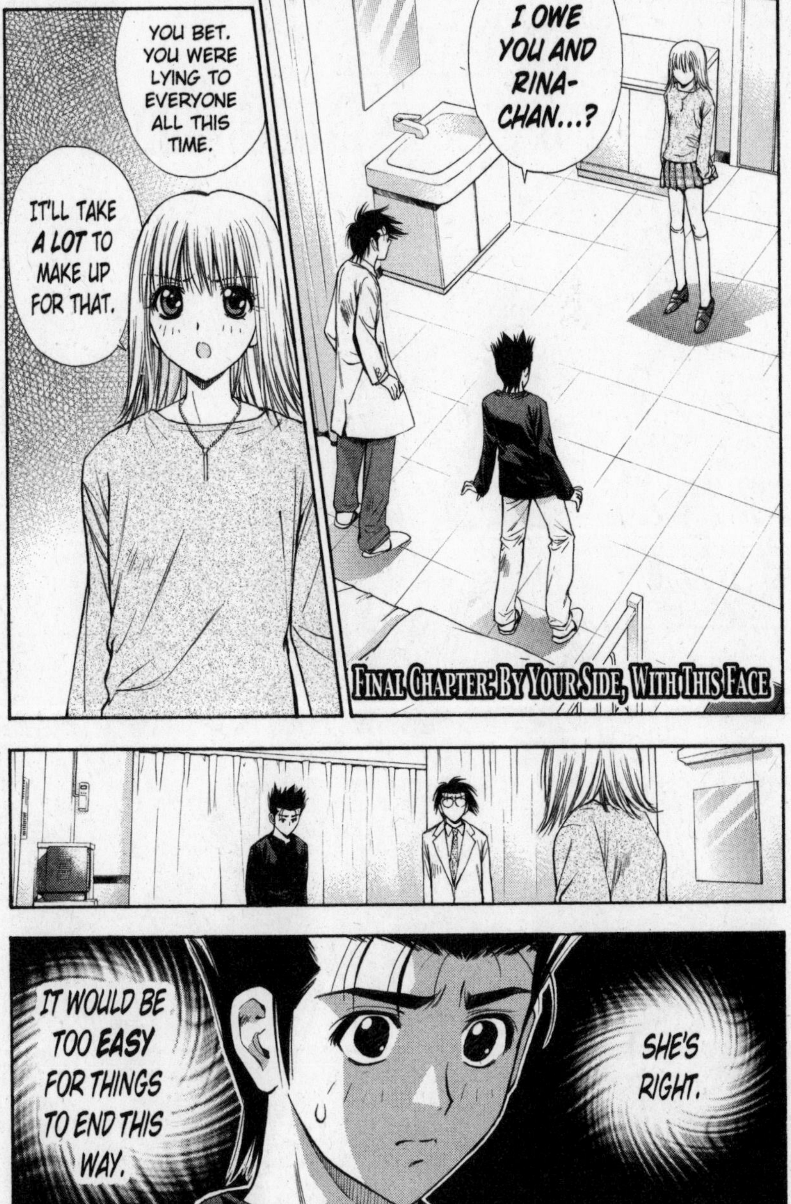
I OWE YOU AND RINA-CHAN...?
FINAL CHAPTER: BY YOUR SIDE, WITH THIS FACE
YOU BET. YOU WERE LYING TO EVERYONE ALL THIS TIME.
IT'LL TAKE A LOT TO MAKE UP FOR THAT.
SHE'S RIGHT.
IT WOULD BE TOO EASY FOR THINGS TO END THIS WAY.

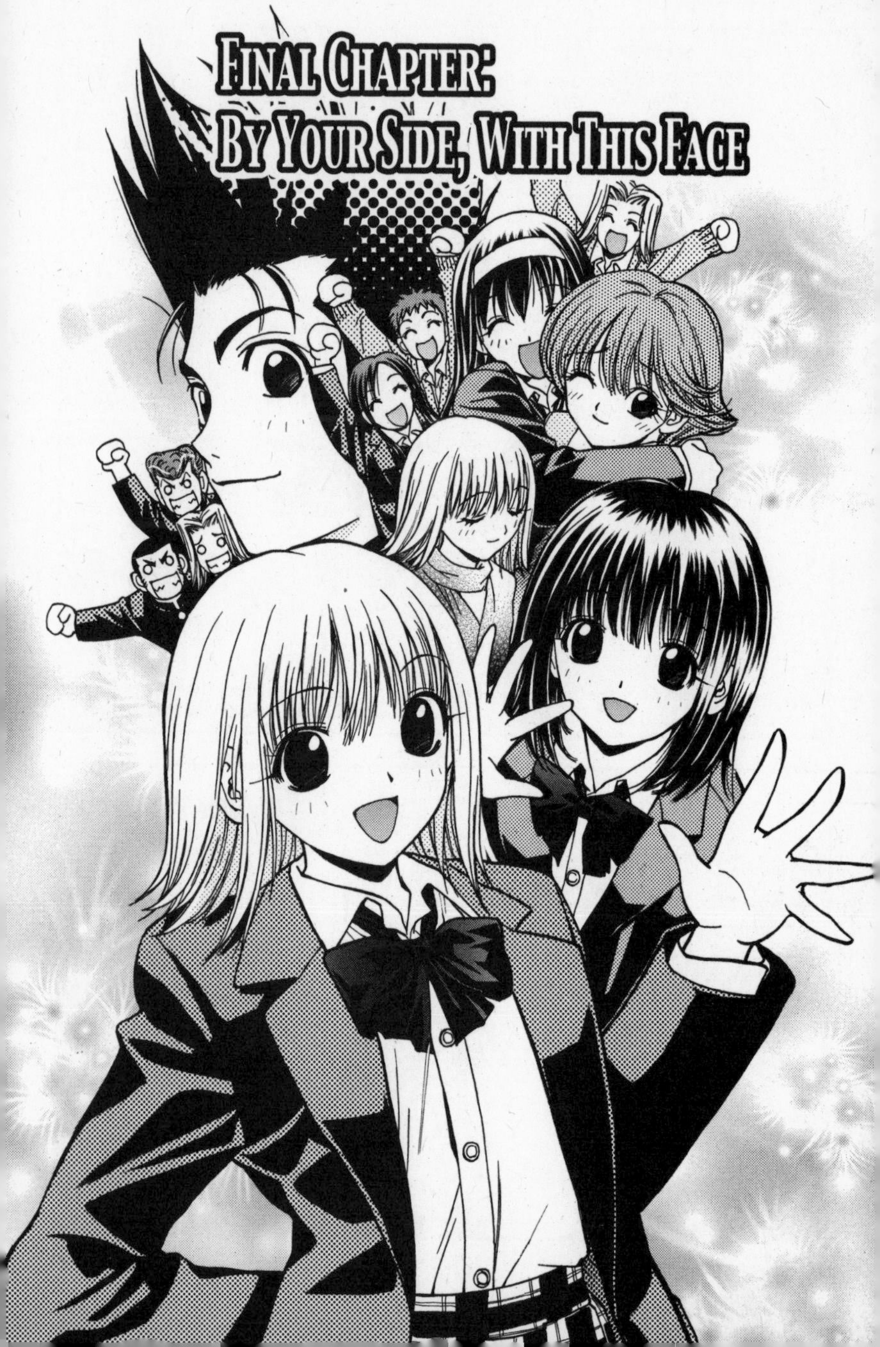
FINAL CHAPTER:
BY YOUR SIDE, WITH THIS FACE

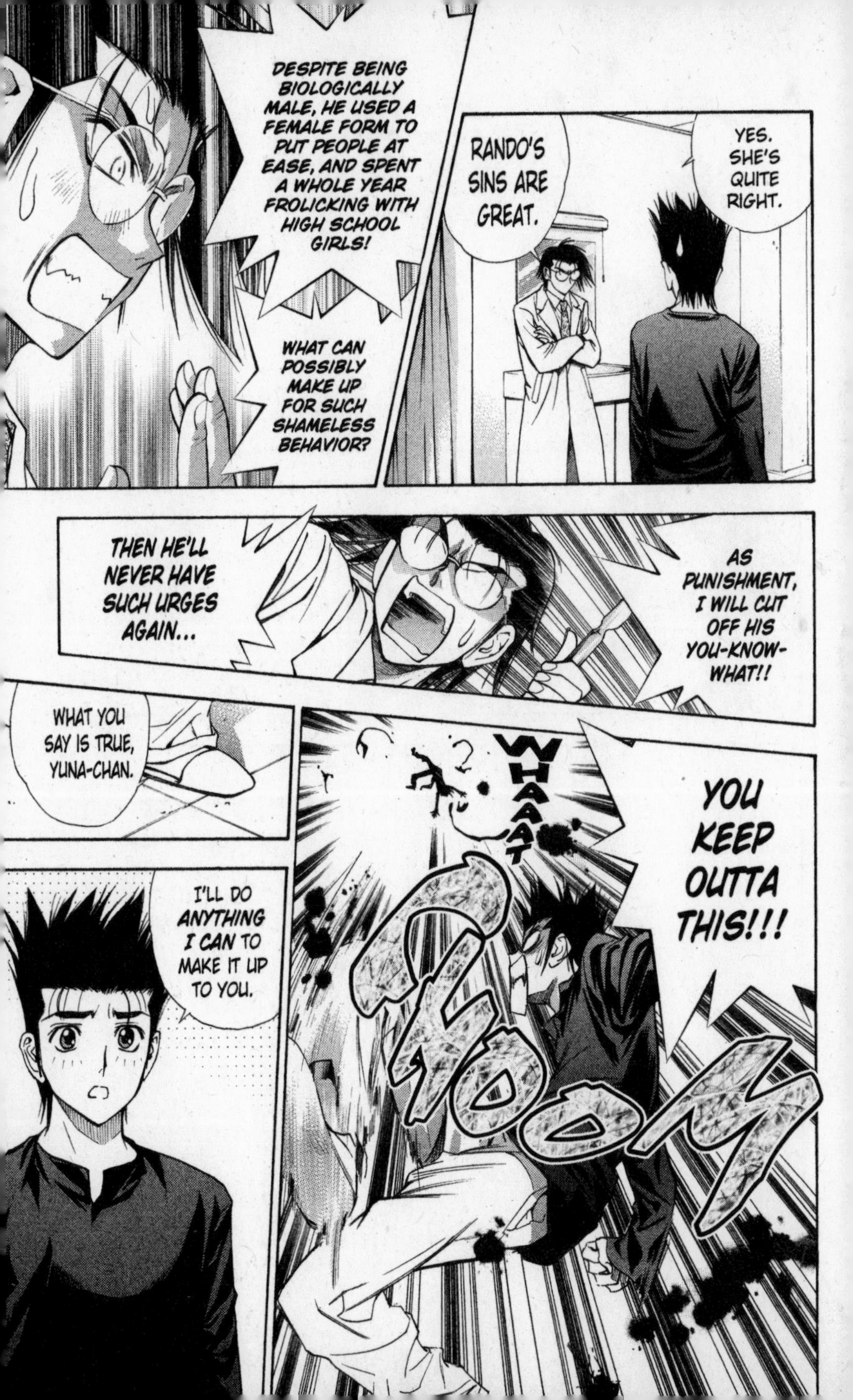
YES. SHE'S QUITE RIGHT.
RANDO'S SINS ARE GREAT.
DESPITE BEING BIOLOGICALLY MALE, HE USED A FEMALE FORM TO PUT PEOPLE AT EASE, AND SPENT A WHOLE YEAR FROLICKING WITH HIGH SCHOOL GIRLS!
WHAT CAN POSSIBLY MAKE UP FOR SUCH SHAMELESS BEHAVIOR?
AS PUNISHMENT, I WILL CUT OFF HIS YOU-KNOW-WHAT!!
THEN HE'LL NEVER HAVE SUCH URGES AGAIN...
YOU KEEP OUTTA THIS!!!
WHAAAT
WHAT YOU SAY IS TRUE, YUNA-CHAN.
I'LL DO ANYTHING I CAN TO MAKE IT UP TO YOU.

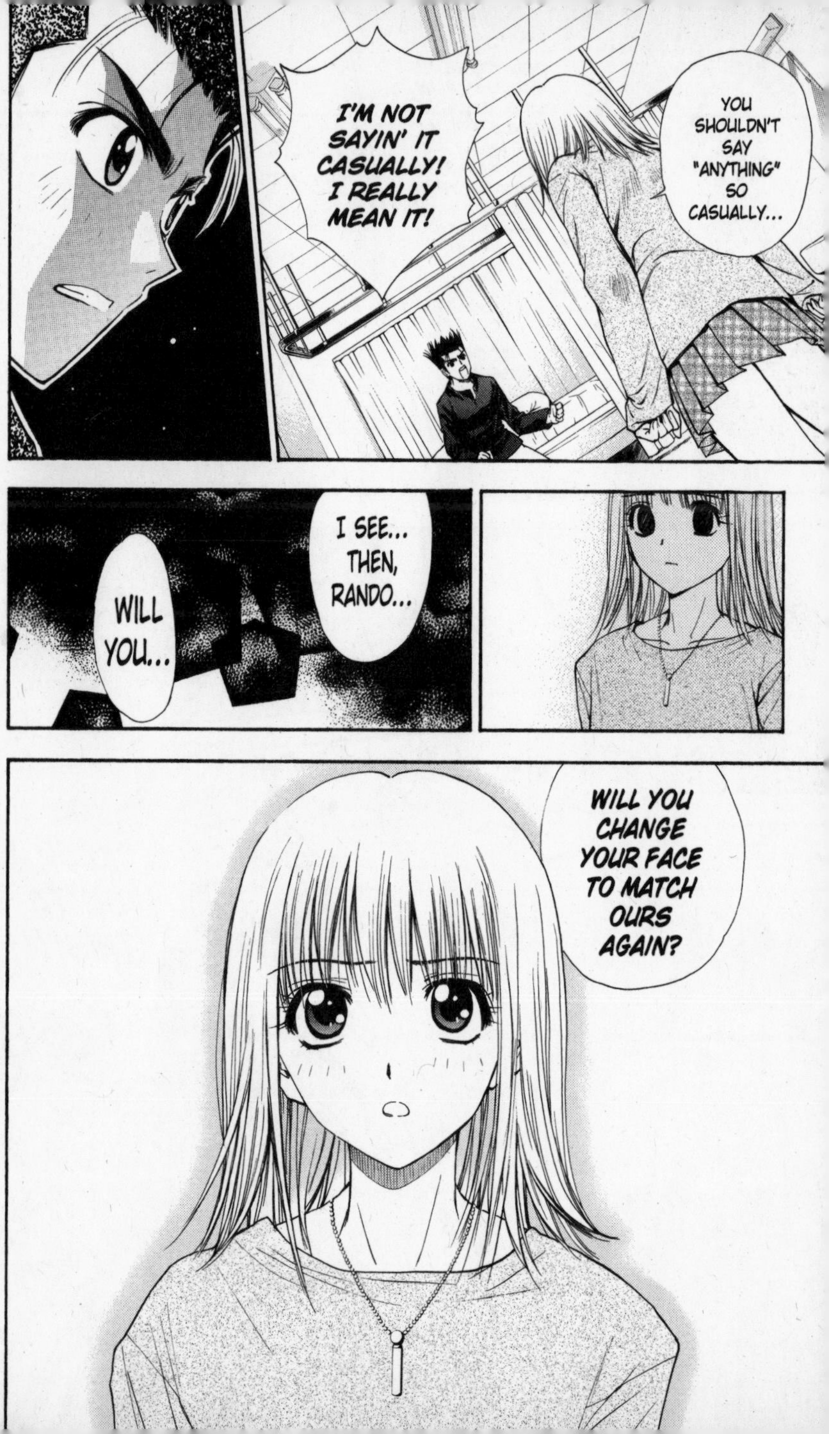
YOU SHOULDN'T SAY "ANYTHING" SO CASUALLY...
I'M NOT SAYIN' IT CASUALLY! I REALLY MEAN IT!
I SEE... THEN, RANDO...
WILL YOU...
WILL YOU CHANGE YOUR FACE TO MATCH OURS AGAIN?

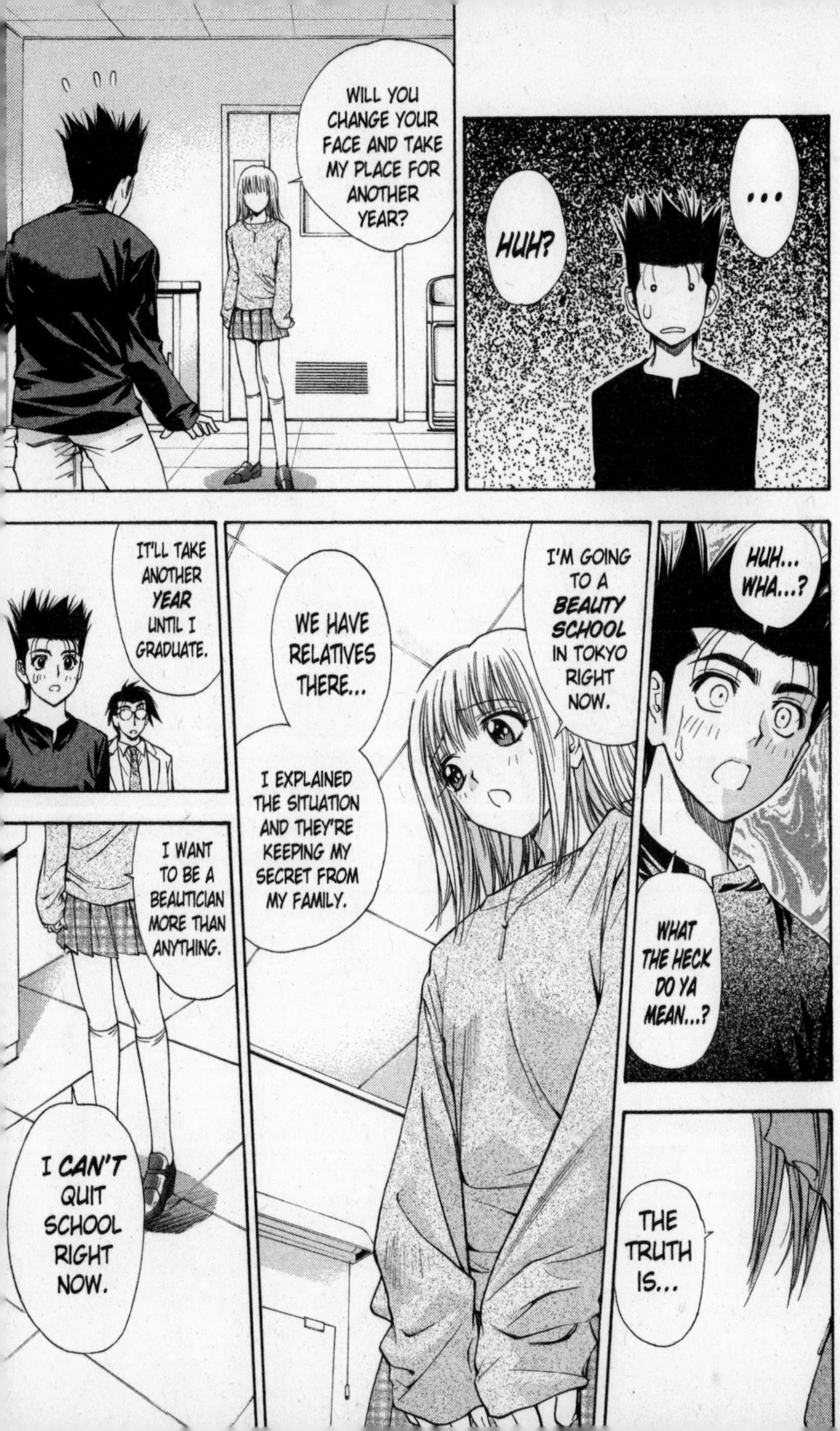
...
HUH?
WILL YOU CHANGE YOUR FACE AND TAKE MY PLACE FOR ANOTHER YEAR?
HUH... WHA...?
WHAT THE HECK DO YA MEAN...?
THE TRUTH IS...
I'M GOING TO A BEAUTY SCHOOL IN TOKYO RIGHT NOW.
WE HAVE RELATIVES THERE...
I EXPLAINED THE SITUATION AND THEY'RE KEEPING MY SECRET FROM MY FAMILY.
IT'LL TAKE ANOTHER YEAR UNTIL I GRADUATE.
I WANT TO BE A BEAUTICIAN MORE THAN ANYTHING.
I CAN'T QUIT SCHOOL RIGHT NOW.

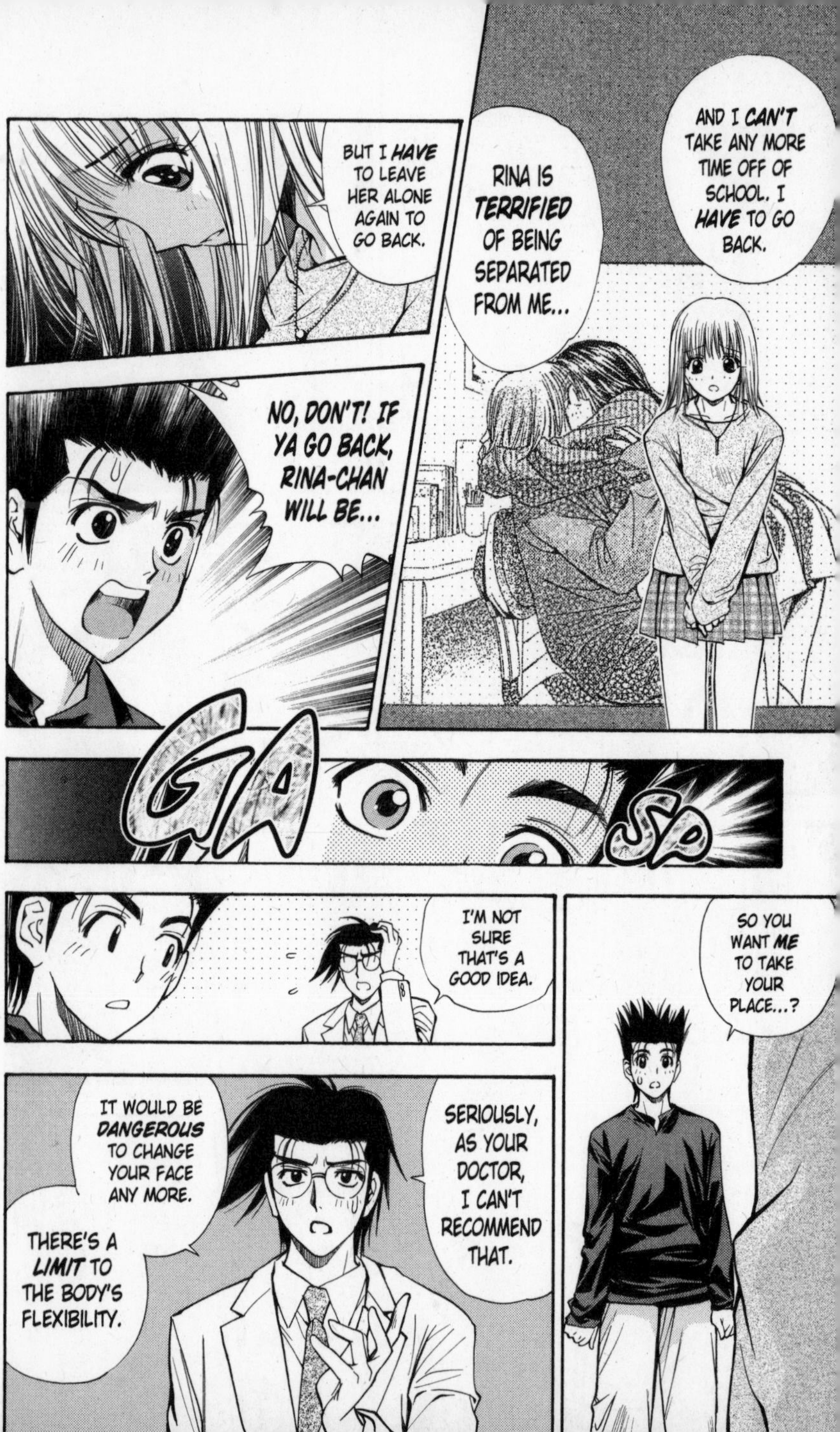
AND I CAN'T TAKE ANY MORE TIME OFF OF SCHOOL. I HAVE TO GO BACK.
RINA IS TERRIFIED OF BEING SEPARATED FROM ME...
BUT I HAVE TO LEAVE HER ALONE AGAIN TO GO BACK.
NO, DON'T! IF YA GO BACK, RINA-CHAN WILL BE...
GASP
SO YOU WANT ME TO TAKE YOUR PLACE...?
I'M NOT SURE THAT'S A GOOD IDEA.
SERIOUSLY, AS YOUR DOCTOR, I CAN'T RECOMMEND THAT.
IT WOULD BE DANGEROUS TO CHANGE YOUR FACE ANY MORE.
THERE'S A LIMIT TO THE BODY'S FLEXIBILITY.

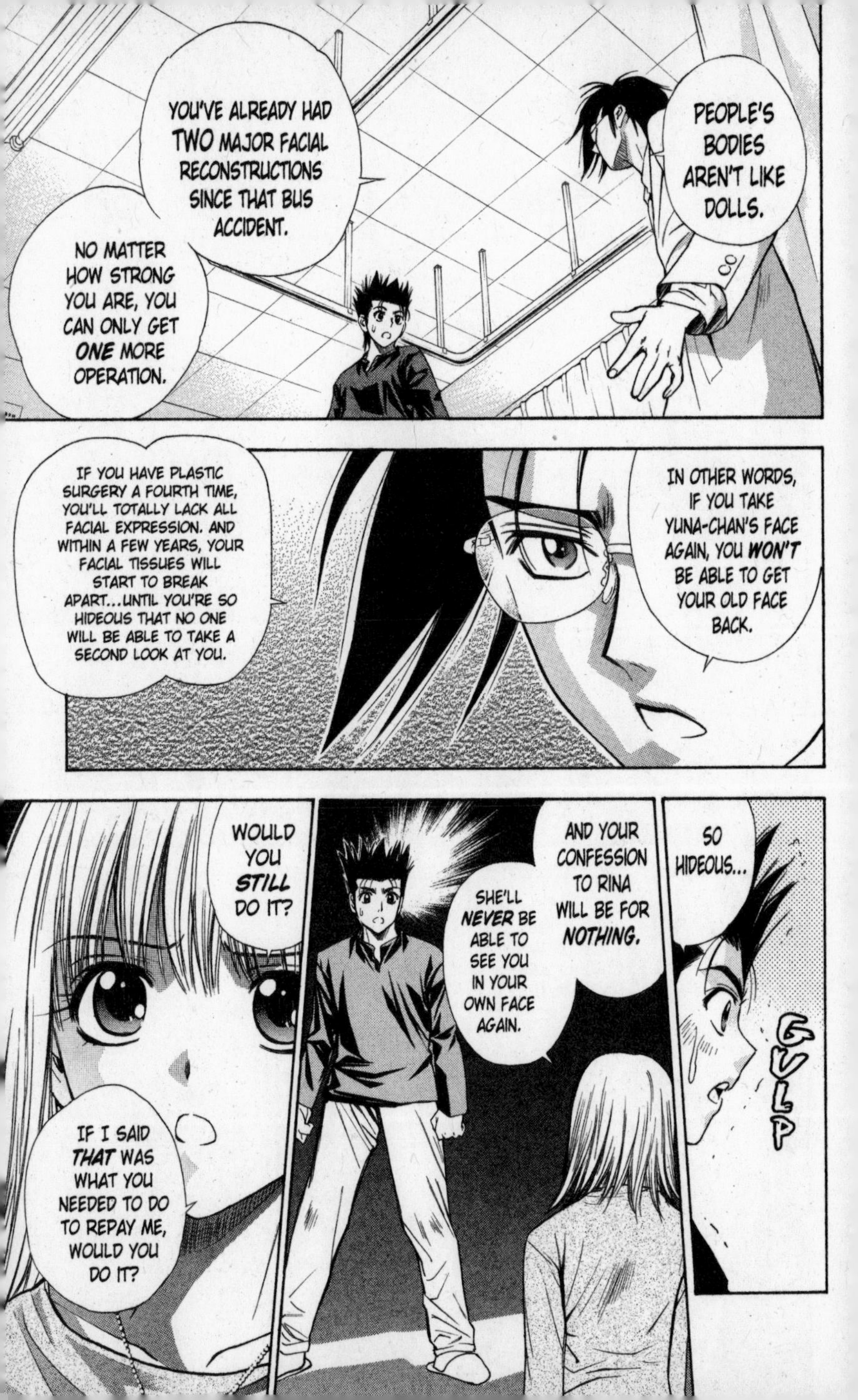
PEOPLE'S BODIES AREN'T LIKE DOLLS.
YOU'VE ALREADY HAD TWO MAJOR FACIAL RECONSTRUCTIONS SINCE THAT BUS ACCIDENT.
NO MATTER HOW STRONG YOU ARE, YOU CAN ONLY GET ONE MORE OPERATION.
IN OTHER WORDS, IF YOU TAKE YUNA-CHAN'S FACE AGAIN, YOU WON'T BE ABLE TO GET YOUR OLD FACE BACK.
IF YOU HAVE PLASTIC SURGERY A FOURTH TIME, YOU'LL TOTALLY LACK ALL FACIAL EXPRESSION. AND WITHIN A FEW YEARS, YOUR FACIAL TISSUES WILL START TO BREAK APART...UNTIL YOU'RE SO HIDEOUS THAT NO ONE WILL BE ABLE TO TAKE A SECOND LOOK AT YOU.
SO HIDEOUS...
GULP
AND YOUR CONFESSION TO RINA WILL BE FOR NOTHING.
SHE'LL NEVER BE ABLE TO SEE YOU IN YOUR OWN FACE AGAIN.
WOULD YOU STILL DO IT?
IF I SAID THAT WAS WHAT YOU NEEDED TO DO TO REPAY ME, WOULD YOU DO IT?

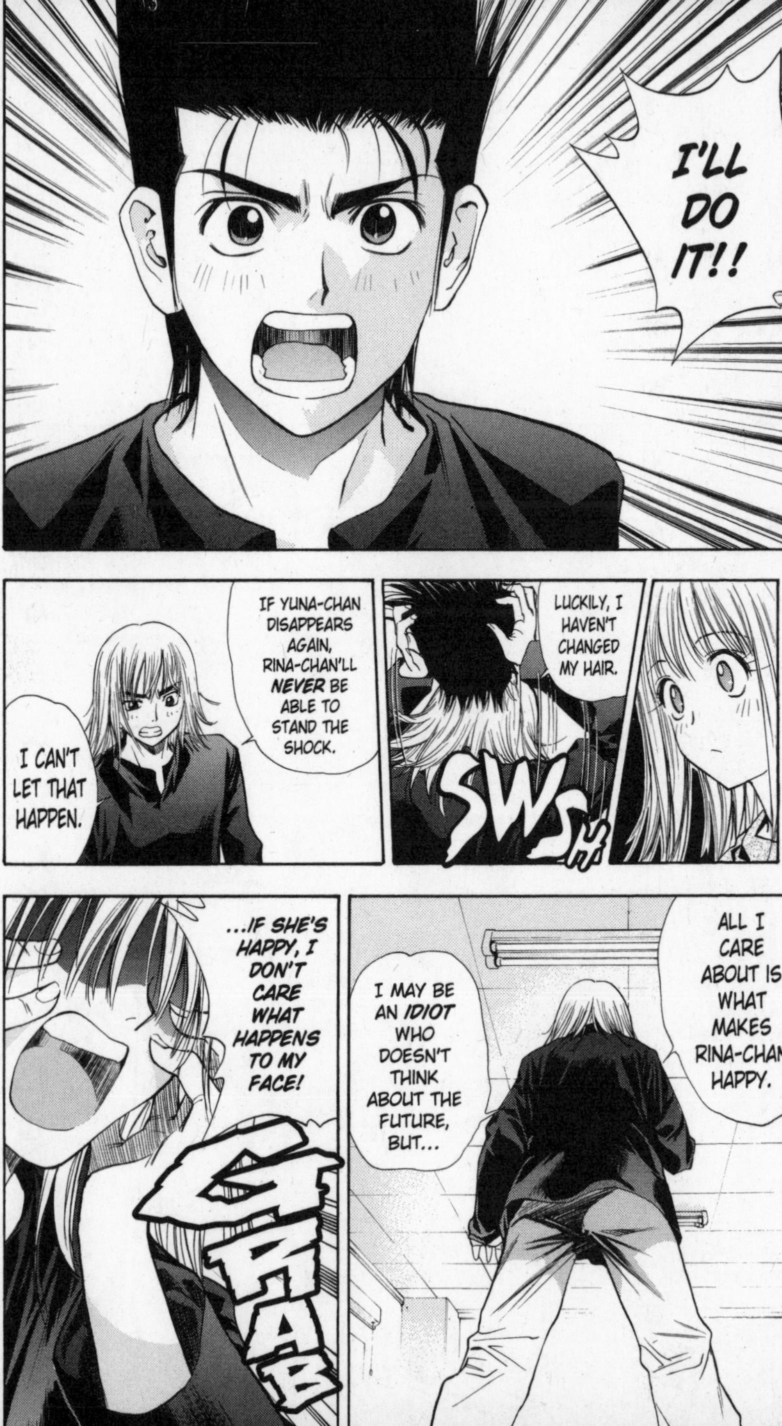
I'LL DO IT!!
LUCKILY, I HAVEN'T CHANGED MY HAIR.
SWSH
IF YUNA-CHAN DISAPPEARS AGAIN, RINA-CHAN'LL *NEVER* BE ABLE TO STAND THE SHOCK.
I CAN'T LET THAT HAPPEN.
ALL I CARE ABOUT IS WHAT MAKES RINA-CHAN HAPPY.
I MAY BE AN *IDIOT* WHO DOESN'T THINK ABOUT THE FUTURE, BUT...
...IF SHE'S HAPPY, I DON'T CARE WHAT HAPPENS TO MY FACE!
GRAB

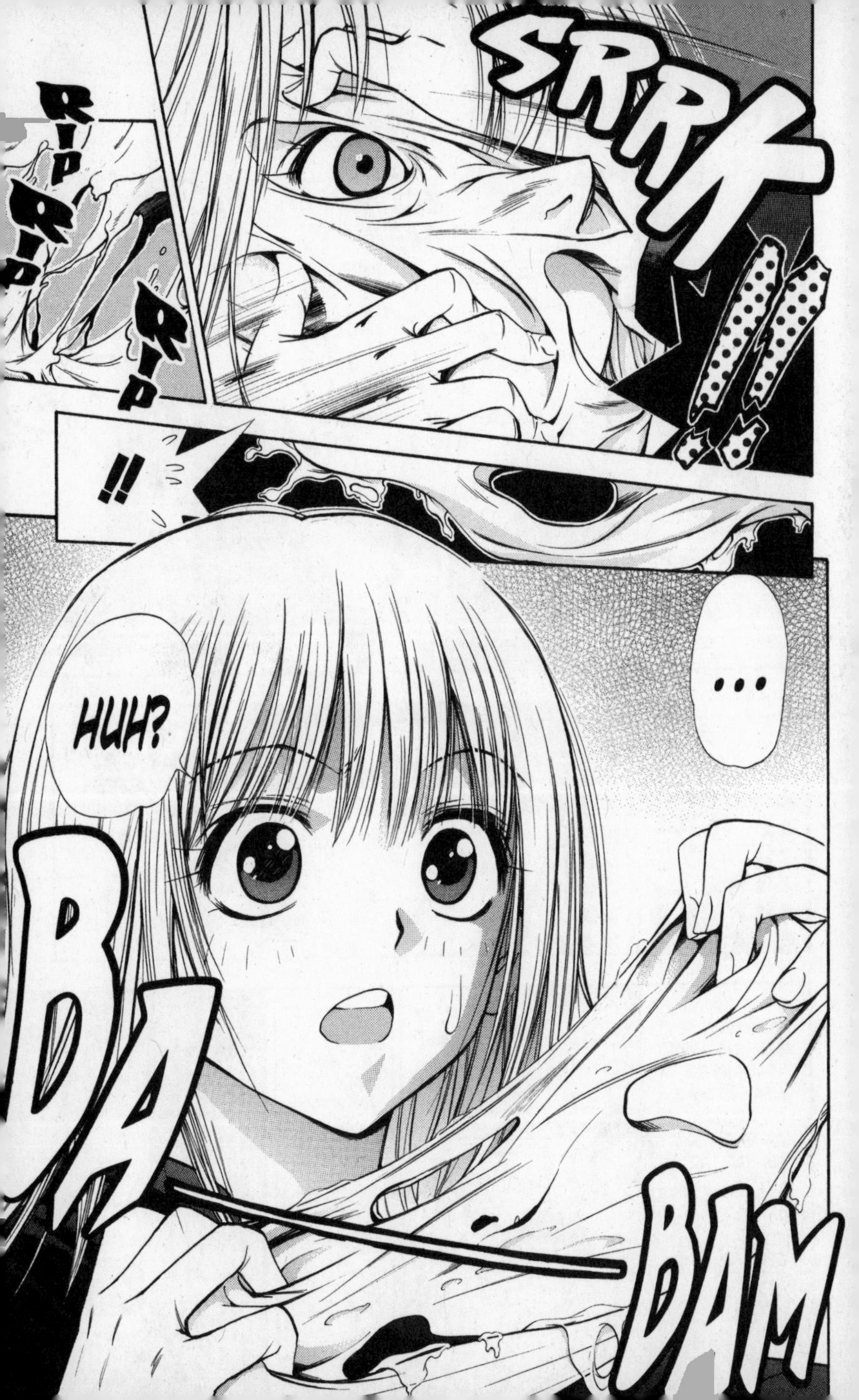
SRRK!!
RIP RIP
RIP RIP
!!
...
HUH?
BAM
BA

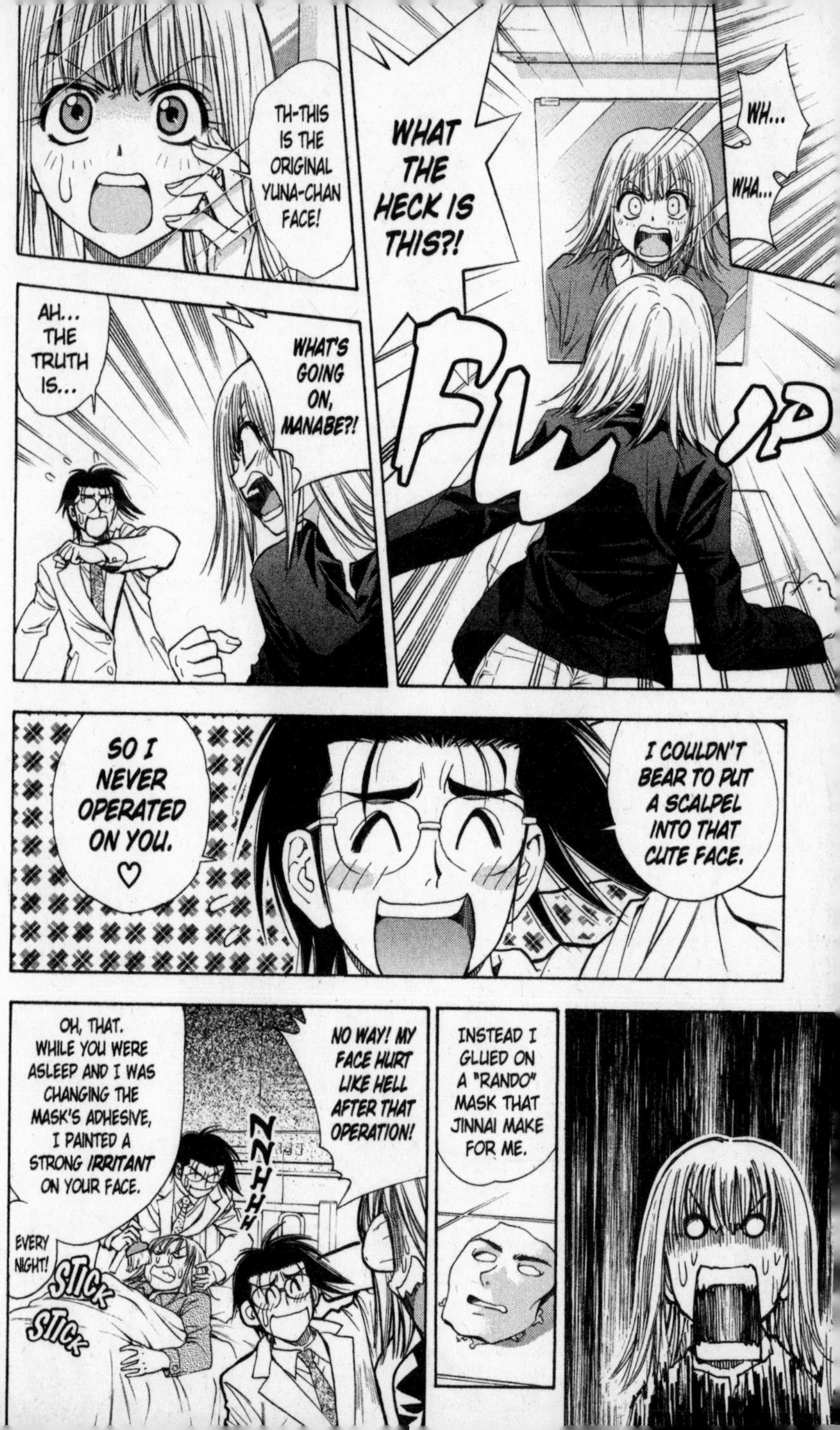
WH...
WHA...
WHAT THE HECK IS THIS?!
FLIP
TH-THIS IS THE ORIGINAL YUNA-CHAN FACE!
WHAT'S GOING ON, MANABE?!
AH... THE TRUTH IS...
I COULDN'T BEAR TO PUT A SCALPEL INTO THAT CUTE FACE.
SO I NEVER OPERATED ON YOU. ♡
INSTEAD I GLUED ON A "RANDO" MASK THAT JINNAI MAKE FOR ME.
NO WAY! MY FACE HURT LIKE HELL AFTER THAT OPERATION!
OH, THAT. WHILE YOU WERE ASLEEP AND I WAS CHANGING THE MASK'S ADHESIVE, I PAINTED A STRONG IRRITANT ON YOUR FACE.
NNHHHH
EVERY NIGHT!
STICK
STICK

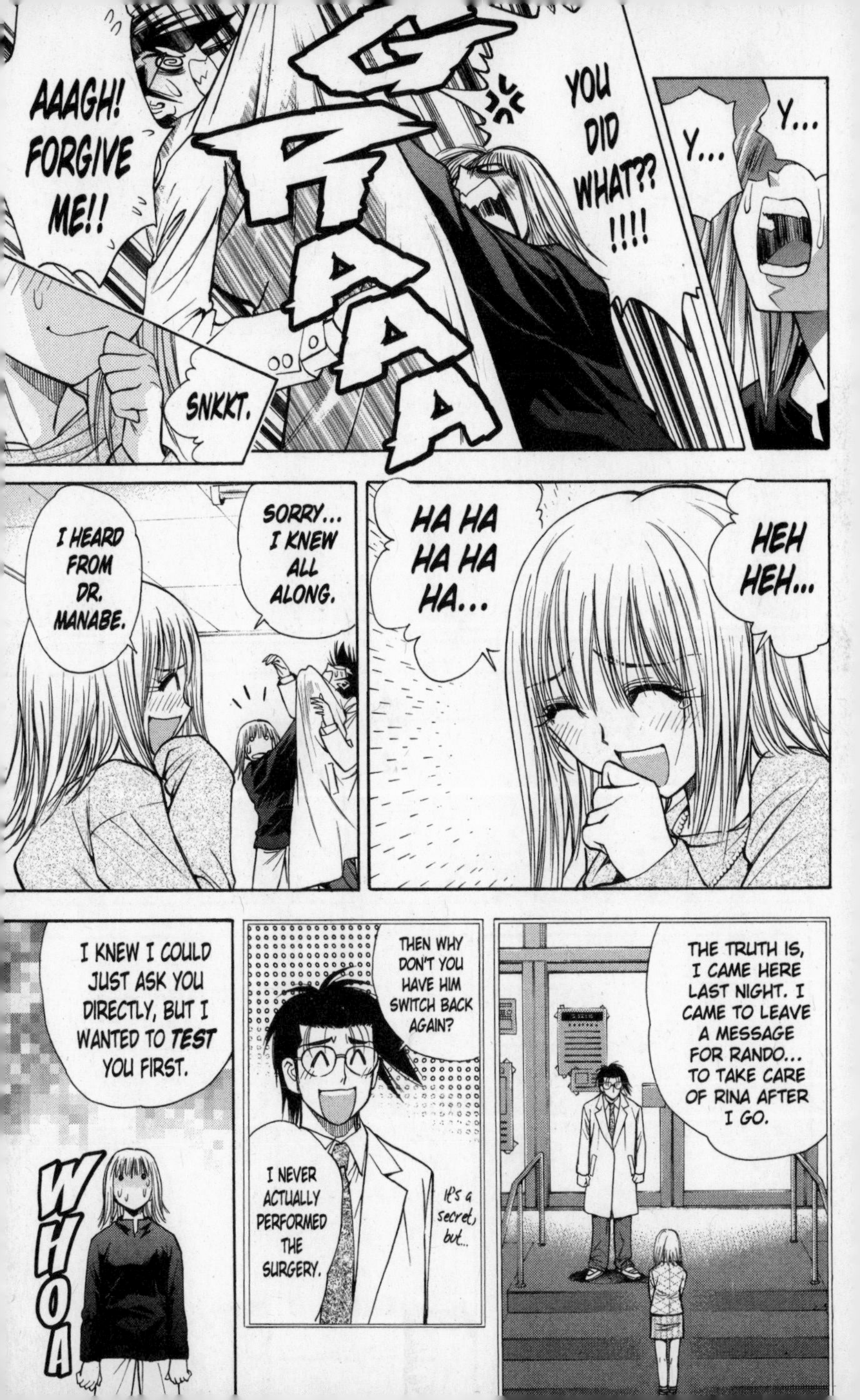
Y... Y...
YOU DID WHAT?? !!!!
GAAAA
AAAGH! FORGIVE ME!!
SNKKT.
HEH HEH...
HA HA HA HA HA...
SORRY... I KNEW ALL ALONG.
I HEARD FROM DR. MANABE.
THE TRUTH IS, I CAME HERE LAST NIGHT. I CAME TO LEAVE A MESSAGE FOR RANDO... TO TAKE CARE OF RINA AFTER I GO.
THEN WHY DON'T YOU HAVE HIM SWITCH BACK AGAIN?
It's a secret, but...
I NEVER ACTUALLY PERFORMED THE SURGERY.
I KNEW I COULD JUST ASK YOU DIRECTLY, BUT I WANTED TO TEST YOU FIRST.
WHOA

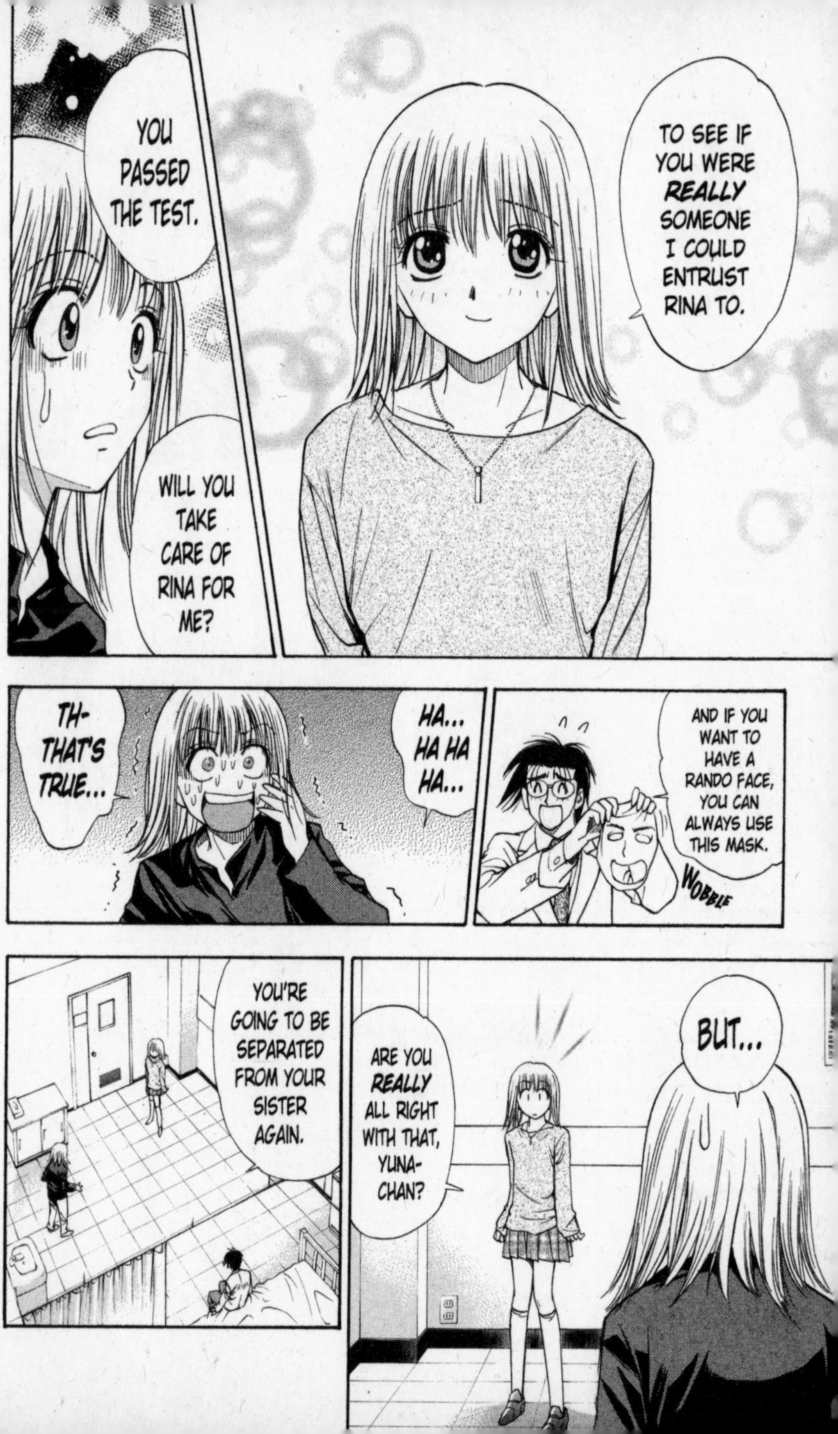
TO SEE IF YOU WERE REALLY SOMEONE I COULD ENTRUST RINA TO.
YOU PASSED THE TEST.
WILL YOU TAKE CARE OF RINA FOR ME?
AND IF YOU WANT TO HAVE A RANDO FACE, YOU CAN ALWAYS USE THIS MASK.
WOBBLE
HA... HA HA HA...
TH- THAT'S TRUE...
BUT...
ARE YOU REALLY ALL RIGHT WITH THAT, YUNA-CHAN?
YOU'RE GOING TO BE SEPARATED FROM YOUR SISTER AGAIN.

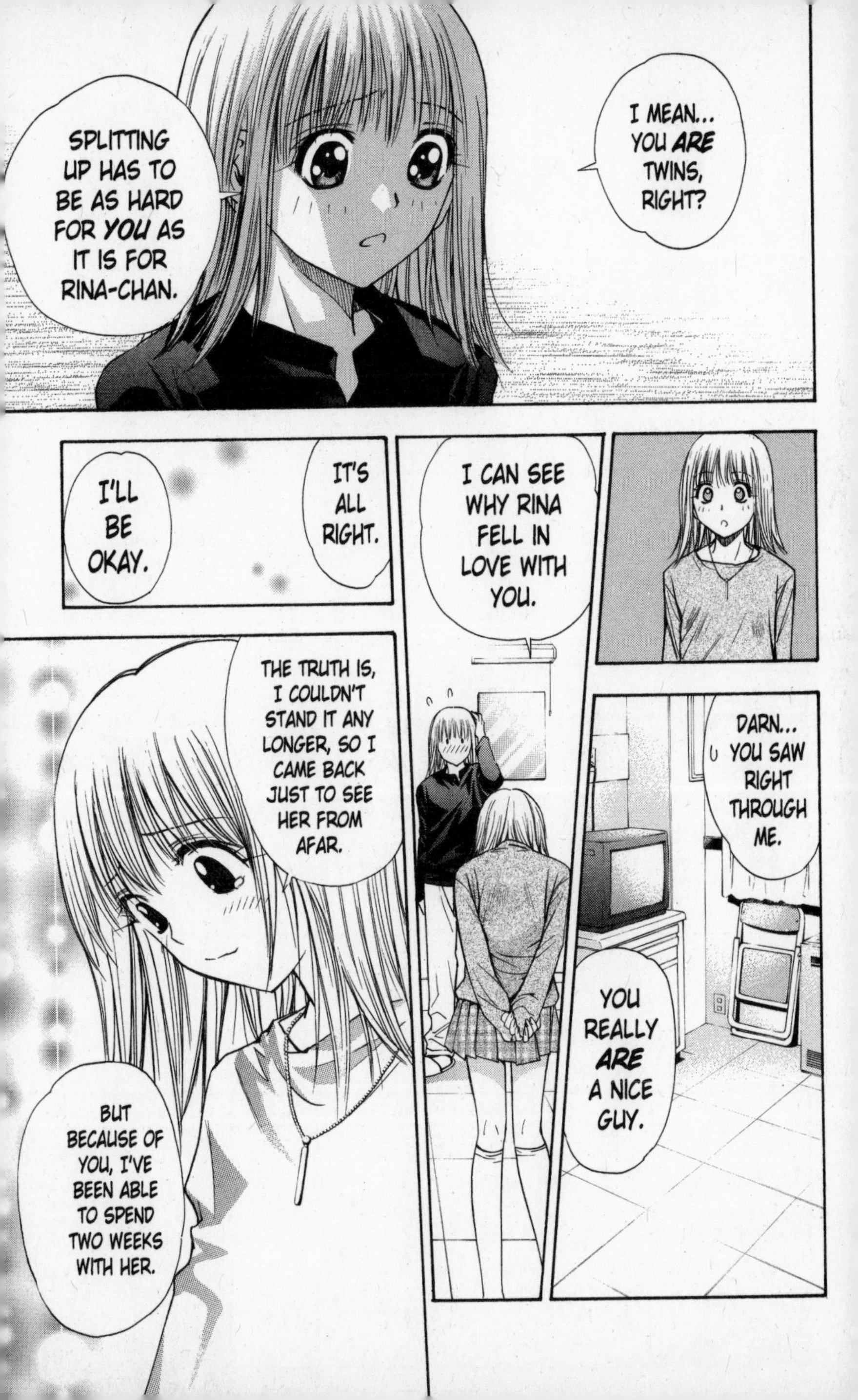
I MEAN... YOU ARE TWINS, RIGHT?
SPLITTING UP HAS TO BE AS HARD FOR YOU AS IT IS FOR RINA-CHAN.
DARN... YOU SAW RIGHT THROUGH ME.
YOU REALLY ARE A NICE GUY.
I CAN SEE WHY RINA FELL IN LOVE WITH YOU.
IT'S ALL RIGHT.
I'LL BE OKAY.
THE TRUTH IS, I COULDN'T STAND IT ANY LONGER, SO I CAME BACK JUST TO SEE HER FROM AFAR.
BUT BECAUSE OF YOU, I'VE BEEN ABLE TO SPEND TWO WEEKS WITH HER.

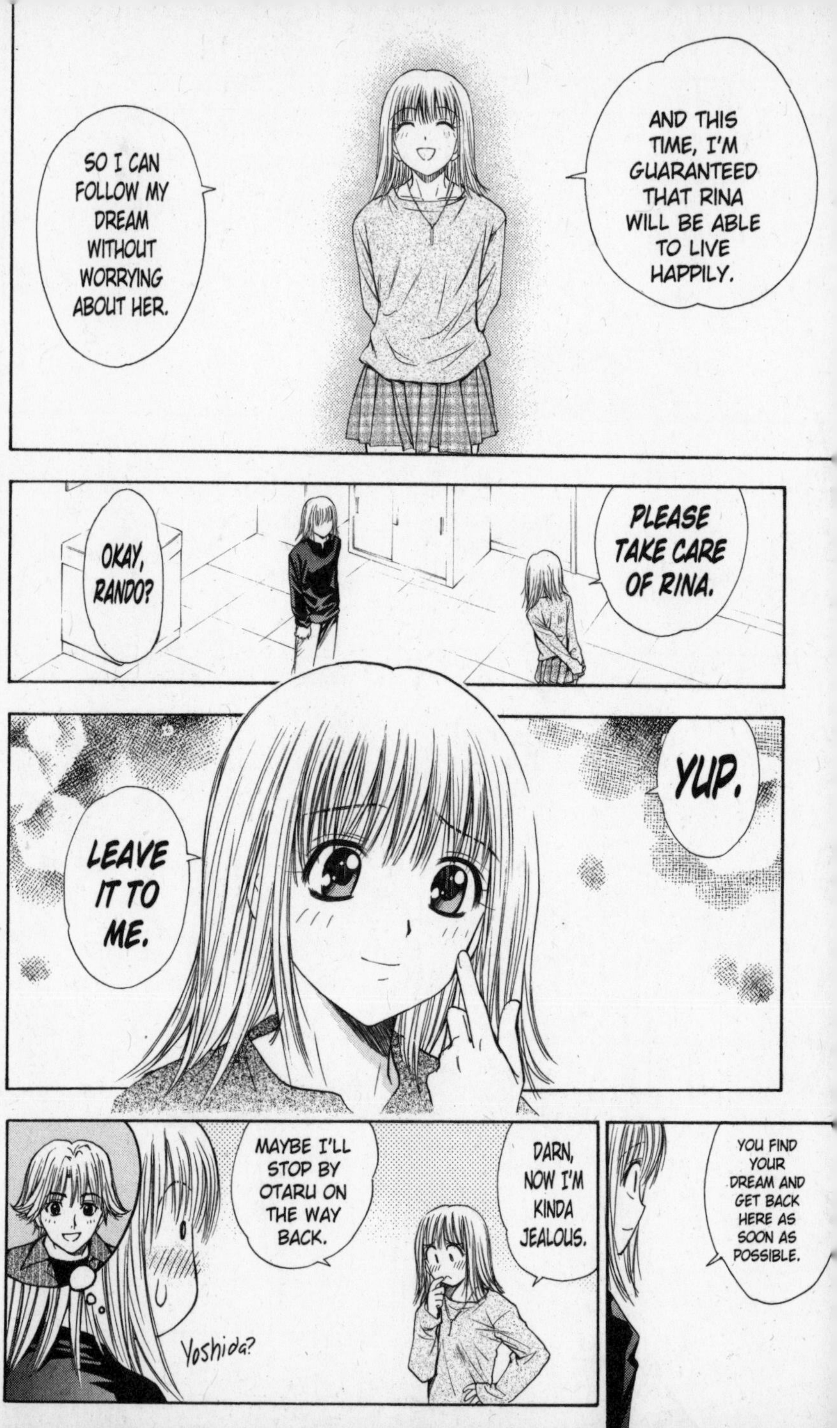
AND THIS TIME, I'M GUARANTEED THAT RINA WILL BE ABLE TO LIVE HAPPILY.
SO I CAN FOLLOW MY DREAM WITHOUT WORRYING ABOUT HER.
PLEASE TAKE CARE OF RINA.
OKAY, RANDO?
YUP.
LEAVE IT TO ME.
YOU FIND YOUR DREAM AND GET BACK HERE AS SOON AS POSSIBLE.
DARN, NOW I'M KINDA JEALOUS.
MAYBE I'LL STOP BY OTARU ON THE WAY BACK.
Yoshida?

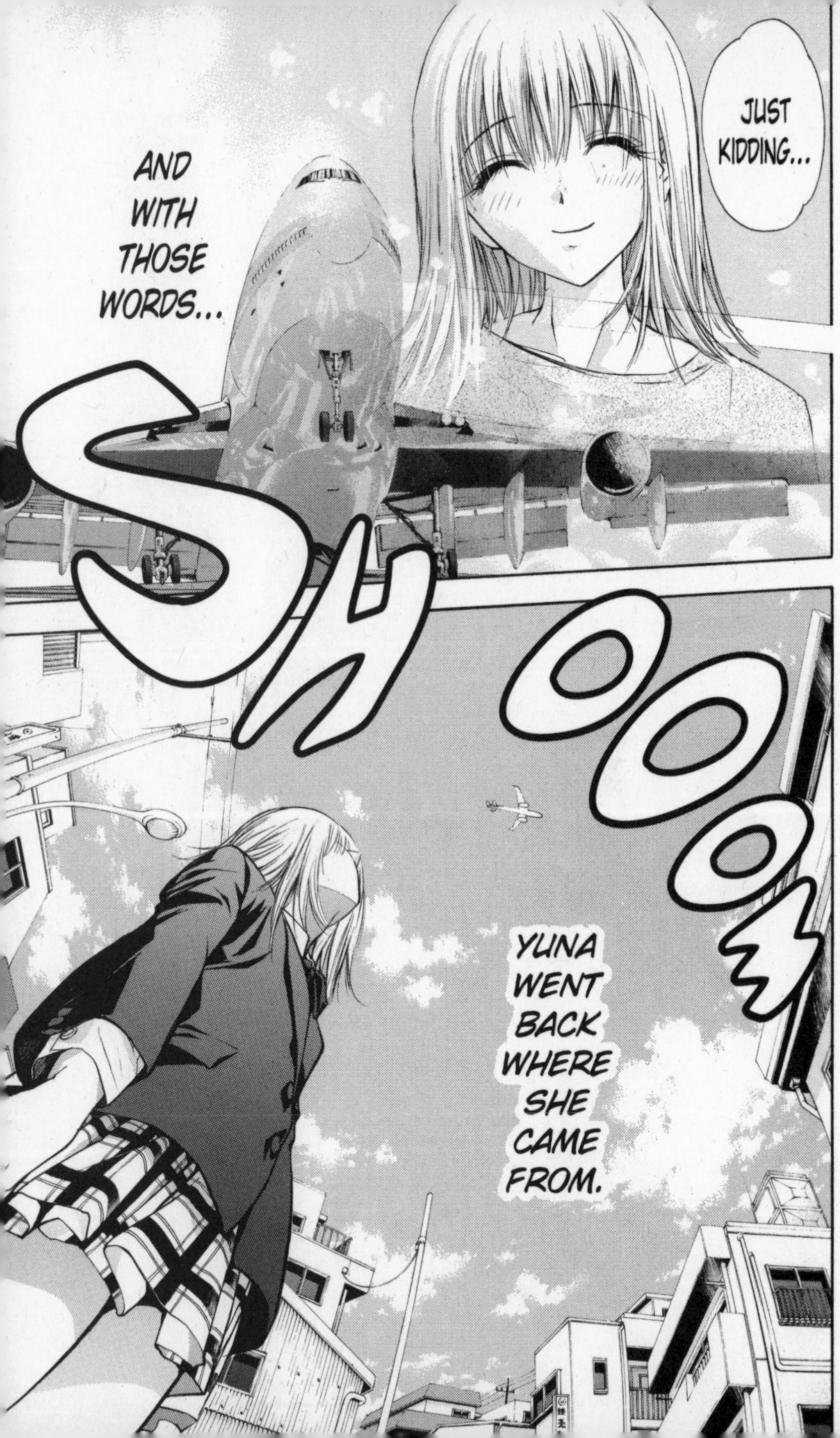
JUST KIDDING...
AND WITH THOSE WORDS...
SHOOOOOM
YUNA WENT BACK WHERE SHE CAME FROM.

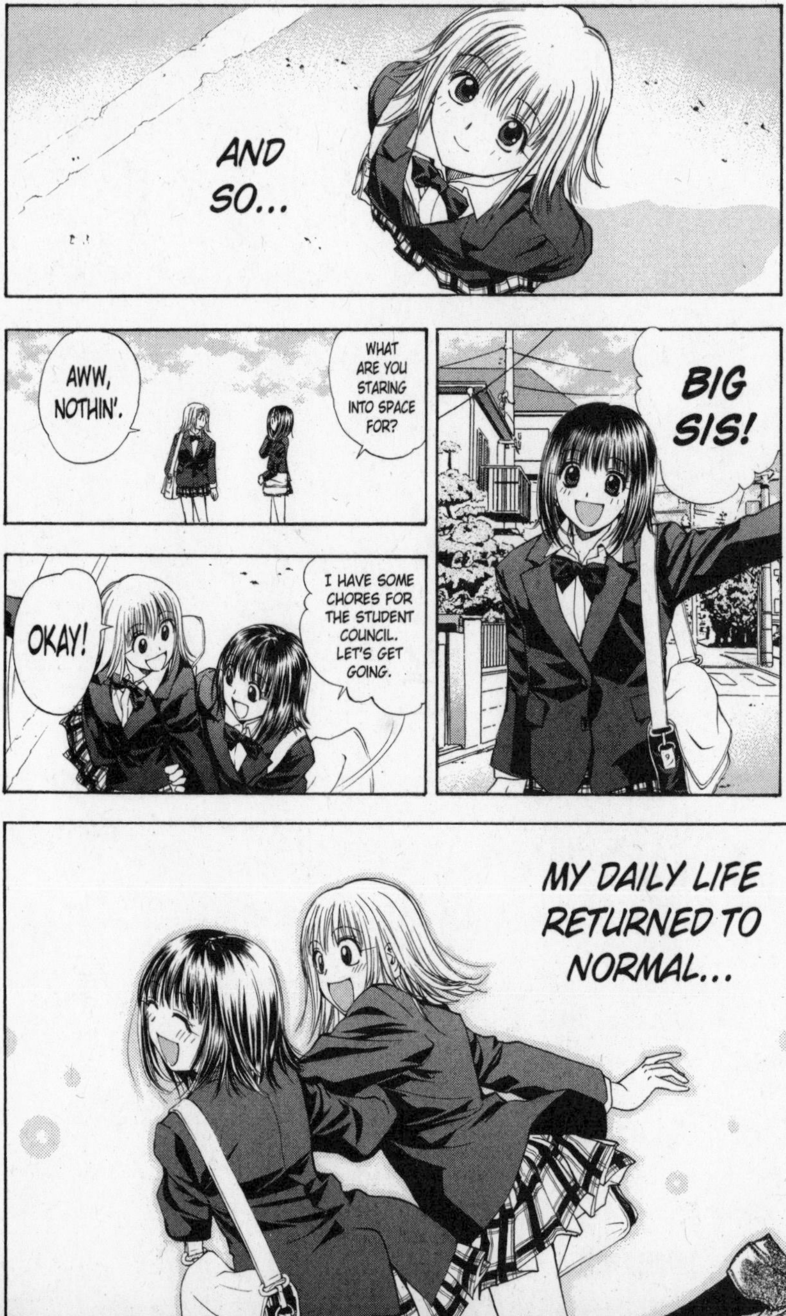
AND SO...
BIG SIS!
WHAT ARE YOU STARING INTO SPACE FOR?
AWW, NOTHIN'.
I HAVE SOME CHORES FOR THE STUDENT COUNCIL. LET'S GET GOING.
OKAY!
MY DAILY LIFE RETURNED TO NORMAL...

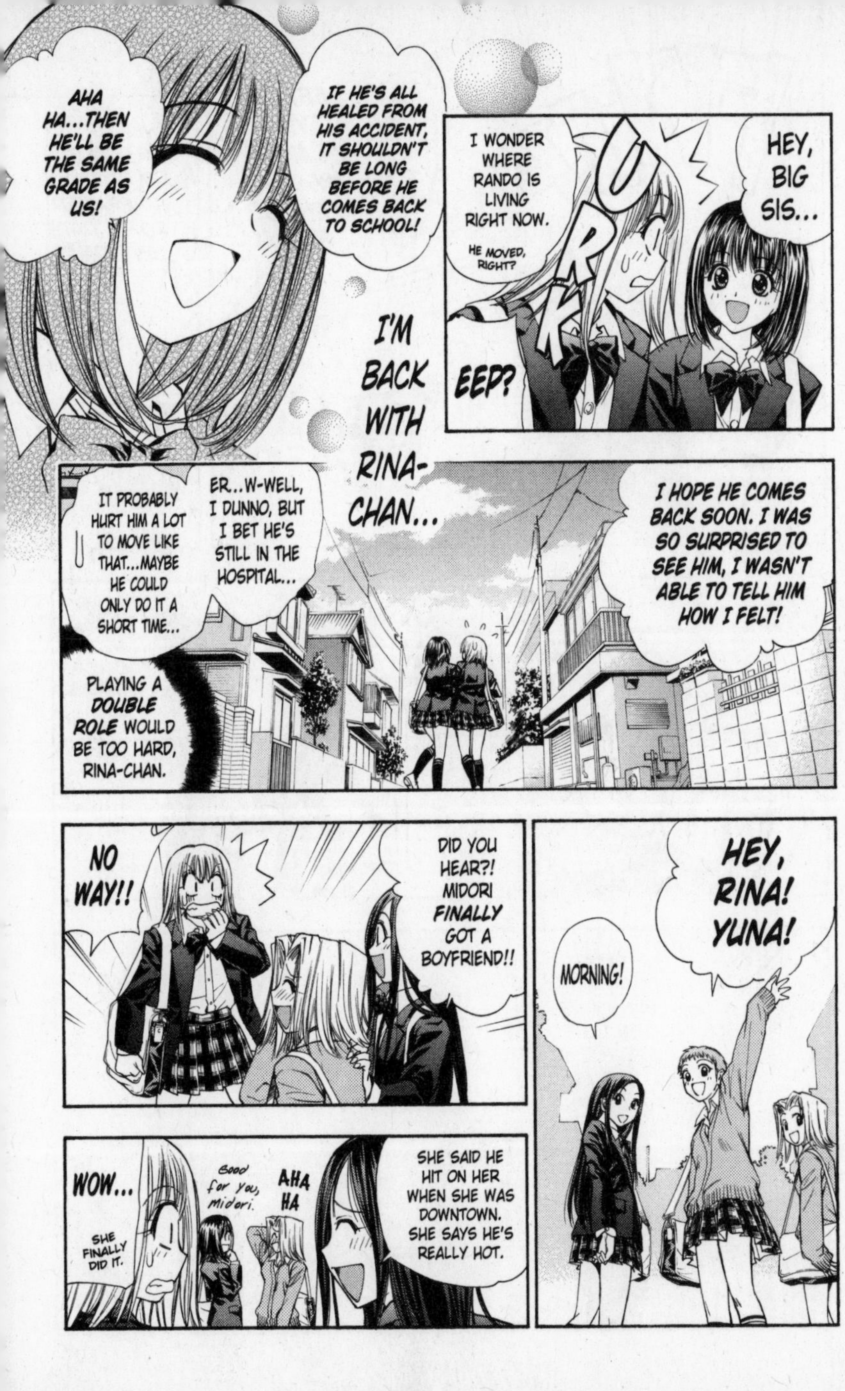

HEY, BIG SIS...
I WONDER WHERE RANDO IS LIVING RIGHT NOW.
HE MOVED, RIGHT?
URK
EEP?
IF HE'S ALL HEALED FROM HIS ACCIDENT, IT SHOULDN'T BE LONG BEFORE HE COMES BACK TO SCHOOL!
AHA HA...THEN HE'LL BE THE SAME GRADE AS US!
I'M BACK WITH RINA-CHAN...
I HOPE HE COMES BACK SOON. I WAS SO SURPRISED TO SEE HIM, I WASN'T ABLE TO TELL HIM HOW I FELT!
ER...W-WELL, I DUNNO, BUT I BET HE'S STILL IN THE HOSPITAL...
IT PROBABLY HURT HIM A LOT TO MOVE LIKE THAT...MAYBE HE COULD ONLY DO IT A SHORT TIME...
PLAYING A DOUBLE ROLE WOULD BE TOO HARD, RINA-CHAN.
HEY, RINA! YUNA!
MORNING!
DID YOU HEAR?! MIDORI FINALLY GOT A BOYFRIEND!!
NO WAY!!
SHE SAID HE HIT ON HER WHEN SHE WAS DOWNTOWN. SHE SAYS HE'S REALLY HOT.
AHA HA
Good for you, midori.
WOW...
SHE FINALLY DID IT.

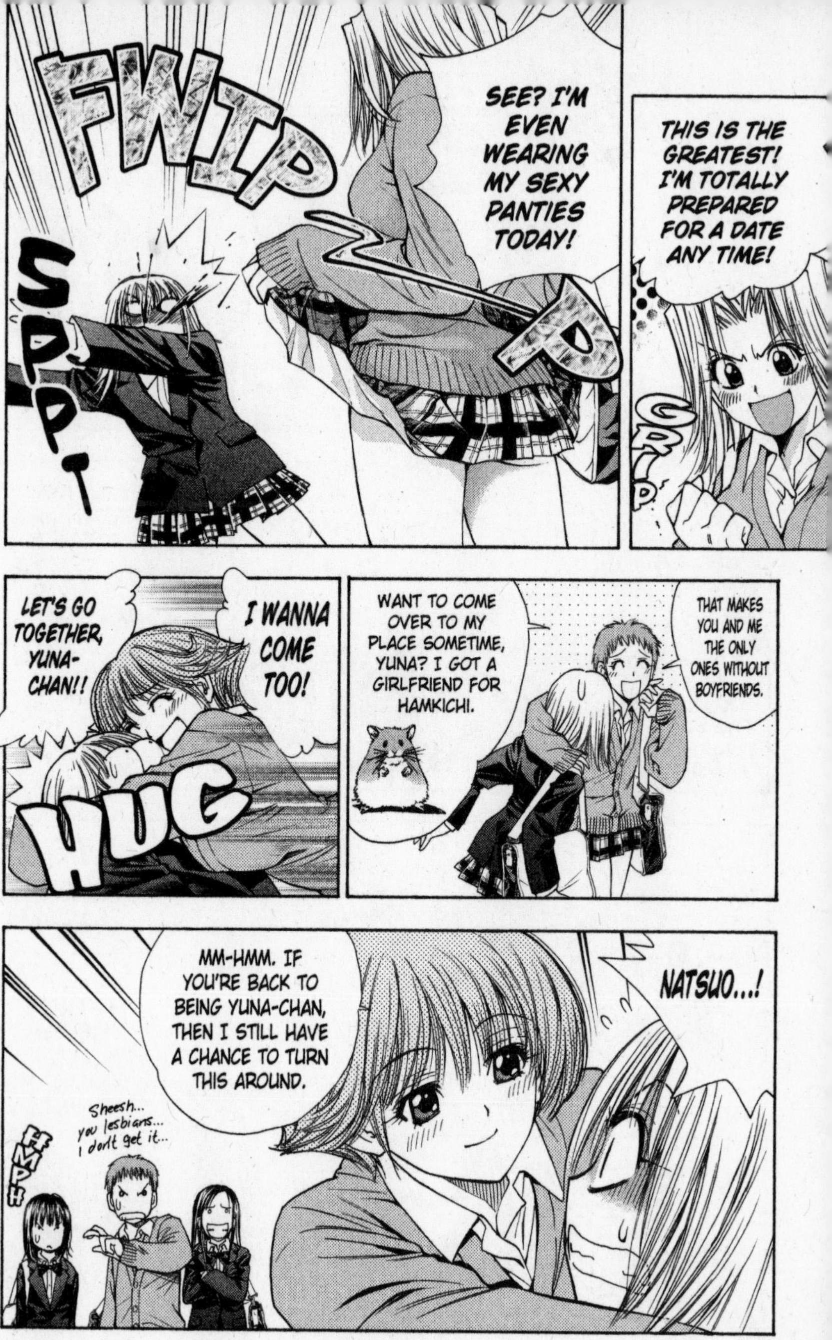
THIS IS THE GREATEST! I'M TOTALLY PREPARED FOR A DATE ANY TIME!
GRIP
SEE? I'M EVEN WEARING MY SEXY PANTIES TODAY!
FWIP
FWIP
SPPT
THAT MAKES YOU AND ME THE ONLY ONES WITHOUT BOYFRIENDS.
WANT TO COME OVER TO MY PLACE SOMETIME, YUNA? I GOT A GIRLFRIEND FOR HAMKICHI.
I WANNA COME TOO!
LET'S GO TOGETHER, YUNA-CHAN!!
HUG
NATSUO...!
MM-HMM. IF YOU'RE BACK TO BEING YUNA-CHAN, THEN I STILL HAVE A CHANCE TO TURN THIS AROUND.
Sheesh... you lesbians... I don't get it...
HMPH

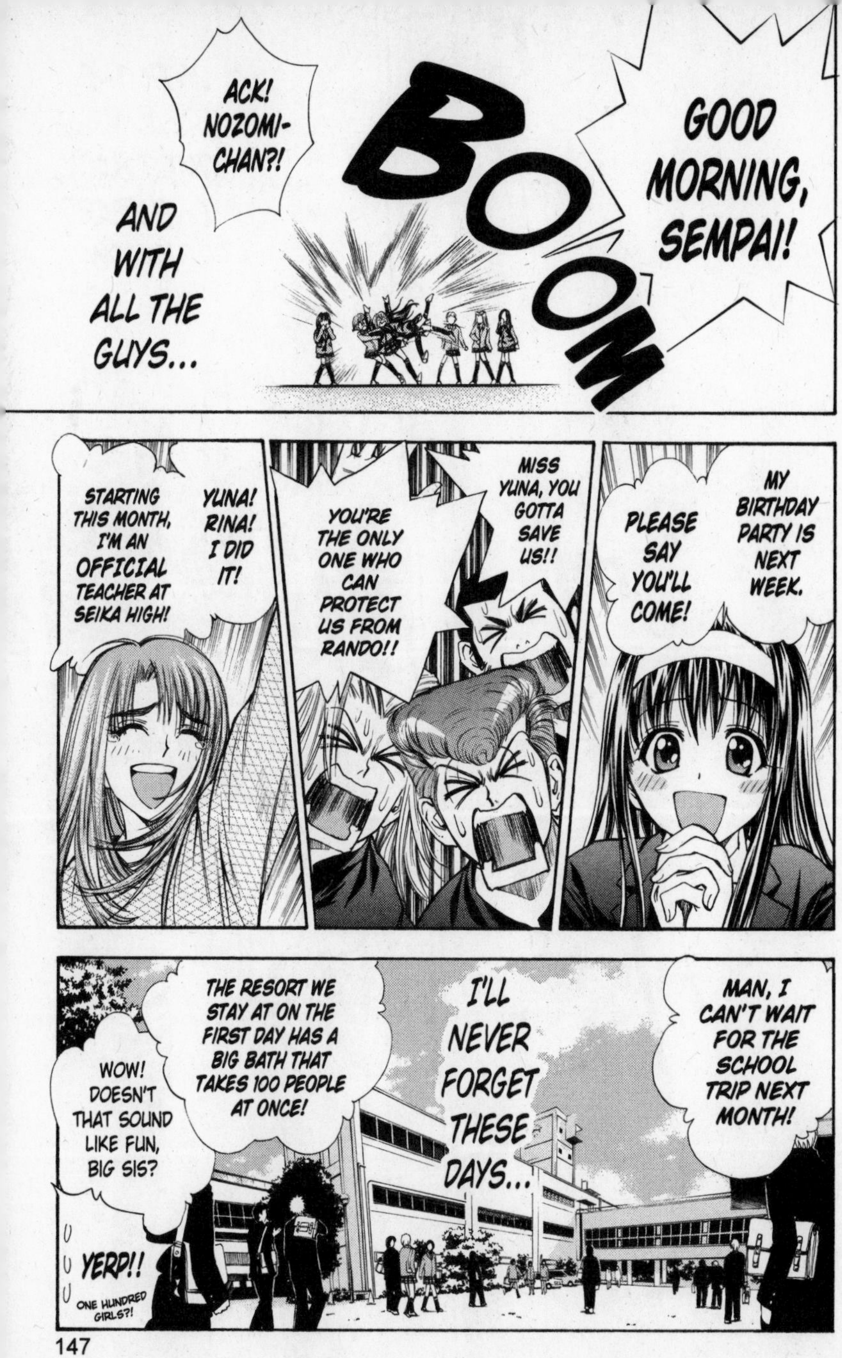
GOOD MORNING, SEMPAI!
BOOM
ACK! NOZOMI-CHAN?!
AND WITH ALL THE GUYS...
MY BIRTHDAY PARTY IS NEXT WEEK.
PLEASE SAY YOU'LL COME!
MISS YUNA, YOU GOTTA SAVE US!!
YOU'RE THE ONLY ONE WHO CAN PROTECT US FROM RANDO!!
YUNA! RINA! I DID IT!
STARTING THIS MONTH, I'M AN OFFICIAL TEACHER AT SEIKA HIGH!
MAN, I CAN'T WAIT FOR THE SCHOOL TRIP NEXT MONTH!
I'LL NEVER FORGET THESE DAYS...
THE RESORT WE STAY AT ON THE FIRST DAY HAS A BIG BATH THAT TAKES 100 PEOPLE AT ONCE!
WOW! DOESN'T THAT SOUND LIKE FUN, BIG SIS?
YERP!!
ONE HUNDRED GIRLS?!

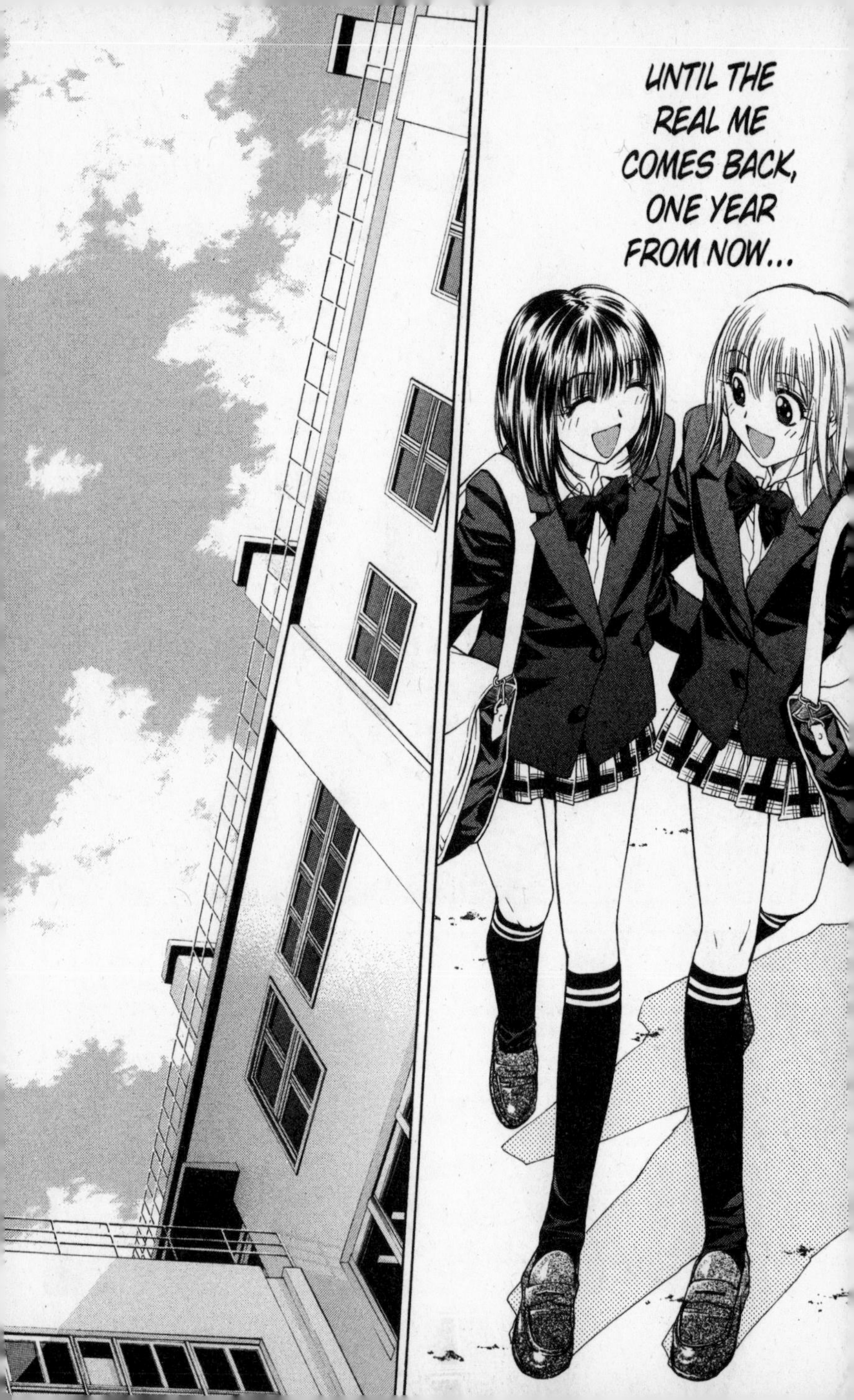
UNTIL THE REAL ME COMES BACK, ONE YEAR FROM NOW...

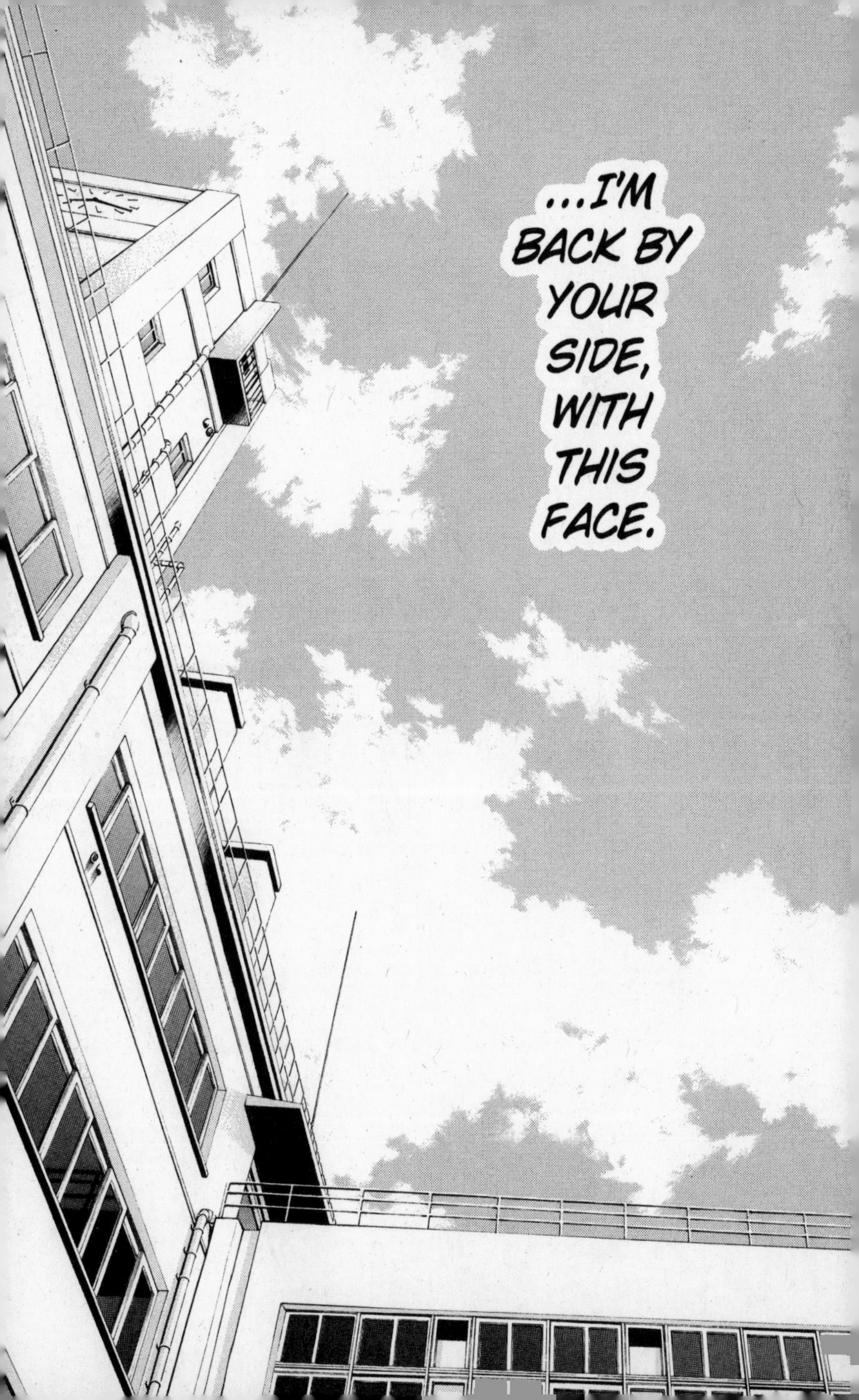
...I'M BACK BY YOUR SIDE, WITH THIS FACE.

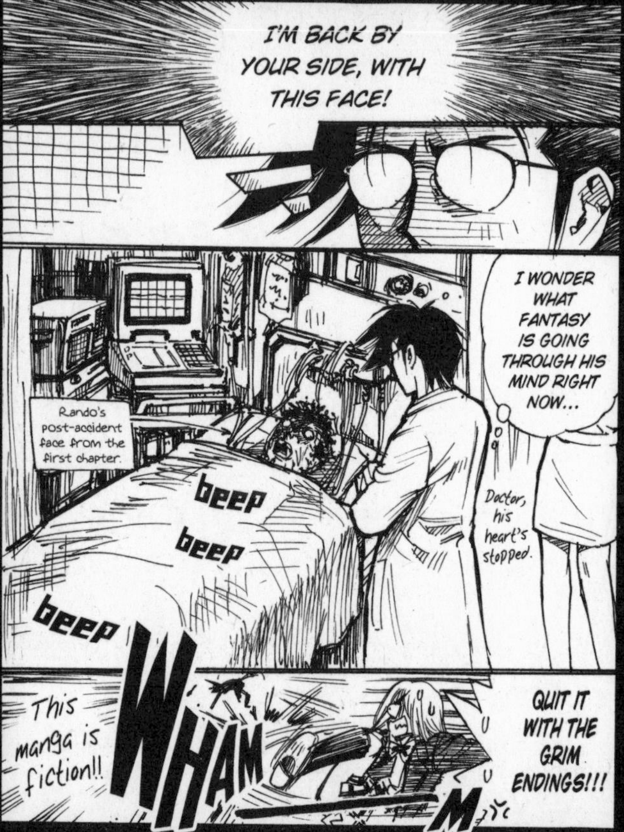
I'M BACK BY YOUR SIDE, WITH THIS FACE!
I WONDER WHAT FANTASY IS GOING THROUGH HIS MIND RIGHT NOW...
Doctor, his heart's stopped.
beep
beep
beep
Rando's post-accident face from the first chapter.
QUIT IT WITH THE GRIM ENDINGS!!!
WHAM
This manga is fiction!!

# ALTERNATE ENDING #2

THE TWIST WAS THAT THE WHOLE STORY WAS EITHER MANABE'S IMAGINATION OR RANDO'S DREAM WHILE HE WAS IN A COMA. IT'S PRETTY COMMON AS TWIST ENDINGS GO, BUT I'M SURE IT WOULD HAVE HAD QUITE AN IMPACT IF I'D DONE IT. WELL, IT GOT REJECTED ANYWAY (HEH). I REALLY THOUGHT OF DOING IT RIGHT UP UNTIL THE END.

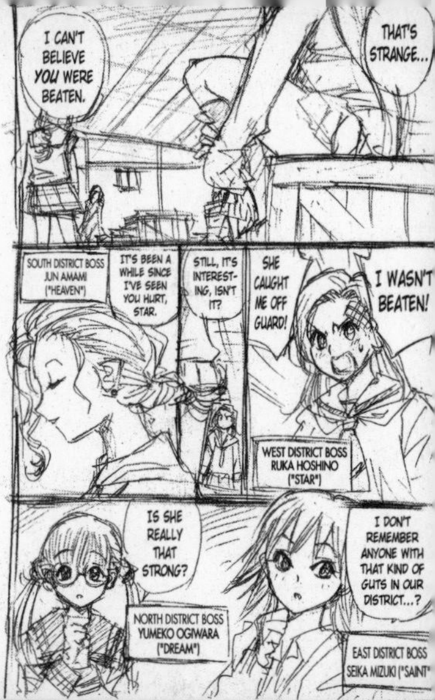
THAT'S STRANGE...
I CAN'T BELIEVE YOU WERE BEATEN.
I WASN'T BEATEN!
SHE CAUGHT ME OFF GUARD!
WEST DISTRICT BOSS RUKA HOSHINO ("STAR")
STILL, IT'S INTEREST-ING, ISN'T IT?
IT'S BEEN A WHILE SINCE I'VE SEEN YOU HURT, STAR.
SOUTH DISTRICT BOSS JUN AMAMI ("HEAVEN")
I DON'T REMEMBER ANYONE WITH THAT KIND OF GUTS IN OUR DISTRICT...?
EAST DISTRICT BOSS SEIKA MIZUKI ("SAINT")
IS SHE REALLY THAT STRONG?
NORTH DISTRICT BOSS YUMEKO OGIWARA ("DREAM")

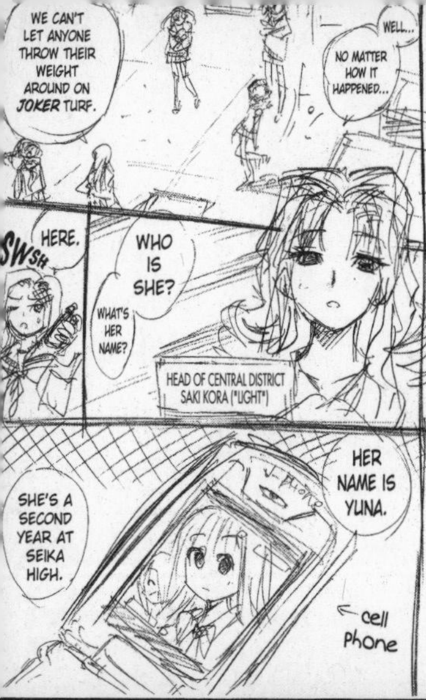
WELL...
NO MATTER HOW IT HAPPENED...
WE CAN'T LET ANYONE THROW THEIR WEIGHT AROUND ON JOKER TURF.
WHO IS SHE?
HEAD OF CENTRAL DISTRICT SAKI KORA ("LIGHT")
WHAT'S HER NAME?
HERE.
SWSH
HER NAME IS YUNA.
SHE'S A SECOND YEAR AT SEIKA HIGH.
← cell Phone

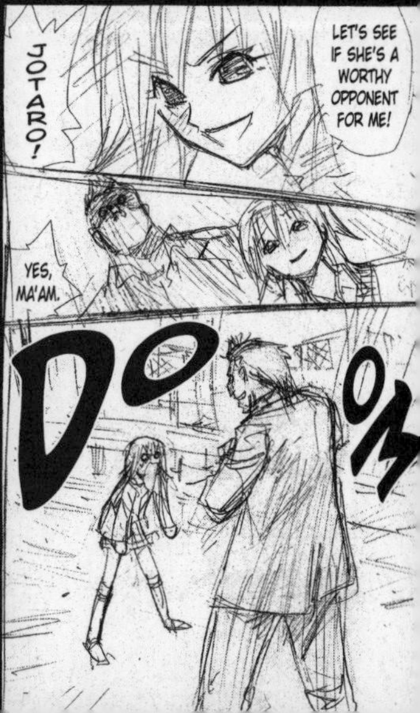
LET'S SEE IF SHE'S A WORTHY OPPONENT FOR ME!
JOTARO!
YES, MA'AM.
DOOM

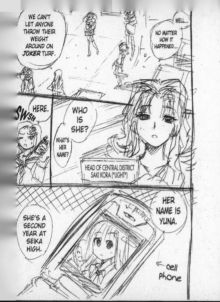

THIS WAS AN EPISODE WHERE RANDO FOUGHT THE GIRL GANG WHO CONTROLLED THE AREA AROUND SEIKA HIGH. I THOUGHT IT WAS A FUN STORY, BUT IT WAS THOUGHT THAT A FIGHT BETWEEN GIRLS WOULDN'T FLY IN A BOY'S MAGAZINE, SO IT GOT DROPPED. SIGH...MAYBE IF I'D MADE THE FIGHT INTO A KIND OF COMEDY SEQUENCE, IT WOULD HAVE WORKED...I REALLY LIKED THE DUMB NICKNAMES OF EACH OF THE CHARACTERS AND THE GANG NAME "JOKER" (WRITTEN WITH THE KANJI "JO"= YOUNG LADY AND "KA"= FLOWER).

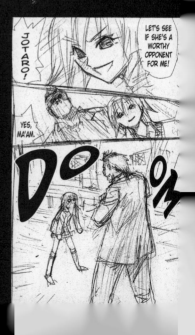

# BONUS: REJECTED STORIES (PART 5)

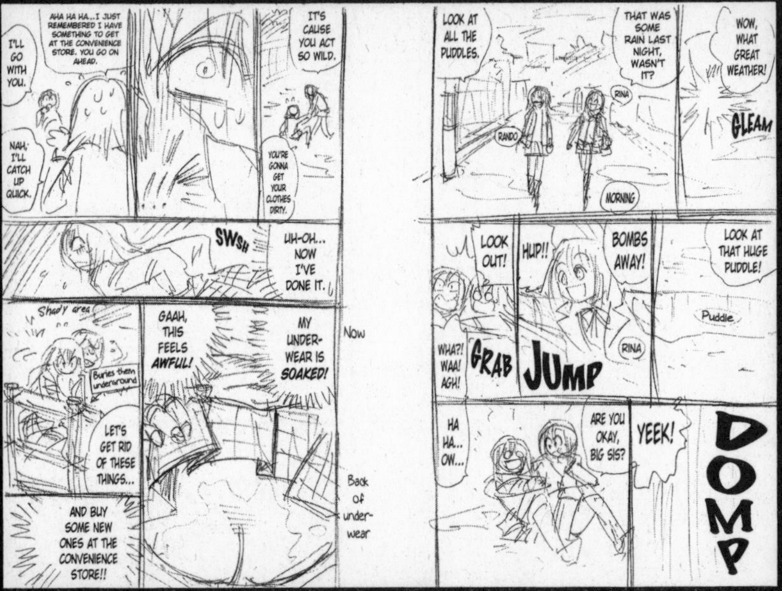
WOW, WHAT GREAT WEATHER!
GLEAM
THAT WAS SOME RAIN LAST NIGHT, WASN'T IT?
RINA
LOOK AT ALL THE PUDDLES.
RANDO
MORNING
LOOK AT THAT HUGE PUDDLE!
Puddle
BOMBS AWAY!
HUP!!
RINA
JUMP
LOOK OUT!
WHA?! WAA! AGH!
GRAB
DOMP
YEEK!
ARE YOU OKAY, BIG SIS?
HA HA... OW...
IT'S CAUSE YOU ACT SO WILD.
YOU'RE GONNA GET YOUR CLOTHES DIRTY.
AHA HA HA...I JUST REMEMBERED I HAVE SOMETHING TO GET AT THE CONVENIENCE STORE. YOU GO ON AHEAD.
I'LL GO WITH YOU.
NAH, I'LL CATCH UP QUICK.
UH-OH... NOW I'VE DONE IT.
SWSH
Now
Back of under-wear
MY UNDER-WEAR IS SOAKED!
GAAH, THIS FEELS AWFUL!
Shady area
Buries them underground
LET'S GET RID OF THESE THINGS...
AND BUY SOME NEW ONES AT THE CONVENIENCE STORE!!

RANDO GETS HIS UNDERWEAR WET ON THE WAY TO SCHOOL, AND RUNS TO A CONVENIENCE STORE, BUT FOR SOME REASON THEY'RE SOLD OUT. WITHOUT ANY OTHER RECOURSE, RANDO GOES TO SCHOOL WITH NO UNDERWEAR ON. ON TOP OF THAT, THE PHOTOGRAPHY CLUB HAS BAD THINGS PLANNED...AND SO GOES THE STORY. IT WAS A SILLY STORY THAT DIDN'T MATTER AT ALL (OR DID IT?), SO I THOUGHT I COULD FIT IT IN ANYTIME, AND I ENDED UP FINISHING THE SERIES WITHOUT USING IT.

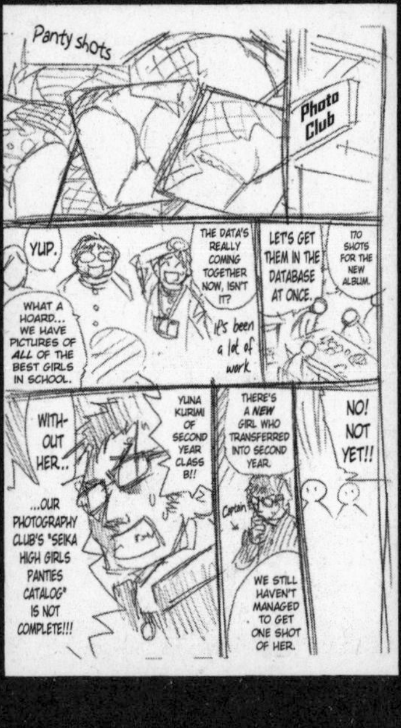
Panty shots
Photo Club
170 SHOTS FOR THE NEW ALBUM.
LET'S GET THEM IN THE DATABASE AT ONCE.
THE DATA'S REALLY COMING TOGETHER NOW, ISN'T IT?
It's been a lot of work
YUP.
WHAT A HOARD... WE HAVE PICTURES OF ALL OF THE BEST GIRLS IN SCHOOL.
NO! NOT YET!!
THERE'S A NEW GIRL WHO TRANSFERRED INTO SECOND YEAR.
Captain
WE STILL HAVEN'T MANAGED TO GET ONE SHOT OF HER.
YUNA KURIMI OF SECOND YEAR CLASS B!!
WITH-OUT HER..
...OUR PHOTOGRAPHY CLUB'S "SEIKA HIGH GIRLS PANTIES CATALOG" IS NOT COMPLETE!!!

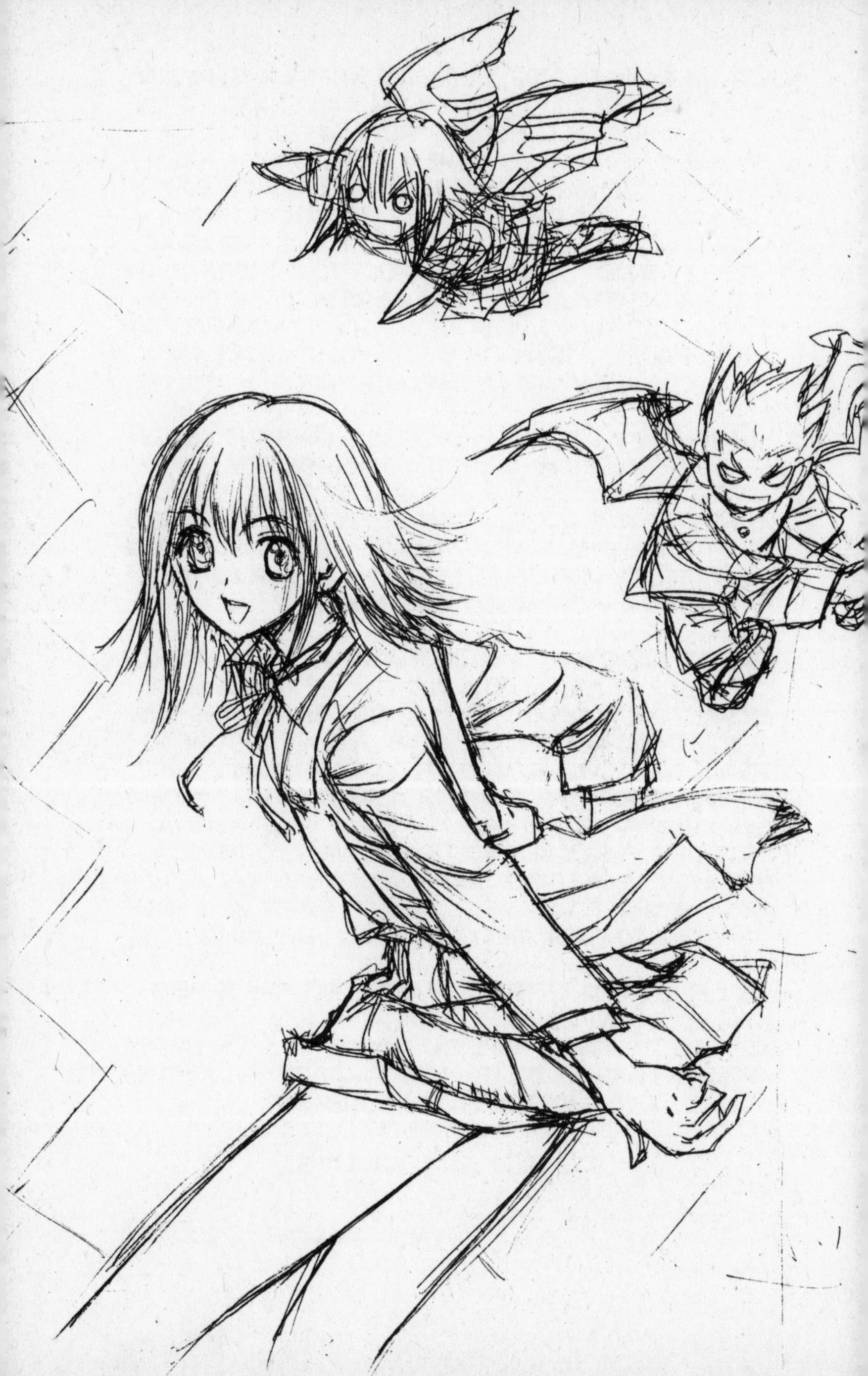

FOR THE FINAL EPISODE, I DEBATED WHETHER TO REVEAL WHAT HAPPENED TO RANDO'S FAMILY AND WHETHER TO HAVE RANDO TELL RINA THE TRUTH. AFTER A LOT OF THOUGHT, IT TURNED OUT THE WAY YOU SAW. I COULD HAVE GONE THE WAY OF REVEALING THE UNREVEALED PLOT ELEMENTS, BUT I FELT LIKE IF I DID THAT THEN THIS WORLD WOULD REALLY END. I FELT REALLY SAD ABOUT THAT, SO I ENDED THE STORY WITHOUT TOUCHING ON THEM. I'M SURE THERE ARE SOME READERS WHO ARE DISAP- POINTED, BUT WHEN I HEAR ABOUT THE RESPONSE TO THE LAST EPISODE, I THINK I MADE THE RIGHT CHOICE AND I COMFORT MYSELF WITH THAT.

I RECEIVED A LOT OF FAN LETTERS DURING THE SERIES AND THAT CHEERED ME A LOT. I WAS ESPECIALLY PLEASED THAT PEOPLE LIKED THE MAIN CHARACTER RANDO SO MUCH. AT FIRST, I WAS WORRIED THAT HE MIGHT GET BRUSHED OFF WITH THE SINGLE WORD "SICKO." I WAS HARDLY ABLE TO WRITE ANY REPLIES, BUT I READ ALL YOUR LETTERS. THANK YOU VERY MUCH.

*PRETTY FACE* WAS CREATED IN A GREAT ENVIRONMENT, BLESSED BY ITS READERS AND ALL THE PEOPLE WHO WORKED ON IT. EVERY WEEK THE EDITORS WORRIED AND FRETTED WITH ME, AND THE STAFF FOUGHT WITH ME TO REACH THE DEADLINE. MY STAFF AND ASSISTANTS WERE INCREDIBLY TALENTED, AND THEY WERE ALL GREAT PEOPLE WHO HELPED ME OUT. ALSO OF GREAT HELP WERE MY EDITORS, THE COMICS EDITORS AND MANY OTHERS. A MANGA ISN'T SOMETHING THAT IS WRITTEN BY THE AUTHOR ALONE. WITHOUT THEIR HELP, I WOULD NEVER HAVE BEEN ABLE TO FINISH THIS. THANK YOU VERY MUCH.

AS I FINISH THIS LETTER, I REALIZE THAT THIS IS FARE- WELL TO RANDO AND THE OTHERS. IT WAS A LONG YEAR AND A SHORT YEAR. I HOPE THE DAY COMES SOON WHEN I CAN WORK HARD TO CREATE MORE CHARACTERS LIKE THEM WHO INSPIRE SUCH ATTACHMENT.

LET'S MEET AGAIN SOMETIME.

YASUHIRO KANO    2003.9.1

IT'S BEEN ONE YEAR SINCE THIS STORY BEGAN, AND I MANAGED TO FINISH IT, SO I'M RELIEVED.

THINKING BACK, IT WAS MY THIRD EDITOR SHIMADA'S COMMENT "I'D LIKE TO SEE SOMETHING LIKE A SCHOOL COMEDY" THAT WAS THE INSPIRATION. I THOUGHT "THAT'S A GOOD GENRE FOR FIRST-TIME MANGA CREATORS. IT SEEMS LIKE SOMETHING I WOULD BE GOOD AT." SO JUST TO TRY IT, I DREW A ONE-SHOT STORY AND THAT WAS THE BEGINNING. BEFORE I REALIZED IT, THAT STORY HAD TURNED INTO A SERIES AND *PRETTY FACE* WAS BORN. BUT ALTHOUGH I'D MANAGED TO START IT, HOW SHOULD I GO ON? IT WAS A TOUGH PROCESS OF TRIAL AND ERROR. I HAD THE DRAWING ABILITY TO MAKE GIRLS CUTE ENOUGH TO CATCH THE EYE. THE STORY FELL INTO A LOVE COMEDY PATTERN, AND ENDED UP BEING A "CHAPTER BY CHAPTER, GAG-FILLED SCHOOL COMEDY" SERIES. I LIKED COMING UP WITH RIDICULOUS STORIES, SO OVERALL THE WORK WAS FUN. ON THE OTHER HAND, I WORKED SO SLOW THAT THE DEADLINE WAS ALWAYS HARSH. (HEH)

MY FAVORITE STORIES, FROM TOP TO BOTTOM, WERE:
"IF YOU GET PAST THE IMPOSSIBLE,
THEN IT SOUNDS PLAUSIBLE."
"PRETTY FACE"
"YUKIE-CHAN IN LOVE"
"MANABE(RANDO+2$\pi$)=$\pi$R"

THAT'S ABOUT IT. AS AN AUTHOR, I THINK I WRITE BETTER STORIES WHEN THE TENSION IS HIGH. THE THINGS I REGRET ARE NOT BEING ABLE TO WRITE STORIES ABOUT RANDO AND RINA WHEN RANDO WAS A GUY, AN EPISODE WHERE RANDO'S YOUNGER BROTHER ENTERS THE SCHOOL (I PLANNED TO PAIR HIM WITH NATSUO), RANDO (YUNA) WINNING THE NATIONAL HIGH SCHOOL KARATE COMPETITION, THE DAY YUNA OFFICIALLY RETURNS, AND ALL SORTS OF OTHER STORIES THAT I COULDN'T DRAW BEFORE THE SERIES ENDED. IF IT HAD GONE ON A LITTLE LONGER I WOULD HAVE WRITTEN "THE REVENGE OF APOLLO" (A CONTINUATION OF CHAPTER 8).

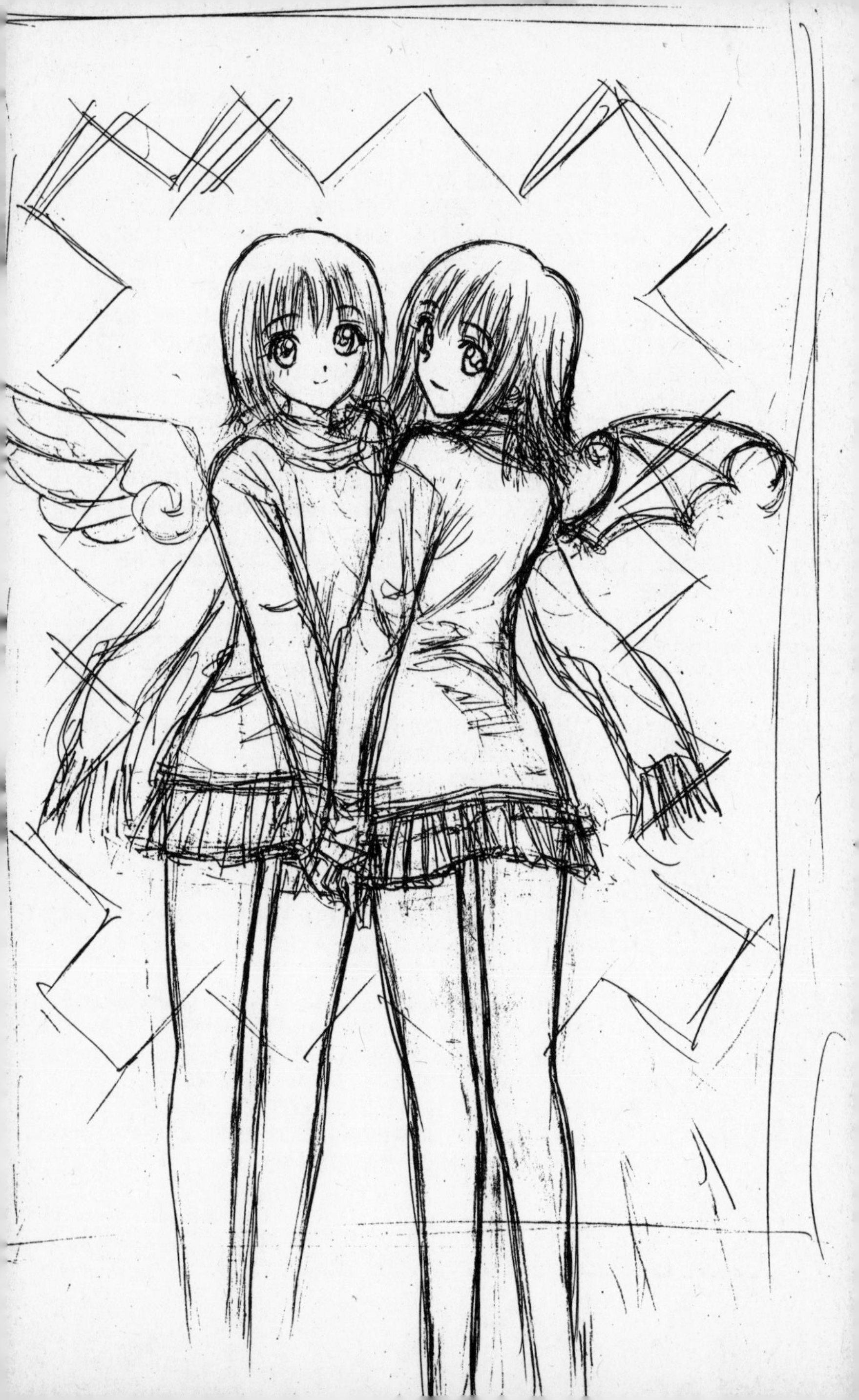

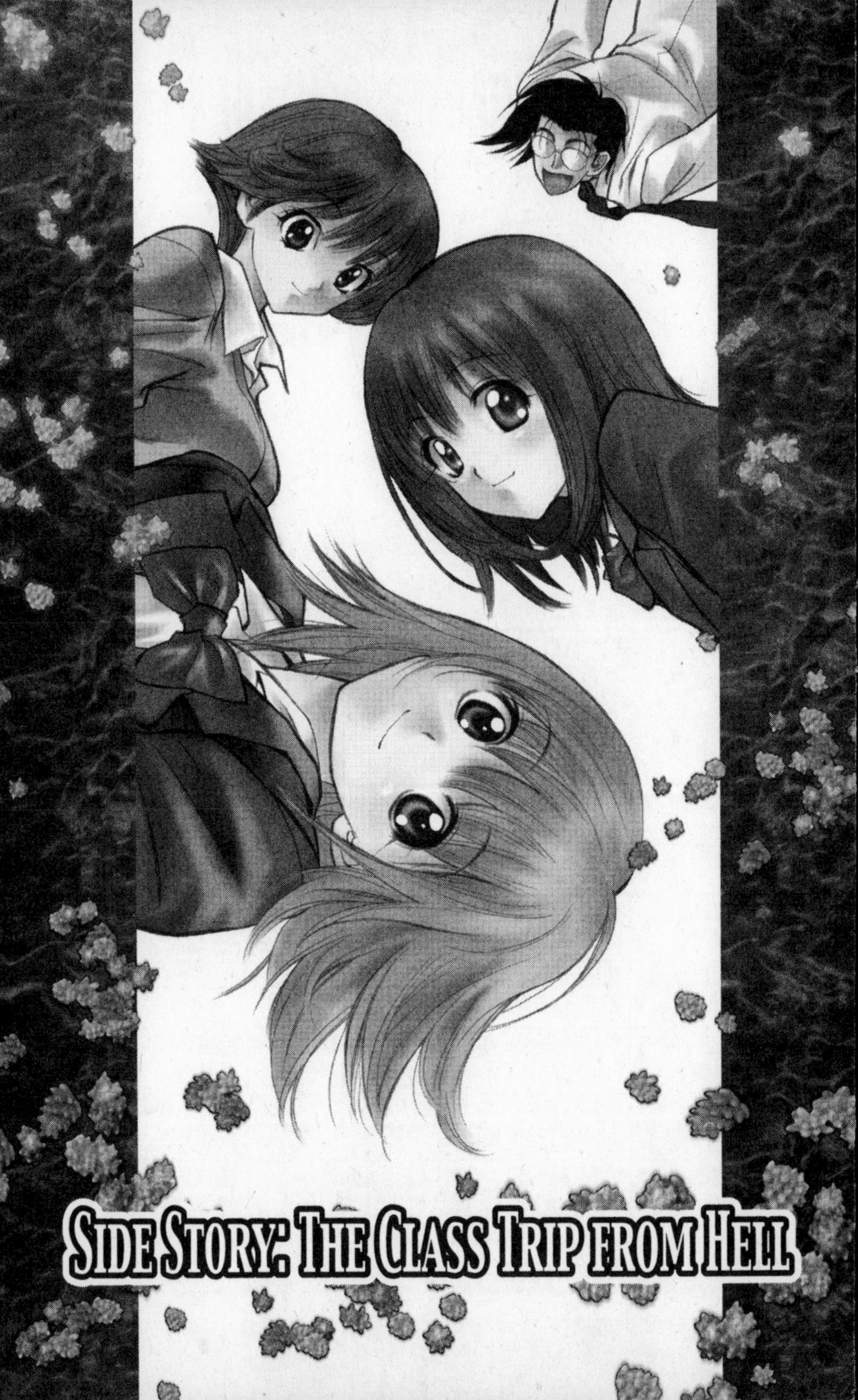

# Side Story: The Class Trip from Hell

# PRETTY FACE CHARACTER CONTEST RESULTS!!

*PRETTY FACE* ENDED WHILE IT WAS STILL VERY POPULAR. HERE ARE THE RESULTS OF THE POPULARITY CONTEST. WHAT PLACE DID YOUR FAVORITE CHARACTER GET?

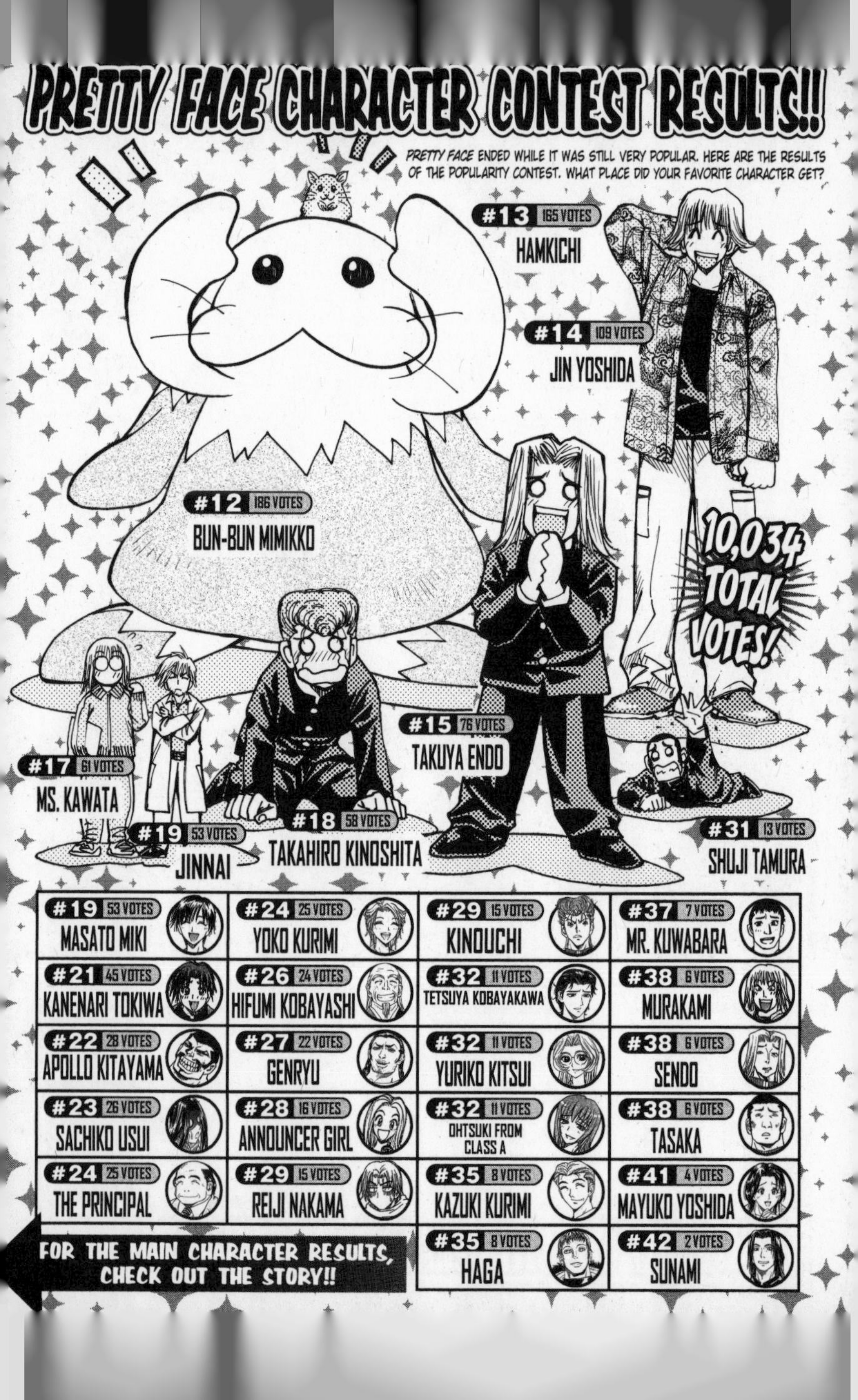
#13 165 VOTES
HAMKICHI
#14 109 VOTES
JIN YOSHIDA
#12 186 VOTES
BUN-BUN MIMIKKO
10,034 TOTAL VOTES!
#15 76 VOTES
TAKUYA ENDO
#17 61 VOTES
MS. KAWATA
#19 53 VOTES
JINNAI
#18 58 VOTES
TAKAHIRO KINOSHITA
#31 13 VOTES
SHUJI TAMURA

| | | | |
|---|---|---|---|
| #19 53 VOTES MASATO MIKI | #24 25 VOTES YOKO KURIMI | #29 15 VOTES KINOUCHI | #37 7 VOTES MR. KUWABARA |
| #21 45 VOTES KANENARI TOKIWA | #26 24 VOTES HIFUMI KOBAYASHI | #32 11 VOTES TETSUYA KOBAYAKAWA | #38 6 VOTES MURAKAMI |
| #22 28 VOTES APOLLO KITAYAMA | #27 22 VOTES GENRYU | #32 11 VOTES YURIKO KITSUI | #38 6 VOTES SENDO |
| #23 26 VOTES SACHIKO USUI | #28 16 VOTES ANNOUNCER GIRL | #32 11 VOTES OHTSUKI FROM CLASS A | #38 6 VOTES TASAKA |
| #24 25 VOTES THE PRINCIPAL | #29 15 VOTES REIJI NAKAMA | #35 8 VOTES KAZUKI KURIMI | #41 4 VOTES MAYUKO YOSHIDA |
| | | #35 8 VOTES HAGA | #42 2 VOTES SUNAMI |

FOR THE MAIN CHARACTER RESULTS, CHECK OUT THE STORY!!

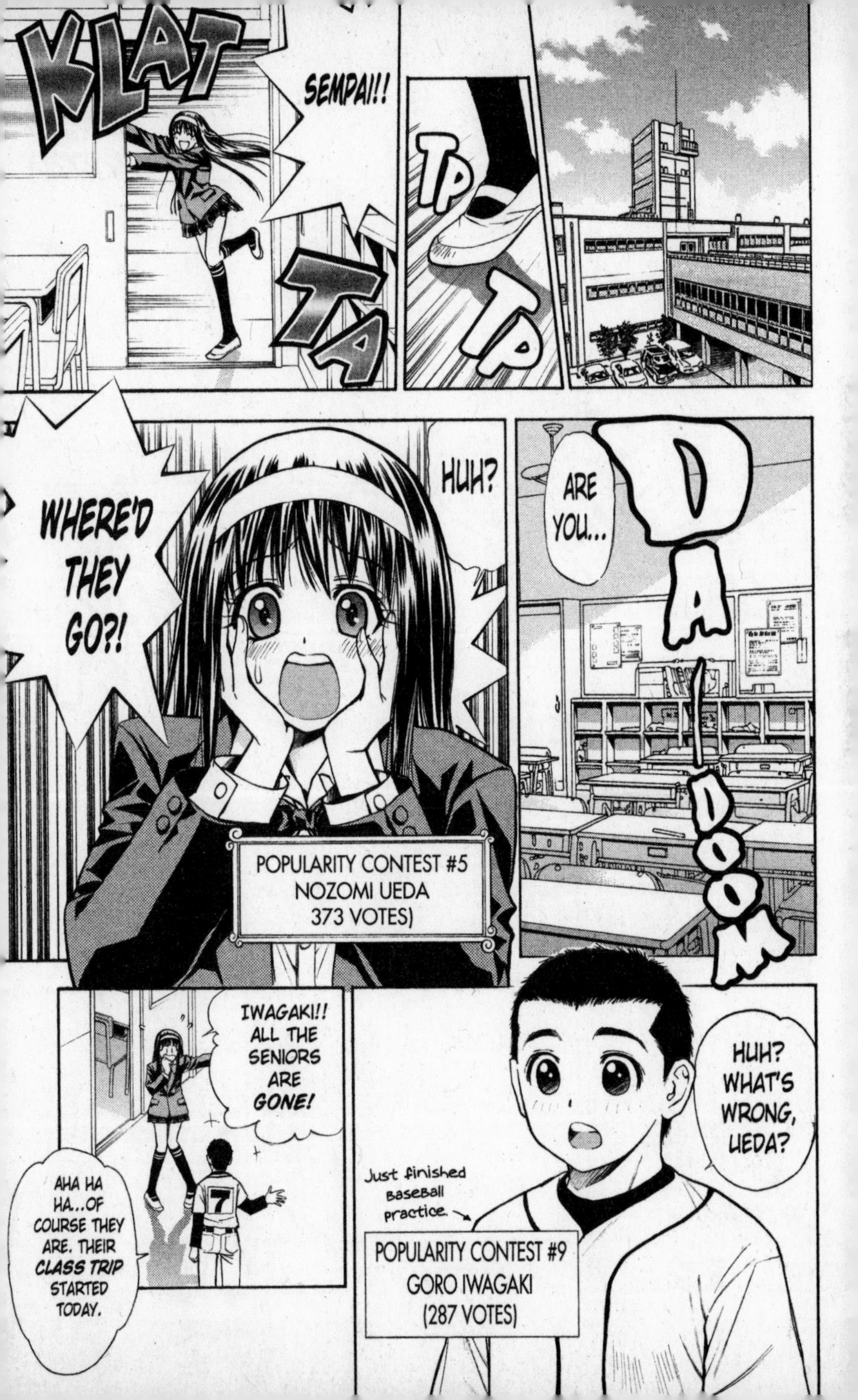
TP
TP
KLAT
SEMPAI!!
TA
ARE YOU...
DA-DOOM
HUH?
WHERE'D THEY GO?!
POPULARITY CONTEST #5 NOZOMI UEDA 373 VOTES)
HUH? WHAT'S WRONG, UEDA?
Just finished baseball practice.
POPULARITY CONTEST #9 GORO IWAGAKI (287 VOTES)
IWAGAKI!! ALL THE SENIORS ARE GONE!
AHA HA HA...OF COURSE THEY ARE. THEIR CLASS TRIP STARTED TODAY.

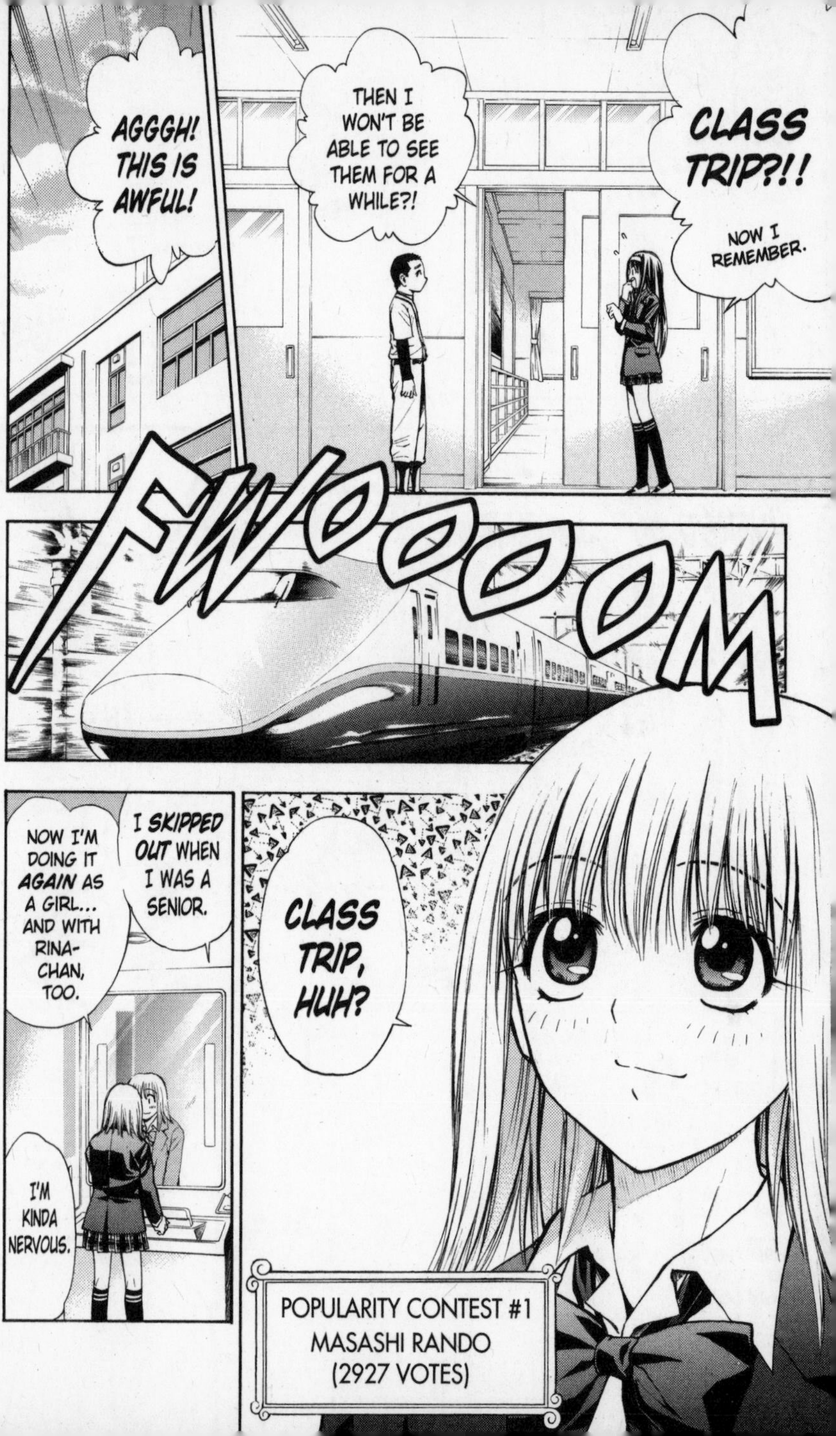
CLASS TRIP?!!
NOW I REMEMBER.
THEN I WON'T BE ABLE TO SEE THEM FOR A WHILE?!
AGGGH! THIS IS AWFUL!
FWOOOOM
CLASS TRIP, HUH?
POPULARITY CONTEST #1
MASASHI RANDO
(2927 VOTES)
I SKIPPED OUT WHEN I WAS A SENIOR.
NOW I'M DOING IT AGAIN AS A GIRL... AND WITH RINA-CHAN, TOO.
I'M KINDA NERVOUS.

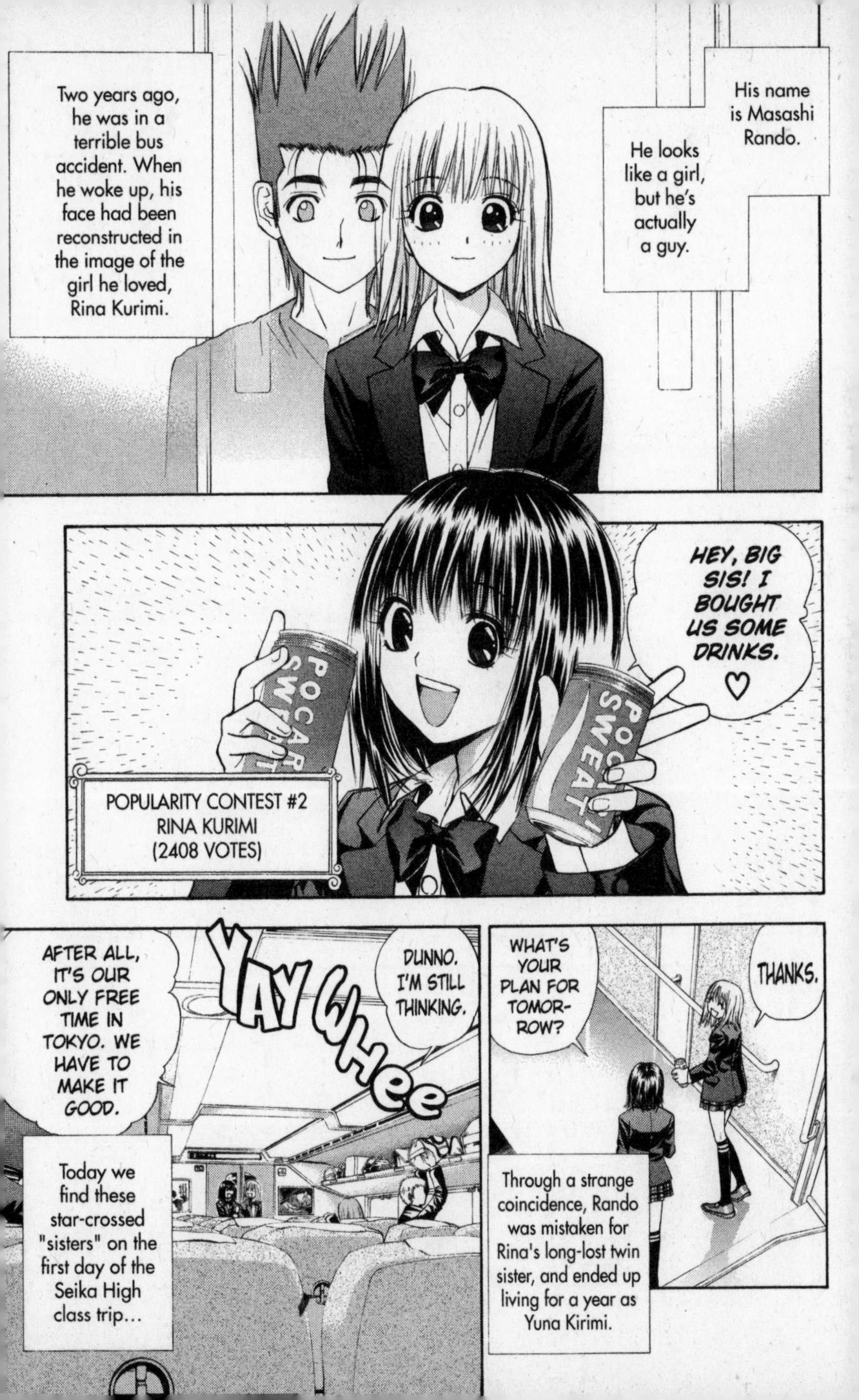
His name is Masashi Rando.
He looks like a girl, but he's actually a guy.
Two years ago, he was in a terrible bus accident. When he woke up, his face had been reconstructed in the image of the girl he loved, Rina Kurimi.
HEY, BIG SIS! I BOUGHT US SOME DRINKS. ♡
POPULARITY CONTEST #2
RINA KURIMI
(2408 VOTES)
THANKS.
WHAT'S YOUR PLAN FOR TOMOR-ROW?
Through a strange coincidence, Rando was mistaken for Rina's long-lost twin sister, and ended up living for a year as Yuna Kirimi.
DUNNO. I'M STILL THINKING.
YAY WHEE
AFTER ALL, IT'S OUR ONLY FREE TIME IN TOKYO. WE HAVE TO MAKE IT GOOD.
Today we find these star-crossed "sisters" on the first day of the Seika High class trip...

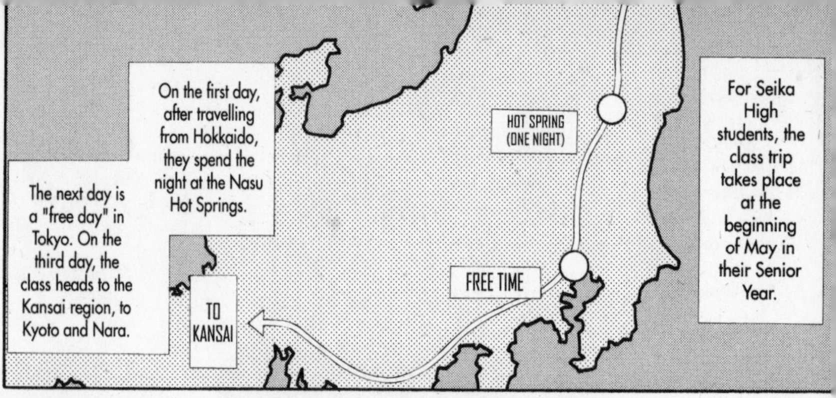
For Seika High students, the class trip takes place at the beginning of May in their Senior Year.
HOT SPRING (ONE NIGHT)
FREE TIME
On the first day, after travelling from Hokkaido, they spend the night at the Nasu Hot Springs.
TO KANSAI
The next day is a "free day" in Tokyo. On the third day, the class heads to the Kansai region, to Kyoto and Nara.

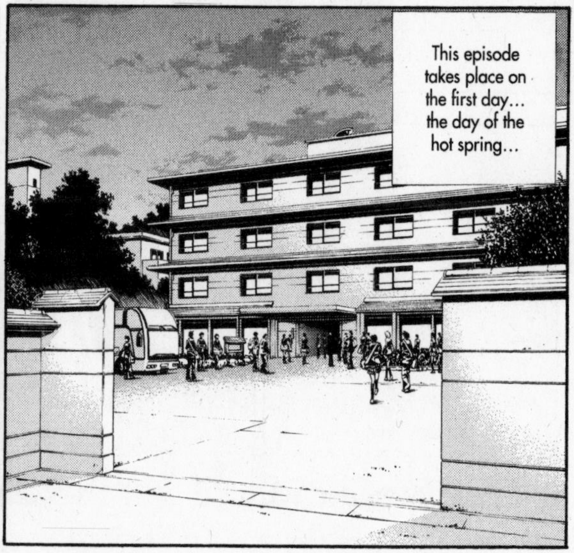
This episode takes place on the first day... the day of the hot spring...

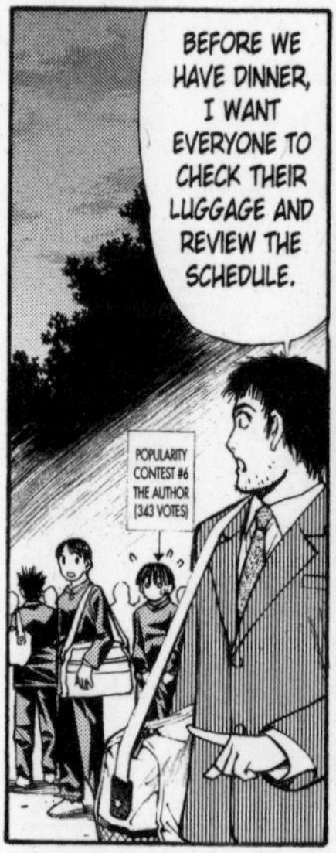
BEFORE WE HAVE DINNER, I WANT EVERYONE TO CHECK THEIR LUGGAGE AND REVIEW THE SCHEDULE.
POPULARITY CONTEST #6 THE AUTHOR (343 VOTES)

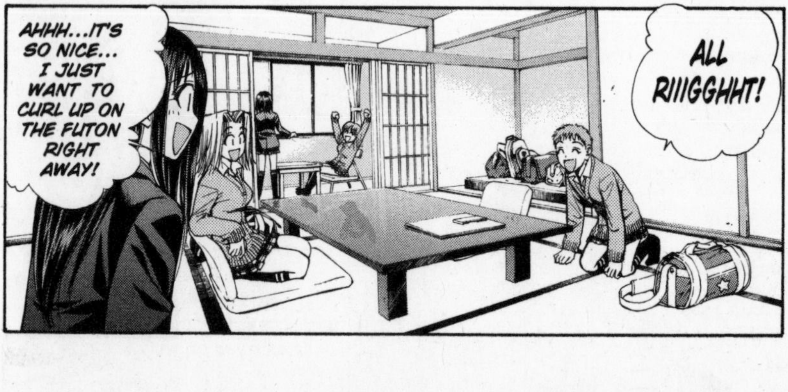
ALL RIIIGGHHT!
AHHH...IT'S SO NICE... I JUST WANT TO CURL UP ON THE FUTON RIGHT AWAY!

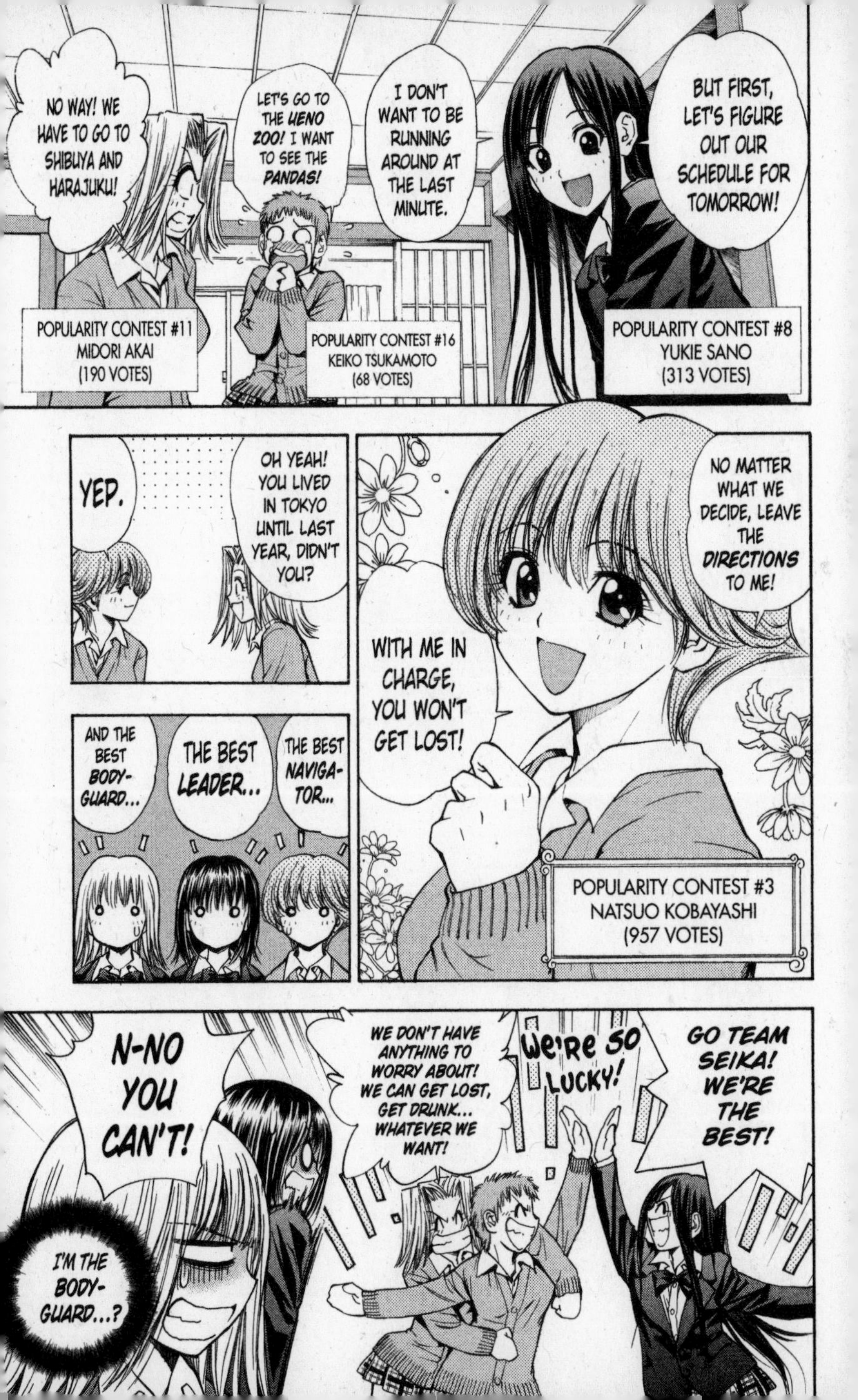
BUT FIRST, LET'S FIGURE OUT OUR SCHEDULE FOR TOMORROW!
I DON'T WANT TO BE RUNNING AROUND AT THE LAST MINUTE.
LET'S GO TO THE UENO ZOO! I WANT TO SEE THE PANDAS!
NO WAY! WE HAVE TO GO TO SHIBUYA AND HARAJUKU!
POPULARITY CONTEST #8 YUKIE SANO (313 VOTES)
POPULARITY CONTEST #16 KEIKO TSUKAMOTO (68 VOTES)
POPULARITY CONTEST #11 MIDORI AKAI (190 VOTES)
NO MATTER WHAT WE DECIDE, LEAVE THE DIRECTIONS TO ME!
WITH ME IN CHARGE, YOU WON'T GET LOST!
POPULARITY CONTEST #3 NATSUO KOBAYASHI (957 VOTES)
OH YEAH! YOU LIVED IN TOKYO UNTIL LAST YEAR, DIDN'T YOU?
YEP.
THE BEST NAVIGATOR...
THE BEST LEADER...
AND THE BEST BODYGUARD...
GO TEAM SEIKA! WE'RE THE BEST!
We're so LUCKY!
WE DON'T HAVE ANYTHING TO WORRY ABOUT! WE CAN GET LOST, GET DRUNK... WHATEVER WE WANT!
N-NO YOU CAN'T!
I'M THE BODYGUARD...?

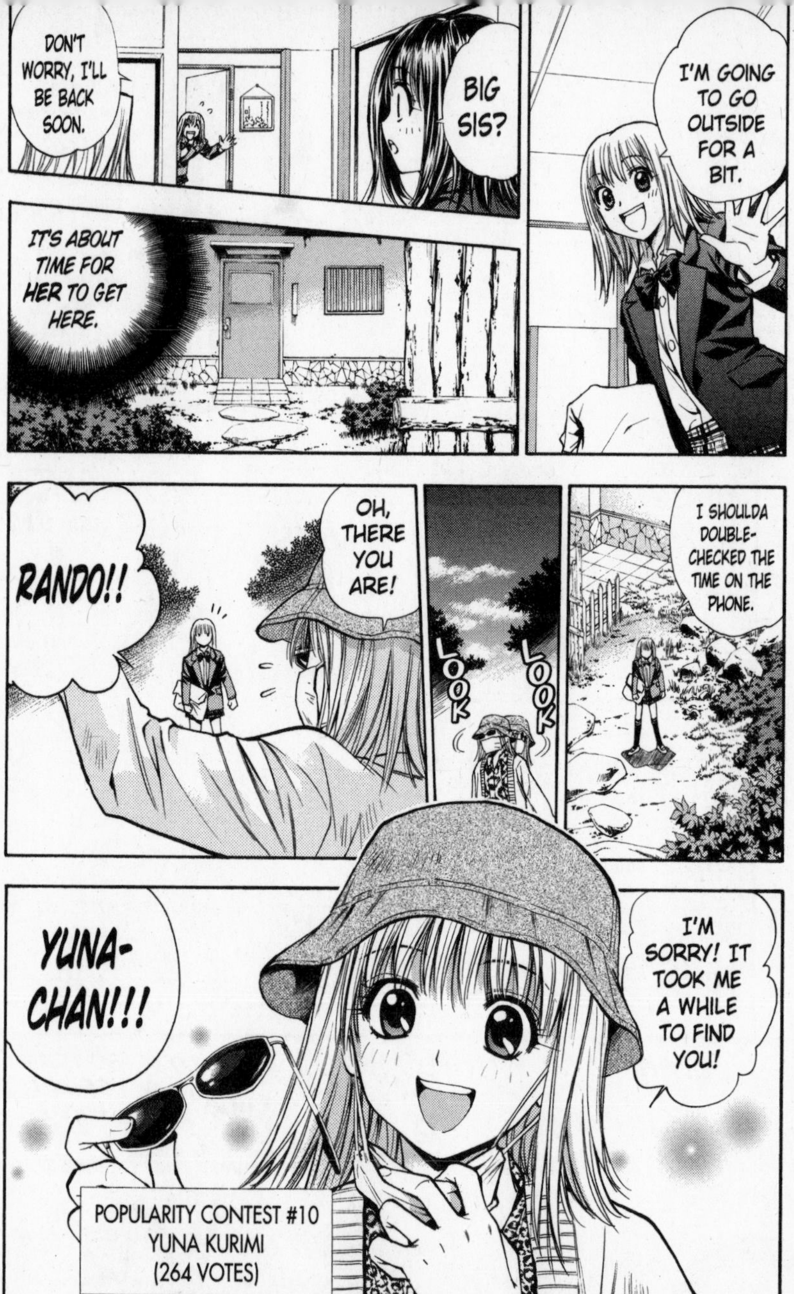
I'M GOING TO GO OUTSIDE FOR A BIT.
BIG SIS?
DON'T WORRY, I'LL BE BACK SOON.
IT'S ABOUT TIME FOR HER TO GET HERE.
I SHOULDA DOUBLE-CHECKED THE TIME ON THE PHONE.
LOOK
LOOK
OH, THERE YOU ARE!
RANDO!!
I'M SORRY! IT TOOK ME A WHILE TO FIND YOU!
YUNA-CHAN!!!
POPULARITY CONTEST #10
YUNA KURIMI
(264 VOTES)

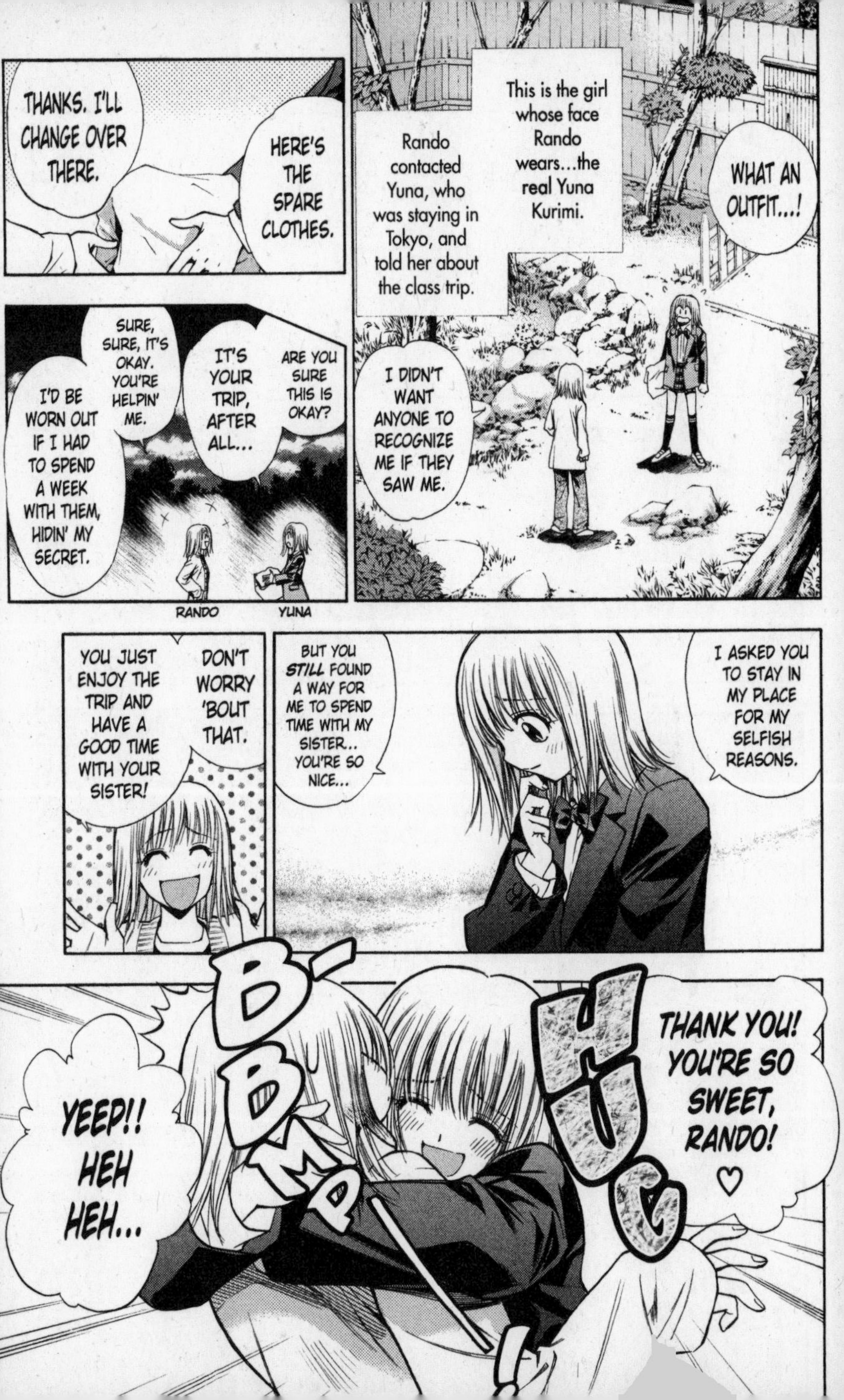
WHAT AN OUTFIT...!
This is the girl whose face Rando wears...the real Yuna Kurimi.
Rando contacted Yuna, who was staying in Tokyo, and told her about the class trip.
I DIDN'T WANT ANYONE TO RECOGNIZE ME IF THEY SAW ME.
HERE'S THE SPARE CLOTHES.
THANKS. I'LL CHANGE OVER THERE.
ARE YOU SURE THIS IS OKAY?
IT'S YOUR TRIP, AFTER ALL...
SURE, SURE, IT'S OKAY. YOU'RE HELPIN' ME.
I'D BE WORN OUT IF I HAD TO SPEND A WEEK WITH THEM, HIDIN' MY SECRET.
RANDO
YUNA
I ASKED YOU TO STAY IN MY PLACE FOR MY SELFISH REASONS.
BUT YOU *STILL* FOUND A WAY FOR ME TO SPEND TIME WITH MY SISTER... YOU'RE SO NICE...
DON'T WORRY 'BOUT THAT.
YOU JUST ENJOY THE TRIP AND HAVE A GOOD TIME WITH YOUR SISTER!
THANK YOU! YOU'RE SO SWEET, RANDO! ♡
HUG
B-BMP
YEEP!! HEH HEH...

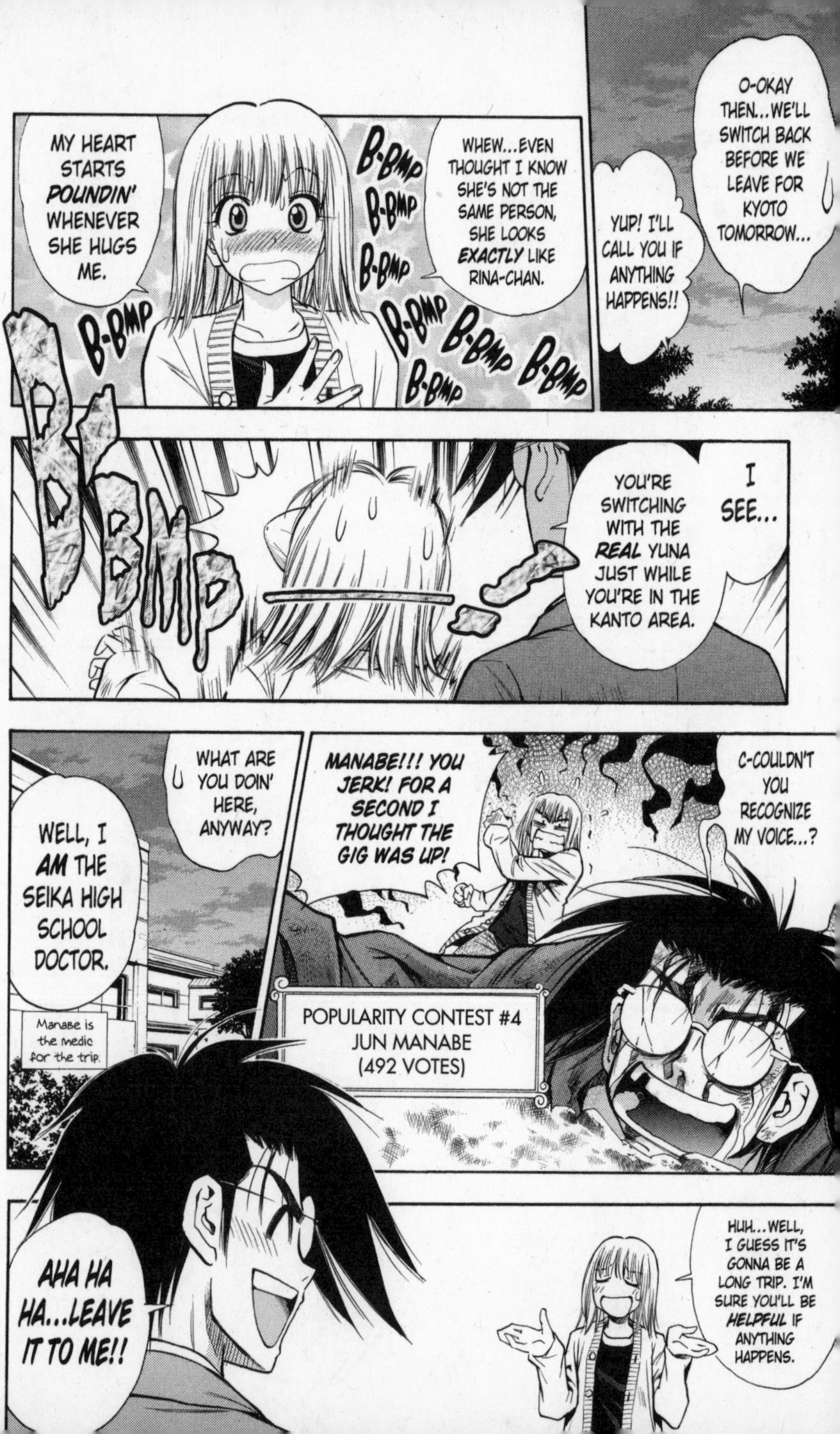
O-OKAY THEN...WE'LL SWITCH BACK BEFORE WE LEAVE FOR KYOTO TOMORROW...
YUP! I'LL CALL YOU IF ANYTHING HAPPENS!!
WHEW...EVEN THOUGHT I KNOW SHE'S NOT THE SAME PERSON, SHE LOOKS EXACTLY LIKE RINA-CHAN.
B-BMP B-BMP B-BMP
MY HEART STARTS POUNDIN' WHENEVER SHE HUGS ME.
B-BMP B-BMP B-BMP B-BMP B-BMP B-BMP
I SEE...
YOU'RE SWITCHING WITH THE REAL YUNA JUST WHILE YOU'RE IN THE KANTO AREA.
B-BMP
C-COULDN'T YOU RECOGNIZE MY VOICE...?
MANABE!!! YOU JERK! FOR A SECOND I THOUGHT THE GIG WAS UP!
WHAT ARE YOU DOIN' HERE, ANYWAY?
WELL, I AM THE SEIKA HIGH SCHOOL DOCTOR.
Manabe is the medic for the trip.
POPULARITY CONTEST #4
JUN MANABE
(492 VOTES)
HUH...WELL, I GUESS IT'S GONNA BE A LONG TRIP. I'M SURE YOU'LL BE HELPFUL IF ANYTHING HAPPENS.
AHA HA HA...LEAVE IT TO ME!!

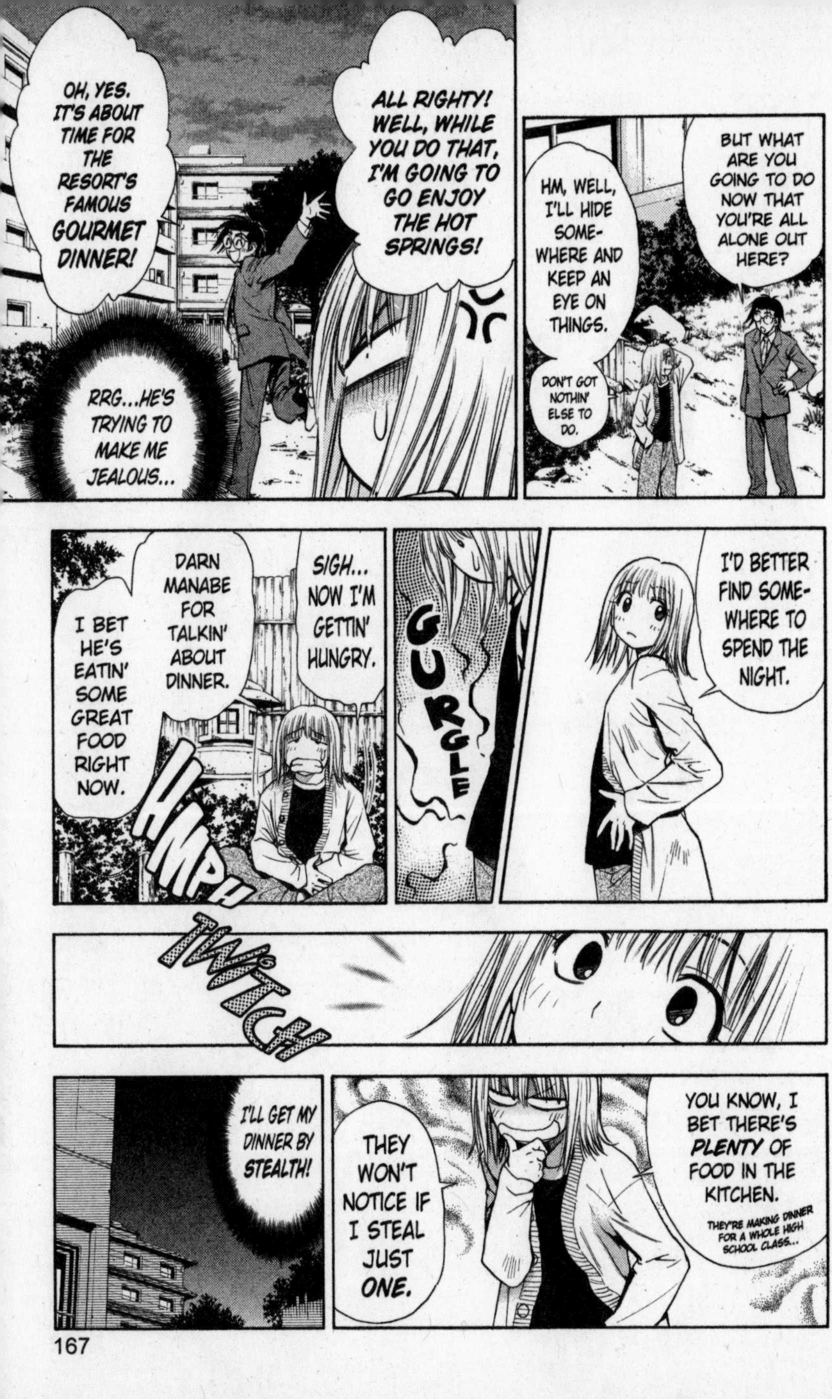
BUT WHAT ARE YOU GOING TO DO NOW THAT YOU'RE ALL ALONE OUT HERE?
HM, WELL, I'LL HIDE SOME-WHERE AND KEEP AN EYE ON THINGS.
DON'T GOT NOTHIN' ELSE TO DO.
ALL RIGHTY! WELL, WHILE YOU DO THAT, I'M GOING TO GO ENJOY THE HOT SPRINGS!
OH, YES. IT'S ABOUT TIME FOR THE RESORT'S FAMOUS GOURMET DINNER!
RRG...HE'S TRYING TO MAKE ME JEALOUS...
I'D BETTER FIND SOME-WHERE TO SPEND THE NIGHT.
GURGLE
SIGH... NOW I'M GETTIN' HUNGRY.
DARN MANABE FOR TALKIN' ABOUT DINNER.
I BET HE'S EATIN' SOME GREAT FOOD RIGHT NOW.
HMPH
TWITCH
YOU KNOW, I BET THERE'S PLENTY OF FOOD IN THE KITCHEN.
THEY'RE MAKING DINNER FOR A WHOLE HIGH SCHOOL CLASS...
THEY WON'T NOTICE IF I STEAL JUST ONE.
I'LL GET MY DINNER BY STEALTH!

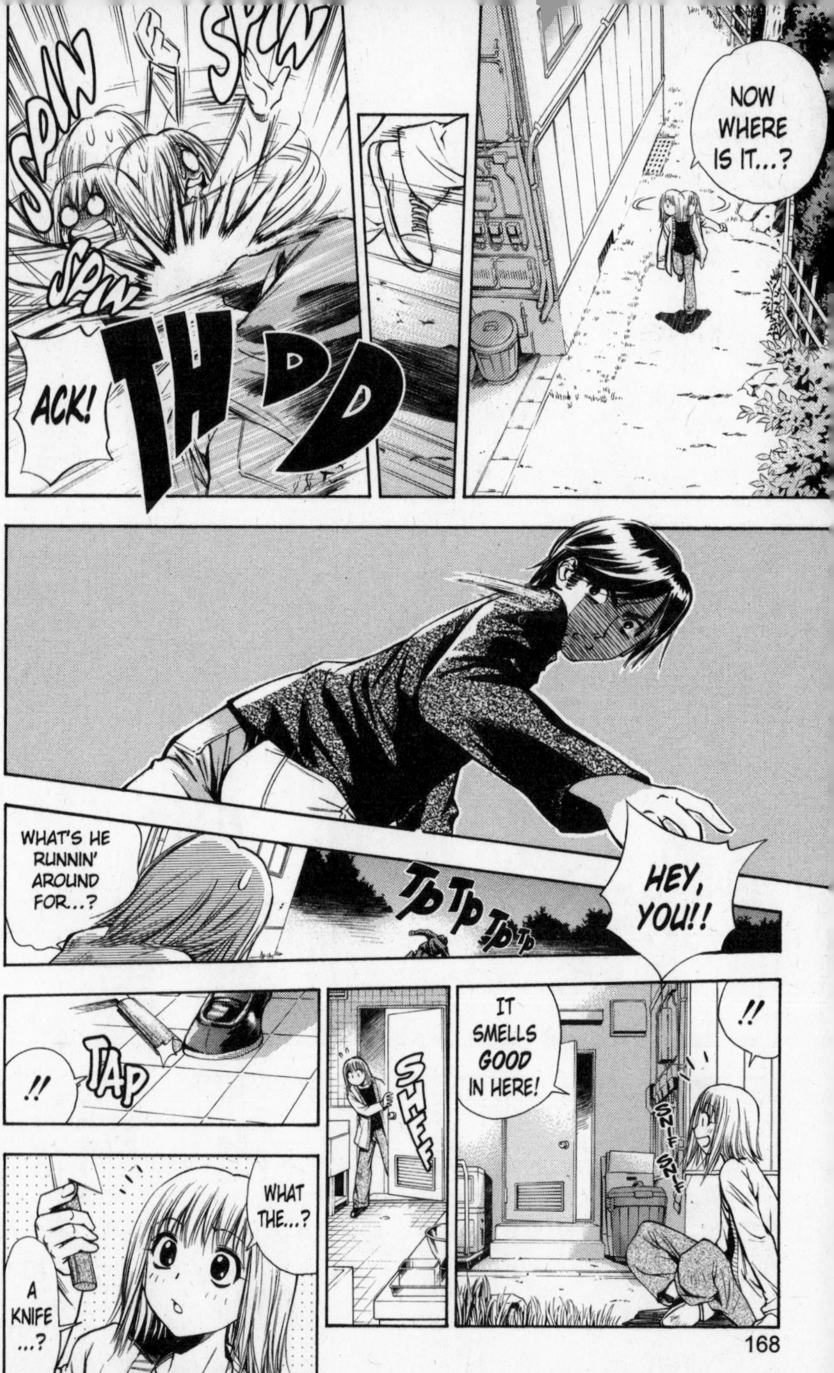
NOW WHERE IS IT...?
SPIN
SPIN
SPIN
ACK!
THDD
HEY, YOU!!
TP TP TP TP
WHAT'S HE RUNNIN' AROUND FOR...?
!!
SNIF SNIF
IT SMELLS GOOD IN HERE!
SHFF
TAP
!!
WHAT THE...?
A KNIFE ...?

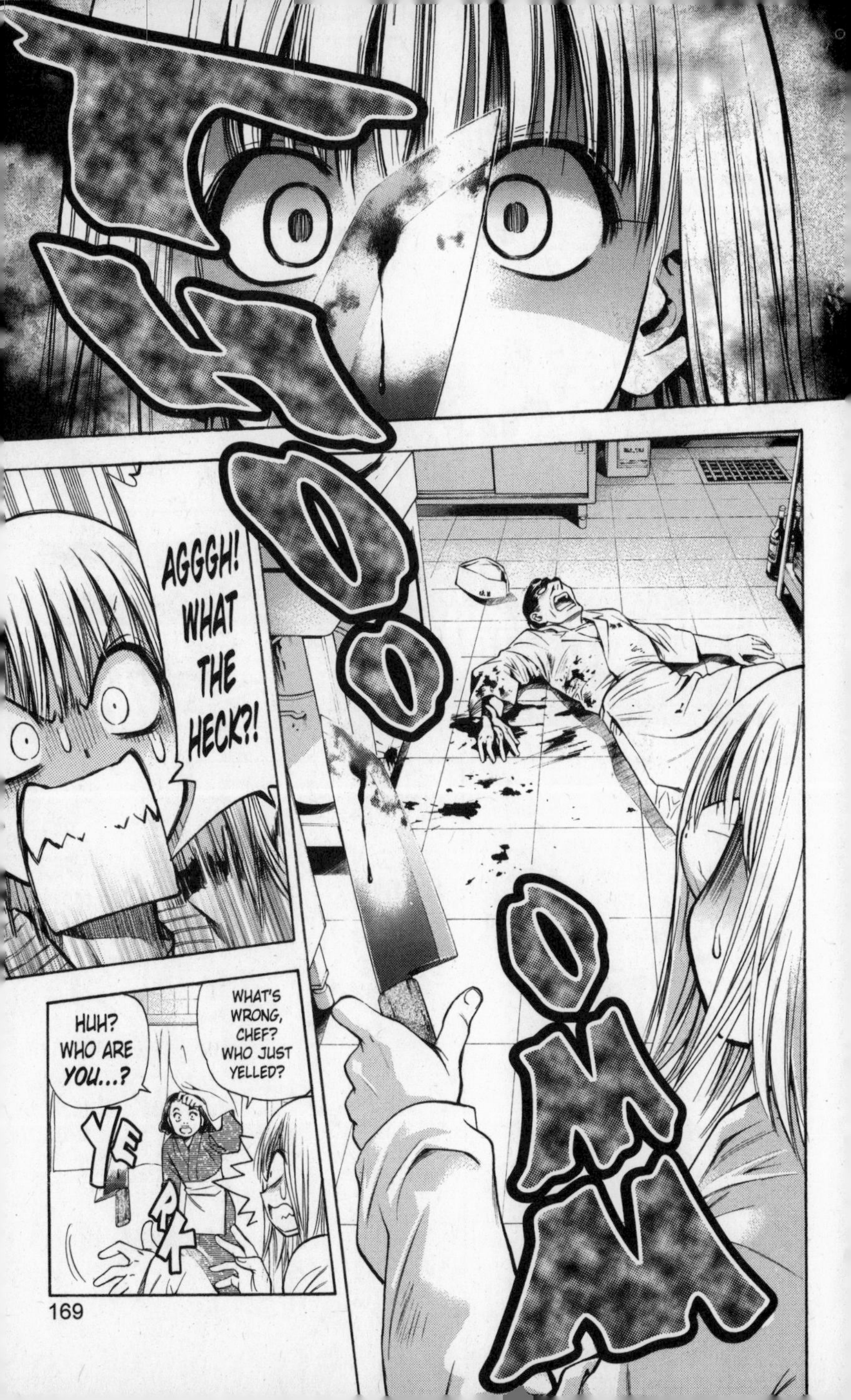
AGGGH! WHAT THE HECK?!
WHAT'S WRONG, CHEF? WHO JUST YELLED?
HUH? WHO ARE YOU...?
YERK

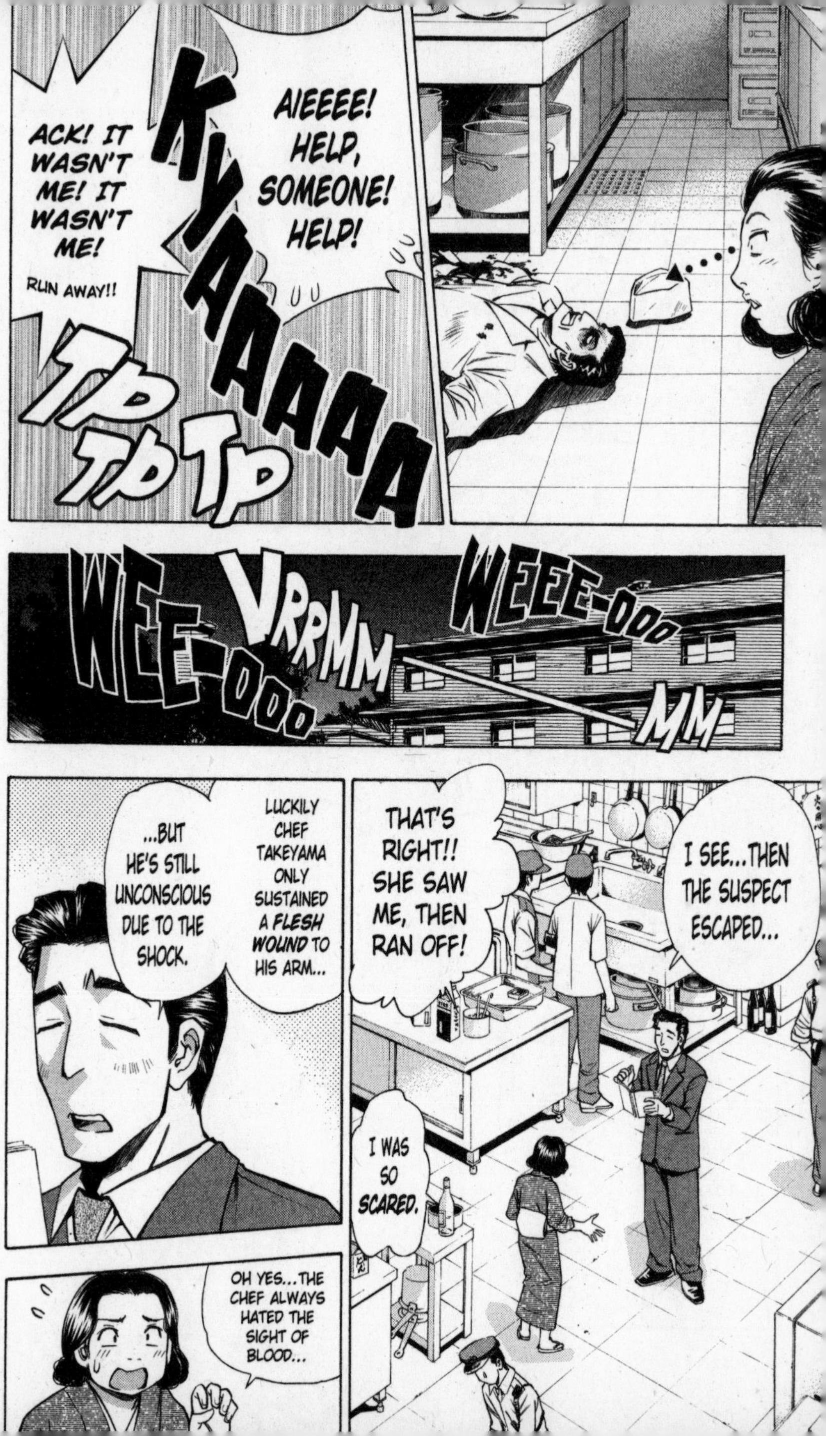
AIEEEE! HELP, SOMEONE! HELP!
KYAAAAAA
ACK! IT WASN'T ME! IT WASN'T ME!
RUN AWAY!!
TP TP TP
WEEE-OOO
VRRMMMM
WEE-OOO
I SEE...THEN THE SUSPECT ESCAPED...
THAT'S RIGHT!! SHE SAW ME, THEN RAN OFF!
I WAS SO SCARED.
LUCKILY CHEF TAKEYAMA ONLY SUSTAINED A FLESH WOUND TO HIS ARM...
...BUT HE'S STILL UNCONSCIOUS DUE TO THE SHOCK.
OH YES...THE CHEF ALWAYS HATED THE SIGHT OF BLOOD...

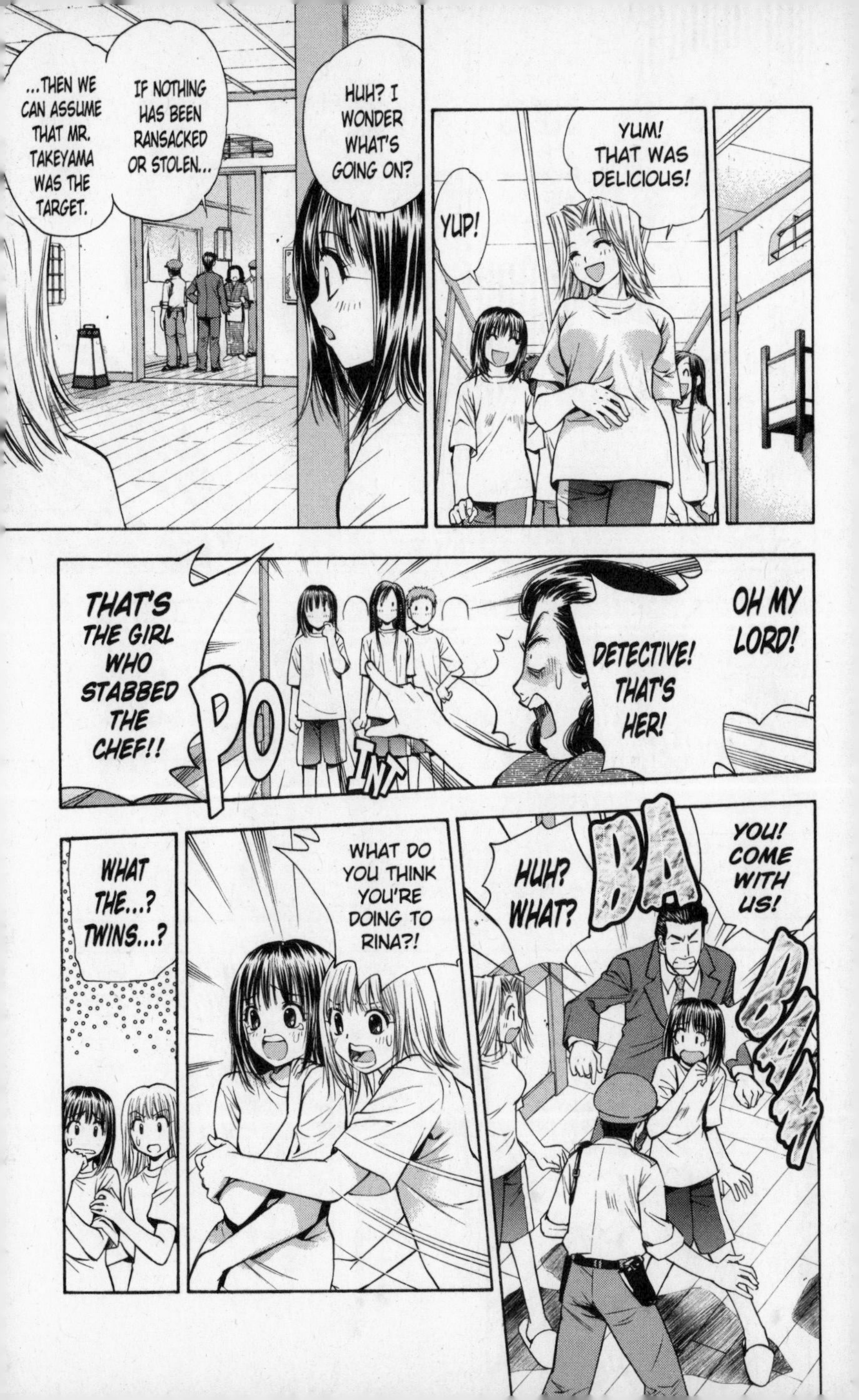
YUM! THAT WAS DELICIOUS!
YUP!
HUH? I WONDER WHAT'S GOING ON?
IF NOTHING HAS BEEN RANSACKED OR STOLEN...
...THEN WE CAN ASSUME THAT MR. TAKEYAMA WAS THE TARGET.
OH MY LORD!
DETECTIVE! THAT'S HER!
POINT
THAT'S THE GIRL WHO STABBED THE CHEF!!
YOU! COME WITH US!
BA
HUH? WHAT?
WHAT DO YOU THINK YOU'RE DOING TO RINA?!
WHAT THE...? TWINS...?

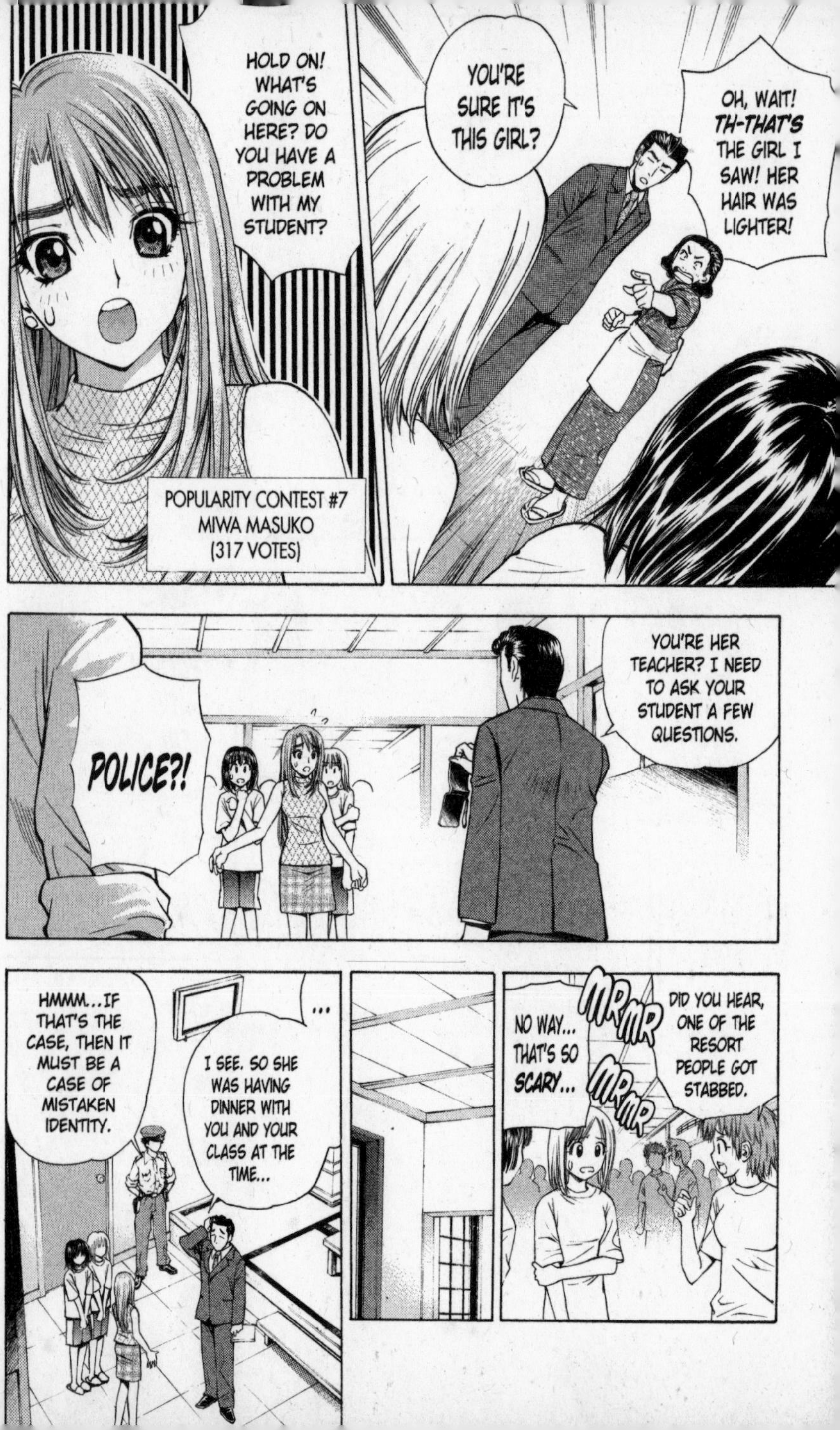
OH, WAIT! TH-THAT'S THE GIRL I SAW! HER HAIR WAS LIGHTER!
YOU'RE SURE IT'S THIS GIRL?
HOLD ON! WHAT'S GOING ON HERE? DO YOU HAVE A PROBLEM WITH MY STUDENT?
POPULARITY CONTEST #7
MIWA MASUKO
(317 VOTES)
YOU'RE HER TEACHER? I NEED TO ASK YOUR STUDENT A FEW QUESTIONS.
POLICE?!
DID YOU HEAR, ONE OF THE RESORT PEOPLE GOT STABBED.
MRMR
MRMR
NO WAY... THAT'S SO SCARY...
...
I SEE. SO SHE WAS HAVING DINNER WITH YOU AND YOUR CLASS AT THE TIME...
HMMM...IF THAT'S THE CASE, THEN IT MUST BE A CASE OF MISTAKEN IDENTITY.

READ THIS WAY

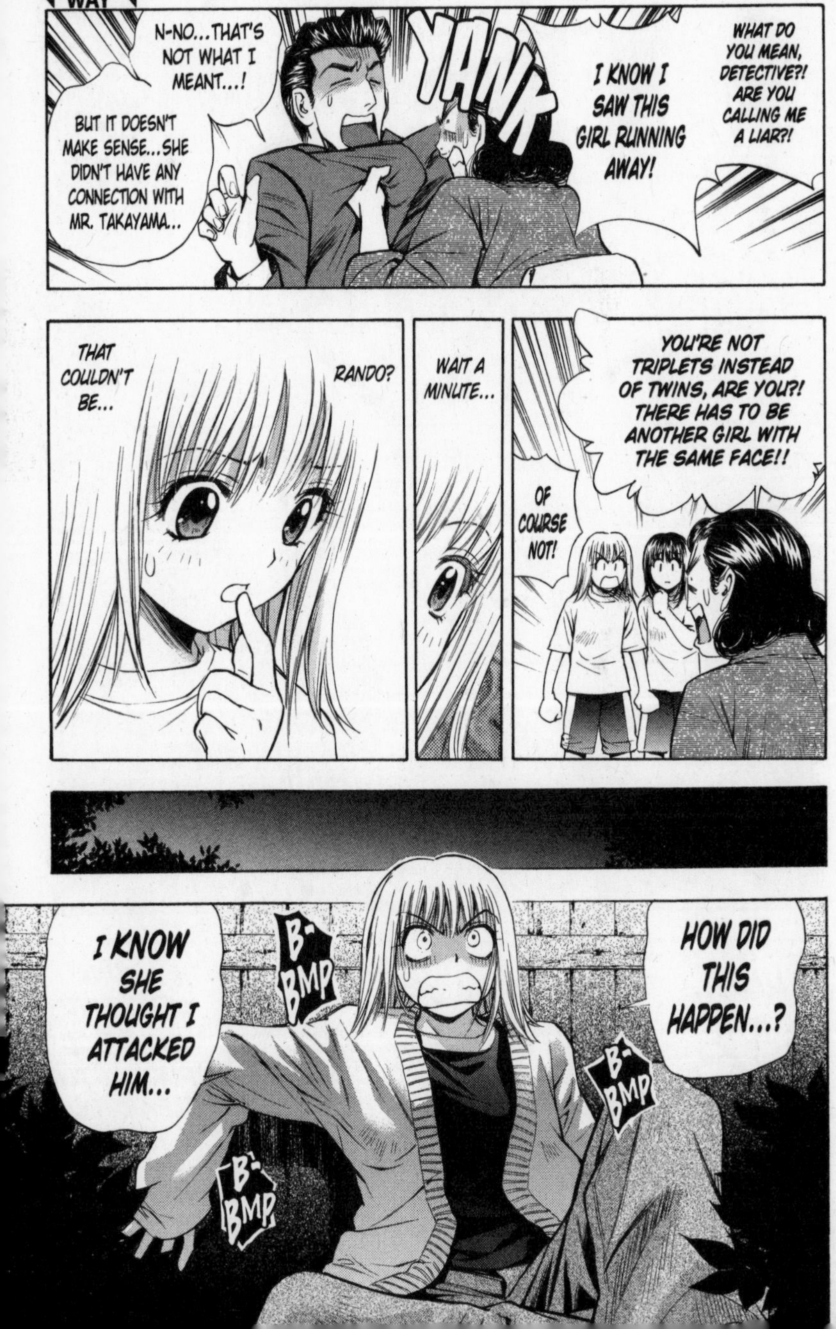
WHAT DO YOU MEAN, DETECTIVE?! ARE YOU CALLING ME A LIAR?!
I KNOW I SAW THIS GIRL RUNNING AWAY!
YANK
N-NO...THAT'S NOT WHAT I MEANT...!
BUT IT DOESN'T MAKE SENSE...SHE DIDN'T HAVE ANY CONNECTION WITH MR. TAKAYAMA...
YOU'RE NOT TRIPLETS INSTEAD OF TWINS, ARE YOU?! THERE HAS TO BE ANOTHER GIRL WITH THE SAME FACE!!
OF COURSE NOT!
WAIT A MINUTE...
RANDO?
THAT COULDN'T BE...
HOW DID THIS HAPPEN...?
B-BMP
I KNOW SHE THOUGHT I ATTACKED HIM...
B-BMP
B-BMP

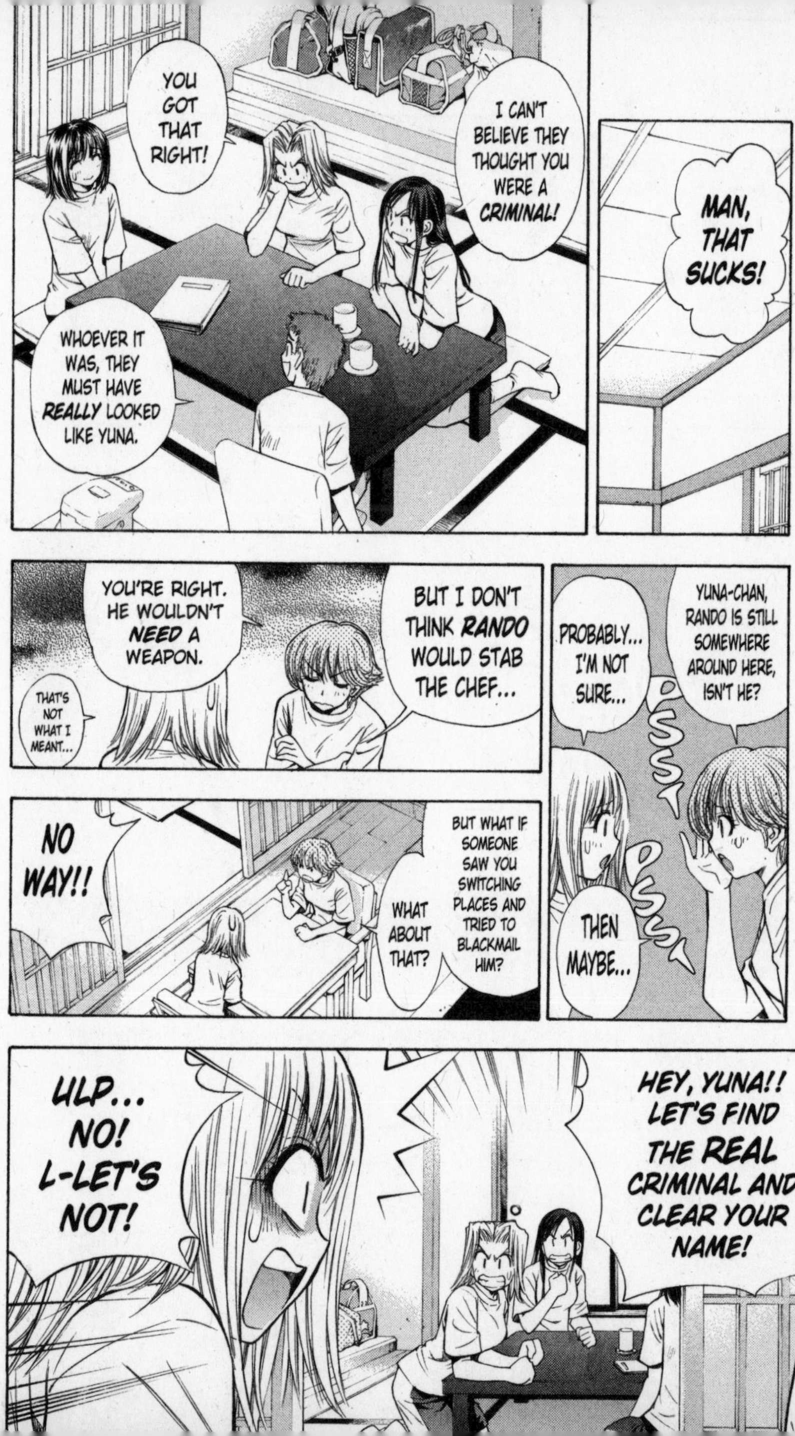
MAN, THAT SUCKS!
I CAN'T BELIEVE THEY THOUGHT YOU WERE A CRIMINAL!
YOU GOT THAT RIGHT!
WHOEVER IT WAS, THEY MUST HAVE REALLY LOOKED LIKE YUNA.
YUNA-CHAN, RANDO IS STILL SOMEWHERE AROUND HERE, ISN'T HE?
PROBABLY... I'M NOT SURE...
THEN MAYBE...
BUT I DON'T THINK RANDO WOULD STAB THE CHEF...
YOU'RE RIGHT. HE WOULDN'T NEED A WEAPON.
THAT'S NOT WHAT I MEANT...
BUT WHAT IF SOMEONE SAW YOU SWITCHING PLACES AND TRIED TO BLACKMAIL HIM?
WHAT ABOUT THAT?
NO WAY!!
HEY, YUNA!! LET'S FIND THE REAL CRIMINAL AND CLEAR YOUR NAME!
ULP... NO! L-LET'S NOT!

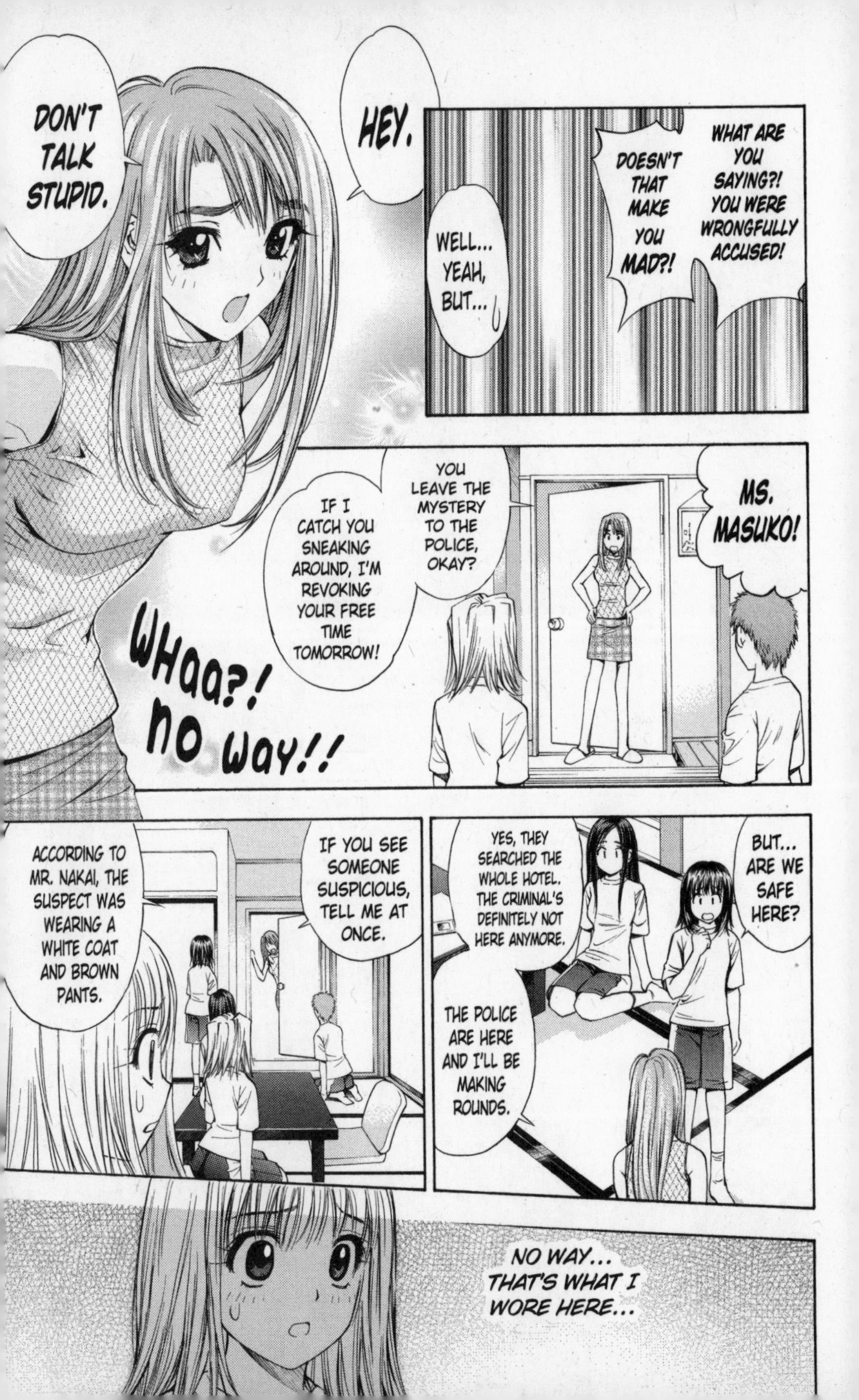
WHAT ARE YOU SAYING?! YOU WERE WRONGFULLY ACCUSED!
DOESN'T THAT MAKE YOU MAD?!
WELL... YEAH, BUT...
HEY.
DON'T TALK STUPID.
MS. MASUKO!
YOU LEAVE THE MYSTERY TO THE POLICE, OKAY?
IF I CATCH YOU SNEAKING AROUND, I'M REVOKING YOUR FREE TIME TOMORROW!
WHAA?! NO WAY!!
BUT... ARE WE SAFE HERE?
YES, THEY SEARCHED THE WHOLE HOTEL. THE CRIMINAL'S DEFINITELY NOT HERE ANYMORE.
THE POLICE ARE HERE AND I'LL BE MAKING ROUNDS.
IF YOU SEE SOMEONE SUSPICIOUS, TELL ME AT ONCE.
ACCORDING TO MR. NAKAI, THE SUSPECT WAS WEARING A WHITE COAT AND BROWN PANTS.
NO WAY... THAT'S WHAT I WORE HERE...

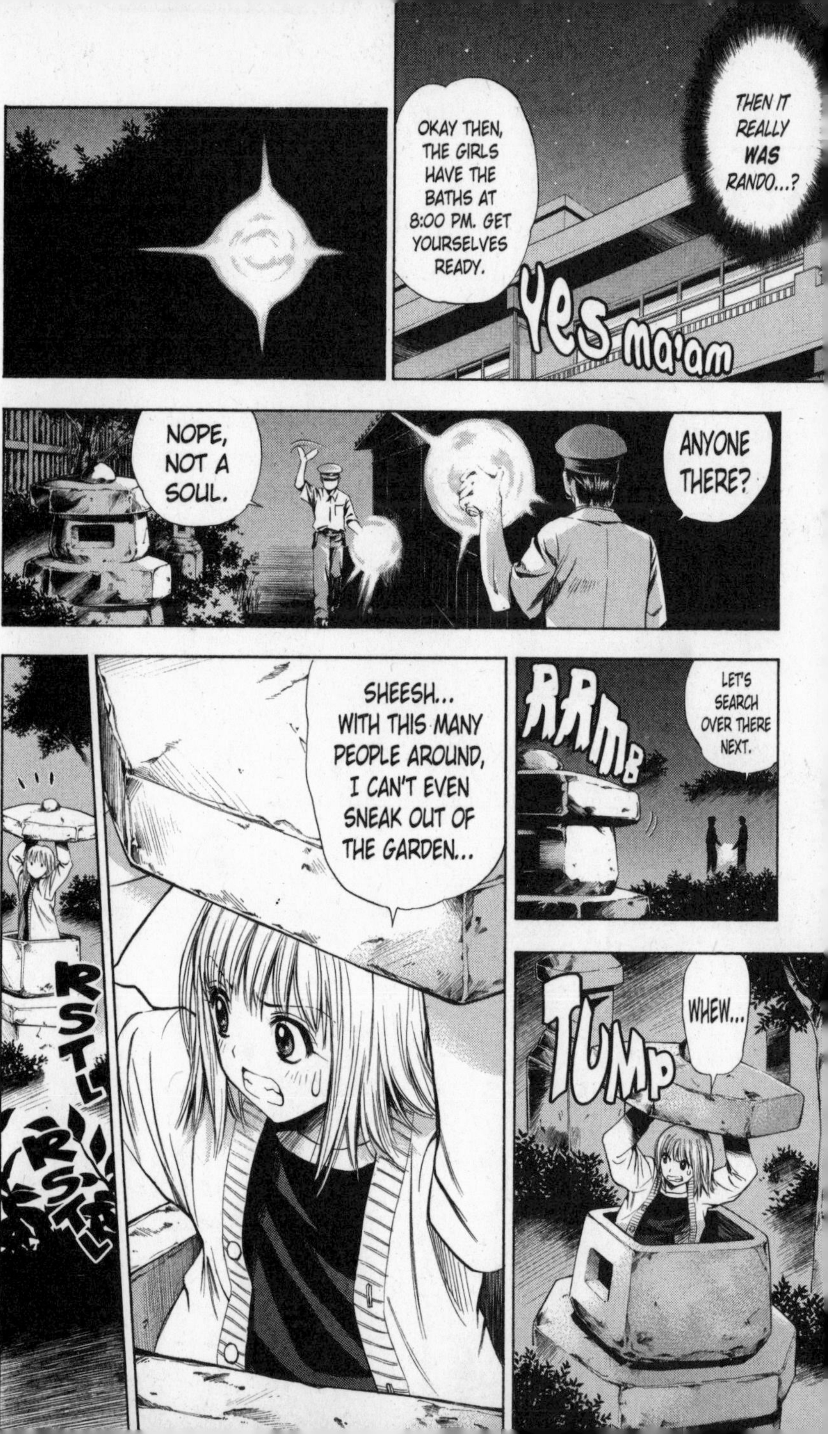
THEN IT REALLY WAS RANDO...?
OKAY THEN, THE GIRLS HAVE THE BATHS AT 8:00 PM. GET YOURSELVES READY.
YES MA'AM
ANYONE THERE?
NOPE, NOT A SOUL.
RRMB
LET'S SEARCH OVER THERE NEXT.
TUMP
WHEW...
SHEESH... WITH THIS MANY PEOPLE AROUND, I CAN'T EVEN SNEAK OUT OF THE GARDEN...
RSTL
RSTL

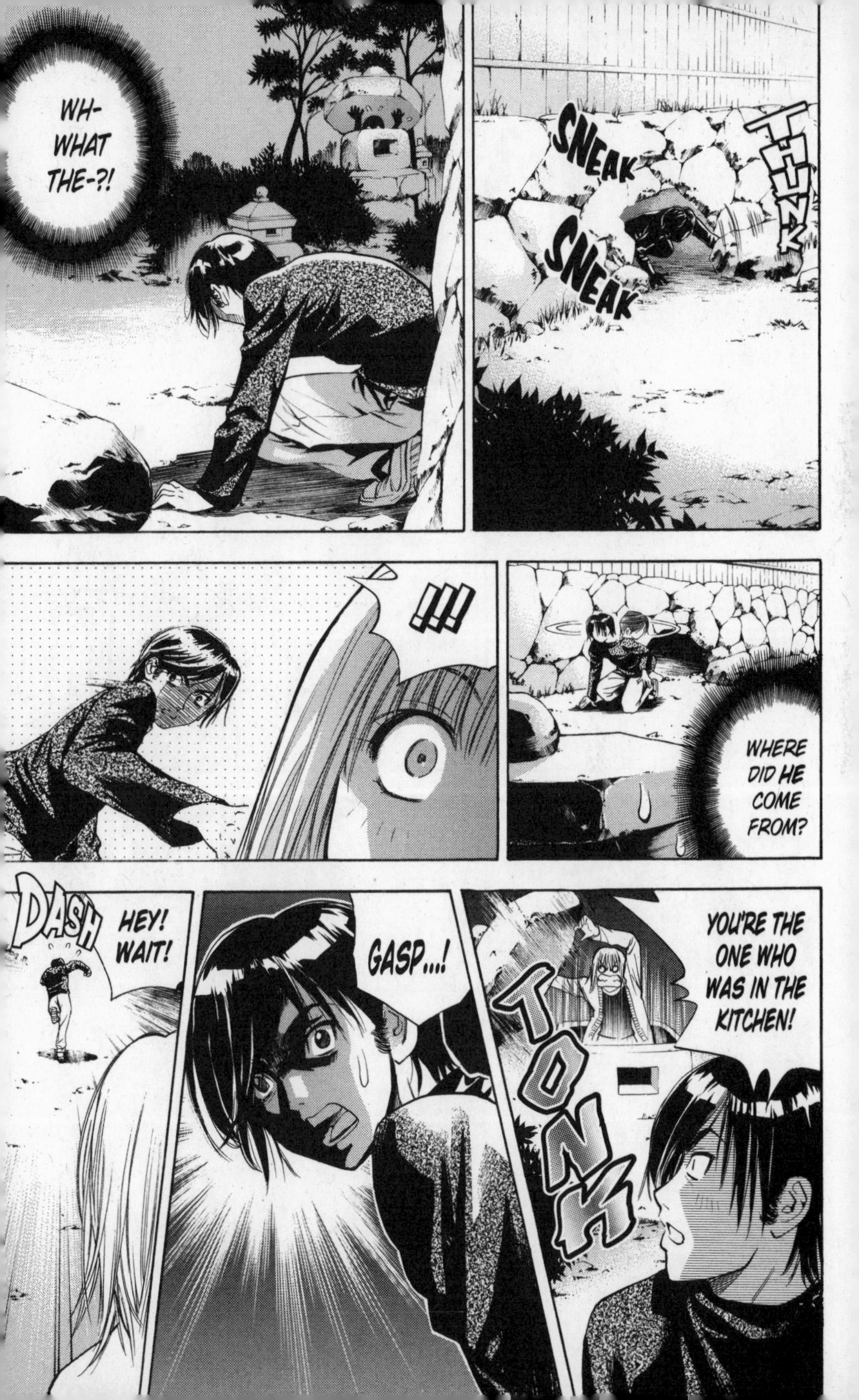

SNEAK
SNEAK
THUNK
WH- WHAT THE-?!
WHERE DID HE COME FROM?
!!!
YOU'RE THE ONE WHO WAS IN THE KITCHEN!
TONK
GASP...!
HEY! WAIT!
DASH

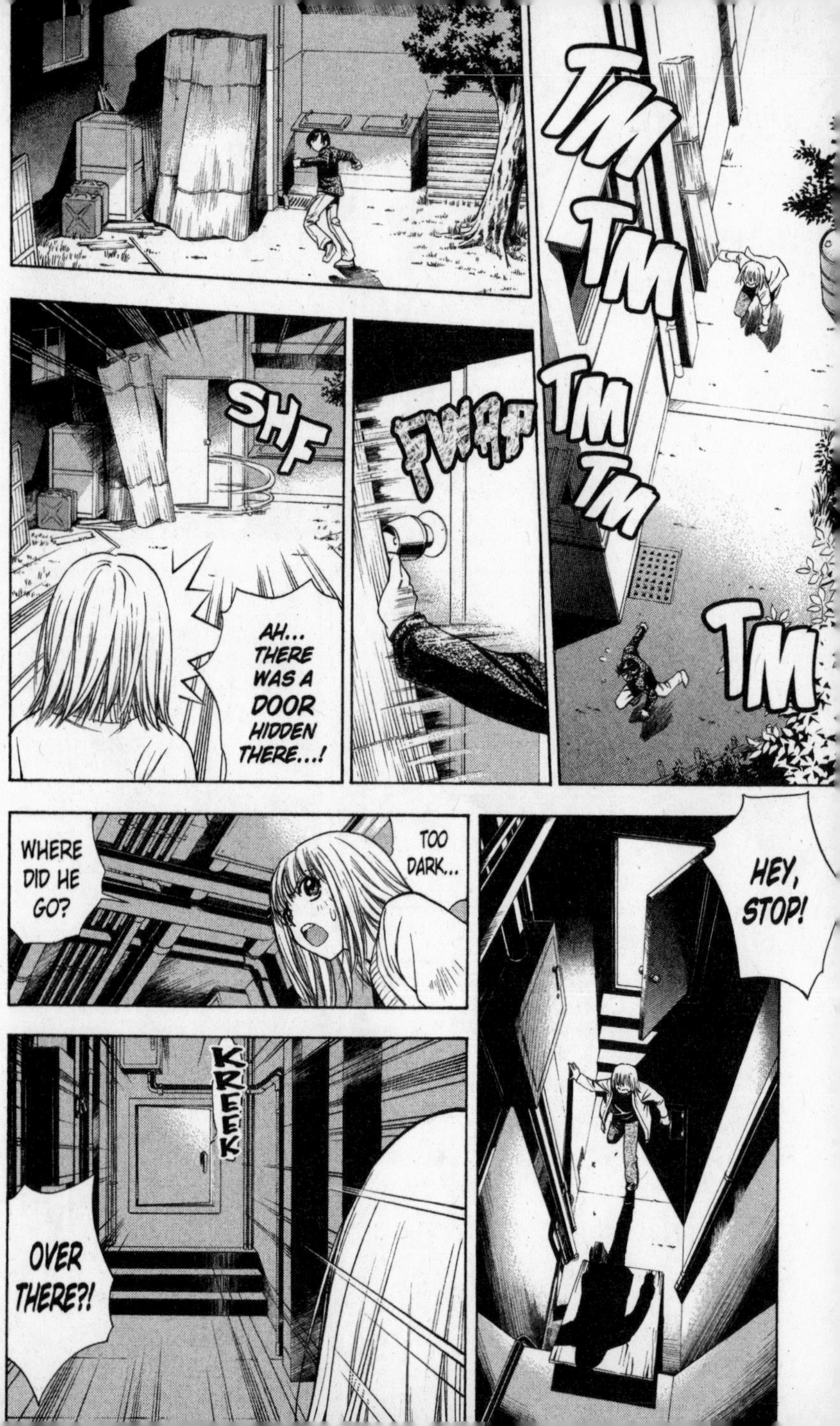

TM
TM
TM
TM
TM
FWAP
SHF
AH... THERE WAS A DOOR HIDDEN THERE...!
HEY, STOP!
TOO DARK...
WHERE DID HE GO?
KREEK
OVER THERE?!

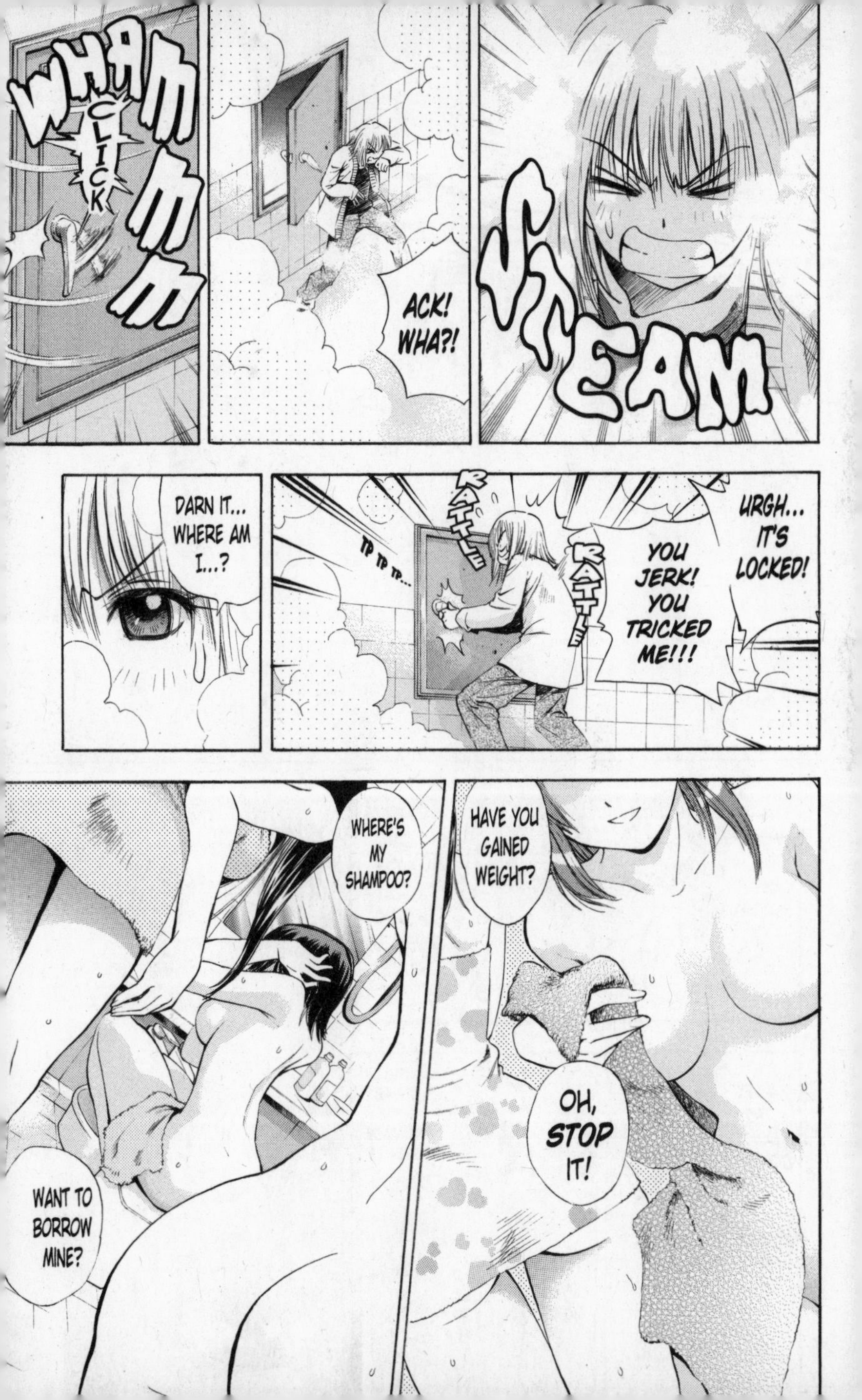
STEAM
ACK! WHA?!
WHAM
CLICK
URGH... IT'S LOCKED!
YOU JERK! YOU TRICKED ME!!!
RATTLE
RATTLE
TP TP TP...
DARN IT... WHERE AM I...?
HAVE YOU GAINED WEIGHT?
OH, STOP IT!
WHERE'S MY SHAMPOO?
WANT TO BORROW MINE?

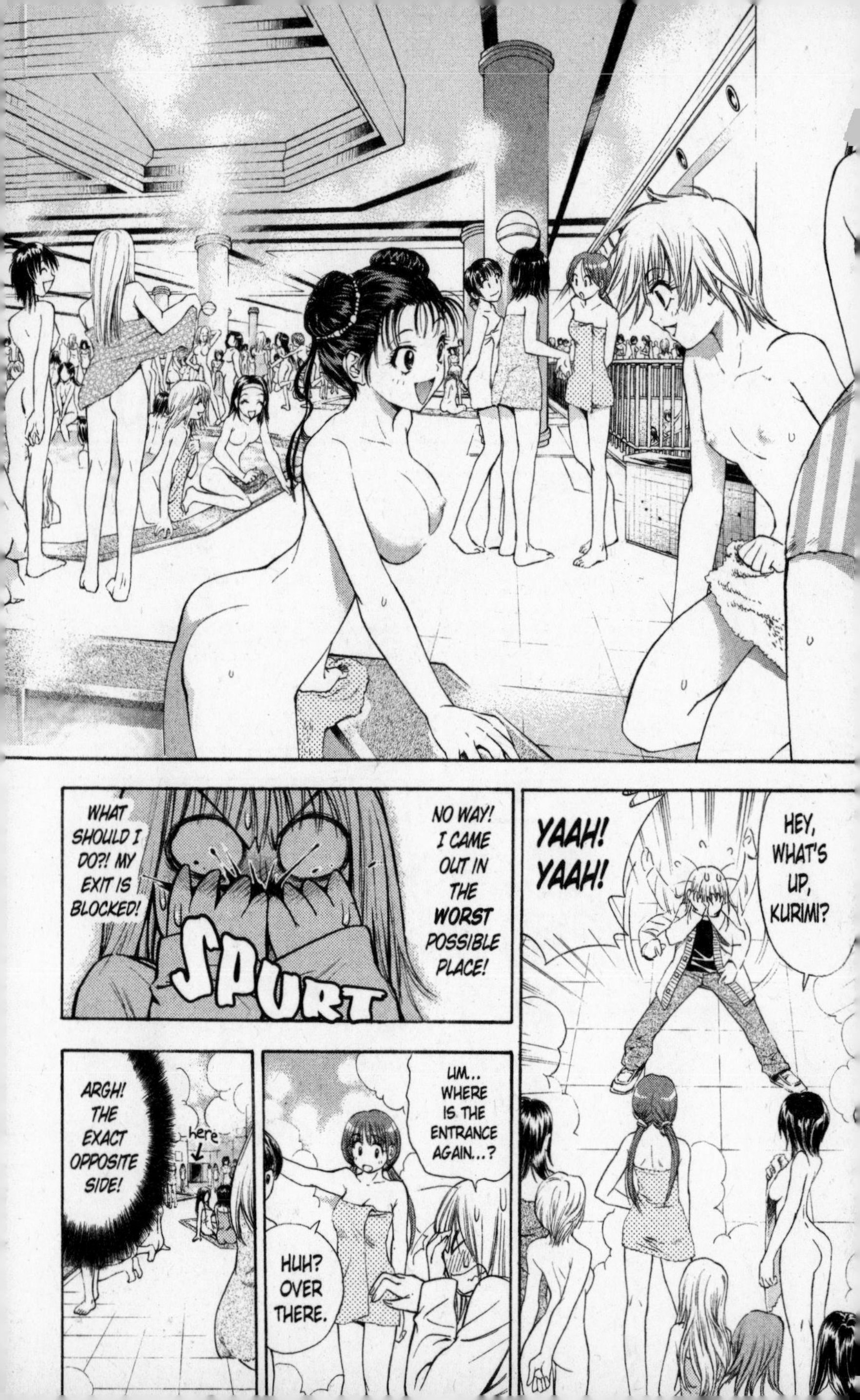
HEY, WHAT'S UP, KURIMI?
YAAH! YAAH!
NO WAY! I CAME OUT IN THE WORST POSSIBLE PLACE!
WHAT SHOULD I DO?! MY EXIT IS BLOCKED!
SPURT
UM.. WHERE IS THE ENTRANCE AGAIN...?
HUH? OVER THERE.
ARGH! THE EXACT OPPOSITE SIDE!
here

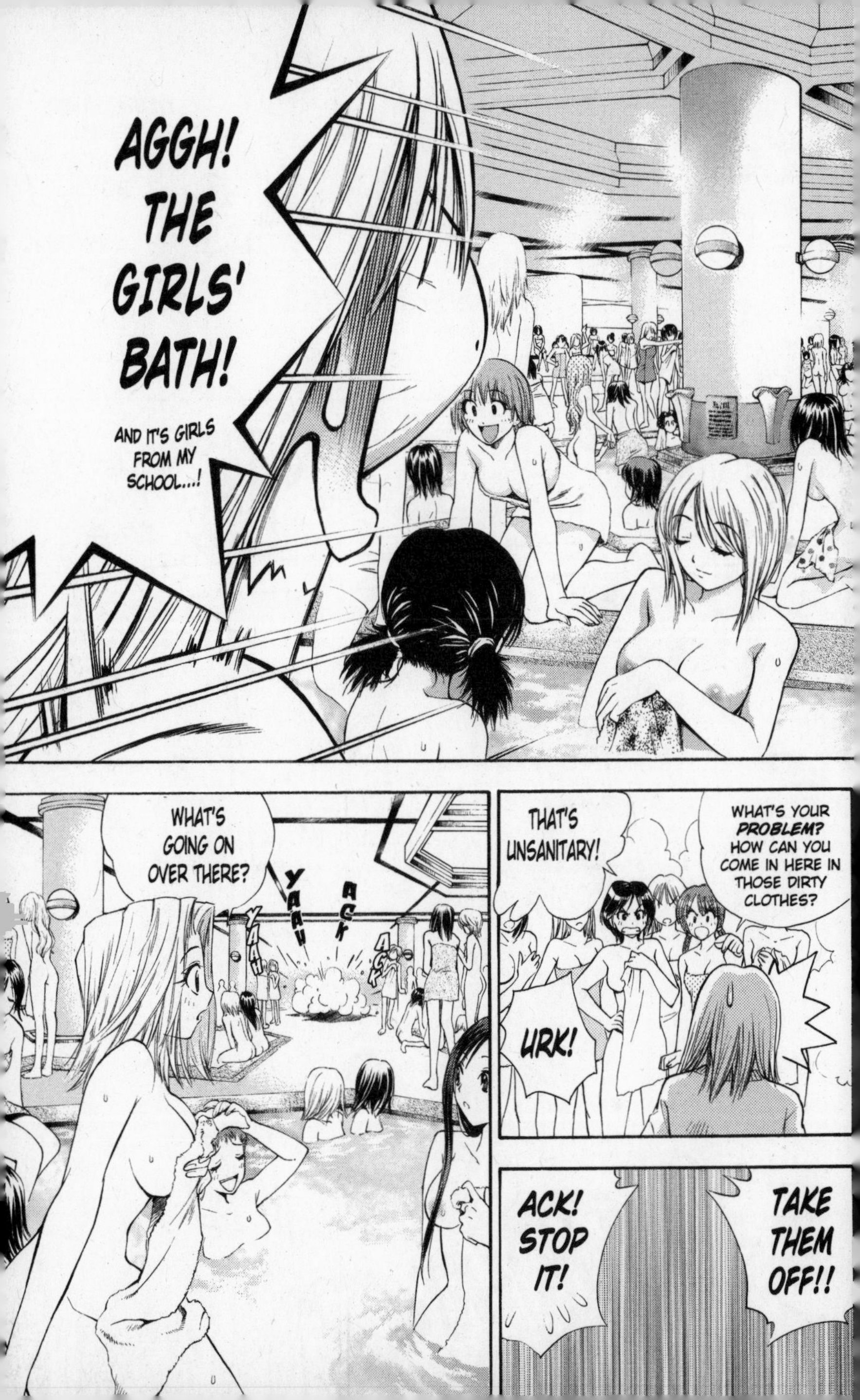
AGGH! THE GIRLS' BATH!
AND IT'S GIRLS FROM MY SCHOOL...!
WHAT'S YOUR *PROBLEM?* HOW CAN YOU COME IN HERE IN THOSE DIRTY CLOTHES?
THAT'S UNSANITARY!
URK!
TAKE THEM OFF!!
ACK! STOP IT!
WHAT'S GOING ON OVER THERE?
ACK
ACK
YAAH
YAAH

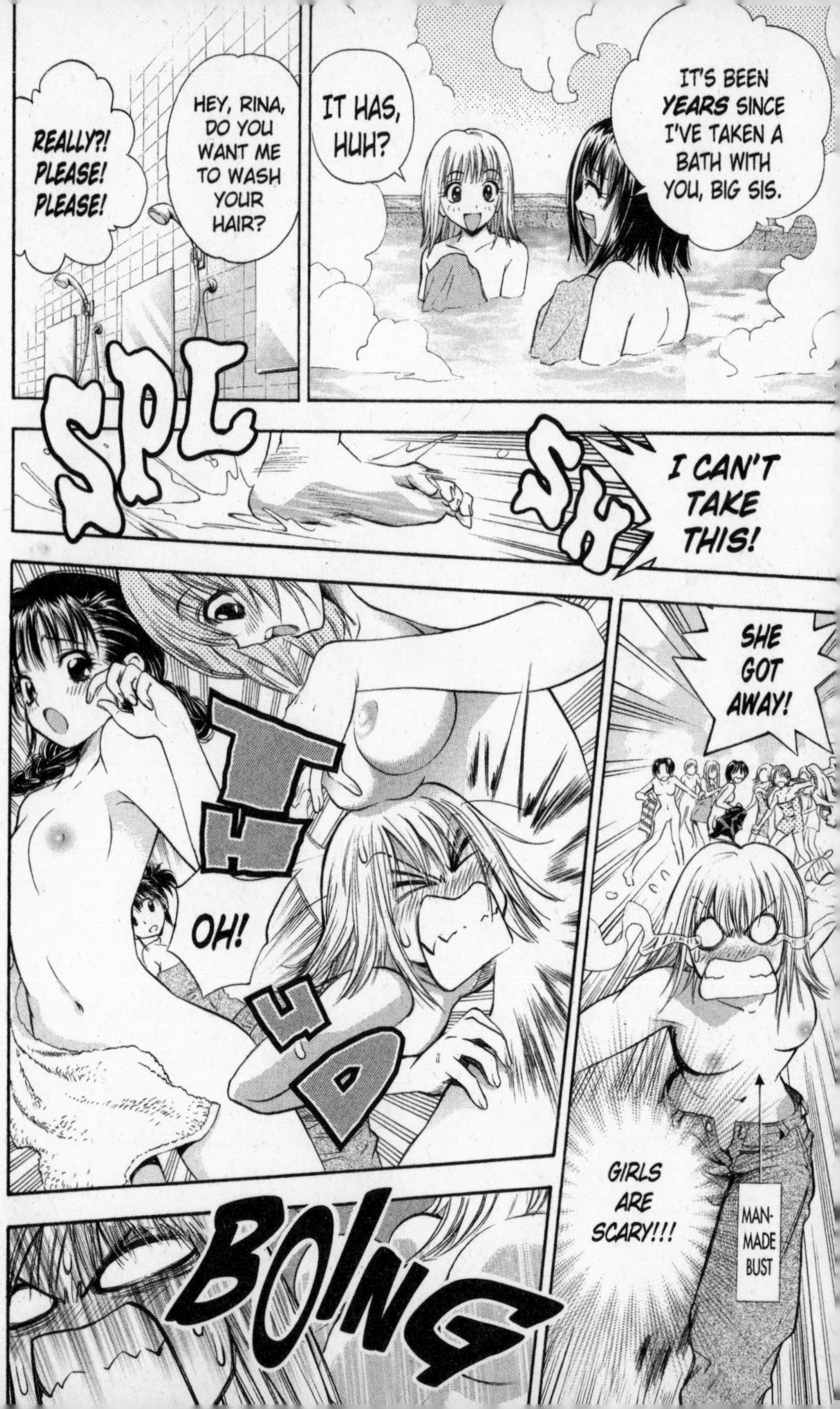
IT'S BEEN YEARS SINCE I'VE TAKEN A BATH WITH YOU, BIG SIS.
IT HAS, HUH?
HEY, RINA, DO YOU WANT ME TO WASH YOUR HAIR?
REALLY?! PLEASE! PLEASE!
I CAN'T TAKE THIS!
SH
SPL
SHE GOT AWAY!
GIRLS ARE SCARY!!!
MAN-MADE BUST
THUD
OH!
BOING

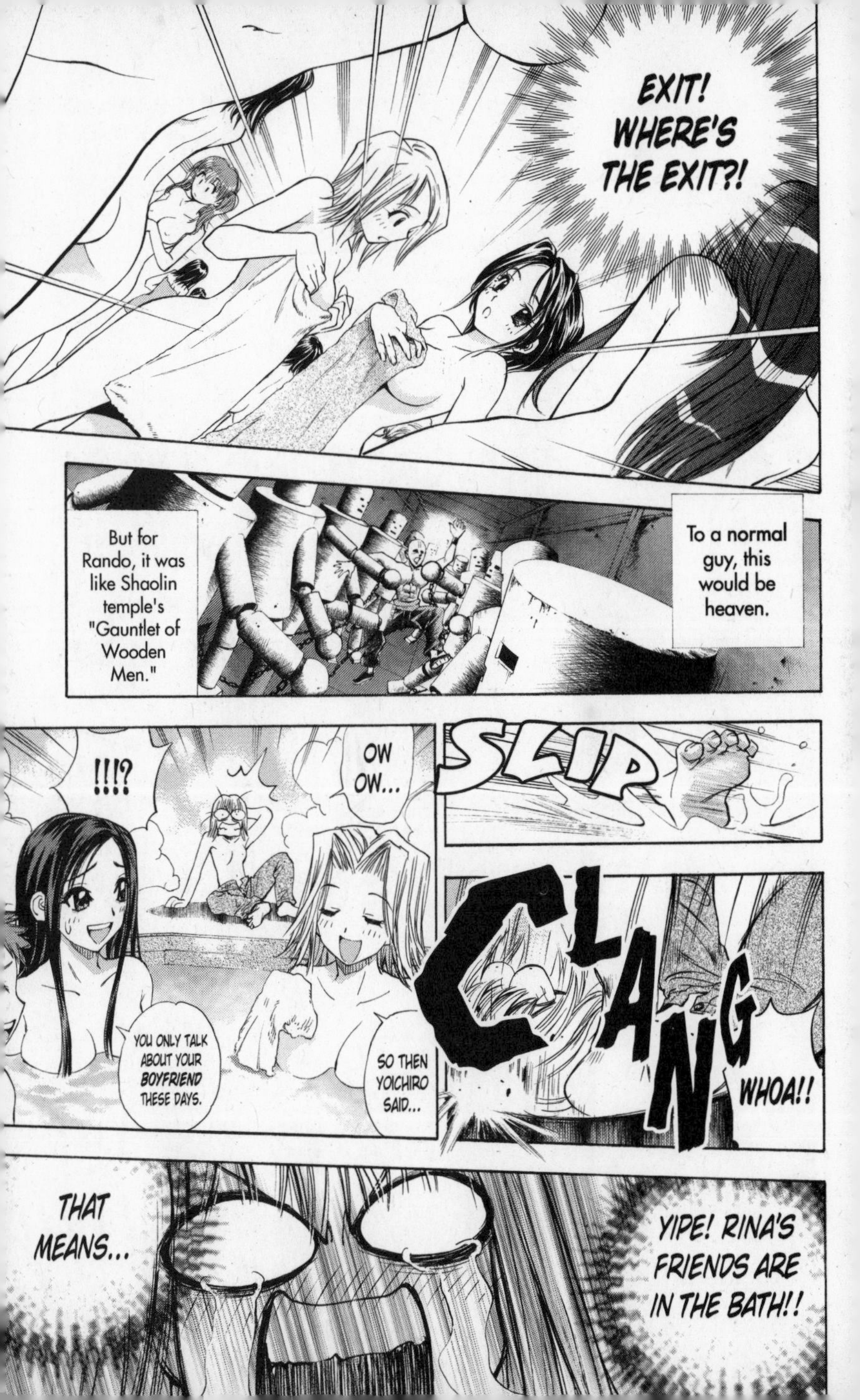
EXIT! WHERE'S THE EXIT?!
To a normal guy, this would be heaven.
But for Rando, it was like Shaolin temple's "Gauntlet of Wooden Men."
SLIP
CLANG
WHOA!!
OW OW...
!!!?
SO THEN YOICHIRO SAID...
YOU ONLY TALK ABOUT YOUR BOYFRIEND THESE DAYS.
THAT MEANS...
YIPE! RINA'S FRIENDS ARE IN THE BATH!!

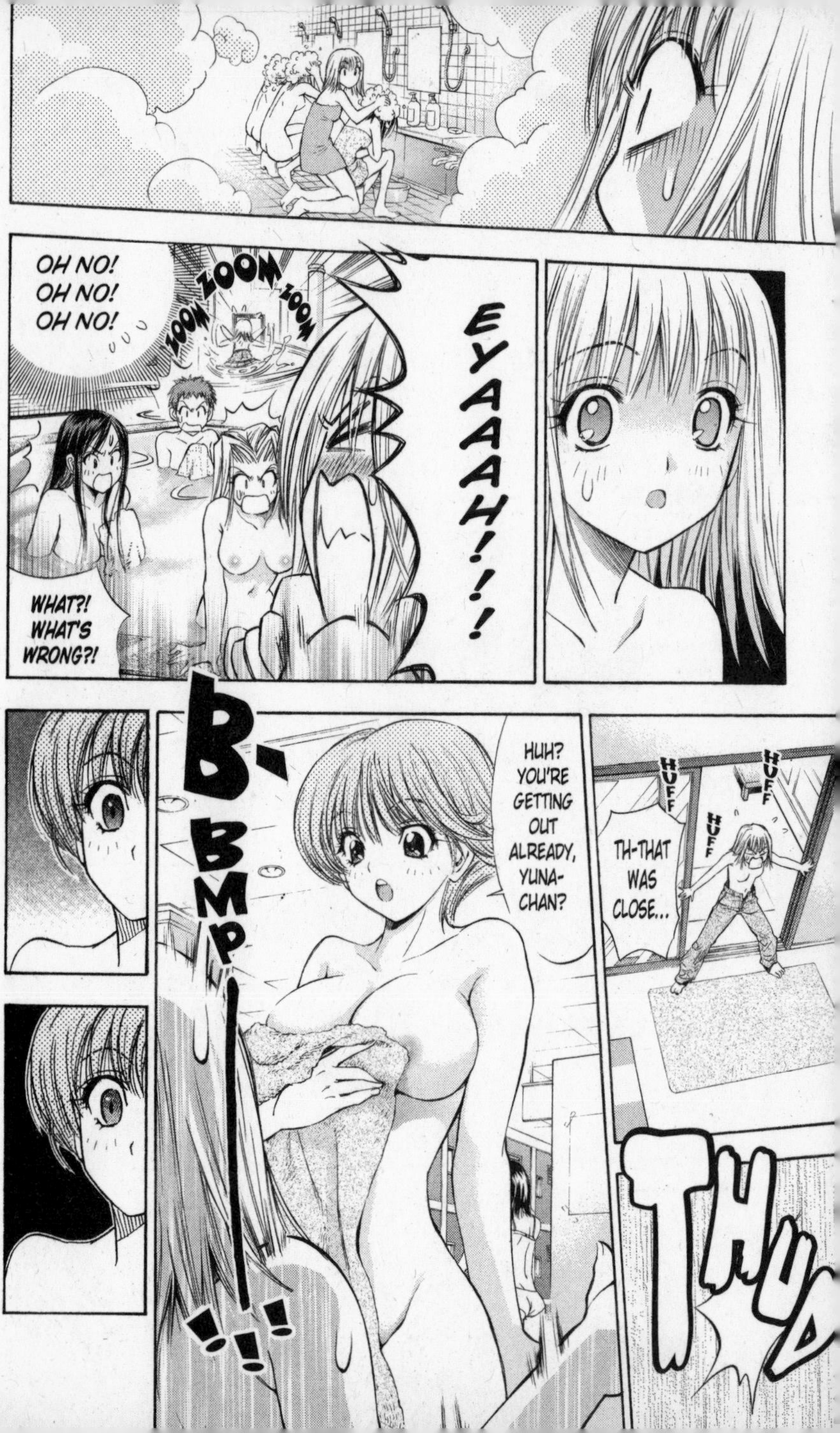
EYAAAAH!!!
ZOOM ZOOM ZOOM ZOOM
OH NO! OH NO! OH NO!
WHAT?! WHAT'S WRONG?!
HUFF HUFF HUFF
TH-THAT WAS CLOSE...
THUD
HUH? YOU'RE GETTING OUT ALREADY, YUNA-CHAN?
B-BMP!!!!

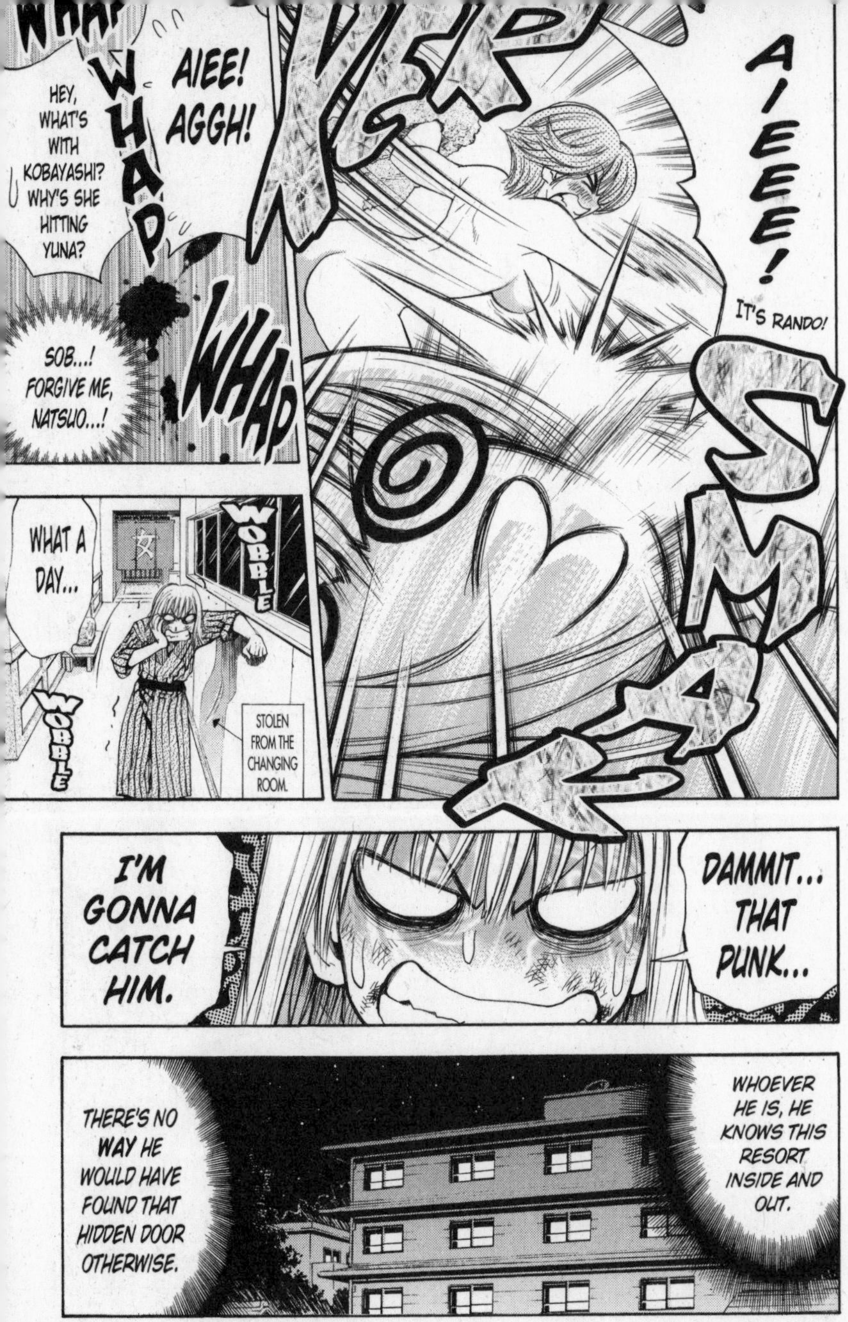
AIEEE!
IT'S RANDO!
SMAAK
WHAP
AIEE! AGGH!
WHAP
HEY, WHAT'S WITH KOBAYASHI? WHY'S SHE HITTING YUNA?
WHAP
SOB...! FORGIVE ME, NATSUO...!
WOBBLE
WHAT A DAY...
WOBBLE
STOLEN FROM THE CHANGING ROOM.
DAMMIT... THAT PUNK...
I'M GONNA CATCH HIM.
WHOEVER HE IS, HE KNOWS THIS RESORT INSIDE AND OUT.
THERE'S NO WAY HE WOULD HAVE FOUND THAT HIDDEN DOOR OTHERWISE.

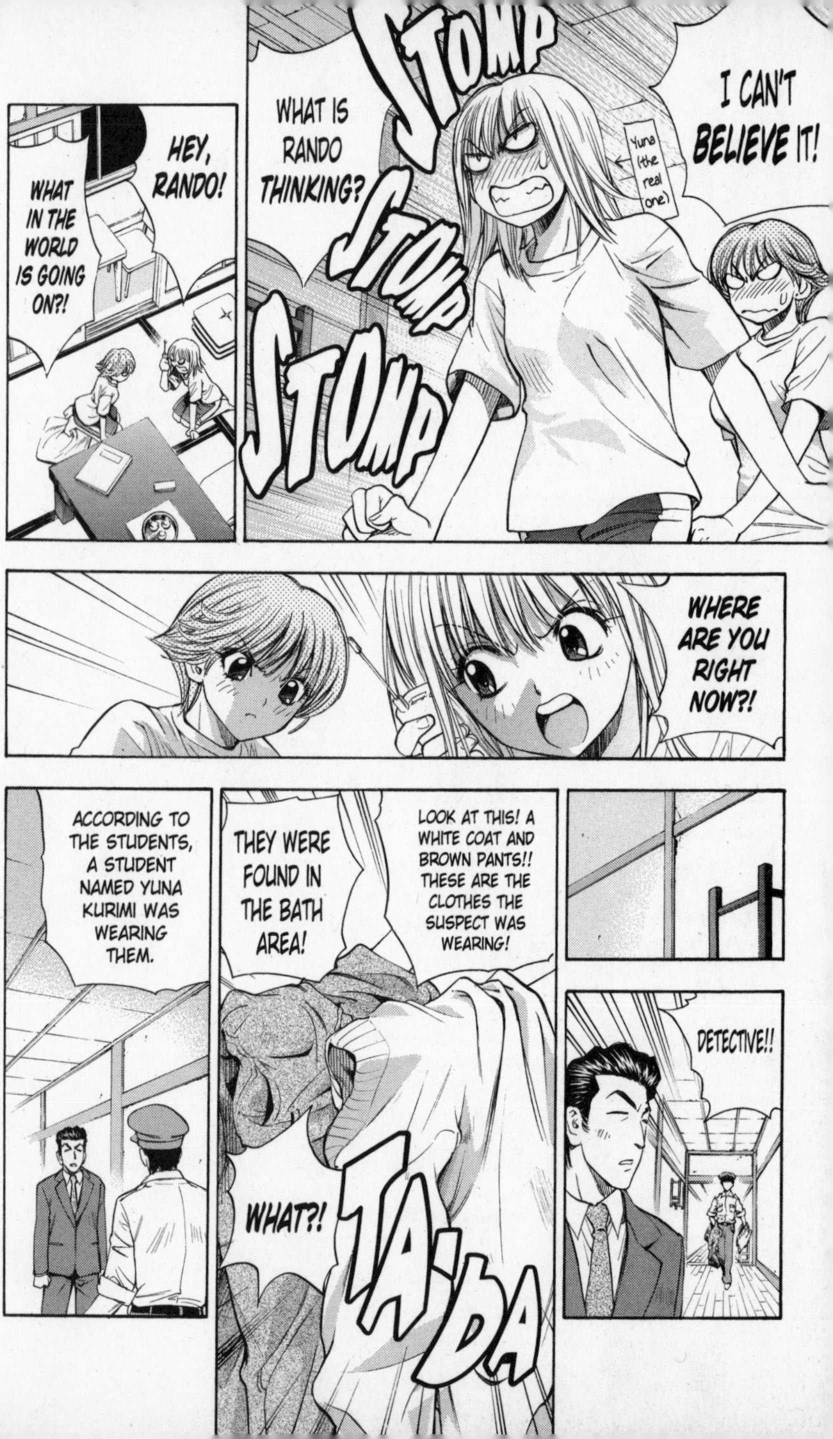
STOMP
I CAN'T BELIEVE IT!
Yuna (the real one)
STOMP
WHAT IS RANDO THINKING?
STOMP
STOMP
HEY, RANDO!
WHAT IN THE WORLD IS GOING ON?!
WHERE ARE YOU RIGHT NOW?!
DETECTIVE!!
LOOK AT THIS! A WHITE COAT AND BROWN PANTS!! THESE ARE THE CLOTHES THE SUSPECT WAS WEARING!
THEY WERE FOUND IN THE BATH AREA!
TA-DA
WHAT?!
ACCORDING TO THE STUDENTS, A STUDENT NAMED YUNA KURIMI WAS WEARING THEM.

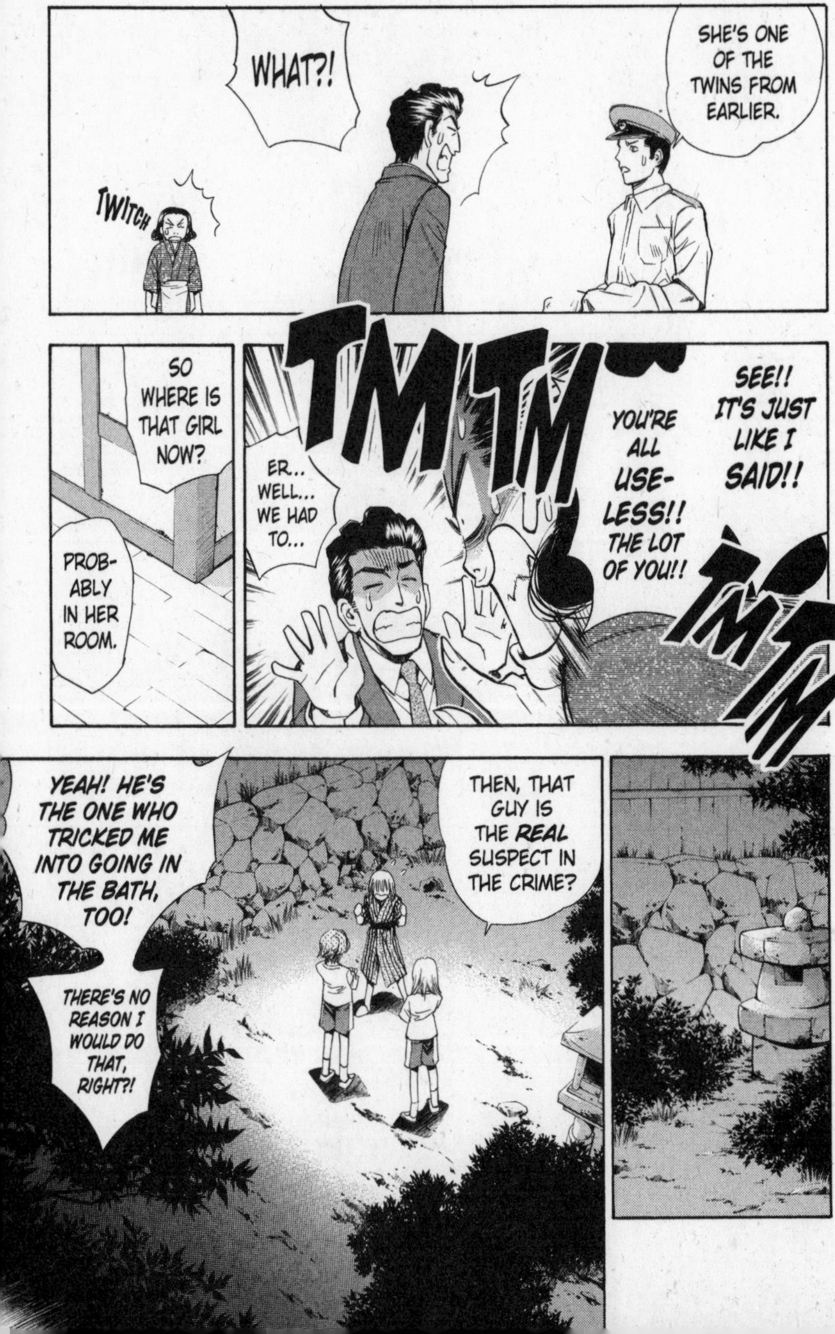
SHE'S ONE OF THE TWINS FROM EARLIER.
WHAT?!
TWITCH
SEE!! IT'S JUST LIKE I SAID!!
YOU'RE ALL USE-LESS!! THE LOT OF YOU!!
TMTM
ER... WELL... WE HAD TO...
TMTM
SO WHERE IS THAT GIRL NOW?
PROB-ABLY IN HER ROOM.
THEN, THAT GUY IS THE REAL SUSPECT IN THE CRIME?
YEAH! HE'S THE ONE WHO TRICKED ME INTO GOING IN THE BATH, TOO!
THERE'S NO REASON I WOULD DO THAT, RIGHT?!

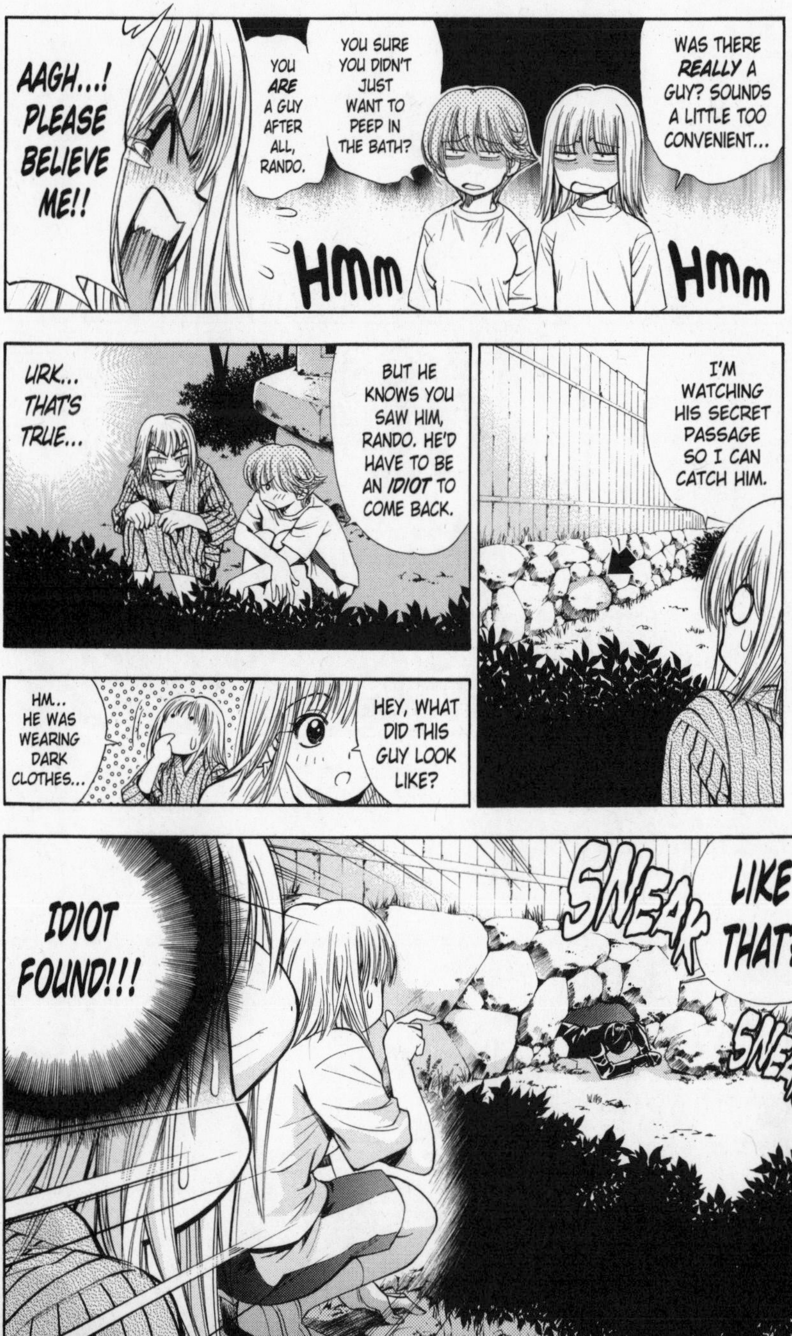
WAS THERE REALLY A GUY? SOUNDS A LITTLE TOO CONVENIENT...
Hmm
YOU SURE YOU DIDN'T JUST WANT TO PEEP IN THE BATH?
YOU ARE A GUY AFTER ALL, RANDO.
Hmm
AAGH...! PLEASE BELIEVE ME!!
I'M WATCHING HIS SECRET PASSAGE SO I CAN CATCH HIM.
BUT HE KNOWS YOU SAW HIM, RANDO. HE'D HAVE TO BE AN IDIOT TO COME BACK.
URK... THAT'S TRUE...
HEY, WHAT DID THIS GUY LOOK LIKE?
HM... HE WAS WEARING DARK CLOTHES...
LIKE THAT?
SNEAK
SNEAK
IDIOT FOUND!!!

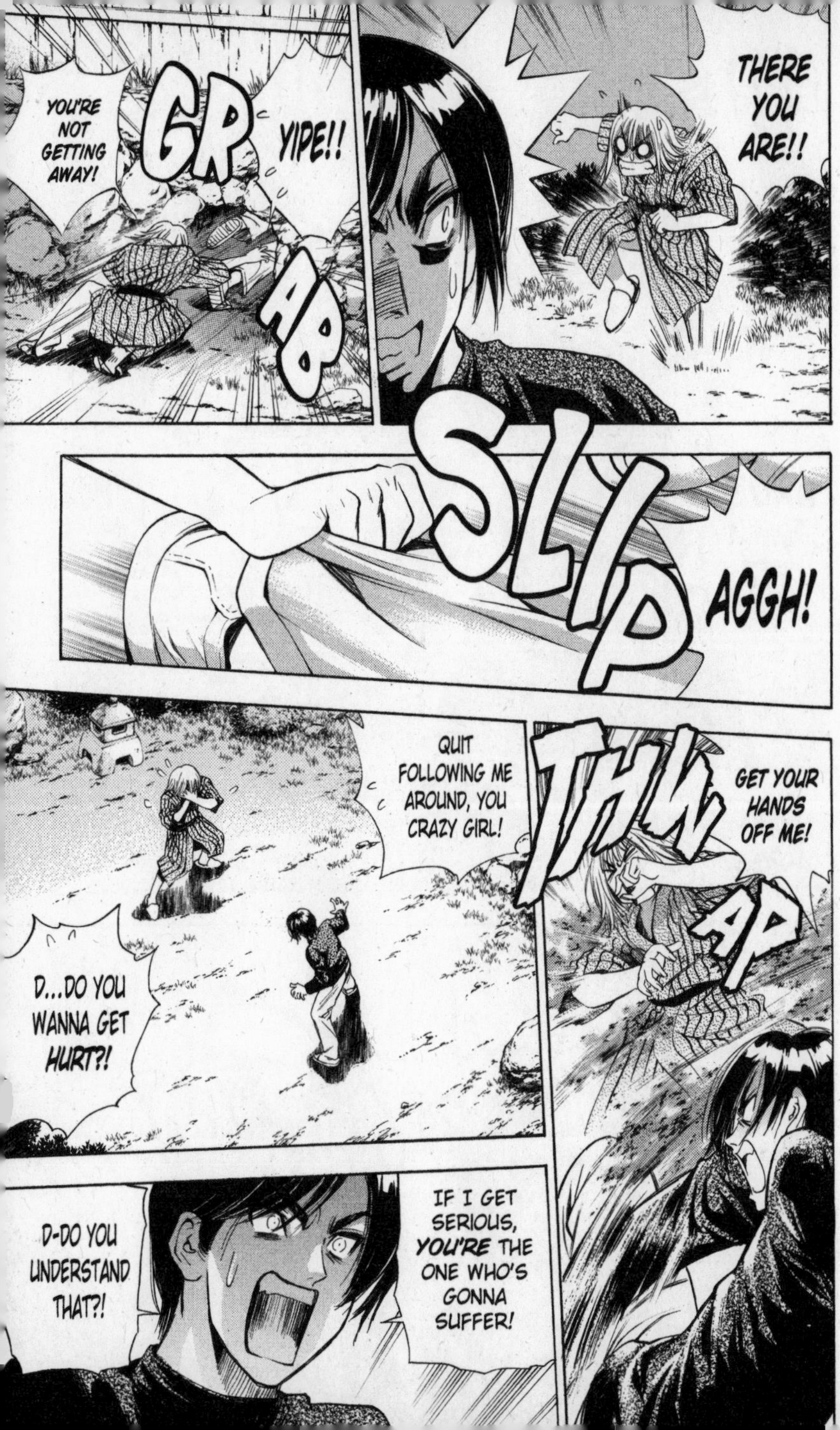
THERE YOU ARE!!
YIPE!!
GRAB
YOU'RE NOT GETTING AWAY!
AGGH!
SLIP
GET YOUR HANDS OFF ME!
THWAP
QUIT FOLLOWING ME AROUND, YOU CRAZY GIRL!
D...DO YOU WANNA GET *HURT*?!
IF I GET SERIOUS, *YOU'RE* THE ONE WHO'S GONNA SUFFER!
D-DO YOU UNDERSTAND THAT?!

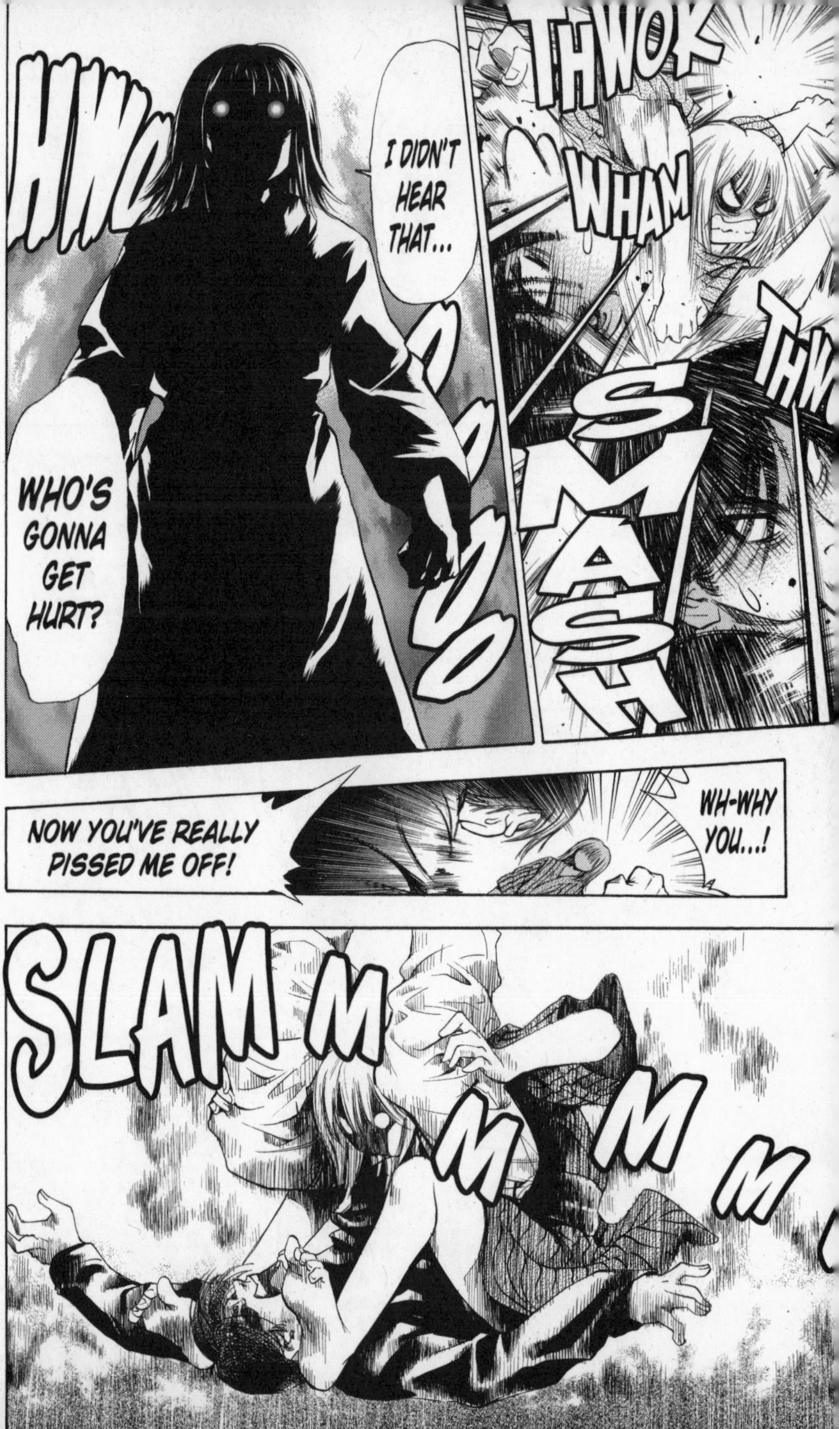
THWOK
WHAM
THWO
SMASH
I DIDN'T HEAR THAT...
HWO
WHO'S GONNA GET HURT?
OOOOO
WH-WHY YOU...!
NOW YOU'VE REALLY PISSED ME OFF!
SLAM
MMMMM

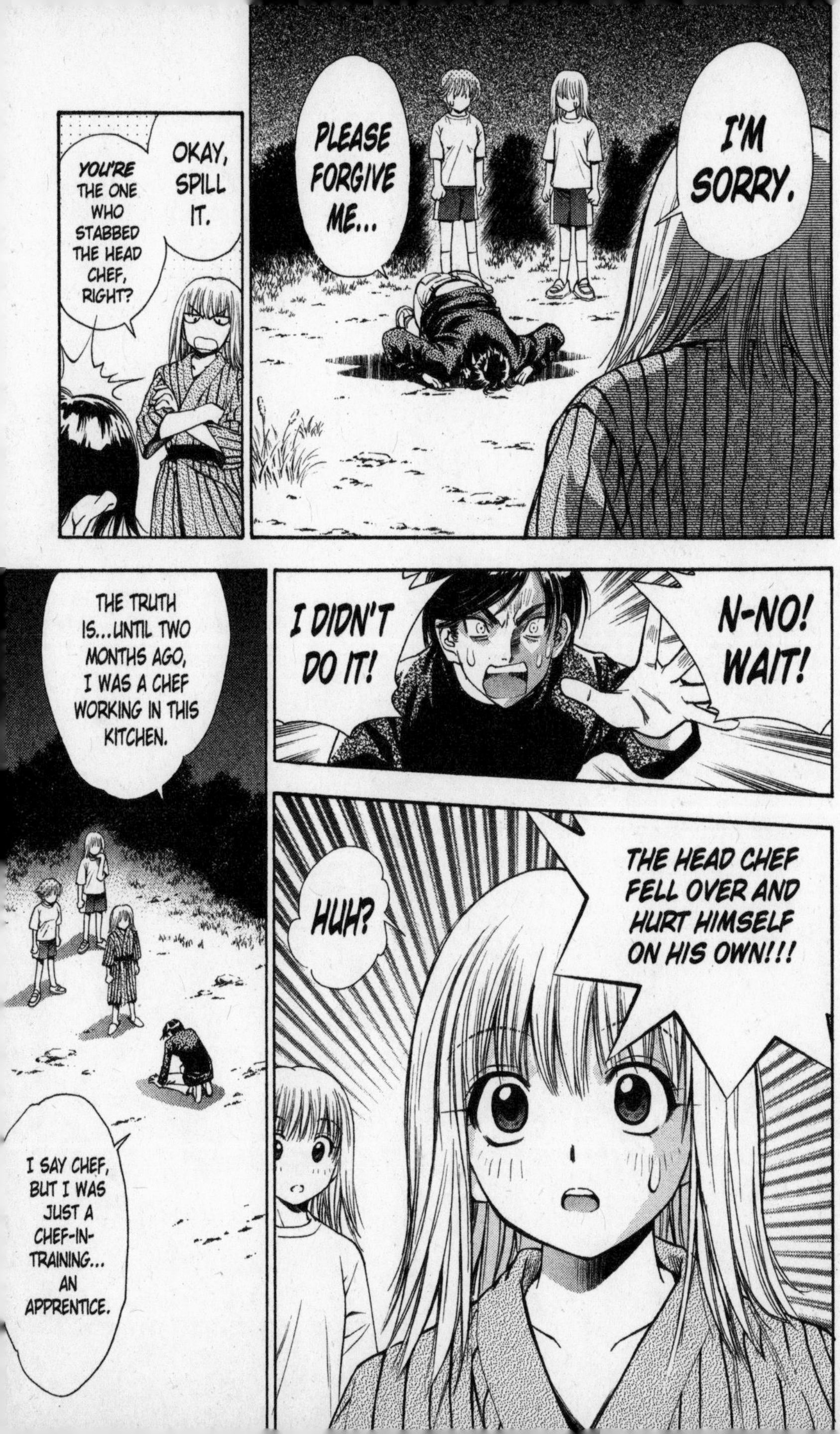
I'M SORRY.
PLEASE FORGIVE ME...
OKAY, SPILL IT.
*YOU'RE* THE ONE WHO STABBED THE HEAD CHEF, RIGHT?
N-NO! WAIT!
I DIDN'T DO IT!
THE HEAD CHEF FELL OVER AND HURT HIMSELF ON HIS OWN!!!
HUH?
THE TRUTH IS...UNTIL TWO MONTHS AGO, I WAS A CHEF WORKING IN THIS KITCHEN.
I SAY CHEF, BUT I WAS JUST A CHEF-IN-TRAINING... AN APPRENTICE.

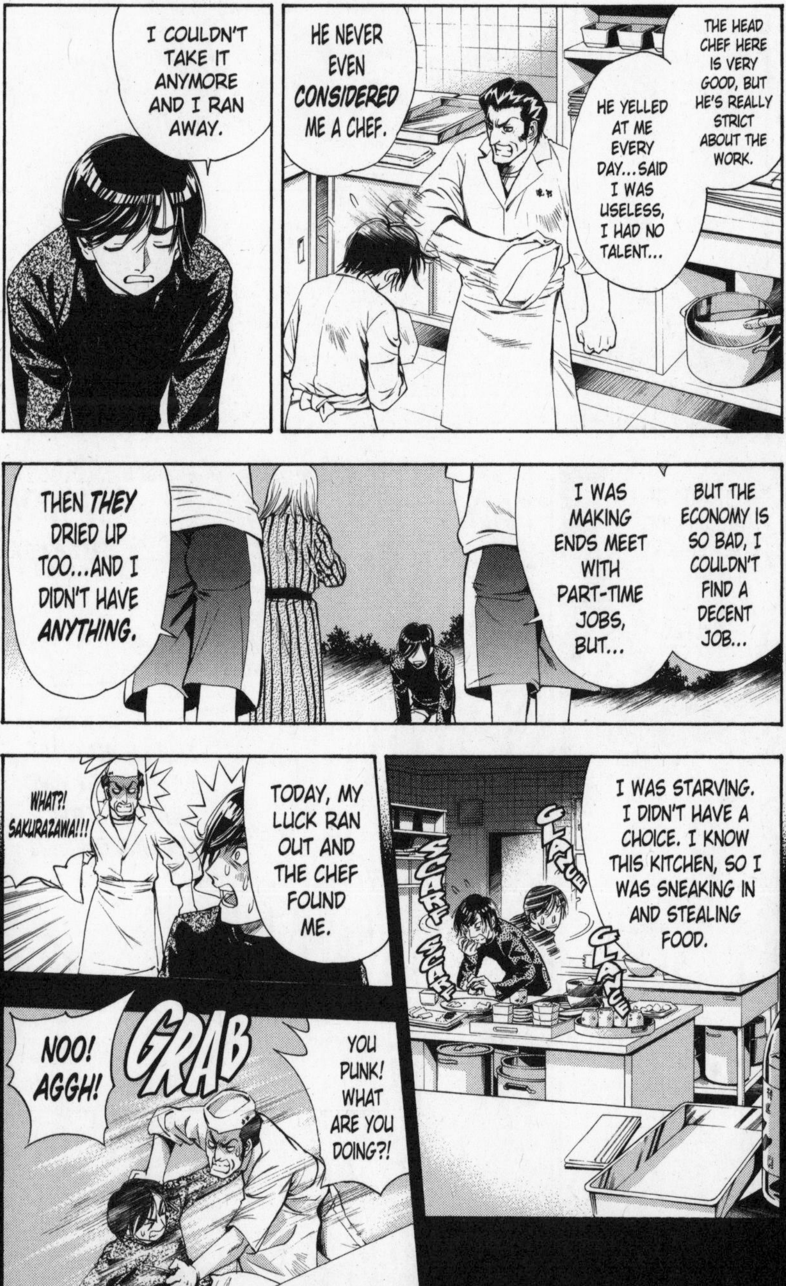
THE HEAD CHEF HERE IS VERY GOOD, BUT HE'S REALLY STRICT ABOUT THE WORK.
HE YELLED AT ME EVERY DAY...SAID I WAS USELESS, I HAD NO TALENT...
HE NEVER EVEN CONSIDERED ME A CHEF.
I COULDN'T TAKE IT ANYMORE AND I RAN AWAY.
BUT THE ECONOMY IS SO BAD, I COULDN'T FIND A DECENT JOB...
I WAS MAKING ENDS MEET WITH PART-TIME JOBS, BUT...
THEN THEY DRIED UP TOO...AND I DIDN'T HAVE ANYTHING.
I WAS STARVING. I DIDN'T HAVE A CHOICE. I KNOW THIS KITCHEN, SO I WAS SNEAKING IN AND STEALING FOOD.
GLANCE
GLANCE
SCARF SCARF
TODAY, MY LUCK RAN OUT AND THE CHEF FOUND ME.
WHAT?! SAKURAZAWA!!!
YOU PUNK! WHAT ARE YOU DOING?!
GRAB
NOO! AGGH!

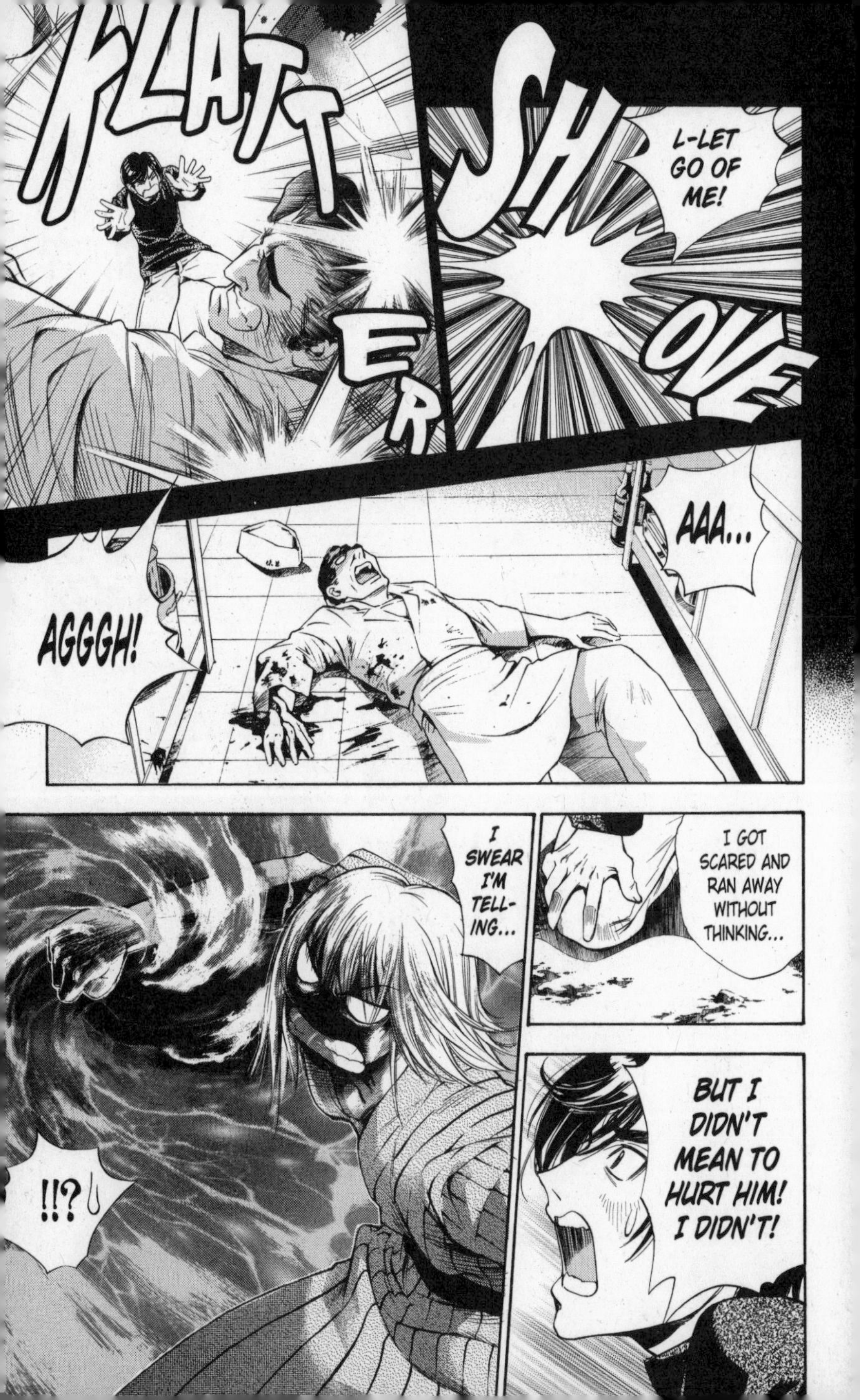
SHOVE
L-LET GO OF ME!
KLATTTER
AAA...
AGGGH!
I GOT SCARED AND RAN AWAY WITHOUT THINKING...
I SWEAR I'M TELLING...
BUT I DIDN'T MEAN TO HURT HIM! I DIDN'T!
!!?

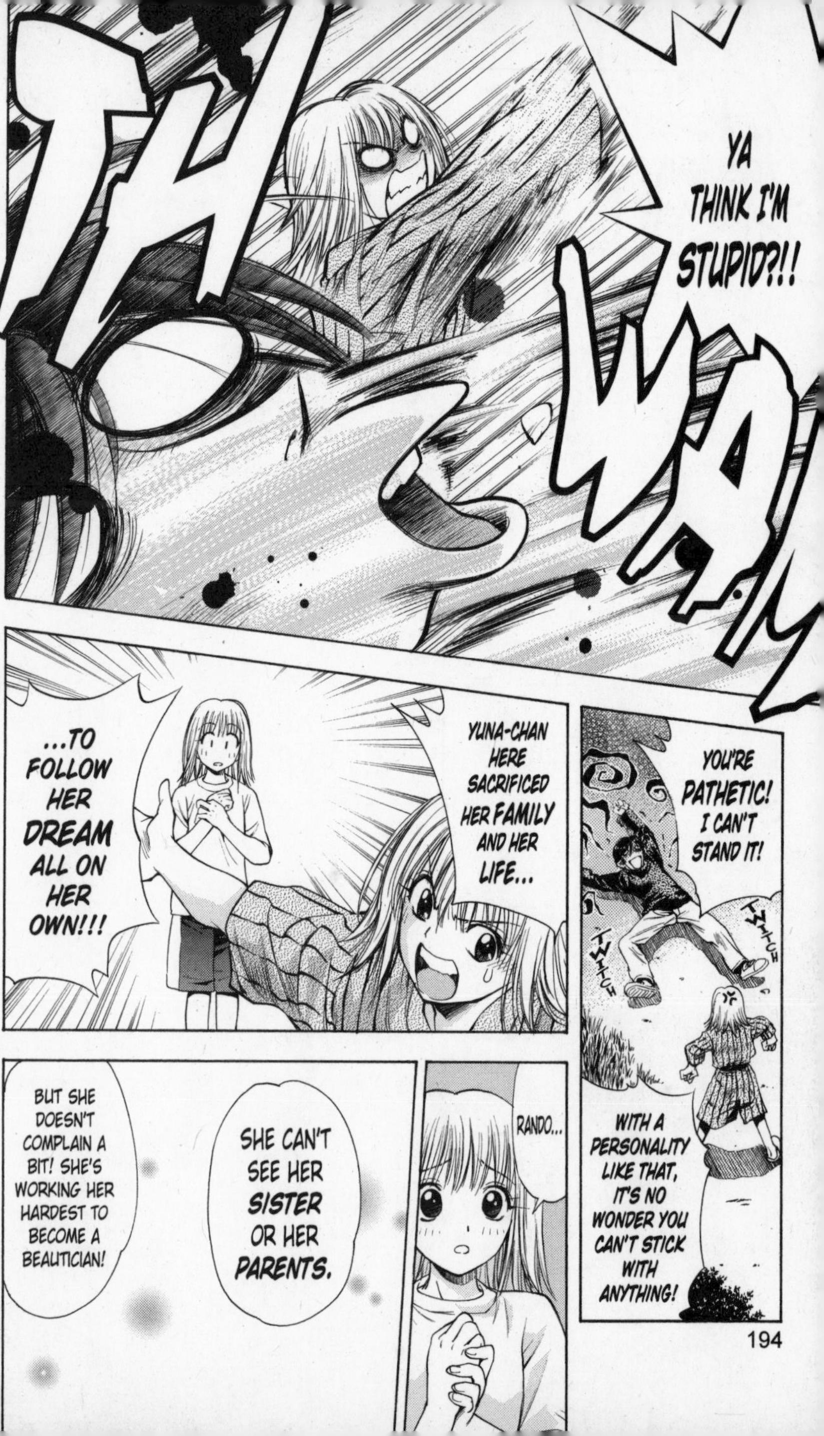
YA THINK I'M STUPID?!!
TH
WAM
YOU'RE PATHETIC! I CAN'T STAND IT!
TWITCH
TWITCH
WITH A PERSONALITY LIKE THAT, IT'S NO WONDER YOU CAN'T STICK WITH ANYTHING!
YUNA-CHAN HERE SACRIFICED HER FAMILY AND HER LIFE...
...TO FOLLOW HER DREAM ALL ON HER OWN!!!
RANDO...
SHE CAN'T SEE HER SISTER OR HER PARENTS.
BUT SHE DOESN'T COMPLAIN A BIT! SHE'S WORKING HER HARDEST TO BECOME A BEAUTICIAN!

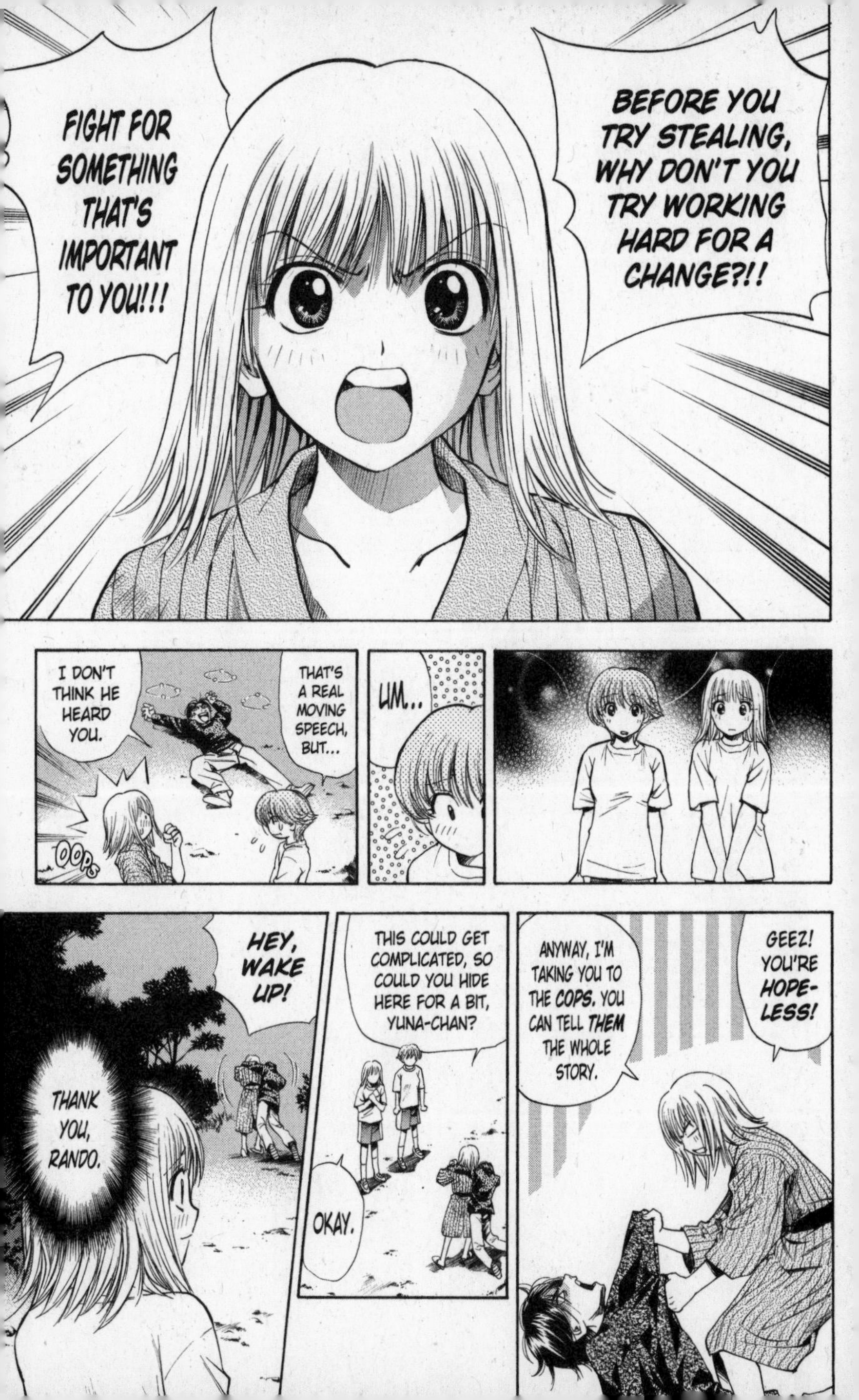
BEFORE YOU TRY STEALING, WHY DON'T YOU TRY WORKING HARD FOR A CHANGE?!!
FIGHT FOR SOMETHING THAT'S IMPORTANT TO YOU!!!
UM...
THAT'S A REAL MOVING SPEECH, BUT...
I DON'T THINK HE HEARD YOU.
OOPS
GEEZ! YOU'RE HOPE-LESS!
ANYWAY, I'M TAKING YOU TO THE COPS. YOU CAN TELL THEM THE WHOLE STORY.
THIS COULD GET COMPLICATED, SO COULD YOU HIDE HERE FOR A BIT, YUNA-CHAN?
OKAY.
HEY, WAKE UP!
THANK YOU, RANDO.

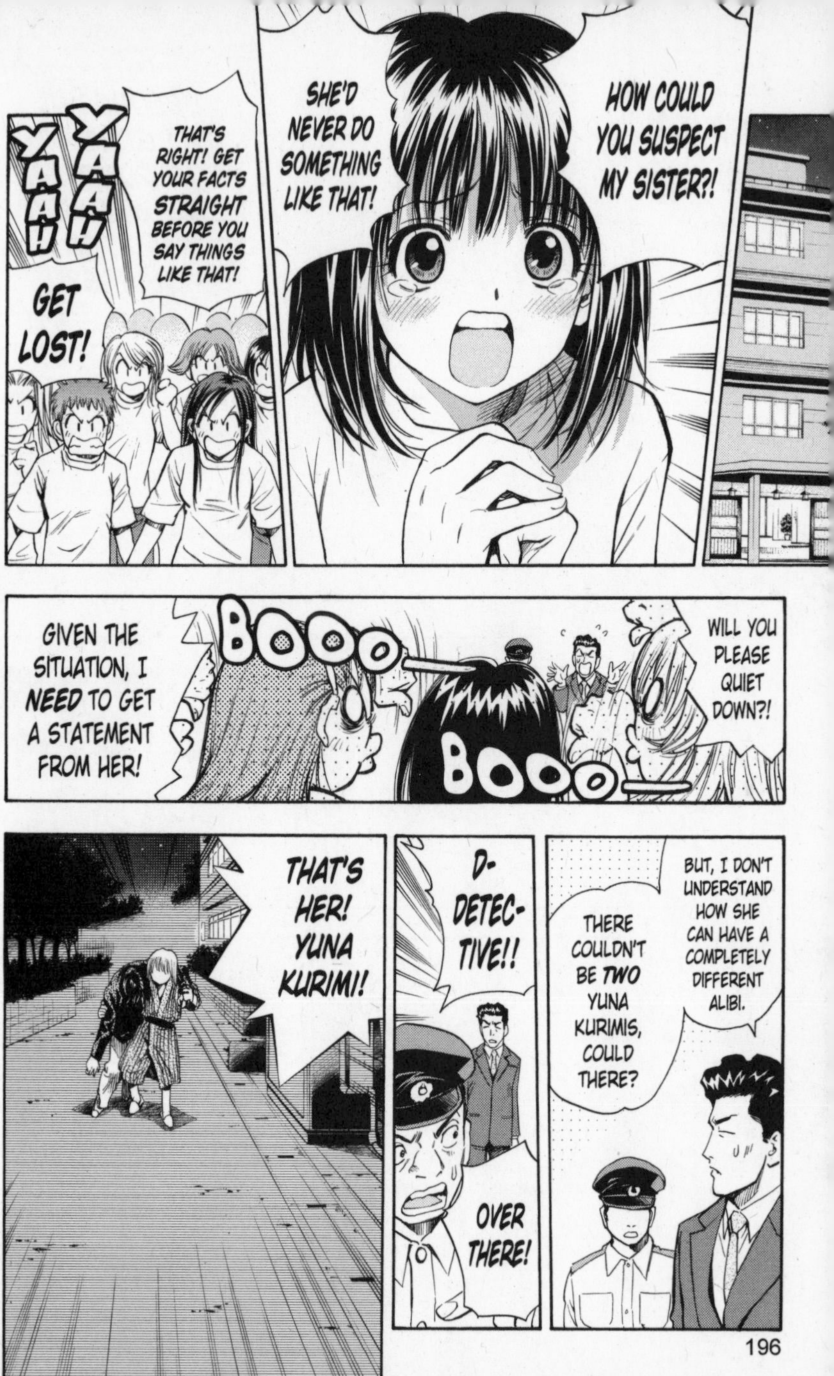
HOW COULD YOU SUSPECT MY SISTER?!
SHE'D NEVER DO SOMETHING LIKE THAT!
THAT'S RIGHT! GET YOUR FACTS STRAIGHT BEFORE YOU SAY THINGS LIKE THAT!
YAAAH
YAAAH
GET LOST!
WILL YOU PLEASE QUIET DOWN?!
BOOO
BOOO—
GIVEN THE SITUATION, I NEED TO GET A STATEMENT FROM HER!
BUT, I DON'T UNDERSTAND HOW SHE CAN HAVE A COMPLETELY DIFFERENT ALIBI.
THERE COULDN'T BE TWO YUNA KURIMIS, COULD THERE?
D-DETECTIVE!!
OVER THERE!
THAT'S HER! YUNA KURIMI!

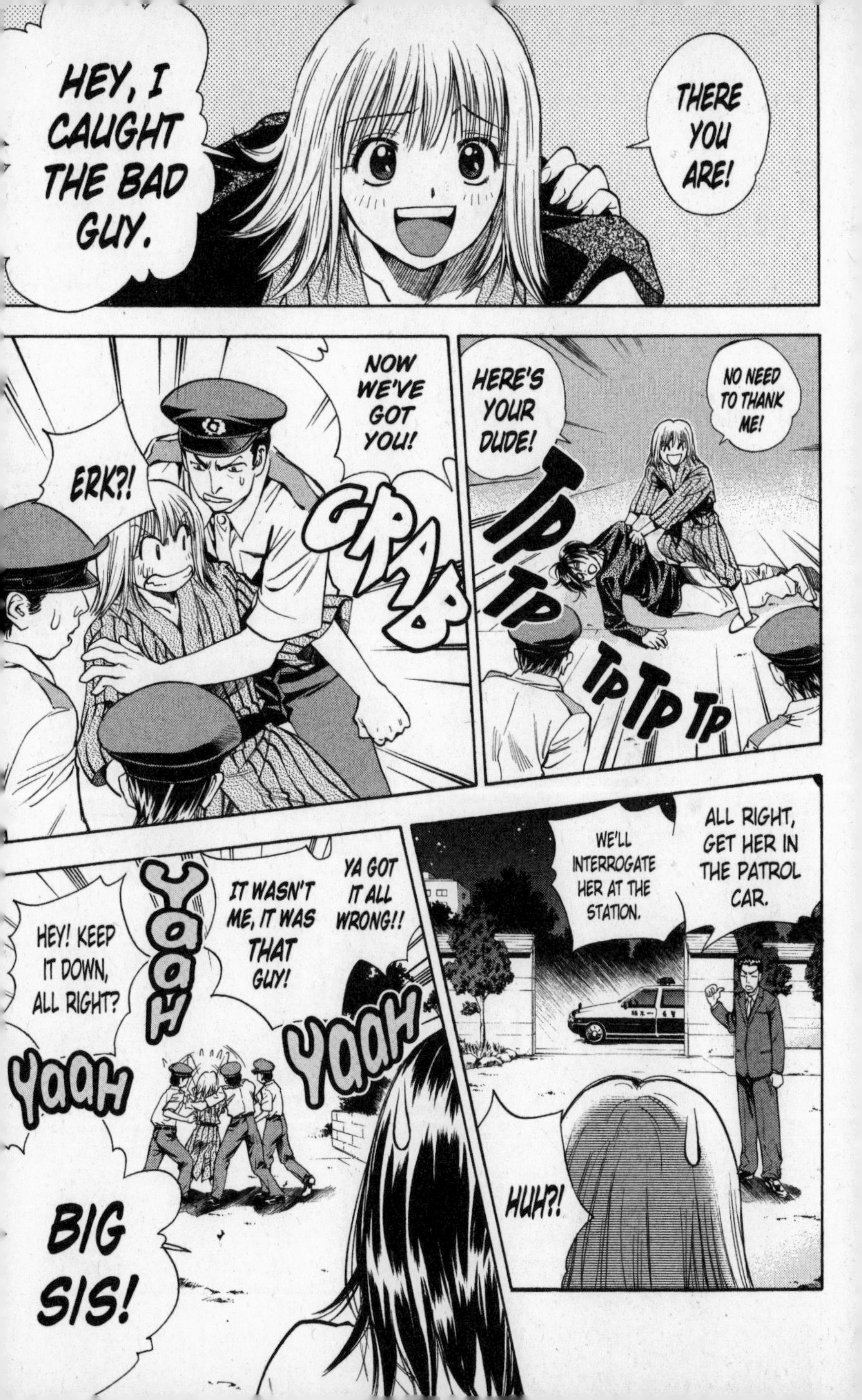
THERE YOU ARE!
HEY, I CAUGHT THE BAD GUY.
NO NEED TO THANK ME!
HERE'S YOUR DUDE!
TP TP
TP TP TP TP
NOW WE'VE GOT YOU!
GRAB
ERK?!
ALL RIGHT, GET HER IN THE PATROL CAR.
WE'LL INTERROGATE HER AT THE STATION.
HUH?!
YA GOT IT ALL WRONG!!
IT WASN'T ME, IT WAS THAT GUY!
YAAH
YAAH
HEY! KEEP IT DOWN, ALL RIGHT?
YAAH
BIG SIS!

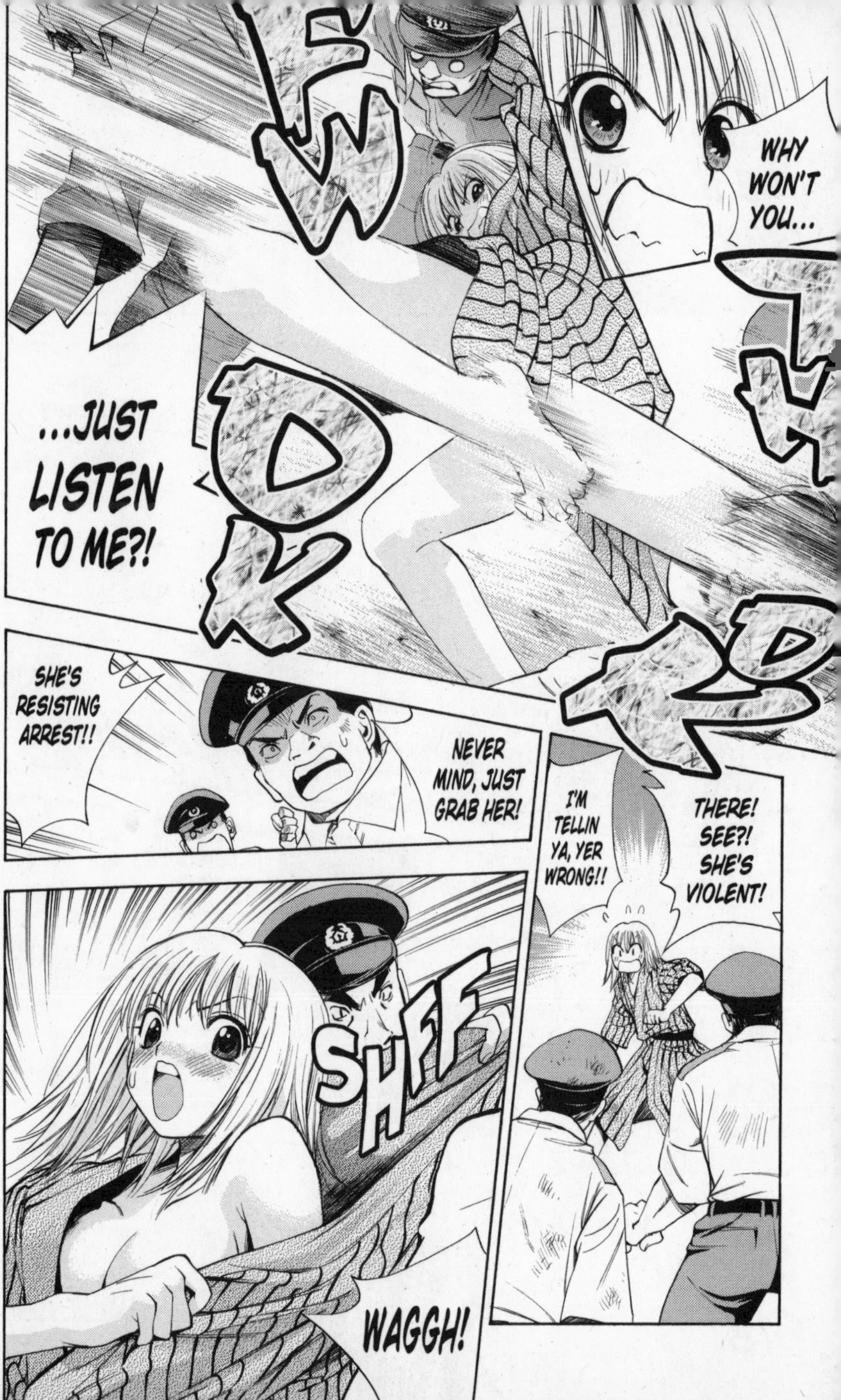
WHY WON'T YOU...
...JUST LISTEN TO ME?!
THERE! SEE?! SHE'S VIOLENT!
I'M TELLIN YA, YER WRONG!!
SHE'S RESISTING ARREST!!
NEVER MIND, JUST GRAB HER!
SHFF
WAGGH!

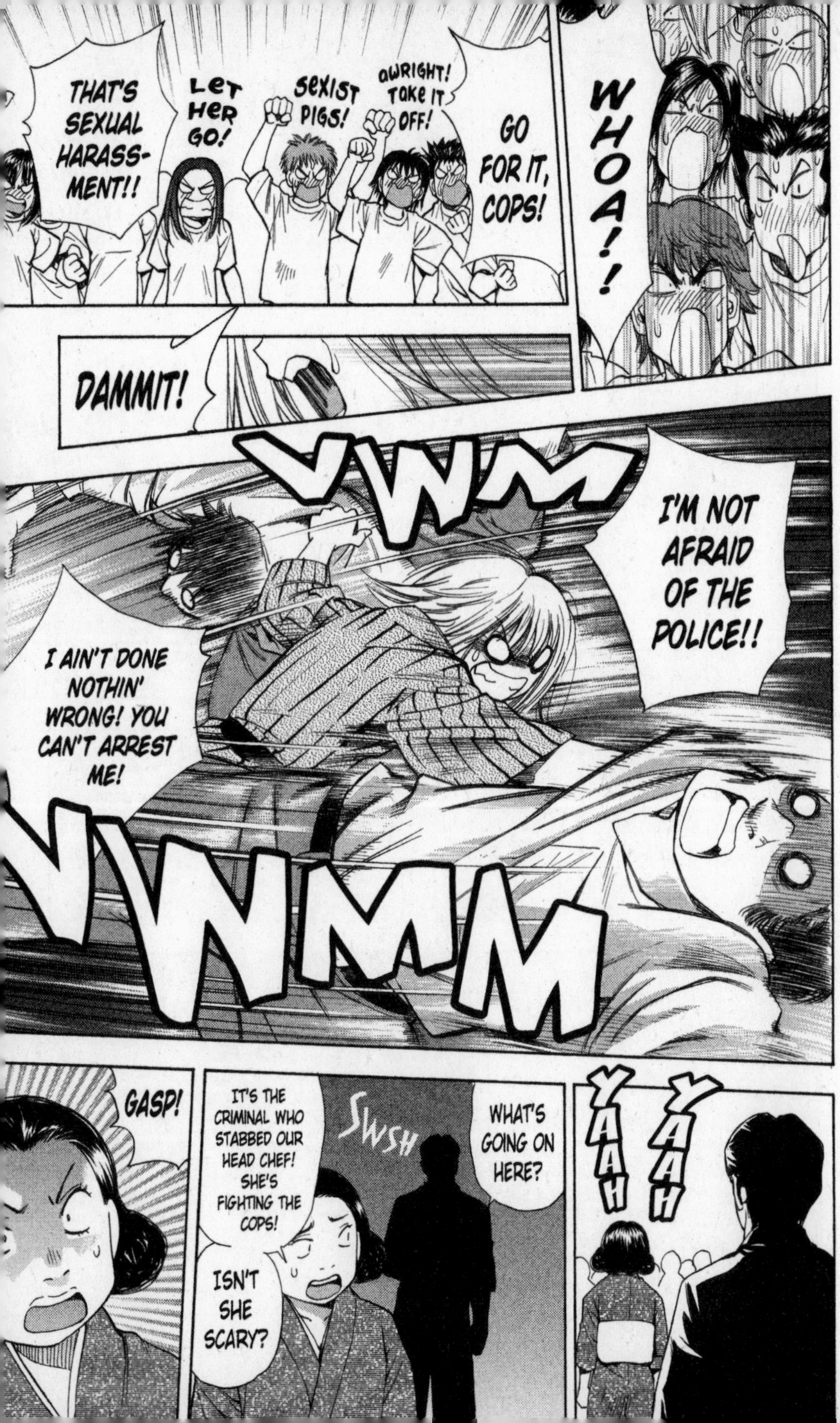
WHOA!!
GO FOR IT, COPS!
AWRIGHT! TAKE IT OFF!
SEXIST PIGS!
LET HER GO!
THAT'S SEXUAL HARASS-MENT!!
DAMMIT!
VWM
I'M NOT AFRAID OF THE POLICE!!
I AIN'T DONE NOTHIN' WRONG! YOU CAN'T ARREST ME!
VWMM
YAAAH YAAAH
WHAT'S GOING ON HERE?
SWSH
IT'S THE CRIMINAL WHO STABBED OUR HEAD CHEF! SHE'S FIGHTING THE COPS!
ISN'T SHE SCARY?
GASP!

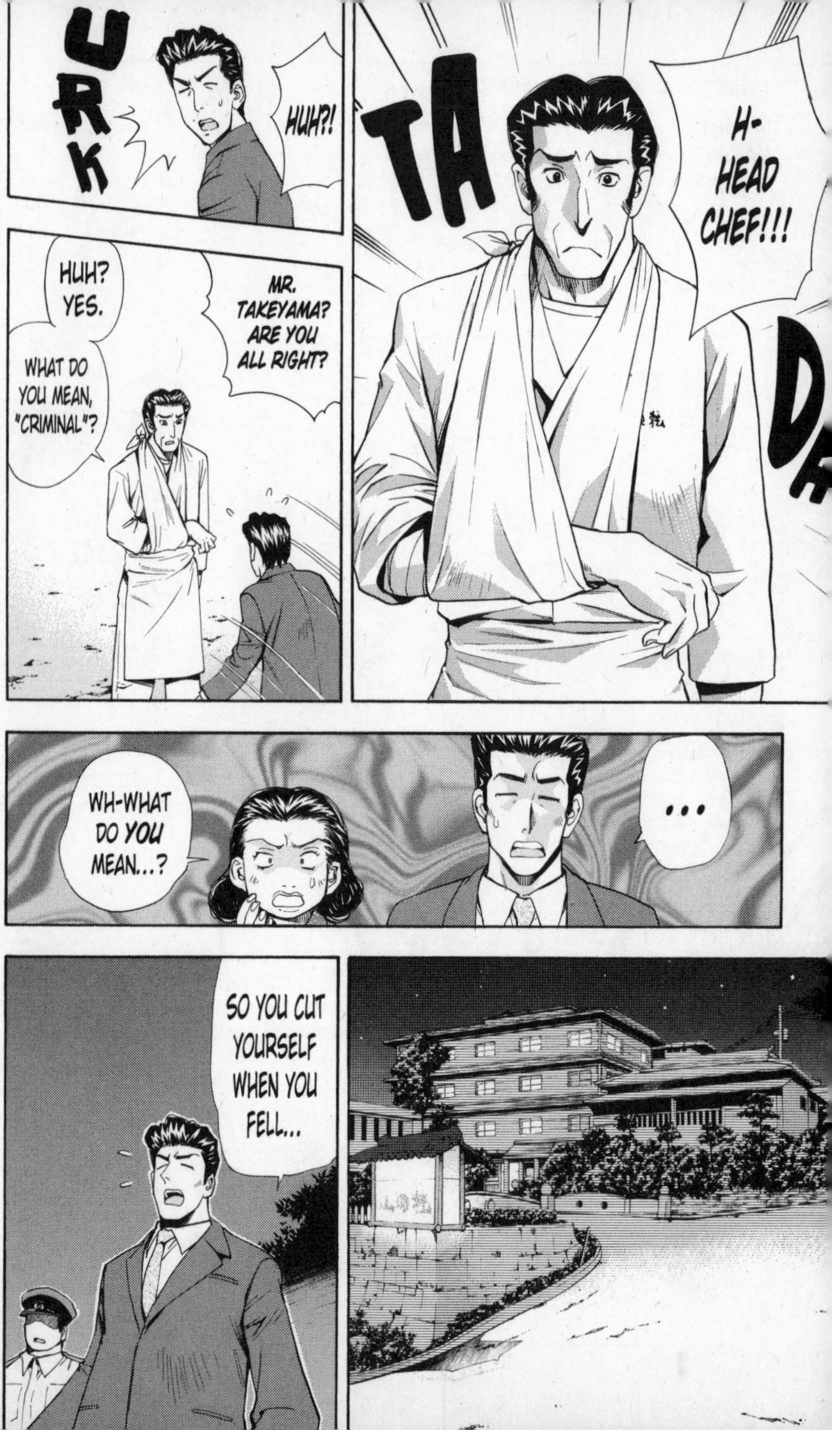
H-HEAD CHEF!!!
TA
DA
URK
HUH?!
MR. TAKEYAMA? ARE YOU ALL RIGHT?
HUH? YES.
WHAT DO YOU MEAN, "CRIMINAL"?
...
WH-WHAT DO YOU MEAN...?
SO YOU CUT YOURSELF WHEN YOU FELL...

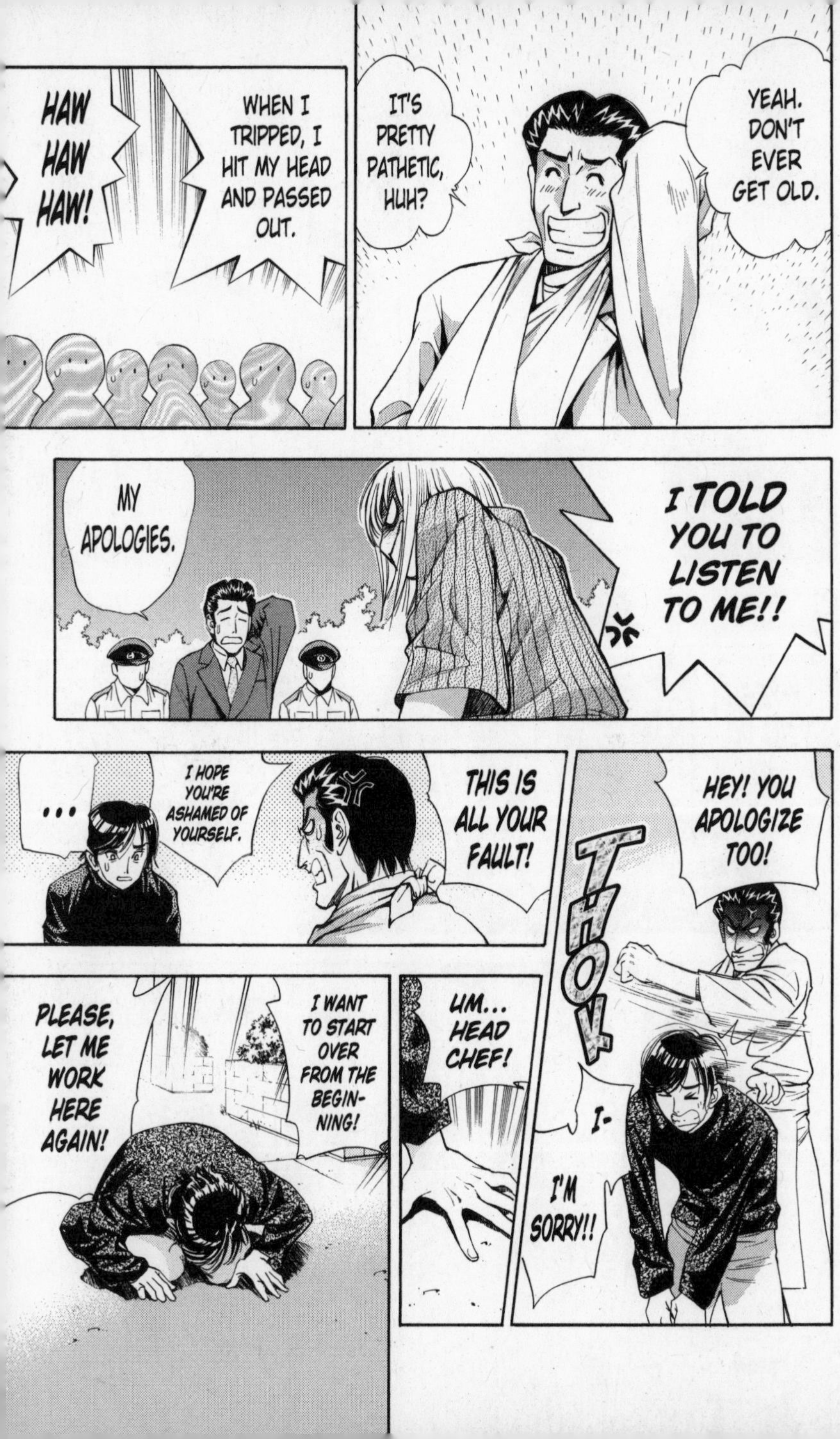
YEAH. DON'T EVER GET OLD.
IT'S PRETTY PATHETIC, HUH?
WHEN I TRIPPED, I HIT MY HEAD AND PASSED OUT.
HAW HAW HAW!
I TOLD YOU TO LISTEN TO ME!!
MY APOLOGIES.
HEY! YOU APOLOGIZE TOO!
THOK
I-
I'M SORRY!!
THIS IS ALL YOUR FAULT!
I HOPE YOU'RE ASHAMED OF YOURSELF.
...
UM... HEAD CHEF!
I WANT TO START OVER FROM THE BEGIN-NING!
PLEASE, LET ME WORK HERE AGAIN!

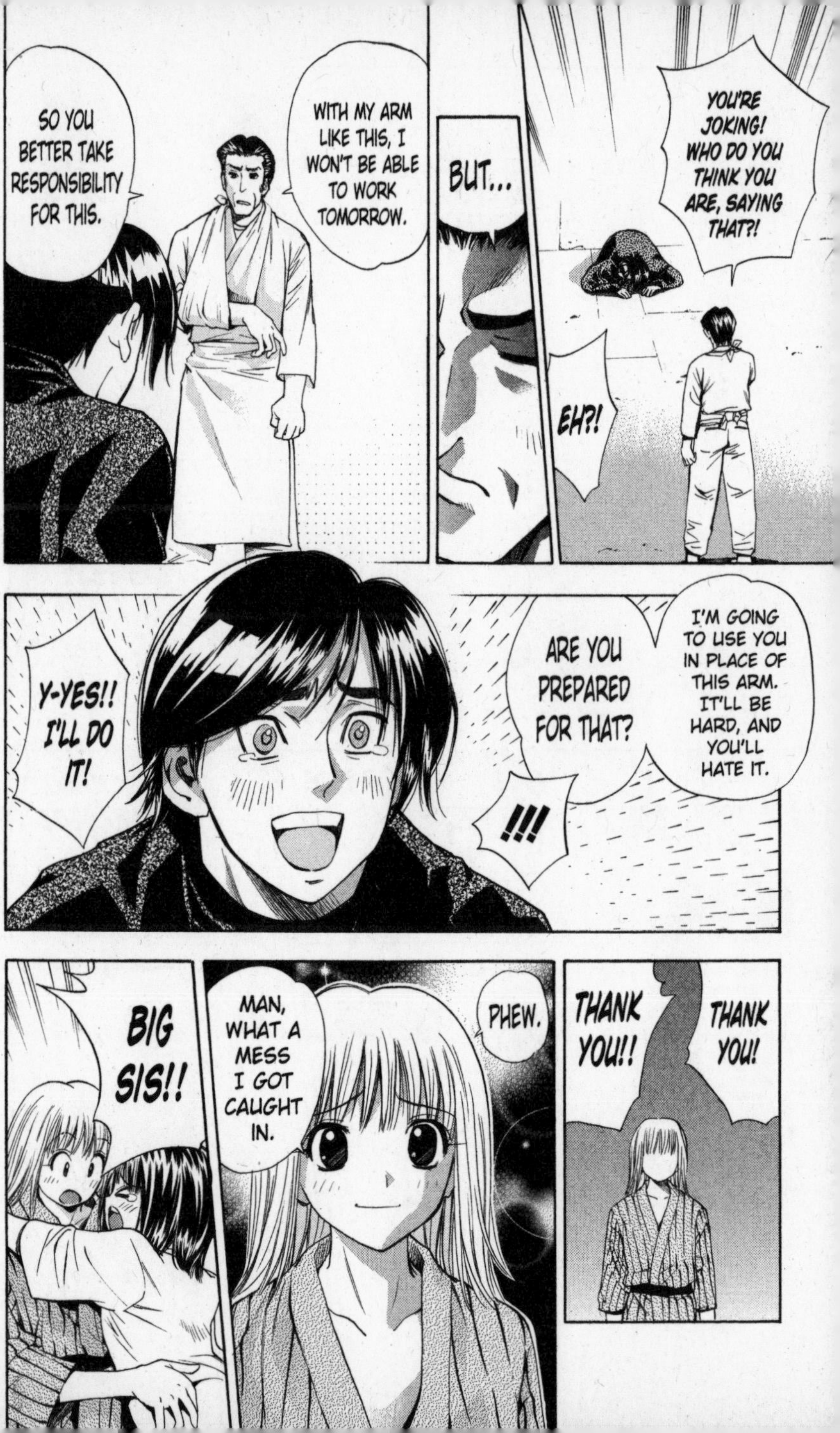
YOU'RE JOKING! WHO DO YOU THINK YOU ARE, SAYING THAT?!
EH?!
BUT...
WITH MY ARM LIKE THIS, I WON'T BE ABLE TO WORK TOMORROW.
SO YOU BETTER TAKE RESPONSIBILITY FOR THIS.
I'M GOING TO USE YOU IN PLACE OF THIS ARM. IT'LL BE HARD, AND YOU'LL HATE IT.
ARE YOU PREPARED FOR THAT?
!!!
Y-YES!! I'LL DO IT!
THANK YOU!
THANK YOU!!
PHEW.
MAN, WHAT A MESS I GOT CAUGHT IN.
BIG SIS!!

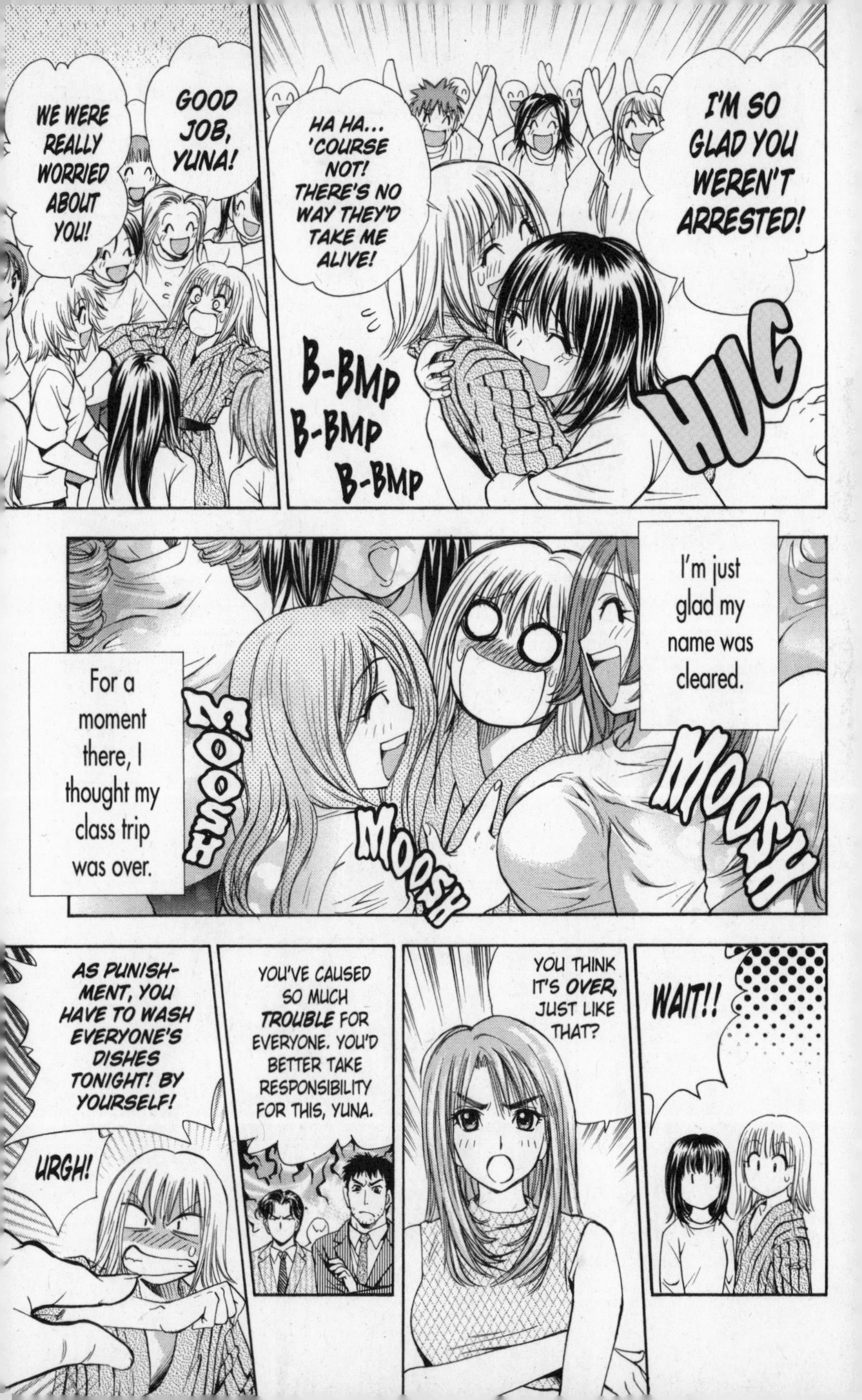
I'M SO GLAD YOU WEREN'T ARRESTED!
HUG
HA HA... 'COURSE NOT! THERE'S NO WAY THEY'D TAKE ME ALIVE!
B-BMP B-BMP B-BMP
GOOD JOB, YUNA!
WE WERE REALLY WORRIED ABOUT YOU!
I'm just glad my name was cleared.
MOOSH
MOOSH
MOOSH
For a moment there, I thought my class trip was over.
WAIT!!
YOU THINK IT'S OVER, JUST LIKE THAT?
YOU'VE CAUSED SO MUCH TROUBLE FOR EVERYONE. YOU'D BETTER TAKE RESPONSIBILITY FOR THIS, YUNA.
AS PUNISHMENT, YOU HAVE TO WASH EVERYONE'S DISHES TONIGHT! BY YOURSELF!
URGH!

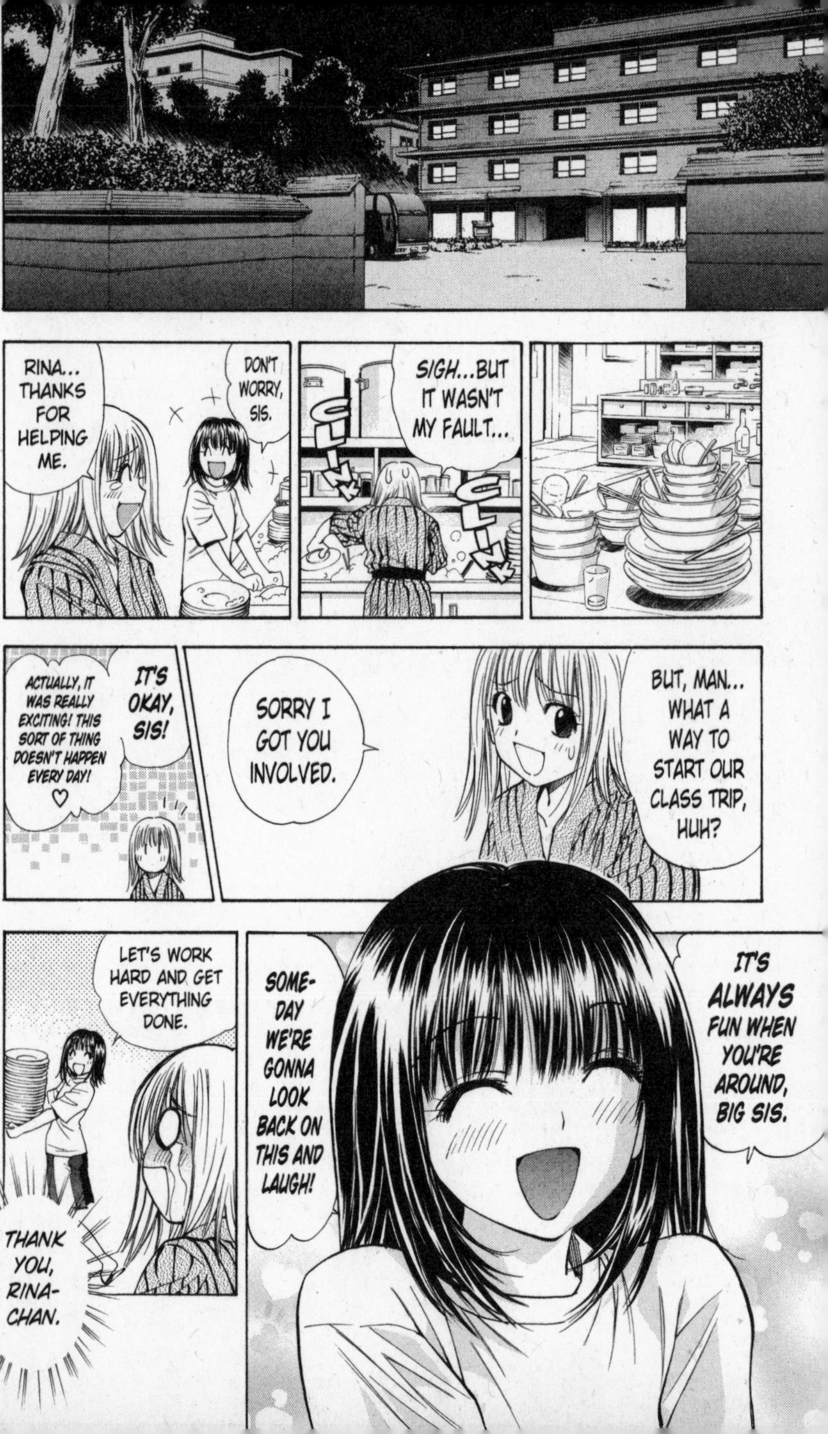
SIGH...BUT IT WASN'T MY FAULT...
CLINK
CLINK
DON'T WORRY, SIS.
RINA... THANKS FOR HELPING ME.
BUT, MAN... WHAT A WAY TO START OUR CLASS TRIP, HUH?
SORRY I GOT YOU INVOLVED.
IT'S OKAY, SIS!
ACTUALLY, IT WAS REALLY EXCITING! THIS SORT OF THING DOESN'T HAPPEN EVERY DAY! ♡
IT'S ALWAYS FUN WHEN YOU'RE AROUND, BIG SIS.
SOME-DAY WE'RE GONNA LOOK BACK ON THIS AND LAUGH!
LET'S WORK HARD AND GET EVERYTHING DONE.
THANK YOU, RINA-CHAN.

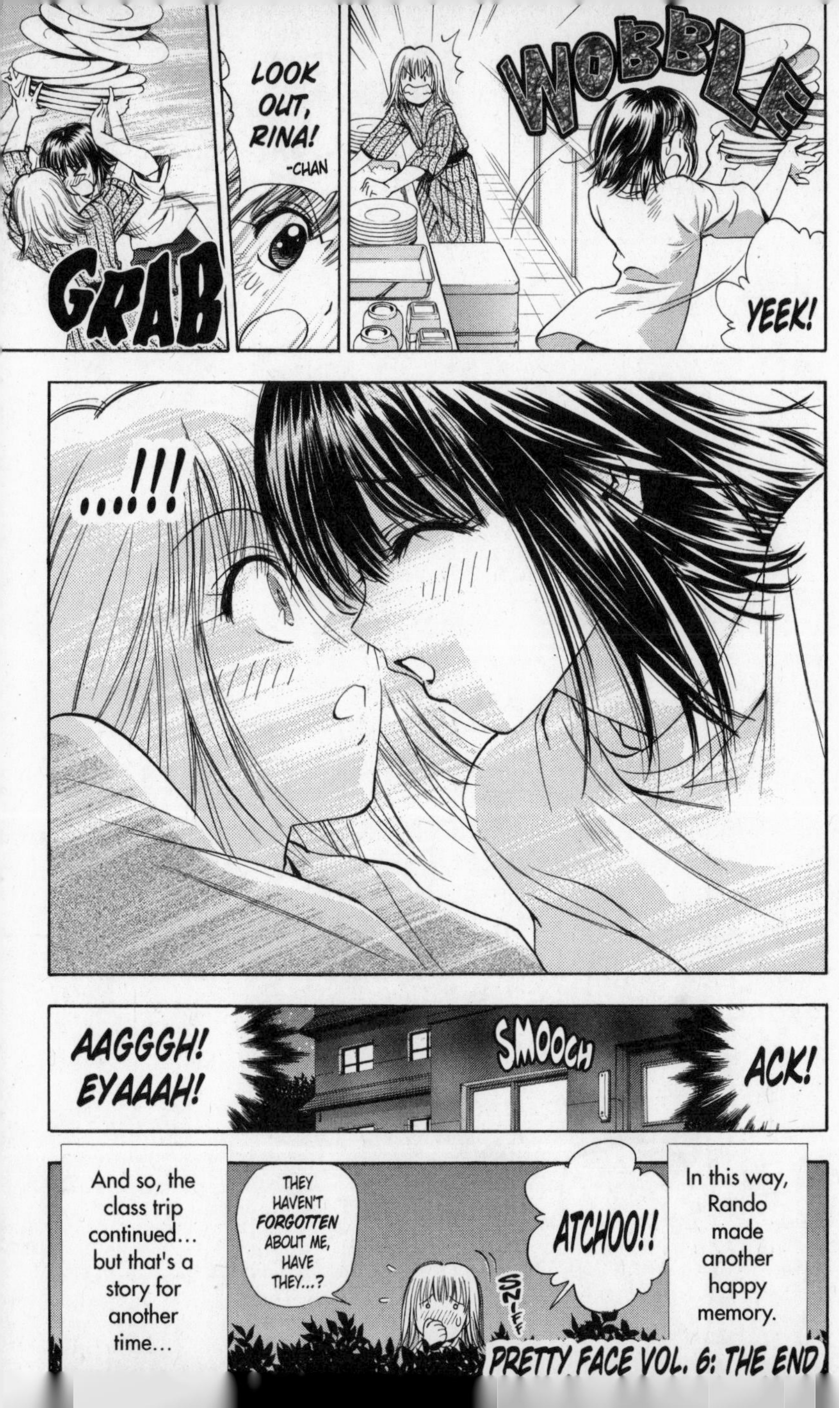
WOBBLE
YEEK!
LOOK OUT, RINA! -CHAN
GRAB
...!!!
ACK!
SMOOCH
AAGGGH! EYAAAH!
In this way, Rando made another happy memory.
ATCHOO!!
SNIFF
THEY HAVEN'T FORGOTTEN ABOUT ME, HAVE THEY...?
And so, the class trip continued... but that's a story for another time...
PRETTY FACE VOL. 6: THE END

# Pretty Face

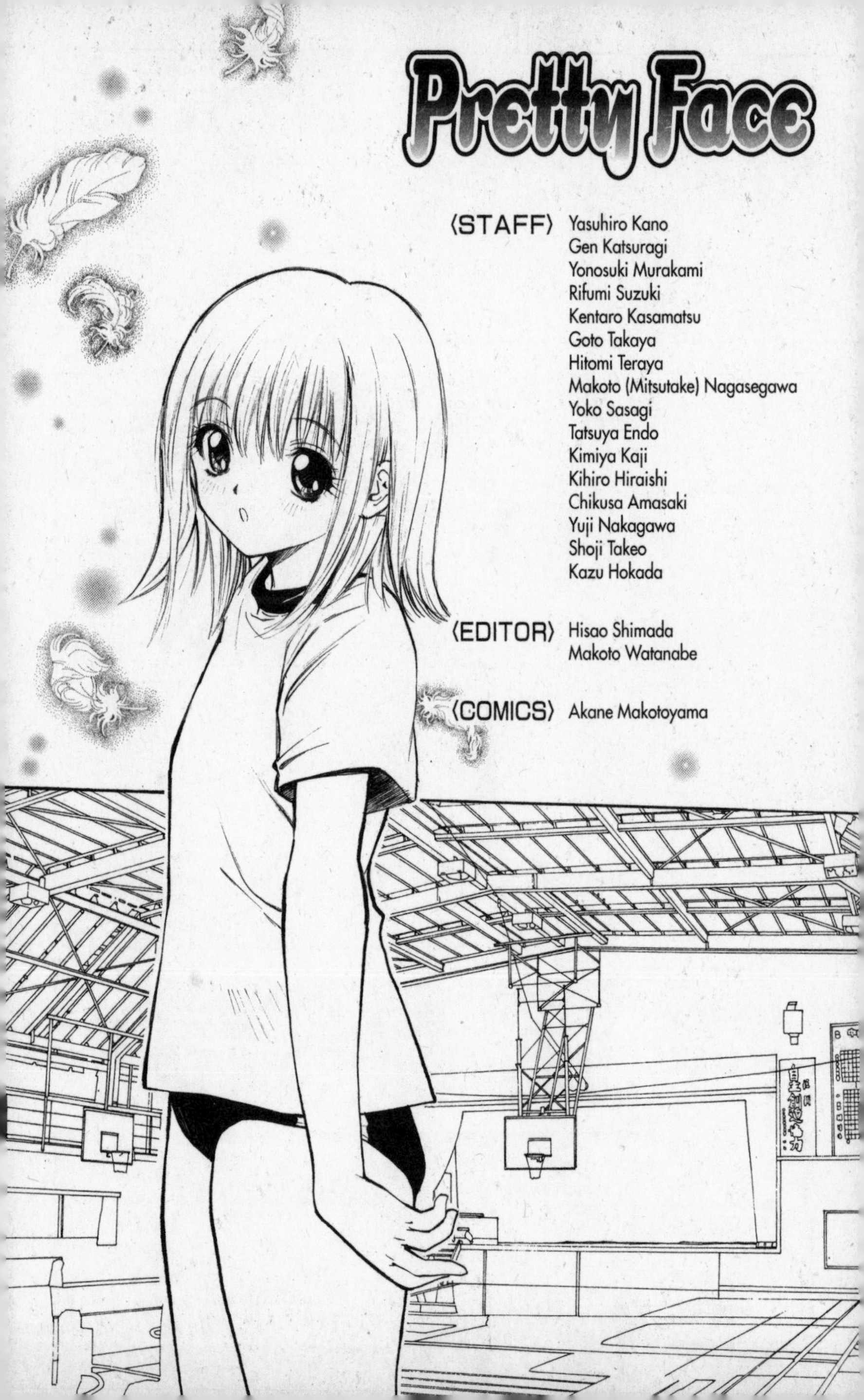

〈STAFF〉 Yasuhiro Kano
Gen Katsuragi
Yonosuki Murakami
Rifumi Suzuki
Kentaro Kasamatsu
Goto Takaya
Hitomi Teraya
Makoto (Mitsutake) Nagasegawa
Yoko Sasagi
Tatsuya Endo
Kimiya Kaji
Kihiro Hiraishi
Chikusa Amasaki
Yuji Nakagawa
Shoji Takeo
Kazu Hokada

〈EDITOR〉 Hisao Shimada
Makoto Watanabe

〈COMICS〉 Akane Makotoyama

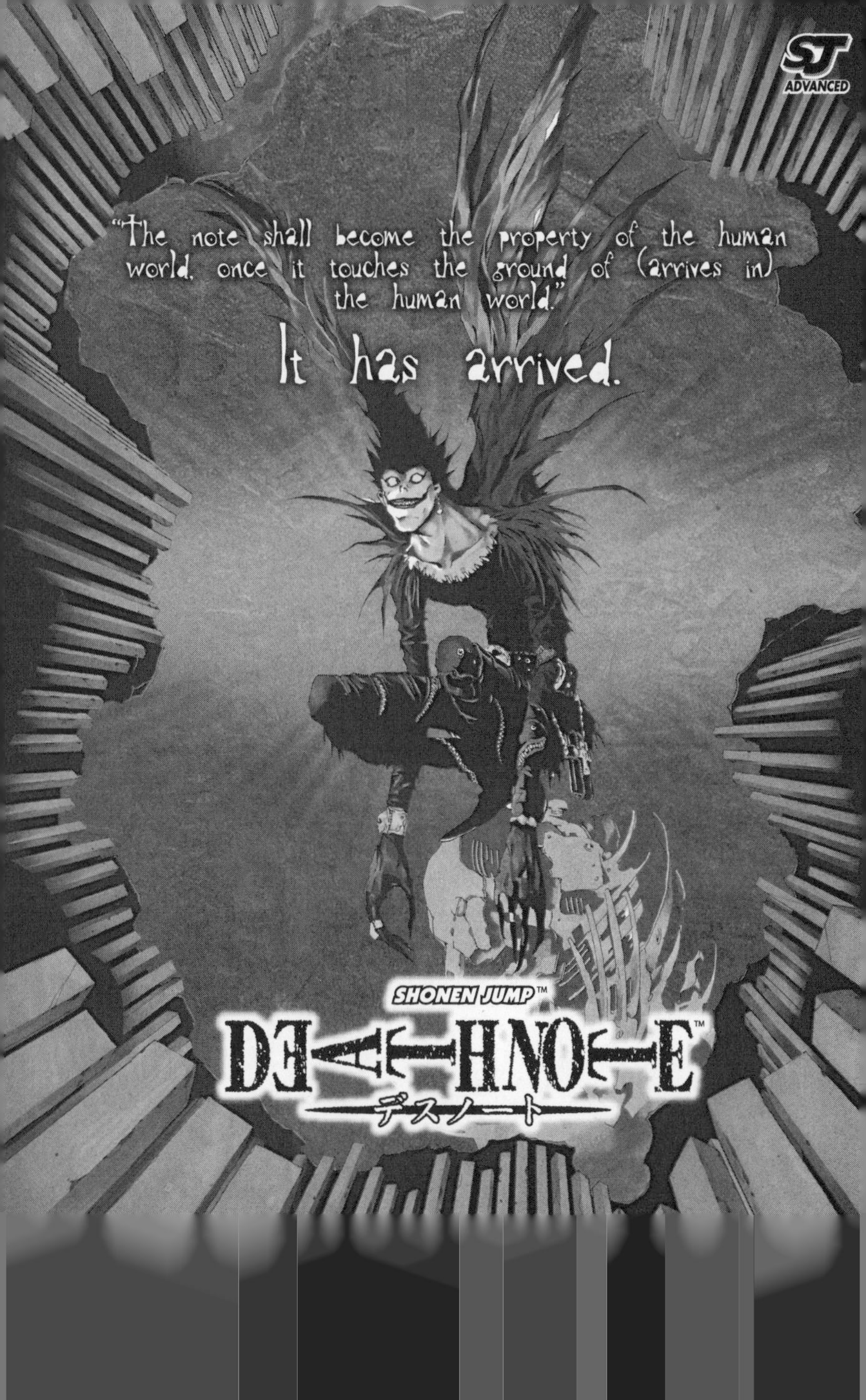
SJ
ADVANCED
"The note shall become the property of the human world, once it touches the ground of (arrives in) the human world."
It has arrived.
SHONEN JUMP™
DEATH NOTE™
デスノート

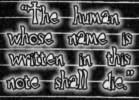

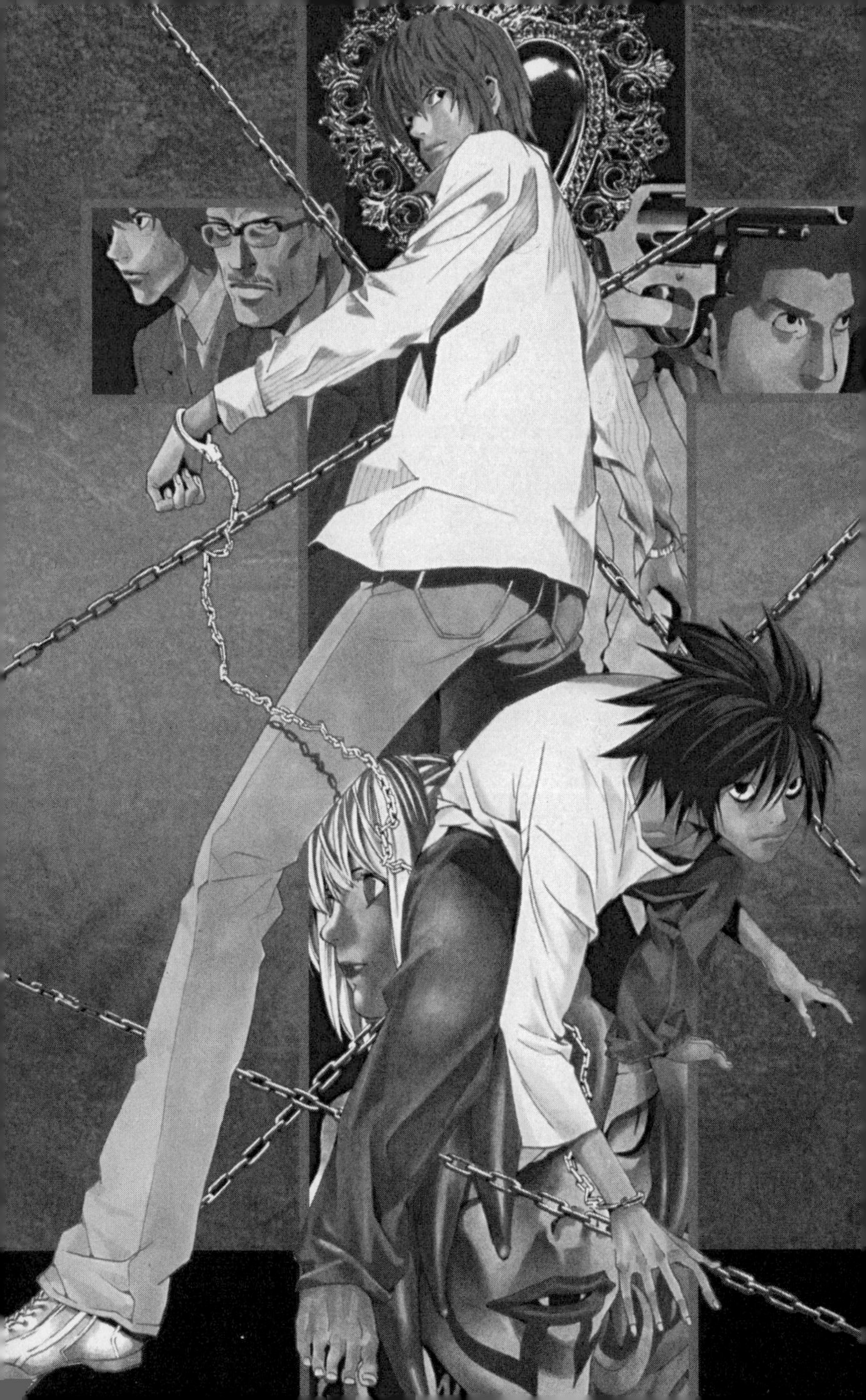

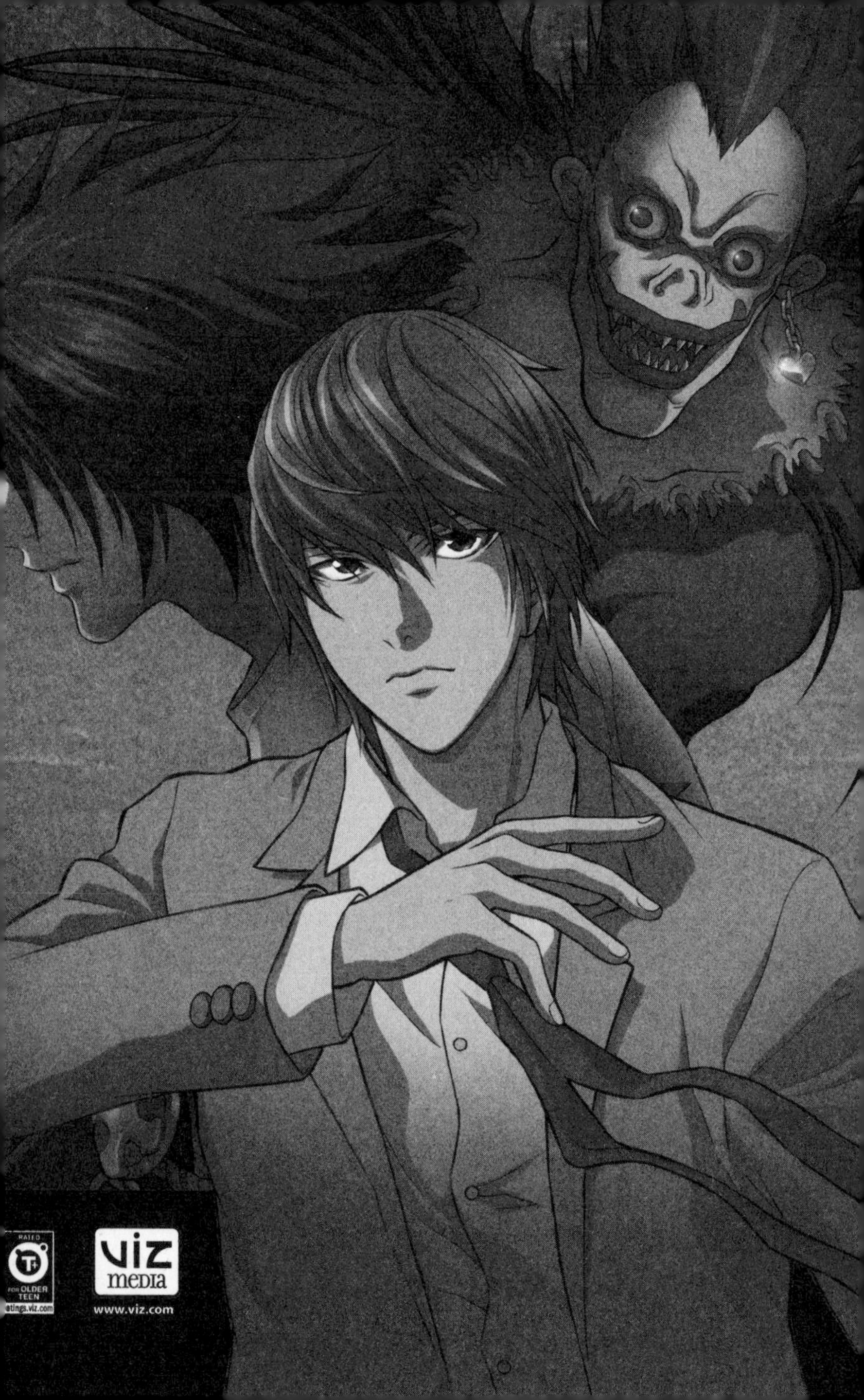
RATED
T+
FOR OLDER TEEN
atings.viz.com
VIZ media
www.viz.com

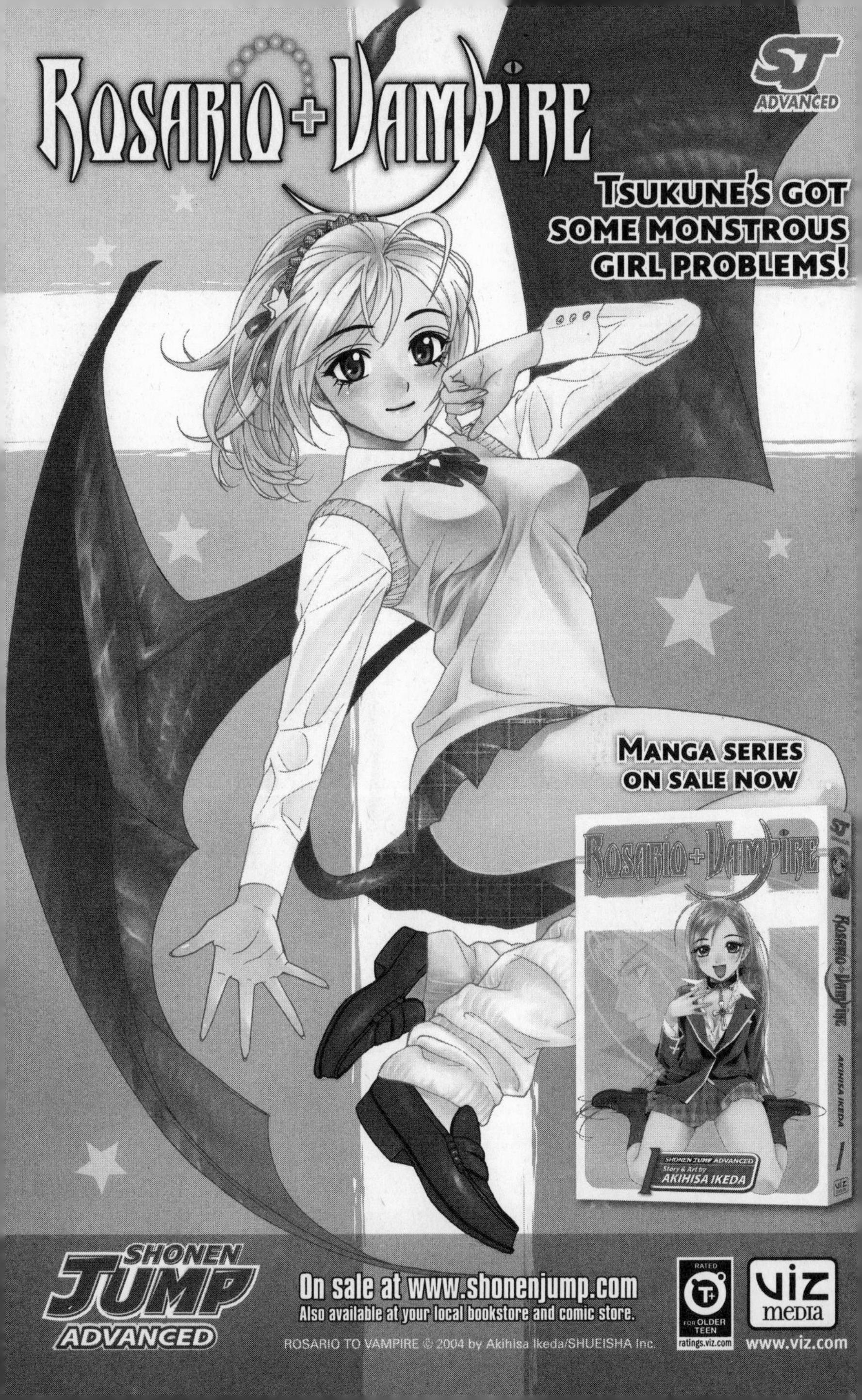

Tell us what you think about SHONEN JUMP manga!

Our survey is now available online.
Go to: www.SHONENJUMP.com/mangasurvey

Help us make our product offering better!

THE REAL ACTION STARTS IN...

SHONEN JUMP
THE WORLD'S MOST POPULAR MANGA
www.shonenjump.com

ST ADVANCED

ST

VIZ MEDIA